CA Antony Mason

BRUSSELS

Cadogan Books plc
London House, Parkgate Road, London SW11 4NQ, UK

The Globe Pequot Press
6 Business Park Road, PO Box 833, Old Saybrook, Connecticut 06475–0833

Copyright © Antony Mason 1995
Illustrations © Veronica Wood 1995

Book and cover design by Animage
Cover illustrations by Robin Harris
Maps © Cadogan Guides, drawn by Thames Cartographic Ltd

Series Editors: Rachel Fielding and Vicki Ingle

Editing: Rachel Fielding, Jane Middleton and Linda McQueen
Proofreading: Louisa McDonnell
Indexing: Judith Wardman
Production: Rupert Wheeler Book Production Services
DTP: Jacqueline Lewin and Linda McQueen

A catalogue record for this book is available from the British Library
ISBN 0–94–7754–55–5

US Library of Congress Cataloging-in-Publication Data
Mason, Antony.
    Brussels, Bruges, Ghent & Antwerp/Antony Mason
    p. cm. -- (Cadogan guides)
    Includes index.
    ISBN 1–56440–273–8
    1. Brussels (Belgium)--Guidebooks. 2. Bruges (Belgium)--Guidebooks.
    3. Ghent (Belgium)--Guidebooks. 4. Antwerp (Belgium)--Guidebooks.
    I. Title. II. Title: Brussels, Bruges, Ghent and Antwerp. III. Series.
DH804.M39   1995
914.9304'43--dc20   93-47110   CIP

Output by Bookworm Ltd.
Printed and bound in Great Britain by Redwood Books Ltd. on Challenger Cartridge supplied by McNaughton Publishing Papers Ltd.

About the Author

Antony Mason is the author of some 25 books, which include biographies of great artists, children's atlases, and books on exploration, great civilizations, the Wild West, houseplants, volleyball, spying—as well as travel guides. He has also written (with Felicity Goulden) the Cadogan Guide to Bali, a book inspired by sitting on a beach in Bali and wondering if there was any way he might be able to make a living out of doing just that (he couldn't). Having travelled to most parts of the world, he now lives and works in London, but for many years has been a frequent visitor to Brussels and Belgium. So convinced is he of the virtues and charms of the Belgians that he has married one.

Please help us keep this guide up to date

We have done our best to ensure that the information in this guide is correct at the time of going to press. But places and facilities are constantly changing, and standards and prices in hotels and restaurants fluctuate. We would be delighted to receive any comments concerning existing entries or omissions. Significant contributions will be acknowledged in the next edition, and authors of the best letters will receive a copy of the Cadogan Guide of their choice.

Dedication

To the memory of my father, Captain Ian Godson Mason, RN (1913–92), who set me on the path to travel.

Contents

Maps

Introduction

DETAIL FROM GRAND PLACE.

Every year the British Diagram Group holds a competition to find the oddest title of a published book. Recent contenders have included *Thirty Years of Bananas*; *Lights! Catalogue of Worldwide Matchbox Labels with the Word 'Light' in the Title*; and *Construction of an Egyptian Wig in the British Museum*. It was once suggested that the competition should be widened to include CD titles as well, citing as an example the title *Great Moments in Belgian Jazz*.

It is not a joke that most Belgians would understand—not that they can't laugh at themselves: they just would not see the incongruity. The fact is, none of us may find this particularly amusing in a few years' time. Belgium, and Belgian culture, is suddenly being pushed out of the backstage and into the limelight, and undergoing radical reappraisal. Belgian restaurants, Belgian beer, Belgian chocolates have now achieved virtual cult status. New fashion collections by members of the Antwerp Six group of couturiers have buyers and commentators positively salivating beside the international catwalks, where the very name 'Belgique' has acquired a cachet. In 1994 the Royal Academy in London felt brave enough to mount an exhibition devoted entirely to Belgian art, which was warmly received. Nowadays journalists strive to rework the time-worn clichés and produce headlines such as 'Belgium isn't boring any more!' And even the French these days seem less inclined to make jokes about the Belgians.

This comes as little surprise to anyone who already knows and loves Belgium. But the new mood also brings a tinge of regret: like all aficionados, admirers of Belgium are jealous of the object of their affections. The tired custom of belittling Belgium was—by love's inverted logic—music to their ears: it only served to increase the value of their appreciation, and to keep all but genuine converts outside the temple doors.

Devotees of Belgium have no difficulty in identifying what it is that attracts them. Food is always high on the agenda. Belgian cooking is among the best in Europe—and generally very reasonably priced. Built on a solid foundation of market fare, it is rarely tainted by highfalutin' *gastronomie*: succulent steaks, seafood straight out of the bracing North Sea, unparalleled *frites* (chips/french fries), supreme *pâtisseries*, and, of course, the world-famous chocolates. Belgian beer is the Bordeaux and Burgundy of brewing; many leading brands are still produced under the auspices of Trappist monks, who infuse their brews with a vision of heaven. This excellence of Belgian food and drink has not evolved in isolation. It belongs to a long tradition of sociability and *joie de vivre*, captured so infectiously by Flemish artists such as Pieter Bruegel the Elder and Jacob Jordaens. The Dutch have a word for this uniquely Belgian style of life, pronounced with a hint of envy: *Bourgondisch*—Burgundian, reflecting the robust, luxurious and immensely wealthy period when the Low Countries were ruled by the Dukes of Burgundy.

Brussels, Bruges, Ghent and Antwerp all developed as trading cities, fattened on the wealth of the merchants, craftsmen and their guilds, who were responsible for their great collections of art as well as their squares of sparkling, ornamented town halls and guildhouses. Ultimate power may have rested in the hands of the colonial rulers of Belgium—the Burgundians, the Spanish, the Austrians, the French, the Dutch—but the essential character of the nation was shaped by the broad band of the middle classes. A patrician culture dominated feudal Britain and France into the industrial age, producing the palaces and grand stately homes, laden with sumptuous finery. In Flanders, Brussels and Wallonia, by contrast, the arbiter and manufacturer of taste was always the burgher: well-to-do, democratic, moderate in tastes and needs, mindful that pleasure is as important a priority as education, domestic security and social cohesion—and sometimes vociferously independent, idiosyncratic and downright odd. It was this culture that produced the beer, the lace, the luminescent painting of Jan van Eyck, and it later formed the backdrop to the flourish of Art Nouveau homes for the middle classes, the quirky art of the Symbolists and James Ensor, the surrealism of Magritte and Delvaux, and the Atomium. It also accounts for the way that Belgians have taken the concept of European Union to their heart.

'Capital of Europe' is Brussels' sobriquet, a just claim in view of its role as the focal point of Euro-administration. For some, indeed, Brussels has become a synonym for bureaucratic centralism—and for Eurosceptics the very word can induce a life-threatening rise in blood-pressure. In fact Brussels is not simply the capital city of the EU, but a honeypot which has also attracted a vast number of multinationals, businesses, banks, inter-governmental agencies and media companies from all over the world. It is a truly multicultural city, and it has been successful in its transformation into its modern form because it has been so accommodating. Virtually everyone in Brussels is genuinely pleased that the city has made such a success of it, and foreigners—businessmen and tourists alike— are made to feel welcome. As it turns out, however, the label 'Capital of Europe' paints an oddly inaccurate picture. Brussels is an altogether more modest, down-to-earth city than this would suggest—and herein lies its charm. Its attractions are found as much in the lively bars and cafés and welcoming family bistros as in its civic monuments, its art galleries and literally dozens of museums—many of which reflect Belgium's refreshingly skewed vision of the world from the inner rim of European history.

It is a strange paradox, furthermore, that Brussels, 'Capital of Europe', should also be a capital of a country that is inexorably pulling itself apart. Flemish-speaking Flanders and French-speaking Wallonia have drifted towards increasing levels of self-rule and autonomy—accompanied by regular exchanges of insults and some unedifyingly vicious antagonism. In this light, 'Belgium' sometimes seems a rather remote concept, precariously roped together by national government and national institutions and to some extent by the capital city itself. When visiting Bruges, Ghent and Antwerp after Brussels you might be forgiven if you thought you were in another country. There again, each of these Flemish cities has its own flavour, quite distinct from the next, reflecting the days when they were among the largest and most wealthy in Europe and virtually independent city states.

But paradoxes, it could be argued, are part of the very nature of Belgium. For example, Belgium happens to have some of the best jazz festivals in Europe—but let's keep that a secret among ourselves, shall we?

A Note on the Use of French and Flemish

Belgium has two main languages, and in Brussels all street names, place names and the names of museums and so on have both French and Flemish versions. In this volume, however, these names have generally been given in French only. The Flemish equivalents are cited only in exceptional cases (*see* p.378 for a list of equivalent place names). No prejudice or offence is intended: this is for reasons of space, and because it is assumed that readers, for better or worse, are more likely to be familiar with French than Flemish.

Acknowledgements

This guide would have been quite impossible to write without the help of numerous people. First and foremost I thank my wife, Myriam, for putting up with this prolonged enquiry into her mother country, and also our son Lawrence who provided many intriguing and disarming insights. Heartfelt thanks also to my in-laws, Mariette and Paul Gervy, who not only provided generous hospitality, but tolerated my ceaseless questioning with a patience that went far beyond the call of family duty. Equally heartfelt thanks also to my aunt, Georgette de Petter, for her help on many aspects of Belgian life, and especially on the Flemish language and *bruxellois*. A big thank-you also to: Kurt Debroux, Isabelle Bielen, Monique André, Jean Gervy and Béatrice Van Parys, Annick Kellen, Sjoerd Koopman, Bruno Martin of *The Bulletin* and Tom Hoenig—all of whom must forgive me for doing no more than list their names in a manner that does scant justice to the help they have given to me. The various tourist offices of Brussels, Bruges, Ghent, Antwerp and elsewhere, and the Belgian tourist office in London have all been extremely helpful in supplying information and answering my queries: to them many thanks, and special thanks to Elisabeth Puttaert and Tina Vanhoye in Brussels, and Pierre Claus in London, who have known of this project for several years and always offered their encouragement. Special thanks also to Paul Cornelis of the Antwerp tourist office. Last but by no means least, many thanks indeed to all members of the friendly, engaging, hard-working and dedicated team at Cadogan Books, whose support through the trials and tribulations of this book I much appreciate; particularly warm thanks to Rachel Fielding and Linda McQueen, and also to Jane Middleton for her firm, patient and always well-judged editing.

Travel

By Air

As you might expect, Brussels, 'the capital of Europe', is well served by the world's airlines, jostling to harness the ceaseless ebb and flow of Eurocrats, multinational business travellers and a large population of expatriates—as well as tourists. There are many flights from all points of the globe, and they tend to be packed. If you are on a tight schedule, book early. International flights to Brussels arrive at Belgium's main airport at Zaventem, just 14km from the city centre.

From the UK

The main carriers to Brussels are British Airways, ℂ (Linkline 0345) 222111, and the Belgian national airline Sabena, ℂ (0181) 780 1444. Each offers up to seven flights daily from London Heathrow, and there are also daily flights from London Gatwick, Bristol, Manchester, Birmingham, Leeds, Newcastle, Glasgow and Edinburgh. Sabena also runs a daily service (exc. Sats) from London City Airport. British Midland flies direct from Heathrow, Birmingham and East Midlands.

The full London–Brussels fare for unrestricted economy travel is around £200 return. However, if your journey includes a Saturday night, prices for APEX fares drop to about £130 if you travel midweek, and £145 if you travel during a weekend. It is worth asking British Airways if they are running one of their occasional special offers called 'G-Class Consolidated Fares'. Under the scheme, London–Brussels return tickets are available for about £90, but they have to be purchased seven days in advance.

The flight from London to Brussels takes about 40 minutes. Since the check-in time is usually one hour before take-off, you will spend more time in the departure lounge than in the air—except at London City Airport, where the minimum check-in time is just 15 minutes. An airport tax of £9.10 is payable when you purchase your ticket.

From Ireland

Aer Lingus, ℂ Dublin (01) 8444 747, runs up to five flights a day direct to Brussels from Dublin. Prices start at around IR £200 for a return midweek flight if your journey includes a Saturday night, rising to £258 if you fly over a weekend. Add IR £11 to all fares to cover airport tax.

From North America

There are direct flights to Brussels from just about all the major gateway cities of the USA. Prices vary enormously but, to give some kind of yardstick, the round-trip price quoted by airlines for New York–Brussels is around $540 in the low season (winter), and rises to about $780 in the high season (summer). All fares are subject to additional airport taxes, which amount to about $40. Numerous agencies in the USA offer more competitive prices through charter flights or consolidated fares on scheduled flights; look in the travel pages of your Sunday newspaper. Canadians are rather less well served: travellers have to take a two-stage journey, changing in the USA or in Europe to continue to Brussels.

From Australia and New Zealand

There are no direct flights to Brussels. Travellers from Australia and New Zealand are normally advised to fly to London or Frankfurt and then to take an onward flight with a local carrier. Prices quoted by Qantas, ☏ (02) 957 0111, for Sydney–Brussels return, start at about A$2100 return in low season, but much cheaper deals can be struck with local travel agents, or indeed at Qantas Travel Centres. The same applies to flights from Auckland with Air New Zealand, ☏ (09) 357 3000, which officially quotes a low-season price of NZ$2899.

transport from the airport

Taxis from Zaventem airport to the city centre cost 1400 BF, but taxis with a white aeroplane sticker in the top right-hand corner of their windscreens offer special reduced rates. It is, however, far cheaper to travel by train. Special train services run three times an hour throughout the day from around 5.40am to 11.40pm, and connect with the Gare du Nord and the Gare Centrale (some trains go on to the Gare du Midi). The journey takes 20 minutes to the Gare du Nord. Tickets cost 70 BF and can be purchased at the airport station.

airline addresses in Brussels

Aer Lingus: 91–93 Avenue Louise, 1050 Brussels, ☏ 511 90 30

Air Canada: 131 Boulevard Lemmonier, 1000 Brussels, ☏ 725 39 81

Air France: 48–50 Boulevard Adolphe Max, 1000 Brussels, ☏ 220 08 00

American Airlines: 98 Rue du Trône, 1050 Brussels, ☏ 508 77 00

British Airways: Centre International Rogier, 1210 Brussels, ☏ 725 60 00 or 725 30 00

British Midland: 15 Avenue de Pléiades, 1200 Brussels, ☏ 771 77 66

Delta Airlines: 228 Avenue Louise, 1050 Brussels, ☏ 646 46 00

Lufthansa: 1 Boulevard Anspach, 1000 Brussels, ☏ 212 09 22

Sabena: 35 Rue Cardinal Mercier, 1000 Brussels, ☏ 511 90 30 or 723 31 11

Brussels is only about an hour's drive from the coast, and is connected by good motorways as well as rail services. There are three principal ports serving Belgium: Ostend, Zeebrugge and Dunkirk (Dunkerque), which is just over the border in France. From Britain, the main routes are: Ramsgate to Dunkirk (2½ hours); Ramsgate to Ostend (5 hours, or 1¾ hours by jetfoil); Felixstowe to Zeebrugge (5¾ hours, or 8 hours overnight); and Hull to Zeebrugge (14 hours).

The choice of which Channel-crossing route to take will depend on how far you want to drive, and how much time you want to spend at sea. By and large, the longer the sea journey, the less driving you have to do either end. These days the ferries are fairly luxurious, with a range of restaurants, shops and special facilities for children. Crossing the Channel on a clear, calm day can be a real pleasure, and a relaxing start to a holiday. On a stormy winter's day it can be a nightmare.

The Ramsgate–Dunkirk route is operated by Sally Line, ✆ (01843) 595522 or (0181) 858 1127. There is no direct rail link on the French side for this service: it is primarily for car and coach passengers. Standard return fares for two adults and a car range from about £120 to £255, depending on the season and time of travel, but there are considerable reductions for three-day and five-day return journeys. There are two motorway routes from Dunkirk to Brussels, one via Veurne and Ghent, the other (slightly longer) via Lille and Tournai. Both should take about 2 hours. Drivers on the return journey should be aware that the ferry port at Dunkirk is actually 15km west of the town—so do leave enough time.

Sally Line has also recently set up the Ramsgate–Ostend route, which has train connections on both sides of the Channel operated by British Rail International (*see* 'By Train', p.5). Standard fares for a foot passenger on this route (without rail connections) start at £50 return. For drivers, a motorway connects Ostend to Brussels, and the journey should take little more than an hour. Sally Line operates the jetfoil service from Ramsgate to Ostend, too. This is a passenger-only service, and is more vulnerable to cancellation on account of poor weather than the normal ferry services. Prices are the same as the standard passenger fares for the ferry, with an additional supplement of £6 return in the low season, rising to £18 return in the high season.

The Felixstowe–Zeebrugge crossing is operated by P&O, ✆ (0181) 575 8555, (01304) 203388 or (01394) 604040. There are usually two crossings per day, one an overnight crossing for which cabin accommodation is available. Crossings for two adults and a car range from £118 to £285 return, and two-berth cabins cost an additional £16 or so per crossing. Like Ostend, Zeebrugge is about an hour away from Brussels on the motorway.

The overnight crossing from Hull to Zeebrugge is operated by North Sea Ferries, ✆ Hull (01482) 377177. All prices include dinner and breakfast. Standard passenger fares (with reclining seat) start at £94 return in the low season, and £114 for a car, and rise to £110 in the high season and £138 for the car. Allow an additional £25 or so per person for the use of a cabin.

Via the Channel Tunnel

The Channel Tunnel, crossing the Channel between Folkestone and Calais, opens up entirely new prospects for travellers between Britain and the Continent. Using the tunnel, travellers with cars can cross the Channel in just 35 mins, whatever the weather.

The Tunnel is a rail link, but offers two separate services to Belgium: one is for rail passengers, who can travel swiftly from London to Brussels on the Eurostar (*see* 'By Train'). The other is for passengers with cars, who use purpose-built car-transporter trains called *Le Shuttle* that travel between Folkestone and Calais only. A standard low-season return costs about £220, rising to £310 in the high season (summer). You pay for the car only, irrespective of the number of passengers. Special five-day return prices are available in the winter months. There is no pre-booking system, but you can pay for tickets in advance if you like. For information about *Le Shuttle* and ticket purchase, ✆ (01303) 273300.

By Train

Rail travel between the UK and Brussels will be radically affected by the Channel Tunnel. However, the service will only reach its full potential in stages. London–Brussels by the Tunnel's Eurostar train currently takes 3 hrs 15 mins, but this will improve to 2 hrs 40 mins when the Belgians complete their high-speed track in 1996. The high-speed link into London St Pancras is unlikely to be completed until some time in the next century, but this will eventually improve the journey time to just 2 hrs 7 mins. In the initial phase, it will be possible to board the train only at London Waterloo, but Ashford International Station, in Kent, is due to open in late 1995. Trains arrive at the Gare du Midi in Brussels. Prices for Eurostar will remain on a par with its direct competitor, air travel: £155 for a standard return fare, £95 return Apex. Tickets are available from British Rail stations, travel agents and from European Passenger Services, ✆ (01233) 617575..

For those who prefer to take the ferry, there are rail connections from London to Brussels via the Ramsgate–Ostend crossing. These are operated by British Rail International, ✆ (0171) 834 2345 for enquiries or (0171) 828 0892 for credit card bookings, and are likely to remain cheaper than the Eurostar service. There are three services a day from London Victoria, connecting with a courtesy bus to the docks in Ramsgate. In Ostend the railway station is within walking distance of the dock. The total journey time from London to Brussels is about nine hours. Fares for an adult passenger range from £57 return for a five-day excursion in low season to £72 return for the full fare (valid for two months). Special rates are available for students and travellers over 60. There are also between two and four rail services a day (depending on the season) that connect with the Ramsgate–Ostend jetfoil, for which a supplement of £6 to £18 is payable. The total journey time from London to Brussels is 6½ hours.

Brussels is also well connected with other European capitals, and TGV links will soon improve the service yet further, reducing journey times from Paris to 1 hour 15 minutes, Amsterdam 1 hour and Cologne 1 hour. The Belgian railway service (SNCB) is run with the kind of dedication and efficiency that will render most British travellers quite nostalgic.

By Bus

The main carrier between London and Brussels is National Express/Eurolines, ℗ (0171) 730 0202 for enquiries or (0171) 730 3499 for credit card bookings. Coaches depart from Victoria Coach Station in central London and arrive at Place de Brouckère in central Brussels. There are usually two departures a day, one in the morning and one at about 6pm, which arrives in Brussels at 6am the following morning. Crossings are via Calais or Ostend and cost £55 return.

By Car

If you want to hire a car to travel around Belgium you will probably get a much better deal if you arrange this in your own country before departure. If you take your own car to Belgium you'll need a valid EC/EU driving licence—or your own national licence or an international driving licence—plus a valid insurance document and your vehicle registration documents. It is advisable to take out an insurance policy to cover your car against the cost of breakdown and rescue while abroad. You are required by law to carry a warning triangle and a first-aid kit. Your headkights should be adjusted for driving on the right-hand side of the road, but they do not need to be yellow.

Belgium once had a reputation for having some of the worst drivers in Europe. It was not entirely unfounded. Driving licences were only introduced in the early 1960s, at which point the government handed them out liberally to anyone over the age of 18 who applied for one. Practical driving tests were introduced for the first time during the 1970s, but the standard of driving today is as good as anywhere else in Europe. The roads are well maintained, and the motorway network (which is free of charge) can whisk you from one end of the country to the other in about 3 hours. There are a few things to watch out for, however. Stopping distance is not a concept that troubles the mind of the average Belgian driver. Cars in the outer lane of the motorway are liable to chase each other nose to tail at speeds well over the maximum 120km/hr. Another warning: *priorité à droite* (priority to vehicles coming from the right) is alive and unwell in Belgium. On unmarked roads (but not on major thoroughfares and motorways) vehicles may quite legally come shooting out from the right, off a minor road, without looking—provided they do not hesitate. Junctions where this is not permissible have white dog-tooth marks across the road where drivers must give way, and orange diamond signs on the major road *after* the junction in question. When driving in the country, or in the city suburbs, you must remain constantly alert to *priorité à droite*.

Do not flash your lights as a signal in Belgium: you are liable to be misunderstood. In the UK this means, 'Go ahead, I'm allowing you to pass.' In Belgium it means, 'Get out of my way, I'm coming through.' Finally, most Belgian drivers are not used to roundabouts. At some roundabouts priority is given to traffic already on the roundabout while at others it is given to traffic joining it; the best advice is to proceed with care. The speed limits are 120km/hr (75mph) on the motorway, 90km/hr (55mph) on major country roads and 50km/hr (30mph) in built-up areas. (If you are caught speeding by police they may issue you with a ticket there and then; this has to be paid within 48 hours.) Seatbelts must be worn. Children under 12 years old must not sit in the front seat of a car if other seats are available. Drinking and driving is against the law (you'll be over the limit after more than one drink) and liable to severe penalties.

Border Formalities

UK citizens and other EC/EU countries just need a valid passport or visitor's card for stays of up to 90 days. Americans, Canadians, Australians and New Zealanders need valid passports, but no visa is required. Strictly speaking you are supposed to be able to produce your passport or identity card at any time, so keep it with you.

If you are staying longer than 90 days you need to apply for registration (*see* **Living and Working in Brussels**, p.263).

Since EU customs controls were relaxed in 1993 there has been virtually no restriction on the amount of alcohol, tobacco and perfume you can bring back to the UK, provided that it is not bought in a duty-free shop and is in quantities deemed reasonable for personal use: i.e. not more than 800 cigarettes, 10 litres of spirits, 90 litres of wine and 110 litres of beer. Goods bought in duty-free shops and taken into another EU country are still subject to restrictions: 200 cigarettes, 2 litres of still table wine, 1 litre of spirits and 60cc of perfume, but you can buy these quantities on both outward and inward journeys and return home with both. US and Canadian citizens are restricted to the familiar limits of 100 cigars, 200 cigarettes and 1 litre of alcoholic beverages. There are no currency restrictions for travellers entering or leaving Belgium.

Getting Around Brussels

Maps

This book should provide you with sufficient maps for a short stay in Brussels. The Brussels Tourist Office (TIB) includes a useful fold-out map of Brussels in its booklet *Brussels Guide and Map* (70 BF). If you want a more detailed map, Eurocart publishes an excellent book-form map, while Girault Gilbert produces a large single-sheet fold-out map with street index, called *Nouveau Plan de Bruxelles et Grande Banlieue*. The best public transport map is the one issued free by the transport authority STIB (Société des Transports Intercommunaux Bruxellois), available from the STIB information offices (at Métro stations Porte de Namur, Rogier and Midi), and the tourist offices (*see* p.27).

On Foot

Brussels is a compact city and most of the main museums and sights are within walking distance of the centre, the Grand' Place. There is no shortage of public transport around the centre, but walking is often quicker and more rewarding.

One word of warning: in Brussels pedestrian crossings appear to be there merely as a suggestion to drivers. Do not assume cars will stop at them for you. Given enough distance, drivers will reluctantly give way once you are on the crossing—but don't count on it. Foreign drivers also take note: other drivers do not expect you to stop at pedestrian crossings. If you do so in traffic, you are liable to incur the wrath of the driver behind you, if not an accident.

Tickets for Public Transport

Tickets for public transport in the Brussels area can be used on the tram, bus and Métro, which all form part of STIB. The price of an *aller simple*, for a single continuous journey, is 50 BF; this permits changes and is valid for one hour.

If you are making several journeys by public transport there is a five-journey card (*carte de cinq voyages*) for 230 BF, but the best buy is the 10-journey card (*carte de dix voyages*), which costs 305 BF. Alternatively, for 180 BF you can buy a card that is valid for 24 hours (*carte de vingt-quatre heures*), during which time you can make as many journeys as you like on the public transport systems of 25 Belgian towns and cities—but it is only really a bargain if you plan to make well over four journeys in that period. Single tickets and five-journey cards are available from bus and tram drivers or at Métro stations; the 10-journey card and 24-hour card are sold at Métro and railway stations, at STIB information offices (*see* 'Maps', p.8), at tourist offices (*see* p.27), and at newsagents displaying the STIB sign. When travelling with an STIB card, you have to validate it—which is to say, have it stamped with the time and date at the start of each part of a journey. As you board your tram or bus, or as you enter a Métro station, drop the ticket face-forward into the machine. The machine can tell if you are using your card to continue your journey on the same unit, or beginning a new journey. Don't be fooled that other passengers are not validating their tickets: they may well have passes.

By Tram

Brussels was once a city of trams: it grew with the tram age. Over the last two decades, however, the trams have been savagely axed and replaced by buses. This process has now more or less abated, and those tram routes that have survived look set to stay. It is a speedy and efficient way to travel—and for anyone from a city without trams it also has the novelty of its historic tradition.

The STIB public transport map (*see* 'Maps', p.8) shows the tram routes. Trams can be boarded only at designated tram stops (red signs). Note that they do not halt at all stops if no one is waiting to board: you can signal that you want to get off at the next stop by pressing one of the black bells on the wall of the tram. Trams, along with buses and the Métro system, operate from about 5.30am to midnight, but services are much reduced after 6pm at weekends.

By Bus

The bus network is now far more extensive than the tram network that it has largely usurped. Buses operate on the same ticket system as trams, and you have to validate your ticket on the bus at the start of your journey. Once you have got the hang of it, the bus system is a very effective way of getting around. The STIB public transport map marks all the routes and the stops, so it is easy to plan your journey and to feel confident about where to board and where to get off.

By Métro

The Métro system in Brussels, constructed since 1965 and still being extended, has the fresh look of something new, and remains both clean and efficient. It has two lines: Line 1 crosses town on an east–west axis and Line 2 curls around the centre of the city. An additional service called the Pré-métro, which in fact is part of the tram network, runs underground in the 'tram tunnel' on a north–south axis, beneath the Boulevards Adolphe Max and Anspach.

To find your way around the Métro system you really need to consult a Métro map (there are maps posted in the stations). The direction of a train is indicated by the terminus towards which it is travelling, and this will be signalled on the platform and by a headcode (and by signs inside the carriages).

By Taxi

Taxis in Brussels are ordinary saloon cars with 'Taxi' written on the top. They can be hired only at a designated taxi rank (or by telephone), and cannot be hailed from the street. The fact that someone is registered as a taxi driver in Brussels does not guarantee that they know any more than just the key destinations and streets in the city: it helps to be able to supply as much information as possible yourself. Don't be surprised if your driver has to resort to a map.

A short journey will cost about 200 BF: this comprises the initial fee of 95 BF and then 38 BF per kilometre (it is advisable to check the metre on departure). It is normal to add 10–15 per cent as a tip, or round up to the nearest 50 BF.

Major Brussels taxi companies:
ATR: ✆ 242 22 22 or 647 22 22
Autolux: ✆ 512 31 23
Taxis Oranges: ✆ 513 62 00
Taxis Verts: ✆ 349 49 49

By Car

Driving in Brussels is no more hair-raising than it is in any other major European city. Two points to watch out for are *priorité à droite* (*see* p.7) and trams. Trams have priority and you have to get out of their way if you can. These days there are fewer roads where trams and cars jostle for position, but where they do, beware!

Parking is comparatively easy, especially in outlying districts. In the centre of town there is a fair number of underground car parks (follow the blue P signs) and parking meters (which take 5 BF and 20 BF coins).

By Bicycle

Although cycling is a national sport and you will see *pelotons* of sleek cyclists on the open road, cyclists in Brussels are a rarity. This is probably an example of evolutionary adaptation: cyclists simply do not survive long enough to reproduce. Not recommended. If, however, you are determined to cycle, you could make use of a network of 'green' car-free routes devised by the environment lobby Ecolo. Apply **Ecolo**, 12 Rue Charles V!I, 1030 Brussels (150 BF). Bicycles can be hired from **Pro-Vélo**, 53 Boulevard du Midi (closed Mon) for about 400 BF per day.

By Horse-drawn Carriage

During the summer months until September, and at weekends at either end of the season, authentic horse-drawn carriages are available for short tours of the city centre. Starting from Rue Charles Buls (off the Grand' Place), the usual tour goes to the Manneken-Pis, then around to the Bourse and across the Grand' Place itself. A 20-minute journey costs around 450 BF (for the carriage, irrespective of the number of passengers).

Travellers with Disabilities

Whatever might be claimed by the authorities, Brussels is not an easy city for the disabled, with its busy, cobbled streets, narrow pavements and hills. That said, people generally show greater respect, sympathy and patience towards the disabled than many of their European counterparts, and their welcome and offers of assistance where required may help to compensate for the absence of lifts and ramps in museums, restaurants and public offices. An excellent publication is available (in French) called *Guide Touristique et des Loisirs à l'Usage des Personnes à Mobilité Réduite* (Tourist and Leisure Guide for People with Reduced Mobility). This is a very thorough compilation of restaurants, sports facilities and shops in Brussels and Wallonia, with an assessment of accessibility. It can be obtained by writing to the Ministre des Affaires Sociales de la Communauté Française, Direction Générale des Affaires Sociales, Manhattan Center, 3 Rue des Croisades, 1210 Brussels.

A number of organizations can provide useful information about travel in Brussels for the disabled. These include:

Croix Rouge de Belgique (Belgian Red Cross): 98 Chaussée de Vleurgat, 1050 Brussels, ✆ 645 44 11. General advice about facilities, loan of wheelchairs and other equipment.

Radar (The Royal Association for Disability and Rehabilitation): 12 City Forum, 250 City Road, London EC1V 8AF, ✆ (0171) 250 3222. General travel advice, accommodation listings, and information about specialist holidays.

Holiday Care Service: 2 Old Bank Chambers, Station Road, Horley, Surrey, RH6 9HW, ✆ (01293) 774535. Accommodation advice.

SATH (Society for the Advancement of Travel for the Handicapped): 347 Fifth Avenue, Suite 610, New York, NY 10016, ✆ (212) 447 7284. General travel advice.

Travel Information Center: Moss Rehab. Hospital, 1200 West Tabor Road, Philadelphia, PA 1914/3099, ✆ (215) 456 9600.

Guided Tours

Several companies offer guided tours of Brussels, ranging from a quick sweep around the highlights in a coach to walks with a guide focusing on special themes. For 700 BF, De Boeck offers a walk in the Grand' Place followed by a coach trip past the Atomium, Palais de Justice, Colonne du Congrès and Parc du Cinquantenaire, all of which is achieved in about 2½ hours flat. ARAU has a list of more specialist trips, such as Art Nouveau, parks and gardens, and industrial archaeology, all for around 500 BF per person.

The Brussels Tourist Office (*see* p.27) has its own expert guides who can take you on walking tours of the centre or on tailor-made tours (about 850 BF per hour per group). In general they like at least two weeks' notice to arrange group tours but it is always worth asking if something can be arranged at shorter notice. Their list of organized walks includes such themes as 'Brussels in the footsteps of famous women', 'Brussels through the eyes of famous people', 'Brussels... Cheers' (beer), and Jewish history in Brussels.

De Boeck: 8 Rue de la Colline, 1000 Brussels, ℂ 513 77 44.

ARAU: 37 Rue Henri Maus, 1000 Brussels, ℂ 513 47 61.

Tour Operators

Various travel companies offer weekend breaks in Brussels and other parts of Belgium, including several of the ferry companies and *Le Shuttle*. The only UK company specializing exclusively in Belgium is the **Belgian Travel Service**, Bridge House, Ware, Herts, ℂ (01920) 467 345. It offers a broad range of holidays to all the most popular Belgian destinations and can also book accommodation for tailor-made trips.

A few tour operators offer specialist tours of Belgium, but most of these are directed towards Flanders and the cities of the north rather than Brussels itself. Themes include river and canal cruising, beer festivals, battlefield tours (Ypres, Waterloo, Passchendaele, the Ardennes), fine arts, even country-and-western weekends. The Belgian Tourist Office (*see* p.27) publishes a list of operators in its annual brochure entitled 'Savour the Flavour of Belgium'. These include:

Swan Hellenic Art Treasures Tours: 77 New Oxford Street, London WC1A 1PP, ℂ (0171) 831 1676.

Holts Battlefield Tours: Golden Key Building, 15 Market Street, Sandwich, Kent CT13 9DA, ℂ (01304) 612248.

Practical A–Z

Belgium is a small country. At 30,000 square km, it's not much bigger than Sicily or Wales. You can drive from north to south in less than three hours.

Its population numbers about 10 million. There are *cities* in the world with more people but, given the size of the country, Belgium has one of the highest average population densities, at over 300 inhabitants per square km. Brussels accounts for one-tenth of them, with a population of about 950,000. Antwerp has 486,000, Ghent 231,000, Charleroi 207,000, Liège 196,000 and Bruges 118,000.

The Flemish speakers in the north of the country outnumber the French speakers in the south by 5,848,000 to 3,303,000 respectively; and there are 67,600 German-speaking Belgians in the east, on the German border (*see* **Language**, p.21). These figures, however, do not include Brussels (Bruxelles in French, Brussel in Flemish), which floats like a multilingual bubble in the southern part of the Flemish-speaking region, and is counted as a separate administrative region. Here the French speakers easily outnumber the Flemish—but a full quarter of the population of Brussels is of foreign extraction.

Children

The first thing you notice about Belgian children is how well behaved they are. Belgium has a comparatively close-knit society, where traditional values are maintained not only by parents but also through the kindly guidance of ever-present older cousins, aunts, great-aunts and grandmothers. Just about all children go to the local state-run school, which therefore has the strong backing of Belgium's mighty middle classes. If a child is unacceptably disruptive, the parents will soon be under pressure to do something about it; parents are also liable to penalties if their children commit offences, such as vandalism.

For all that, this is a child-friendly society, where children are broadly welcomed and generally well catered for. Providing they behave, they will be accepted in all restaurants, cafés and bars. Since lunch in Belgium often lasts well beyond the endurance of most children, many parents wisely take toys, books and colouring kits to the restaurant.

Few of Brussels' attractions are specifically geared to children, apart from the Musée du Jouet, Bruparck and Walibi at Wavre. However, most children will probably enjoy the Atomium, the Manneken-Pis and his costumes in the Musée Communal de Bruxelles, the waxworks at Historium, the air section in the Musée Royal de l'Armée, the old trams at the Musée du Transport Urbain Bruxellois, and the Musée Royal de l'Afrique Centrale (*see* 'Index' for page references).

Belgium shares a similar weather pattern to the UK—that is to say, there are glorious summers of endless sunshine, and there are summers when it never ceases to rain. The average temperature in Brussels is 16°C in summer and 3°C in winter. In winter, however, temperatures can be noticeably colder than in Britain, sometimes dropping to –20°C if the wind is blowing from the Baltic; the north of the country can be shrouded in an eerie cold fog for days.

All the seasons have their merits—even winter, which is brightened by Christmas markets and carnival festivities. Clear, ice-cold winter days can be invigorating; the low-pitched, gilded sunlight throws the Gothic architecture into spellbinding relief, while lakes and canals are thronged with skaters and sprawling children, like a winter scene from Bruegel. The Belgians know how to enjoy themselves: in filthy weather you can always eat well. Autumn is perhaps the most spectacular season, when the huge beech woods (especially to the south of Brussels) are transformed into cathedrals of shimmering gold.

Pack, then, for all weathers. Keep warm by wearing several thin layers rather than one or two heavy ones—in winter, Belgian homes, hotels and restaurants can be heated to hothouse temperatures. Bring a light raincoat and an umbrella, and sturdy walking shoes to tackle all those cobbled streets.

The dress code is fairly relaxed. Generally people dress casually, but with some attention to detail, and they appreciate elegance. Jackets and ties are required only in the smartest of restaurants—the sort of place most Belgians don't normally eat in anyway.

Crime and Police

Every country seems to think that crime today is much worse than it used to be, and Belgium is no exception. In fact crime in Brussels, and in Belgium generally, is no worse than it is in the rest of Europe and, as everywhere, common-sense precautions should see you through.

The Brussels police publish a leaflet in five languages that makes various sensible suggestions: in public places keep your handbag under your arm; don't put your wallet in your back pocket; don't leave your belongings visible in your car. Pickpockets operate among the crowds on public transport, and the Métro has its own breed of nimble handbag slashers who can extricate purses and wallets in a single pass.

There are just a few crime blackspots in Brussels, such as the region around the Gare du Nord. The Jardin Botanique (the park, not the French Cultural Centre in the glasshouses) is the most notorious; it is a mugger's paradise, and even hardened world-travellers speak of it with the awe usually reserved for lawless South American ports. Otherwise, let instinct be your guide.

If you are the victim of crime, go straight away to the Police/Politie (see p.17 for emergency numbers). Officers wear dark blue uniforms and many of them speak English. (A separate national force, the Gendarmerie Nationale/Rijkswacht, deals with major crime and polices the motorways; its officers wear lighter blue uniforms with red trouser stripes.) You can expect a sympathetic hearing.

Remember that you have to report theft to the police in order to claim insurance. Note also that you are obliged to carry your passport or other form of identity at all times, and this is the first thing the police will ask to see. (They can check it, but they are not allowed to take it away from you.)

If you are arrested for any reason, you have the right to insist that your consul is informed (see 'Embassies and Consulates'). Proper legal representation can then be arranged.

Doctors and Pharmacies

Belgium has an excellent medical service, with first-class modern hospitals, well-trained staff and a nursing profession founded on the high standards set by Edith Cavell (see **Topics**, pp.42–3). Funded by the state, national insurance and private medical insurance, it has suffered less from growing constraints on government finance than other European nations, notably Britain.

Under the Reciprocal Health Arrangements, visitors from EU countries are entitled to the same standard of treatment in an emergency as Belgian nationals. To qualify you should travel with the E111 form; application forms are available from post offices in the UK. However, the E111 does not cover all medical expenses, and you are well advised to take out health insurance as well. This will cover the cost of ambulances or being flown home for treatment, for example, and is usually included in travel insurance policies at comparatively small cost.

Hotels have a list of doctors and dentists to whom their guests can apply, but a trip to a pharmacy may be sufficient for minor complaints. Pharmacists have a good knowledge of basic medicine and are able to diagnose: if in doubt they will recommend that you visit a doctor, and can provide you with details.

A list of 24-hour duty pharmacies is posted on every pharmacy door, together with a list of doctors on call. To call a private doctor in Brussels, © 648 80 00; for a dentist, © 426 10 26. For emergency numbers, see p.17.

You will be expected to pay for all medicine and treatment. With an E111 you can claim back about 75 per cent of the cost at the local Belgian sickness office; if you have separate health insurance you can claim the entire cost on your policy, but make sure that you ask for the correct documentation to make your claim.

Electricity

The current is 220 volts, 50 hertz. Standard British equipment requiring 240 volts will operate satisfactorily on this current. Plugs are the standard European two-pin type. Adaptors are available locally, but it is easier to buy a multi-purpose travelling adaptor before you leave home. Visitors from the US will need a voltage converter in order to use their electrical appliances.

Embassies and Consulates

The following embassies are in Brussels.

Australia: 6 Rue Guimard, 1040 Brussels, ✆ 231 05 00

Canada: 2 Avenue de Tervuren, 1040 Brussels, ✆ 735 60 40

Republic of Ireland: 19–21 Rue de Luxembourg, 1040 Brussels, ✆ 513 66 33

New Zealand: 47–48 Boulevard du Régent, 1000 Brussels, ✆ 512 10 40

South Africa: 26 Rue de la Loi, 1040 Brussels, 230 68 45

UK: 85 Rue Arlon, 1040 Brussels, ✆ 287 62 11

USA: 27 Boulevard du Régent, 1000 Brussels, 513 38 30

Emergencies

There are emergency services in every commune or borough of Brussels. The basic ambulance emergency number is ✆ 100. There is always at least one English-speaking operator on call.

Accident emergency/ambulance/fire/rescue, ✆ 100

Police emergency, ✆ 101

Ambulance service, ✆ 649 11 22

Emergency anti-poisoning centre ✆ 354 45 45

Dental emergencies (non-surgery hours), ✆ 426 10 26; 428 58 88

Emergency private ambulance/doctor, ✆ 648 80 00

Brussels standby emergency services, ✆ 479 18 18

Belgium has a long calendar of festivals and events: some are age-old ceremonies and pageants, widely advertised and drawing large crowds; others are religious festivals, including some of disturbing fervour; others still are entirely local excuses for an annual knees-up and binge. Listed below are the most famous of these, as well as others worth the detour, plus some annual traditions observed among family and friends.

6 January

Fête des rois. Epiphany is celebrated with an almond-flavoured cake called the *galette des rois*, which contains a plastic bean. Whoever finds the bean in his or her slice is awarded the paper crown that is sold with the cake.

February/March

This is the carnival season. Strictly speaking, carnival is a last fling before the beginning of Lent (Latin corruption: *carne vale*, farewell to meat), but carnivals take place in Belgium throughout Lent and even before it. The most famous one is at Binche, a town in western Belgium between Charleroi and Mons. After a steady build-up on the Sundays preceding Lent, the town erupts into a three-day feast with street dancing and processions, culminating in the parade of the extraordinary Gilles de Binche on Shrove Tuesday. The Gilles (clowns) dress in extravagant medieval motley with bizarre bespectacled masks. In the afternoon they don massive headdresses of towering ostrich feathers, then walk around town throwing oranges at their friends. The day is rounded off with fireworks and dancing. Parallel pre-Lenten festivities take place in the eastern towns of Eupen (Sat, Sun and Mon) and Malmédy (mainly Sat and Sun).

Easter Sunday

Children look for Easter eggs, which are said to have been hidden in the garden in the early morning by the *cloches de Rome* (the bells of Rome).

Ascension Day

Procession of the Holy Blood in Bruges (*see* p.300).

Second Sunday in May

Kattefeest in Ypres, northwest Belgium. Until 1817 live cats (a symbol of the Devil) were thrown from the tower of the town hall. These have been replaced by cats made of cloth, and the event is accompanied by a large procession on the theme of cats.

First Thursday in July (9–11pm)	*Ommegang* (literally, 'walk-around'). The grand pageant of Brussels, when some 2000 participants dressed in Renaissance costume—as nobles, guildsmen, mounted soldiers, flag-throwers, jesters, peasants—go on a procession through the Grand' Place before the King and the royal family. The ceremony dates back at least as far as 1549, when it was performed in front of Charles V and the infant Prince Philip; it has now become little more than a costume parade and photo opportunity. Nonetheless, seats are at a premium and have to be booked in advance (from early June onwards) through the tourist office (350–800 BF).
Last Sunday in July	*Procession of the Penitents.* A dramatic procession in Veurne, in the northwest, in which barefoot penitents dressed as monks carry heavy crosses through the streets. It dates back to the Spanish occupation of Belgium.
Mid July–3rd week in August	*Foire du Midi.* The great summer funfair of Brussels, which fills one side of the Boulevard du Midi between the Porte de Hal and the Place de la Constitution. It brings together a mass of noisy, gaudy attractions, from rifle galleries and halls of mirrors to dodgems and the big wheel. Good-humoured fun for all the family: there are plenty of children's rides, and grown-ups can always retreat to the mass of makeshift bars and restaurants serving seafood, beer and wine at trestle tables (the fair is often seen as the beginning of the shellfish season).
9 August	*Plantation du Meiboom.* A deracinated may tree is paraded around the centre of Brussels amid much jollity, then planted at the corner of the Rue du Marais and Rue des Sables.
13–14 August	*Tapis de Fleurs.* The Grand' Place in Brussels is covered in an elaborate 'carpet of flowers'.
Fourth weekend in August	*Vêpres Gouyasse* (Parade of the Giants) at Ath, in west Belgium. A famous procession which centres upon giant models of Monsieur and Madame Gouyasse (Goliath) and their retinue. The couple's marriage is blessed at a church before David slays Goliath in front of the town hall.

Second Sunday in September	*Journée du Patrimoine*. All kinds of historic houses, private collections, businesses and craft workshops throw open their doors to the public for a day, in celebration of the national heritage. Ask at the tourist office.
September/October	*Beer festivals* throughout Belgium, for instance at Diksmuide (near Ostend, to the north of Brussels). Bands, marquees and litres of good beer.
1–2 November	*Toussaint* (All Saints' Day and the following day). A time when the Belgians honour their dead by tidying up the cemeteries and filling them with flowers in preparation for 2 November, known as the *Jour des Morts*. An estimated 55 million flowers are sold during this period.
6 December	*Fête de Saint-Nicolas* (Feast of St Nicholas). Saint Nicholas, a.k.a. Santa Claus, walks the streets and markets and enters schools in his guise as the Bishop of Myra. He is usually accompanied by his jolly sidekick, the blacked-up and decidedly un-p.c. Zwarte Peter. This is when many Belgian children receive their main Christmas gifts, as well as traditional *speculoos* biscuits.
24 December	*Réveillon*. Christmas Eve is the main feast day of Christmas: the centrepiece is a sumptuous evening meal, after which good Catholics stagger off to Mass.
25 December	Christmas Day. A day of family visits and more gifts.

Gay Scene

Brussels may not rank as one of the gay centres of Europe—like London, Paris or Amsterdam—but nonetheless it has an active, if discreet, gay scene. There are three gay listings magazines (all in French), giving details of events, bars, contacts, accommodation and so forth: *Gay mag* (every other month; 35 Rue Marché aux Herbes, 1000 Brussels); *Regard* (every other month; BP 215, 1040 Brussels—apply using address only, without the name *Regard*); *Tels Quels* (monthly; 81 Rue du Marché au Charbon, 1000 Brussels). *Tels Quels* also has a café and meeting point, open every day 5pm–2am (4am at weekends), © 512 45 87.

Two further sources of information are: Infor Homo, 57 Avenue de Roodebeek, 1040 Brussels, © 733 10 24, which also has a Gay Switchboard; and AIDE INFO SIDA, © 514 29 65, which gives information and support about AIDS (SIDA in

French) and also publishes a free Gay-Safe brochure listing bars, clubs, associations and so on.

The main area for gay bars in the centre of Brussels is around the Bourse and southwards down Boulevard Lemonnier; for example there is the Why Not, 7 Rue des Riches Claires; Le Big Noise, 44 Rue du Marché au Charbon; Le Féminin, 9 Rue Borgval (Tues and weekends, 10pm–dawn).

Last, but by no means least, the English-speaking Gay Group (EGG) is an informal club for men and women of all nationalities which offers the opportunity to make new friends at relaxed, informal gatherings and monthly parties. It now has a mailing list of 700 members. Write to EGG, BP 198, 1060 Brussels 6.

Insurance

All travellers are strongly advised to take out insurance as soon as they book their tickets. Insurance packages for European travel are not expensive compared to the total cost of a holiday, or the cost of replacing stolen goods or paying any medical bills yourself (*see* 'Doctors and Pharmacies', p.16). Standard packages include insurance to cover all unrefundable costs should you have to cancel, compensation for travel delays, lost baggage, theft, third-party liabilities and medical cover.

Language

Belgium has two main languages: French and Flemish (a form of Dutch known as *Vlaams* in Belgium but often referred to as *Nederlands*). On a language map of Belgium, the border between the French-speaking and the Flemish-speaking parts runs east to west and roughly slices the country in two, with the Flemish speakers to the north and the French speakers to the south. The north is generally referred to as Flanders (Vlaanderen) and the Flemish-speakers as the Flemish or Flemings; the French-speaking south is called Wallonia (La Wallonie), which is inhabited by Walloons, a few of whom still speak the dialect form of French called *wallon*. The people of Brussels are 85 per cent French-speaking, but Brussels is not part of Wallonia.

The third official language, German, reflects the small eastern territories of Eupen, Malmédy and Moresnet ceded to Belgium in 1918 by the Treaty of Versailles.

French was introduced as the language of the ruling classes by the Burgundians in the 14th century, and by the 19th century the French-speaking population held political and economic ascendancy over the Flemish. This has changed radically since the Second World War, partly because of the decline of heavy industry in the south and the growing strength of modern light industries in the north, and partly because to succeed in administration it is now essential to be bilingual. Remarkably few French-speakers have made the effort to be conversant with Flemish, while a larger proportion of the Flemish have learned French. The result is that the Flemish have now gained the upper hand in the civil service, as well as in public services such as the post office and railways.

However, many of the Flemish appear to preserve a residual distaste for the French language. When you address a Belgian—particularly a civil servant—in the north of the country or in Brussels, do not assume that he or she will want to speak in French: if you happen to be talking to a Flemish-speaker, you are likely to be met with a decidedly cool response, and would be better advised to start off in English. It may subsequently turn out that French is, in fact, your most effective common language, but at least you will have established the rules of play. (For a basic guide to both languages, *see* pp.366–78.)

Naturally enough, Flemish speakers in Brussels use the Flemish names for streets and the main sights, and may not volunteer the French equivalent. Hence be ready to be directed to the Grote Markt as opposed to the Grand' Place, the Muntplein as opposed to the Place de la Monnaie, or Nieuwstraat as opposed to Rue Neuve. (For a list of place names in both languages, *see* p.378.)

There is one final complication. The true Bruxellois, whose family has lived in Brussels for generations, may be at home in both Flemish and French, and often occupies a linguistic world somewhere in between, switching from one language to another without even being aware of it. Over time this has given rise to dialect forms of both French and Flemish, generally referred to as *bruxellois*. Although primarily Flemish in origin, *bruxellois* provides a common pool of linguistic inheritance from which both language groups draw, adding spice to their vocabulary. Few people, however, now speak pure *bruxellois*, although efforts are being made to save it from complete extinction. The Toone puppet shows (*see* pp.249–50) are performed in *bruxellois*, for example.

Media

The Belgian media are, naturally enough, divided into the two main language communities, but this is a cosmopolitan society and newspapers are available in just about any language you could want. The main French-language newspapers in Belgium are *Le Soir*, *La Libre Belgique* and *La Dernière Heure*; the main Flemish ones are *Het Laatste Nieuws*, *De Standaard* and *De Morgen*.

An excellent locally produced weekly magazine in English, *The Bulletin*, is worth looking out for. Designed mainly for English-speaking residents of Brussels, it contains general articles, film and theatre reviews, useful tips on eating out, and a thorough what's-on guide.

Belgian televisions not only have Flemish and locally produced French channels, but also receive channels from France, Germany, the Netherlands and the UK. Televisions linked to cable have an even more mesmerizing choice. The two main, state-owned broadcasting bodies in Belgium are RTBF (Radio Diffusion Télévision Belge) and BRT (Belgische Radio en Televisie).

The main Belgian radio stations are also run by RTBF, which broadcasts in French, and BRT, which broadcasts in Flemish. You can receive BBC radio and BBC World Service, as well as numerous other European stations.

Money and Banks

The currency of Belgium is the Belgian franc (abbreviated to BF or simply F), divided into 100 centimes. At the time of writing, the exchange rate is just over 50 BF to £1, or 35 BF to US$1. There are coins of 50 centimes and 1, 5, 20 and 50 BF, and notes of 100, 500, 1000 and 5000 BF.

There is no shortage of banks offering exchange facilities. **Banking hours** are 9.15–3.30 Mon–Fri, although some branches will close for lunch between 12 and 2; some banks in the centre of Brussels are also open on Saturday mornings. Exchange bureaux have extended opening hours, including weekends, but tend to charge higher commission rates than banks. There are **exchange bureaux** at:

Brussels airport: 7am–11pm daily

Gare Centrale: 8am–9pm daily

Gare du Nord: 7am–11pm daily

Gare du Midi: 7am–11pm daily

Thomas Cook Foreign Exchange: 4 Grand' Place, 9am–7pm Mon–Sat

Traveller's cheques are widely accepted not only for exchange, but also in lieu of cash. Eurocheques, backed by a Eurocheque card, can be used in the same way up to a limit of 7000 BF per transaction. Visa, Mastercard/Eurocard, Cirrus and Switch cards can be used to draw cash from banks, but usually only through automatic cash dispensers, which means you must come armed with your PIN code. Visa, Mastercard/Eurocard, Diners Club, American Express and a handful of other leading cards are all widely accepted in shops, restaurants, hotels and petrol stations, but you should always check this first: you are sure to find the occasional surprising exceptions.

American Express: 100 Boulevard du Souverain, 1170 Brussels, ℰ 672 21 11
(lost cards: ℰ 676 23 23 or 676 21 21)

Diners Club: 36 Rue Ravenstein, 1000 Brussels, ℰ 515 95 11
(lost cards: ℰ 515 97 13 or 515 97 14)

Mastercard/Eurocard: 67 Avenue Roodebeek, 1040 Brussels, ℰ 741 66 11
(lost cards: ℰ 741 66 12; fax 732 01 01)

Visa: 148 Chaussée de Charleroi: 1060 Brussels, ℰ 535 27 11
(lost cards: ℰ 535 28 25)

Opening Hours

The standard opening hours for shops are 9–5.30, but many boutiques open 10–6 or 7. Department stores have late-night shopping once a week: in Brussels this is Friday, when they stay open to 8 or 9pm.

On Sundays, supermarkets and high-street shops are closed but *pâtisseries* and other specialist food shops open in the morning to cater for the tradition of Sunday lunchtime indulgence. For bank opening hours *see* 'Money and Banks', above; for post offices *see* below.

The large public museums and galleries are generally open over the weekend but closed on Mondays; other museums are often open on Mondays but may be closed at other times.

Post Offices

The postal service in Belgium can claim to date back to the beginning of the 16th century, and today the PTT provides an efficient and reliable service. Post offices are generally open 9–5, Mon–Fri, but the following branches have extended opening hours:

Brussels X, Gare du Midi, 48a Avenue Fonsny: open 24 hours a day, including weekends (but for fax services normal working hours only).

Centre Monnaie: Mon 9–6, Tues–Fri 9–5, Sat 9–12; special office (for postal services and stamps only) open Mon–Fri 8–9am and 5–7pm, Sat 8–9am and 12–7pm. The Centre Monnaie also offers fax services (charged by the page, and very expensive) and is Brussels' main poste restante address (Poste Restante, 1000 Bruxelles 1, Belgium).

Stamps are also widely available from tobacconists and shops selling postcards; however, for reliable information about the cost of postage, it is best to ask at a post office.

Belgium has a generous number of public holidays. On these days all banks and post offices are closed, as are most shops, bars and cafés and many of the museums and galleries. Where a public holiday falls on a Sunday, the following Monday is taken as a public holiday in lieu.

1 January	New Year's Day (*Nouvel An/Nieuwjaar*)
March/April	Easter Monday (*Pâques/Pasen*)
1 May	Labour Day (*Fête du Travail/Feest van de Arbeid*)
May	Ascension Day (sixth Thurs after Easter) (*Ascension/ Hemelvaart*)
	Whit Monday (seventh Mon after Easter) (*Pentecôte/ Pinksteren*)
21 July	Independence Day (*Fête Nationale/Nationale Feestdag*)
15 August	Assumption (*Assomption/Maria Hemelvaart*)
1 November	All Saints' (*Toussaint/Allerheiligen*)
11 November	Armistice Day (*Armistice/Wapenstilstand*)
25 December	Christmas Day (*Noël/Kerstmis*)

Public offices and institutions are also closed on 15 November (Dynasty Day) and 26 December (Boxing Day).

Religious Affairs

About 90 per cent of Belgians are Roman Catholic. However, the Church is not a dominant feature of Belgian society; it provides the context for all the major rites of passage, but less than a quarter of the population attend Mass on a regular basis. There are facilities for all religious persuasions in Brussels, details of which are published in *Living in Belgium* (*see* p.269). The tourist office (*see* p.27) should also be able to help.

Telephones

Telephoning in Belgium presents few problems. If you are staying in a hotel the switchboard can connect your call, but this is usually far more expensive than using a public telephone. These take 5 BF and 20 BF coins, but if you intend to make a lot of calls a 'Telecard' is a good investment. Telecards are available from tobacconists, newsagents, post offices and public transport ticket offices and cost either 200 BF or 1000 BF. They can be used in any public telephone bearing the Telecard sign; telephone boxes showing a row of foreign flags on the window can be used for international calls. The illustrated instructions in telephone boxes are easy enough to follow, and a liquid-crystal display tells you how many units you have left on your card.

The area code for Brussels is 02, but this does not have to be used within the city. All telephone numbers in this book that are not preceded by a bracketed code are Brussels numbers.

To make an international call from Belgium dial 00, then the country code, then the area code without the initial 0, then the number. The country code for the UK is 44, for Ireland 353, for the USA and Canada 1, for Australia 61 and for New Zealand 64.

There are two specialist telephone centres in Brussels run by the Régie des Télégraphes et Téléphones (RTT), and another at the airport. These provide information and will connect long-distance calls for you if necessary. The one in the Boulevard de l'Impératrice also has a fax service.

RTT: 17 Boulevard de l'Impératrice, 1000 Brussels, 7am–10pm daily

RTT: 30a Rue du Lombard, 1000 Brussels, 10–10 daily

Airport: 8am–10pm daily

In Brussels: directory enquiries within Europe: ✆ 1304

directory enquiries outside Europe: ✆ 1324

person-to-person reverse charge/collect calls: ✆ 1324

Time

Brussels is on Central European Time and is one hour ahead of Britain throughout the year, except for three weeks in October. It is six hours ahead of US Eastern Standard Time, nine hours ahead of California and nine hours behind Sydney.

Tipping

On the question of tipping, relax. Except in the few circumstances listed here, it is not generally expected. In restaurants a 16 per cent service charge is usually included in the bill, along with 19 per cent TVA (Value Added Tax), and so additional tipping is not expected—but if service has been noticeably good a further 5 per cent or so would be appreciated. If you have had table service at a bar or café, it is usual to leave any small change (say 20 BF for a small order), but this is not essential.

Service is included in hotels, so there is no need to tip porters or staff providing room service. In taxis it is usual to round up the total by 10–15 per cent. Ushers showing you to your seat in cinemas will expect a tip of about 20 BF per seat. Similarly, cloakroom attendants may expect 10–50 BF, but the presence or otherwise of a basket of coins will make the position clear. Lastly, attendants in public lavatories will expect 10 BF or so; minimum charges are posted at the entrance, and the attendant herself will usually be there to enforce it.

Tourist Information

The main tourist office in Brussels is a tiny room beneath the arches of the Hôtel de Ville. The staff can offer all kinds of advice about what to see and when, and about special activities and guided tours; they will make hotel reservations for you, and also offer a reservations service for theatres and concerts. They publish various annual brochures, including their useful Guide and Map (100 BF), and a free weekly programme of events. For information about Belgium, there is a separate office in the nearby Rue du Marché-aux-Herbes, where copious literature about the various regions is available. There is also a tourist office at the airport.

The Belgian tourist board has offices in London and New York, which can supply you with information before you leave home.

Brussels: Office de Tourisme et d'Information de Bruxelles (TIB), Hôtel de Ville, Grand' Place, 1000 Brussels, ℂ 513 89 40. Open daily 9–6, Sundays in winter 10–2

Belgium: Commissariat Général au Tourisme/Commissariat General voor Toerisme, 63 Rue du Marché-aux-Herbes/Grasmarkt, 1000 Brussels, ℂ 504 03 90. Open Mon–Sat 9–6 (until 7pm in summer), Sun 1–5 (9–7 in summer)

Belgian Tourist Office, 29 Princes Street, London W1R 7RG, ℂ (0171) 629 0230

Belgian Tourist Office, 780 Third Avenue, Suite 1501, New York 10017, ℂ (212) 758 8130, fax (212) 355 7675

WCs

Public toilets are usually kept scrupulously clean by dedicated middle-aged women with their own brand of hearty chat; for this service you are obliged to pay around 10 BF. There is not a huge number of public toilets: in their absence most Belgians will freely make use of facilities offered by bars and cafés, but it is considered polite to act as a legitimate customer by buying a drink in passing.

Belgium uses the metric system and continental clothing sizes. Below are some conversion factors for the most common metric units. For clothing and shoe sizes it is best simply to ask in the shop and get an assistant to measure you.

1 centimetre (cm)	=	0.39 inches (in)
1 metre (m)	=	3.25 feet (ft)
1 kilometre (km)	=	0.621 miles
1 hectare (ha)	=	2.47 acres
1 litre (l)	=	1.76 UK pints or 2.11 US pints
1 gram (g)	=	0.35 ounces (oz)
1 kilogram (kg)	=	2.2 pounds (lb)
1in	=	2.54cm
1ft	=	305cm
1 mile	=	1.61km
1 acre	=	0.4ha
1 UK pint	=	0.57 litre
1 UK gallon	=	4.55 litre
1 US pint	=	0.47 litre
1 US gallon	=	3.78 litre
1oz	=	28.3g
1lb	=	0.45kg

Belgian Topics

LACE MAKING

The Meaning of Belgian

On 1 April 1992, *The Times* of London announced the start of secret talks between the leaders of Belgium's two main linguistic blocks in an effort to resolve their differences once and for all. The most drastic proposal was the realignment of Flanders with the Netherlands and Wallonia with France, effectively resulting in the dismantlement of Belgium after 162 years of independence. This would, of course, have serious implications for the European Community, although the report mentioned that Brussels itself might become a neutral territory as the capital of Europe, rather like Washington DC. New names had already been discussed, including the possibility of renaming the Grand' Place after the date of this first, historic meeting: Place du 1er Avril.

It was, of course, a cunning *poisson d'avril*, an April fool's joke—but a joke about a subject that to many Belgians is no laughing matter. In recent years the term 'Belgian' has taken on a new significance. '*Il n'y a plus de Belges,*' is a common complaint, '*il n'y a que des Flamands et des Wallons.*' ('There are no more Belgians, only Flemings and Walloons.')

There is a car sticker that announces '*Belge et fier de l'être*' ('Belgian and proud of it'). To an outsider this might seem an odd statement—an affirmation that clearly masks doubt. Why shouldn't one be proud to be Belgian? In fact it is a statement about Belgian unity: 'I am first and foremost Belgian: I believe in Belgian unity and do not want to see my nationality sidelined by regionalism.'

Such sentiments are expressed widely in both Flemish- and French-speaking communities. There are many Belgians who want to preserve the historic union between Flemings and Walloons, and there are plenty of intercommunal, bilingual marriages, friendships and working partnerships to underpin this.

Nonetheless, there are deep historical, social and political reasons for tension between the Flemish and the Walloons (*see* **History**), which emerge in the common unflattering stereotypes that one community holds of the other. This is a gift to politicians, who find it all too easy to exploit the differences. Divide and rule is the pattern of their politics, and in Belgium this has been formalized in constitutional reforms giving increased power to the regions at the expense of central government—a process called federalism. By appeasing regionalist tendencies, the divisions harden, as each community retreats into linguistic, political and cultural isolation.

This process may be acceptable in areas that are unequivocally Walloon or Flemish, but it is troubling to many of the mixed *communes* on the borderlands and around Brussels. Whereas local politics and public life in such areas used to be bilingual, they can now be conducted simply in the language of the majority, a right only too often taken up by regionalist hardliners. In a situation heading towards polarization some unpleasant extremist political groups have emerged—on both sides of the divide—and from time to time otherwise tranquil Belgian *communes* erupt into unedifying outbursts of violence. Meanwhile, on a national level, coalition governments dependent on complex power-brokering for their survival have to appease vociferous separatists at the expense of national cohesion.

The headlong dash towards federalism has caused increasing dismay to those who still regard themselves above all as Belgian. Good Belgians—people who, for instance, have married someone from the other community and are bringing up their children bilingually—suddenly find themselves compromised and their aims called into question. The Belgium that was once considered a model for multi-linguistic unity by other nations struggling with similar problems now seems on the verge of disintegration. (The news that Rwanda was recently seeking a political solution to its bloody turmoil along the lines of the 'Belgian Compromise' was greeted as a sick joke.)

In the summer of 1993 a series of pro-Belgium demonstrations attempted to redress the balance. Then in August 1993 King Baudouin I died. He had been a symbol of Belgian unity, widely respected by both Flemings and Walloons and a quiet and dignified campaigner for harmony within his nation. His sudden death unleashed a tide of public emotion, that was not simply grief at the loss of a deeply admired leader but also an expression of support for what he stood for. It took the nation by surprise: no other event had sounded out public opinion in quite this way before. Belgians (and proud of it) stood up and were counted for the first time, and were found to represent a substantial force that had somehow been overlooked by federalism.

The politicians—Flemish, Walloon and national—should take note. Their past record, however, suggests that they won't. 'Divide and rule' still remains the easier option.

Brussels the Euro-bogeyman

Since the beginning of 1993 the European Community has been called the European Union (EU), much to the alarm of many dissenters in the UK and elsewhere to whom the word union seems like a misnomer laden with a bagful of unwelcome associations—not least the idea of the United States of Europe as envisaged by the Maastricht Treaty of 1992. To many EU citizens, Brussels is a kind of abstract concept signifying centralism, loss of national sovereignty and the gradual eradication of national identity towards a bland Euro-culture. EU rules of product standardization appear to threaten the livelihoods of traditional ham-smokers in the Jura, olive-stuffers in Spain and fish-packers in Cornwall, and to jeopardize outside toilets in British rural pubs. Brussels is the source of the hated Common Agricultural Policy edicts, which provoke enraged farmers to dump cartloads of turnips across rural market squares. In short, to some, Brussels has become a rude word.

In Brussels itself such reservations about the EU are seldom heard. Belgians are, by and large, enthusiastically pro-European. Cars proudly display EU stickers; you can buy flags, labels, postcards, even umbrellas, bearing the EU symbol, a neat circle of stars on a deep blue background. Even the Manneken-Pis has his star-spangled blue Euro-outfit.

Of course, Brussels has much to gain from being the 'Capital of Europe', in terms of both status and financial benefit. But the pro-European fervour of the Belgians is not simply self-seeking. A vision of a united Europe grew directly out of Belgium's unique historical experience, particularly during the Second World War when the country was overrun and mutilated by the Germans for the second time in a quarter of a century. Paul-Henri Spaak, Socialist prime minister just before the war and foreign minister thereafter, battled tirelessly to turn this vision into a reality—a Europe that could build on its common interests and create a structure in which to settle its age-old differences peaceably and constructively.

Belgium, therefore, was at the forefront of the movement to create a united Europe, and Spaak stands beside Robert Schuman and Jean Monnet as one of its founding fathers. Out of the Treaty of Paris, signed by the six founder nations in 1951, grew the European Coal and Steel Community and then the Treaty of Rome in 1957 which established the European Community, augmented to 12 member states in 1986.

Brussels was a natural choice for the EC's headquarters—although of course the European Parliament still meets primarily in Strasbourg, and the European Court of Justice is based in Luxembourg. The city is centrally located, in a country committed to European ideals. Furthermore, Belgium itself is a kind of microcosm of Europe, struggling to promote harmony within its own frontiers between its two main communities. It may be that Belgium owes its very survival to the EU, which has allowed it a broader field upon which to play out its national conflicts. It is hardly surprising, therefore, to find Belgians championing the EU—and to find them incredulous when they see other member nations dragging their heels.

'The king reigns, but he does not govern.' So runs the well-known summary of the role of the Belgian monarchy. The king of the Belgians has a very similar function to that of the British monarch, as head of state and guarantor of the country's constitution, with little real power but a considerable amount of influence.

Today the influence of the Belgian monarchy is largely due to the last king, Baudouin I, who died in 1993. He took over on his twenty-first birthday in a moment of constitutional crisis when his father, Leopold III, abdicated after being unfairly vilified for his role during the war. Baudouin won popular affection for his quiet, understated manner and his fairhanded treatment of both the Flemish and the Walloons, with whom he could converse fluently in both national languages. He and his wife, Fabiola de Mora y Aragon, a member of the Spanish royal family, were the embodiment of low-key royalty, promoting family values with the common touch and entirely suited to modern European constitutional monarchy—like, indeed, their in-laws in Spain. Baudouin showed genuine interest when he talked to war veterans, sportsmen, hospital workers and the many ordinary people whose lives he crossed: when he went to his local golf club, he often played a round with whoever he found free at the first tee. On visits to factories he would eat in the canteen with the workers.

There was a major constitutional crisis in 1990 when Baudouin refused to sign a bill legalizing very limited abortion in Belgium. 'Does freedom of conscience apply to everyone but the king?' he asked. In a classic fudge, he abdicated for 24 hours while parliament passed the law. Most of the nation admired him for having the courage of his convictions, even if they did not share them.

The one great regret of Baudouin and Fabiola was that they could not have any children; Fabiola had two miscarriages and then painfully came to terms with childlessness—which partly explains why they took a growing interest in child welfare, and abortion.

While Britain's House of Windsor stumbles from one crisis to another, the stock of the Belgian royal house rises. Of course its roots go back a mere 160 years, to the accession of Leopold of Saxe-Coburg-Gotha as the first King of the Belgians shortly after independence. Since then the family has married with the aristocracy of just about every European nation—except Britain and, ironically, Belgium itself. The wife of the present king, Albert II, is an Italian princess; his sister is married to the Grand Duke of Luxembourg; his daughter is married to an Austrian Habsburg. Albert's oldest son Philippe (b.1960) is next in line, and as yet unmarried, handing the glossy magazines of Europe a golden vein of speculation.

The Belgian Congo

As a young man, King Leopold II travelled widely, and the idea came to him that Belgium should have colonies. After all, colonies were all the rage in Europe and, as much of the world had already been spoken for, eyes were beginning to turn to Africa. As luck would have it, the great British-American explorer Henry Morton Stanley (1841–1904) was available to take commissions.

Stanley was a human dynamo, a workhouse boy from Britain who had run away to the USA and been adopted by a wealthy patron called Stanley, whose name he in turn adopted. He became a thrusting journalist and was sent on a dangerous mission to Africa by the *New York Herald* in 1871 to search for Dr Livingstone, a media darling who had disappeared from view three years earlier. After a gruelling voyage Stanley found Livingstone in the village of Ujiji and posed the history of exploration's most famous question: 'Dr Livingstone, I presume?'

The voyage gave Stanley a taste for Africa, and in 1874 he began his most ambitious expedition in which he crossed the continent from east to west in 999 days. For the most part he followed the course of the River Congo or Zaire, which he realized had huge potential as a trade route. His expeditions were planned on an imperial scale: he left his east coast base with over 350 porters and locally hired staff, only half of whom completed the journey. The others deserted, died of disease, or were killed in skirmishes with local tribes fearful that the intruders were connected to the slave trade.

In 1878, finding Stanley at a loose end, Leopold commissioned him to carve out a territory for Belgium in Central Africa, which he proceeded to do through a mixture of daring travel, trade negotiations, outrageous trickery and full-blooded thuggery. He made a series of treaties with local tribes which in effect sold trading rights in exchange for land ownership. In his wake came bands of ruthless bounty hunters, who proceeded to make fortunes from this territory's vast natural wealth in diamonds, gold and timber, and from its fertile soil on which plantation crops such as coffee, rubber and palm oil could be grown.

By 1884 Belgium was in control of a vast territory called the Congo Free State, 77 times larger than Belgium itself. Leopold was infuriated to find that the Belgian government would not take responsibility for it (many Europeans in fact believed that trading agreements were more mutually beneficial than colonial possession). So after 1885 he took it over as a personal fiefdom. As a result, he netted huge personal wealth.

Amid much self-congratulatory bluster, slavery was eventually stamped out in the 1890s. The Congo was taken over by the Belgium nation only in 1908, in face of mounting criticism in Europe over the tyrannical way the colony was being run. The local people were subjected to all manner of abuses, including whipping and frequent murders, with little or no attempt by the authorities at intervention. The British Consul played a leading role in exposing the excesses of Belgian colonial rule: he was none other than Sir Roger Casement, the Irish patriot who was hanged by the British in 1916 for plotting a rebellion in Ireland.

There were sporadic outbursts of resistance throughout the period of Belgian rule, notably in the 1890s and during the First World War. These were brutally suppressed; the ringleaders were locked away for decades, while others were sent to internment camps.

After the First World War the former German colonies were redistributed among the victor nations, so Belgian power was extended to Ruanda-Urundi (after 1962, Rwanda and Burundi). This was a boom period for Belgian Africa, as planters, merchants and mining interests consolidated their gains; the period was also accompanied by various humanitarian improvements in education, public health, labour relations and the terms of employment. The Belgian population of the capital of the Congo, Léopoldville (now Kinshasa), rose to some 75,000.

After the Second World War calls for independence became yet more urgent across Africa; in the Belgian Congo they were accompanied by widespread unrest. The country, however, was politically uneducated and riven by tribal conflict. As events spun out of control, Belgium dropped the Congo like a hot brick and hastily granted it its independence in 1960. This was followed by a period of violent anarchy and a bid for secession by the province of Katanga, which was only settled by the intervention of UN troops in 1963. In 1965 General Joseph Désiré Mobutu seized power, which he has clung on to, against growing turmoil, ever since. The ruling élite maintained their contacts with Belgium, travelling frequently to Europe for education, banking, business and hospital treatment, but political relations became increasingly strained. Meanwhile the number of Belgians remaining in the Congo diminished as local conditions deteriorated and their presence and superior attitudes became increasingly resented.

In 1971 the Republic of Congo changed its name to Zaire, and President Mobutu took the name Sese Seko, meaning 'The Warrior Who Knows No Defeat'. Twenty years later, despite its huge natural wealth in diamonds, copper and cobalt, Zaire remains an impoverished and troubled country ruled by a tiny but immensely wealthy élite, buttressed by enduring economic and political ties to its old colonial ruler. When bubonic plague was reported recently, it was found that provincial hospitals lacked the drugs to treat even the most basic diseases.

It's a sorry tale, from which modern Belgium would prefer to distance itself, but like all colonial histories it has its powerful legacies of trading and government contacts, intermarriage and immigration, and a certain rose-tinted nostalgia for a bygone era.

Flemish Tapestry and Brussels Lace

For over five centuries Belgium has been celebrated for two crafts, both requiring the deft skills of its handworkers. Flemish tapestry has been made since the 14th century, while lace came to the fore in the 16th century and, after a lapse of a century or so, is now undergoing a vigorous revival.

Tapestry was a product of the woollen textile industry upon which the thriving medieval economy of Flanders was based. Arras, in northern France, was the first famous centre of production, but this was supplanted by Tournai (in western Belgium) in the mid-15th century. Tapestry was a much prized commodity in the Middle Ages, when virtually all precious works of art and status symbols tended to be portable. As the wealthy feudal aristocracy progressed around their estates, they took their valuables with them—their gold and silver plate, tapestry, luxurious clothing and collapsible beds. Tapestry was not only colourful and attractive, it was also a practical way of providing a measure of insulation in the draughty private chambers of castles and mansions. At his death in 1404, Philip the Bold, Duke of Burgundy, had a collection of 75 tapestries. When his successor, John the Fearless, was negotiating with the English in 1411 and 1416, he was able to use tapestry as a bargaining counter, such was its currency.

Subsequent Dukes of Burgundy encouraged the establishment of a Flemish tapestry industry, and during the 16th century the workshops of Bruges, Antwerp, Oudenarde and particularly Brussels, grew in stature. They generally used the Flemish method of tapestry, in which coloured weft wools are woven on to the warp stretched over a horizontal loom, although the vertical 'high warp' loom was also used. The weavers copied the designs from artist's cartoons, working the reverse side of the image, so the final image was in fact an inverted version of the original design. Mirrors erected on the other side of the loom allowed the weavers to check their progress.

For several centuries, the great artists of the day would gladly turn their hand to designing for the tapestry workshops. Bernard van Orley, who brought the Italian Renaissance to Brussels, is particularly celebrated for the designs he produced there. The Brussels workshops became famous for their ability to handle large, complex designs based on theological, classical or allegorical themes, so when

Pope Leo X wanted tapestry for the Sistine Chapel, it was to Brussels that he turned, sending designs commissioned from Raphael. This had a radical effect on the tapestry world, which thereafter set about imitating fine art, assisted now by a palette of over 150 different colour tones. Rubens and Jordaens likewise produced tapestry designs in the next century.

The tapestry industry continued to thrive until the 18th century, but lost ground when the Baroque period was replaced by more austere neoclassicism, and it never really recovered. Nonetheless, there are plenty of surviving examples of superb Flemish tapestries, in—for example—the Musée Communal de Bruxelles, the Musées Royaux d'Art et Histoire, and hundreds of châteaux and stately homes throughout Europe.

Lace (*dentelle* in French, *kant* in Flemish) was originally made from linen, from the flax fields of central Flanders. It was always a cottage industry, but produced by women from virtually every social rank, notably by the thousands of women living in the *béguinages* of the Low Countries (*see* pp.208–9). Having blossomed in the 16th century, lace remained popular for three centuries, during which fashion for both men and women included lace collars and cuffs. It was also used to make caps, handkerchiefs, shawls, lappets (ribbon-like hair adornments) and bed linen. The Victorian passion for lace with everything, from underwear to the dining-room table, inspired a latter-day Renaissance, but by this time much of the demand was being met by lace-making machines. Nonetheless, even in the mid-19th century there were an estimated 50,000 women lace-makers in Belgium, 10,000 of them in Brussels.

Various lace-making techniques have been used over the centuries. In the 16th century lace-making was essentially a form of embroidery; a hundred years later the dominant technique was needlepoint, which had evolved in Venice. Bobbin embroidery developed during the 18th century in Genoa and Milan and soon spread to the main centres for lace-making elsewhere, notably Brussels and also Mechelen and Bruges. The bobbin technique is the one most widely seen today, but all three techniques survived and were used simultaneously.

Hand-made bobbin lace is extremely slow to make, requiring thousands of carefully planned movements of the bobbins and pins. The intricate patterns are created by moving the threads attached to the bobbins around the pins, which are pressed into a cushion. Complex lace calls for over 100 separate threads and bobbins. Not surprisingly, good lace is expensive; and the industry has been undermined in recent decades by cheap imports from the Far East. That said, plenty of good, hand-made lace is still being produced in Belgium, available in the more respected outlets in Brussels and Bruges, where the staff will be happy to reassure you of its provenance. Cotton lace is more robust and comparatively cheap; linen lace is much finer, and a larger piece with a complex design can cost thousands of Belgian francs. Collections of lace can be seen in a number of Brussels museums, notably the Musée du Costume et de la Dentelle; you can see lace being made at the Louise Verschueren shop in Rue Watteeu in Brussels (*see* pp.139), and at the Kantcentrum in Bruges (*see* pp.310–11).

Tintin

Name the most famous Belgian in the world. Tintin! Translated into some 30 languages, sold in over 100 million volumes worldwide, Tintin's adventures have enthralled countless children and adults around the globe for over half a century.

It is hard to pin down the secret of Tintin's charm: every aficionado will tell a different tale. But his influence is profound: journalists, archaeologists, engineers and aid workers will declare that Tintin was their childhood inspiration. The historical and geographical detail of the stories is carefully researched and the reader travels with Tintin to exotic worlds—Central America (*Tintin and the Picaros*), Tibet, Ancient Egypt (*Cigars of the Pharaoh*), even to the moon.

Tintin, topped by his peculiar blond quiff and accompanied by his faithful white terrier Milou (Snowy in English), first appeared in 1929 in a story called *Tintin au Pays des Soviets*, which was published in *Le Petit Vingtième*, part of the Catholic newspaper *Vingtième Siècle*. His creator was Georges Remi (1907–83), a self-taught illustrator born in the Brussels suburb of Etterbeek, and an early pioneer of the comic-strip form. For his pseudonym he simply reversed his initials and spelled them out as they would be pronounced in French: RG, Hergé.

Tintin featured weekly in *Le Petit Vingtième* for ten years; his brief was to right the wrongs of the world and demonstrate the supremacy of Catholicism, an experience he fortunately survived. As the 1930s advanced, his adventures became more challenging, inspired by contemporary events that clearly affronted Hergé's sense of justice—such as the bloody Gran Chaco War between Paraguay and Bolivia over non-existent oilfields (*The Broken Ear*), and the Japanese invasion of Manchuria (*The Blue Lotus*). In *King Ottokar's Sceptre* the repugnant fascist Iron Guard (led by Musstler) attempts to seize power in a central European state.

It is some wonder, therefore that Hergé was vilified for his performance during the war, during which he produced an inoffensive version of Tintin for *Le Soir*, a newspaper controlled by the occupying German authorities. As for so many Belgians, compromise was simply a question of survival. During this period, paradoxically, the pantomime quality of the Tintin stories was enhanced by the arrival of several new characters, including the English seadog Captain Haddock and Professor Calculus (Tournesol in French). For his pains, Hergé was rewarded by arrest and imprisonment at the end of the war on charges of collaboration—a label that he was never fully able to shed.

He was rescued from his immediate plight by a respected member of the Resistance called Raymond Leblanc, who was not just a Tintin fan, but also a publisher. With Leblanc's help, Hergé began producing the bi-monthly *Journal de Tintin* in 1946, which was an instant success, and the fortunes of Tintin escalated from this point on. However, Leblanc was both a blessing and a burden: Hergé's contractual obligations began to wear him down. He suffered from crippling eczema on his hands, and his marriage came to grief. He battled on, and after 1950 the adventures began to appear in their now-famous volume form. For over two decades Hergé worked constantly on the series, while the public eagerly awaited each successive volume.

Tintin's fiftieth anniversary in 1979 was widely celebrated, but Hergé's health was in decline, and he died on 4 March 1983. Since then Tintin has been transformed for radio, animated cartoons, models and T-shirts, but the publishers have fortunately resisted the temptation to extend his adventures without the hand of his original creator.

Innocent, brave, foolhardy, illuminated by a clear sense of justice, always polite, and tolerant of the foibles of his wayward associates, Tintin no doubt contains much of Hergé himself. He makes an unlikely contender among the comic-book heroes of the modern age, and has never caught on in the USA, but his place in the rest of the world seems assured. Brussels now has a museum devoted to the art of the comic strip, the Centre Belge de la Bande Dessinée, the star of which, needless to say, is Tintin.

Here's a final puzzle: how old do you think Tintin is? He is in fact a 'boy reporter', but part of his success must be that he is any age you want him to be. He is ageless, in more senses than one.

Jacques Brel

French popular entertainment includes a genre that barely exists in the English-speaking world: the truly well-made song. It is a marriage of acutely observed lyrics and a memorable melody. The person who writes and performs such songs acquires the status of something equivalent to a poet; among the small handful of great *chanteurs-compositeurs* of this century stands one of the heroes of modern Belgium, Jacques Brel.

Everyone in Belgium, France and the Netherlands can sing excerpts from their favourite Brel songs. He sang passionately, his rich, mellifluous voice usually accompanied by a simple band consisting of piano, guitar, bass, drums and accordion. His songs paint powerful, unforgettable images, drawing universal qualities out of common experiences, and relishing the textures of ordinary life. In his most famous songs he evokes—with wit, affection and sometimes venom—the rough and ready atmosphere of sailors' dives in Amsterdam, inebriated drinking companions in the small hours of the morning, the awkwardness of impassioned lovers, the ridiculous attitudes of the bourgeoisie, and the triumph of hope over experience in jilted adolescents. Some of his songs are essentially clever musical games, such as *La Valse à Mille Temps*; others are pungent song-pictures, such as *Bruxelles*, a portrait of Brussels in the 1920s combined with an evocation of the silent cinema. He could also produce spellbinding love songs, such as *Ne Me Quitte Pas*. But he is perhaps best remembered for his portraits of Belgium, tender but not always flattering, such as *Le Plat Pays/Mijn Vlakke Land*.

Brel rose to stardom in Paris in the 1950s and was always greatly admired by the French, but he never forgot his Belgian origins. Born in 1929 of Flemish-speaking parents in Brussels, he is celebrated first and foremost for his French songs, but he made Flemish versions of many of these, and some songs, such as *Marieke*, contain words in both languages.

In 1966 Brel abandoned his solo tours, a tragedy for fans who believed he was never better than live in concert. Thereafter he worked in the cinema and took on a series of ambitious projects, including a musical about Don Quixote which became the Broadway hit *The Man of La Mancha*. However, he became increasingly disenchanted with stardom, and spent more and more of his time in retreat in the Marquesas Islands in French Polynesia. Here he fell ill, and was diagnosed as having lung cancer (he was always a heavy smoker). Returning to Europe for treatment, cared for by his wife and a handful of girlfriends, he cut a final album in 1977, and died near Paris in 1978. He was buried in the Marquesas Islands. Today his memory is still revered, and his songs seem as fresh and as inventive as ever. Brussels gave him an unusual accolade for a popular singer: it named a Métro station after him.

Charlotte Brontë

In February 1842 Charlotte Brontë, and her younger sister Emily were despatched from the secure but desultory atmosphere of Haworth parsonage to learn French in Brussels. It was a peculiar move for this strictly Protestant family, but the Reverend Brontë had been told by the chaplain to the British embassy that the

Pensionnat Héger for young ladies was a reliable institution, and he considered it a risk worth taking for the further education of his two daughters, who had now reached the comparatively mature ages of 26 and 24 respectively.

The Pensionnat Héger stood on the present site of the Palais des Beaux-Arts, near the Palais Royal and it was run by Madame Héger, whose husband Constantin taught French literature in the school. By all accounts it was a fairly relaxed and friendly place, where girls from wealthy, respectable families were gently educated to the unambitious standards of women's education of the time.

Charlotte and Emily were not impressed, but nonetheless buckled down to make the most of it. They missed home, and they had nothing but contempt for Belgium and the Belgians, whose manners offended them. Charlotte found their fellow pupils 'singularly cold, selfish, animal, and inferior... and their principles are rotten to the core,'—all of which she attributed to the fact that they were Catholic. However, the sisters threw themselves into their work and, with an industry that surprised their teachers, quickly became fluent in French.

After nine months Charlotte and Emily were recalled to Haworth because their aunt Elizabeth was seriously ill, but in January 1843 Charlotte returned to the Pensionnat Héger alone, not as a pupil but as a teacher of English. This was at the request of Monsieur Héger who had written an elegant and persuasive letter to Charlotte's father extolling her virtues and her potential as a teacher. She was no happier in this guise, and she left at the end of the year on the pretext that her father's growing blindness called for her presence at home.

Charlotte's experiences in Brussels had a profound effect. They provided the inspiration and the thinly-veiled setting for two novels: *The Professor* (written in 1846, and published posthumously in 1857), and a reworking of this book, with the main male character transformed into a girl, entitled *Villette* (published in 1853). Both are sustained and powerful first-person accounts revealing the inner torment of the protagonists as they fall in love with people who cannot return their affection—in the case of *Villette*, this is the older teacher, Monsieur Paul Emanuel. Neither book paints a very flattering picture of Brussels, which in the latter is renamed Villette, the capital of the kingdom of Labassecour.

The reality was yet stranger, and remains shrouded in mystery. Charlotte had clearly developed a strong passion for Monsieur Héger, and once back at Haworth she began writing highly emotional letters to him. After a rare occasion of hearing French being spoken in Yorkshire, she wrote to him that '*chaque mot avait pour moi le plus grand prix, puisqu'il me faisait me souvenir de vous. J'aime le français pour l'amour de vous de tout mon coeur et de toute mon âme*' (every word had the highest value for me because it reminded me of you. I love French because of my love for you, with all my heart and soul). Whatever had gone on between Charlotte and Monsieur Héger in Brussels remains unclear; all evidence suggests she developed this passion from afar, and received little or no encouragement from him. Faced with his reluctant and equivocal responses, Charlotte's letters took on an increasingly desperate tone: '*J'aime mieux subir les plus grandes douleurs physiques que d'avoir toujours le coeur lacéré par des regrets cuisants*' (I would rather suffer the worst physical pain than have my heart torn by bitter regrets); '*Jour et nuit je ne trouve ni repos ni paix*' (Night and day I can find neither rest nor peace). A batch of Charlotte's letters was eventually sold to the British Museum by Monsieur Héger's son, principally to allay rumours that Charlotte had had an affair with his father. Some of these letters had apparently been retrieved from the wastepaper basket by Madame Héger, who had little reason to think highly of Charlotte either then or later: in *Villette* Charlotte portrayed the headmistress as a vain, manipulative and prying woman who was clearly enough identified with Madame Héger to cause great offence. When Mrs Gaskell went to Brussels after Charlotte's death to research her biography, Madame Héger flatly refused to see her, although Monsieur Héger (who has been identified with the character of Paul Emanuel) spoke kindly to her of Charlotte.

Charlotte married after the deaths of her sisters, but she herself died nine months later, after complications arising from pregnancy. Her marriage at the age of 38 to her father's curate, Arthur Bell Nicholls, gave her security and domestic happiness, but it seems unlikely that she ever again experienced the obsessive passion she had felt for Héger.

Edith Cavell

On 12 October 1915 the Germans executed Edith Cavell in Brussels. They could hardly have made a greater mistake. In the UK it was seen as an act of unbelievable barbarity, and military recruitment surged. Shortly thereafter the Americans, who had vainly appealed for a commutation of the sentence, joined the war on the side of the Allies. If Allied propagandists were to be believed, it was a turning point in Germany's fortunes.

Edith Cavell was a rather prim and humourless 49-year-old British nurse—on paper, not obvious material for a heroine. However, she was deeply respected in Brussels even before the war. She had gone there in 1906, and through years of devoted duty had transformed the Belgian nursing system into a proper profession. Her work was acknowledged and supported by Queen Elisabeth of the Belgians, and furthermore did much to promote the respectability of careers for women in general.

At the outbreak of war and German occupation, Edith Cavell was *directrice* of three Brussels hospitals, which she dutifully prepared to receive the wounded, but for various reasons few came to her. In the meantime, a Belgian nobleman and his wife, the Prince and Princesse de Croy, had allowed their estate near Mons to become a refuge for Allied soldiers caught behind enemy lines. These men had to be carefully escorted to freedom by crossing the border to the Netherlands. Before long Edith Cavell had been recruited to provide refuge for Allied soldiers at her nursing institute, and at other safe houses in Brussels. She threw herself into this work with little concern for own safety and was fully aware that penalties would be severe if she was caught.

When the Germans eventually realized that enemy soldiers were crossing out of Belgium, they used an agent to infiltrate the de Croys' network. Edith Cavell was arrested along with other members of her cell, but not before 200 Allied soldiers had won their freedom. She was held in Saint-Gilles prison and told that other detainees had informed the Germans fully of her activities. The Germans had taken the trouble to assemble a convincing body of evidence against Edith Cavell and at a military court she was sentenced to death by firing squad. The international community in Brussels made vigorous protests, to no avail.

Edith Cavell prepared herself for her death with her customary fastidiousness. The English chaplain in Brussels gave her Holy Communion and she said on parting, 'I know now that patriotism is not enough. I must have no hatred and no bitterness toward anyone.' At dawn she was taken by car to the Tir National (shooting range). Here she was made to watch the execution of her colleague in the underground, the architect Philippe Baucq. When her turn came she apparently conducted herself with such dignity that the firing squad aimed above her head. She fainted, and the commander of the squad walked up and shot her in the head. A memorial service was held in a packed Westminster Cathedral on 29 October 1915. At the end of the war Edith Cavell's body was repatriated and taken to Norwich for burial. The funeral cortège passed through London, its silent streets lined with crowds numbering tens of thousands.

In Brussels itself Edith Cavell is remembered with great affection, and one of its most prestigious hospitals is named after her.

Pity the Poor Immigrant

The statistics are remarkably high: over a quarter of Brussels' population is of non-Belgian origin. Many of these are connected to the EU, diplomatic missions or multinational companies, others are immigrant workers from Spain, Portugal, Italy, Greece, the former Yugoslavia and Zaire. But when the Bruxellois speak of *les immigrés* they are thinking primarily of the people who make up about one-third of this immigrant population, the North Africans and Turks.

Immigration into Belgium took place on a large scale during the 1960s, when growing prosperity left the nation short of labour. Workers came from all parts of the world, but particularly from Turkey and the Maghreb—Tunisia, Algeria and Morocco. As the Bruxellois drifted out of the city towards the leafy suburbs, so the inner-city areas began to fill with immigrant workers and their families. Now the population of the Brussels district of Saint-Josse, for example, is 50 per cent immigrant and Schaerbeek 36 per cent.

Many of these immigrant populations are now well into their second generation. The communities are firmly established, with their own shops, restaurants, mosques and language groups—their own closed, exotic world. Yet most non-EU immigrants have no cast-iron rights of residence; they are at the mercy of the prevailing winds of the economy. Whenever there is a downturn, unemployment rises, and so does their dependency on state welfare. Belgians are quick to see the immigrant population as a problem, a drain on national resources, a source of crime; in times of recession, calls for repatriation all too predictably appear on the platforms of extreme political parties.

Belgium has not been very successful at addressing the racial tensions between even its own two native communities, let alone those that surround the immigrant communities. In practice there is little contact between '*les étrangers*' and the Belgians except in the corner shop and on those occasions when the Belgians wish to eat couscous in a North African restaurant (generally considered a cheap night out). Bars—the traditional place of relaxation for Belgians—are off limits for Muslims; the experience of colonialism has taught no lessons, and significantly there are comparatively few *zaïrois* immigrants.

Where one might hope for a will towards integration, one encounters rather suspicion and mutual contempt. Middle-class Belgians will happily bang on about *les immigrés* as if racism was a perfectly acceptable attitude. The gulf widens: many of the immigrants have a poor grasp of the Belgian languages, and send their children to immigrant-dominated schools. Due partly to high levels of unemployment, a class of alienated youth is growing up and, with little to lose, they are becoming increasingly confrontational.

It is a measure of the potential seriousness of this situation that Belgians often express admiration for the level of racial integration they perceive in Britain—which itself is not exactly famous for its racial tolerance.

Léo-Hendrik Baekeland (1863–1944). A key pioneer in the development of modern plastics, famous as the inventor of Bakelite. Developed in 1907, this was the first ever totally synthetic plastic, and from the 1930s to the 1950s it was used for everything from light switches, egg cups and vacuum flasks to telephones and radio sets. A chemist from Ghent, Baekeland spent most of his working life in the USA, where he made a fortune.

Thierry Boutsen (b.1957). Formula 1 racing driver who has scored several Grand Prix victories since his début in 1983.

Jacques Brel (1929–78). One of the greatest French *chanteurs-compositeurs* of this century (*see* pp.39–40).

Pieter Bruegel the Elder (*c.*1525–69). The father of a family of painters, and the most original of all of them—trained in Antwerp but moved to Brussels in 1563. Despite his title, he died at the relatively young age of 44, when his sons Pieter and Jan were still infants.

Hugo Claus (b.1929). Bruges-born poet, playwright and novelist who is widely admired in both Flanders and the Netherlands. His name is consistently put forward as a potential Nobel prizewinner. His most famous work is probably the novel *Het Verdriet van Belgium* ('The Grief of Belgium'). He has a son by the Dutch actress Sylvia Kristel (of *Emmanuelle* fame).

Paul Delvaux (1897–1994). One of the great Belgian Surrealists, noted above all for his haunting night-time scenes of lounging nudes in railway and tram stations.

James Ensor (1860–1949). One of the late 19th century's most remarkable painters. Born in Ostend to a Flemish mother and English father, he showed early talents before ploughing his own furrow with his peculiar brand of colourful, satirical and disturbing images plucked from his imagination and painted in a manner that foreshadowed Expressionism.

César Franck (1822–90). Organist and composer in a romantic style influenced by Beethoven, Liszt and Bach. He lived in Paris after 1844.

Dirk Frimout (b.1941). Engineer and astronaut with the European Space Agency and the first Belgian to go into space, in March 1992, on board the Shuttle, *Atlas 1*.

Michel de Ghelderode (1898–1962). Belgium's most celebrated 20th-century playwright, whose work often explores historic themes.

Zénobe-Théophile Gramme (1826–1901). A self-taught engineer who invented a practical form of direct current dynamo in 1869, which opened the door to the transition from steam power to electrical power.

Arthur Grumiaux (1921–86). One of the great violinists of his generation, noted in particular for his interpretations of Mozart.

Johnny Hallyday (b.1943). A name synonymous with the '*yé-yé*' epoque of French rock 'n' roll in the early 1960s—and still going strong. Born Jean-Philippe Smet, he started on the path to stardom in Paris at the age of 15 and has spent most of his life in France. He has also had a noted film career.

Hergé (1907–83). The creator of Tintin (*see* pp.38–9).

Victor Horta (1861–1947). The presiding genius of Art Nouveau architecture (*see* pp.187–9).

Jacky Ickx (b.1945). One of the great Formula 1 racing drivers, who won eight Grands Prix in a career that lasted from 1966 to 1979. He went on to become one of the world's most successful rally drivers, winning Le Mans six times and the Paris–Dakar Rally in 1983.

René Magritte (1898–1967). One of the great Surrealist painters, famous for his small, technically precise paintings. Their delightful mixture of wit and absurd incongruity has made his paintings some of the most widely reproduced of all 20th-century art.

Gerard Mercator (1512–94). Flemish geographer who devised a way of making the round world look flat. The Mercator projection effectively makes the globe into a cylinder by expanding area proportionately towards the poles. It is still the most familiar way of portraying the world map.

Eddy Merckx (b.1945). Unmatched cycling supremo, winner of the Tour de France five times (1969–72 and 1974) and over 140 other titles; now involved in cycle manufacture. One of the great popular heroes of Belgium.

Pieter Paul Rubens (1577–1640). Leader of a cultural renaissance in Antwerp, and one of the greatest European painters of his day, also much acclaimed in both Spain and Britain, which he visited on diplomatic missions. He had an unrivalled ability to apply a dramatic, sensuous panache even to large-scale paintings. (*See* pp.71–2.)

Adolphe Sax (1814–94). Dinant's favourite son, most famous as the inventor of the saxophone (in 1845), but his experiments with wind instruments and valves also led him to other inventions, such as the bugle-like saxhorn.

Georges Simenon (1903–89). The novelist from Liège whose most famous creation, Inspector Maigret, appeared in 76 of his 300-plus novels, which draw convincingly—and always entertainingly—on a huge breadth of social observation. Simenon ranks among the most read novelists of all time; his books have been translated into 87 languages. He was only more prolific as a womanizer, and claimed to have slept with 10,000 women—although his second wife disputed this. She put the figure at 1200.

Paul-Henri Spaak (1899–1972). Belgium's first socialist prime minister in 1938. After exile in London during the war, Spaak fought tooth and nail for his vision of a united Europe. He was chairman of the six-nation group that signed the Treaty of Rome in 1957, which ultimately led to the creation of the European Community.

Jean-Claude Van Damme (b.1960). Brussels-born actor and former karate champion who went to the USA and delivered pizzas before being adopted by Hollywood and turned into a chisel-chinned star via such films as *No Retreat, No Surrender* (1985), *Bloodsport* (1987), *Kickboxer* (1989) and *Universal Soldier* (1992).

Henri van de Velde (1863–1957). Born in Antwerp and trained as a painter in Paris, Van der Velde ranks beside Horta as one the most inspired designers of the Art Nouveau movement, noted particularly for his stylish furniture and interiors. He moved to Germany in 1899 and later founded the Kunstschule in Weimar, which in 1919 evolved into the Bauhaus and blazed the trail to Modernism.

Jan van Eyck (1390–1441). One of the outstanding north European painters of the late medieval period, Van Eyck (pronounced 'Eck') is credited with the invention of oil paints. This may be exaggerated, but certainly he brought their use to the peak of perfection, applying dazzling technical brilliance to masterpieces such *The Adoration of the Mystic Lamb* in Sint-Baafskathedraal, Ghent (also signed by his otherwise virtually unknown brother, Hubert).

Emile Verhaeren (1855–1916). Symbolist poet, who wrote in French but was noted in particular for his portrayals of Flanders. He was killed by a train in Rouen, France.

Andreas Vesalius (1514–64). Physician to Charles V and Philip II, Vesalius was one of the great scientific figures of the northern Renaissance, famed as the 'father of modern anatomy' through his work in dissecting cadavers, which he wrote up in *De Humani Corporis Fabrica*. He died on a pilgrimage imposed as a punishment by the Inquisition.

Marguerite Yourcenar (1903-87). A major figure of the French literary world, Yourcenar was born in Brussels but became a French national before going to live in the USA in 1939. Best known for historical novels such as *Les Mémoires d'Hadrien*, she was the first woman to be made a member of the Académie Française.

Eugène Ysaÿe (1858–1931). Virtuoso violinist and also a noted composer, whose work included six concertos. He was conductor of the Cincinnati Symphony Orchestra from 1918 to 1922.

History

Belgium has been in existence for only 160 years. Forged as an independent state in 1830, it has had a hard time trying to establish deep historical roots to its nationhood. Before 1830 it had barely seen itself as a nation at all, more the haphazardly constructed filling in a sandwich of powerblocks.

History, however, has a hunger for labels. It likes neatly defined borders, dynasties and empires, big dates and strong storylines. Belgium can provide few of these. Its tale is complex; it has been busy in the wings of mainstream European history, but seldom centre stage. It might be tempting to pretend that Belgium has no history at all—but of course it does, written into the worn bricks of the step-gables of Bruges, into the gilded cornucopias of Brussels' Grand' Place, into the battlefield of Waterloo.

The Bravest of the Gauls

By about 400 BC much of northern Europe was occupied by the Celts, a loosely knit federation of iron-working tribes who had spread out from their original base in southern Germany and Switzerland. The Celts were gifted horsemen and fearless warriors, who would enter battle naked except for a bronze torque around their necks, egged on by the Druids and crowds of women braying like the Furies.

The Romans lived in dread of the Celts, whom they called the **Gauls**. The Gauls hemmed them in across the northern borders of Italy and represented the very opposite of what their civilization stood for. Worse, in 390 BC the Gauls poured into Italy and sacked Rome. The Romans had to wait for the greatest leader of their history, **Julius Caesar** (100–44 BC) to see the Gauls finally subdued. After 59 BC he waged a campaign that pushed the Roman Empire to the North Sea and established his reputation as a general. However, on the eastern fringes of Gaul he came up against furious resistance from the **Belgae**, causing him to comment, '*Horum popularum omnium fortissimi sunt Belgae.*' ('Of all these people [the Gauls], the Belgae are the most courageous.')

The Belgae were subsequently ruled as a part of Roman Gaul, which had its eastern border along the Rhine. After AD 15 Gaul was subdivided, and **Gallia Belgica** became a separate province, which stretched southwards from the North Sea coast and included much of modern Switzerland. As elsewhere in the Roman Empire, the Pax Romana brought a prolonged period of stability and prosperity to the region, once its people had accepted subjugation.

The Franks and Charlemagne (5th–8th centuries)

After the collapse of the Roman Empire, a Germanic tribe called the **Franks**, who had settled as Roman mercenaries in northern Belgium around Tournai, pushed the remnants of the Romans out of Gaul. Their leader, **Clovis I** (r.AD 481–511), founded the Christian Merovingian dynasty (c.500–751), named after his predecessor but one, Merovech.

Throughout the Merovingian period, Tournai was the hub of an empire covering much of France and Germany. Brussels, by contrast, was merely a twinkle in the eye of a Bishop. According to legend, **St Géry**, Bishop of Cambrai, built a chapel on one of the islands in the swampy River Senne in the late 6th century AD. A settlement may then have grown up around it. However, the name Bruocsella, meaning 'house in the swamp', is not recorded before AD 966.

The Merovingian kings ruled until AD 751, when they were ousted by Pepin the Short, who founded the Carolingian dynasty (AD 751–987). Pepin the Short's son, born in Liège in AD 742, was one of the great kings of this transitional period of European history. He was called **Charlemagne** ('Charles the Great', r.AD 768–814). Under his rule the Moors were pushed back from northern Spain, and the Frankish kingdoms were extended into Italy and southern Germany.

Charlemagne saw himself as the heir to the Roman Empire, and the Pope obliged by crowning him Emperor of the West in AD 800. But after his death his heirs squabbled and the Frankish Empire splintered. Under the Treaty of Verdun in AD 843 the River Scheldt, which flows across the middle of Belgium between Tournai and Antwerp, marked the border between lands assigned to rival grandsons of Charlemagne—the German king **Lothair I** (AD 795–855), and the French king **Charles the Bald** (AD 823–77). Charles took West Francia, to the west and north of the Scheldt, and Lothair took lands to the south and east. His kingdom became known as Lotharingia, later Lorraine.

Flanders and Lorraine (9th–11th centuries)

The division of the Frankish Empire along the Scheldt was not simply geographical. In late Roman times, when the Franks had settled in the north of Belgium, the south was occupied by Romanized Celts called the Wala. The language of the Romanized Celts evolved out of Latin to become French, and this was the language of the Wala—later the Walloons. Hence, this was a political and linguistic divide which, broadly speaking, still exists today. Ironically, however, the part assigned to France was Flemish-speaking, while the French-speaking half fell into the orbit of East Francia, which evolved into Germany.

The history of Belgium now follows two different threads for five centuries. Flanders in the north became powerful under a series of notable leaders called Baldwin (Baudouin in French, Boudewijn in Flemish). The first of these, **Baldwin Iron-Arm** challenged the authority of the French king, Charles the Bald, and eloped with his daughter, Judith. The couple fled to Rome, where Pope Nicholas I managed to bring about a reconciliation of all parties, and as a result Charles appointed Baldwin the first Count of Flanders. Although strictly owing allegiance to France, Baldwin and his successors were powers in their own right, and became a force to be reckoned with in French politics. **Bruges** and **Ghent** developed and prospered as their main strongholds.

Meanwhile in East Francia, ruled by German kings, Lorraine became a separate duchy, subdivided into powerful feudal princedoms: Hainaut, Limburg, Namur, Liège and Brabant. In AD 977 **Charles, Duke of Lorraine**, chose the island of St Géry (i.e. **Brussels**) in the Senne as the site of a new fortress. He took up residence there in AD 979—the year given as the official foundation of the city. In 1041 these estates passed into the hands of the **Counts of Leuven** (Louvain), who ruled the surrounding county (subsequently duchy) of Brabant.

During the 11th century Count Lambert II embarked on a major undertaking, building a fortress and residence in Brussels on the high ground above the river. This was the **Coudenberg** ('Cold Hill'), today the site of the Royal Palace and the Musées Royaux des Beaux-Arts. In 1100 the town was fortified by its first ring of defensive walls.

The Battle of the Golden Spurs (1302)

With the decline of feudalism, a powerful merchant class emerged in the towns and cities of Flanders, which were well placed to exploit the trading links that now spread right across northern Europe. The key trade was textiles. **Wool** from England was imported and turned into cloth by Flemish weavers.

Ghent, Bruges and Ypres became virtually independent city states. Their sense of independence put them constantly at odds with the Counts of Flanders, who owed their allegiance to France. After violent confrontations and disputes over succession in the 12th century, the French reasserted their grip on Flanders; but the disdainful behaviour of the Frenchified élite and the cloth merchants, who lorded it over weavers and other workers, became the source of increasing resentment. A mood of rebellion set in, resulting in an uprising against the French in Bruges in 1302, led by **Pieter de Coninck** and **Jan Breydel**, during which anyone unable to speak Flemish was slaughtered.

Later that year, on 11 July, Flemish workers led by Jan Breydel—and armed with little more than lances and staves—took on the full might of the French king, Philip IV (Philip the Fair), near Kortrijk (Courtrai). The French had massively superior and better equipped forces, but the Flemish prepared the marshy ground well, laying branches that acted as traps for the heavily armoured French knights.

The French became completely bogged down and were picked off, one by one. This humiliating rout became known as the Battle of the Golden Spurs, because the Flemish victors collected 700 pairs of golden spurs and exhibited them triumphantly in Kortrijk Cathedral.

As a result of this battle, Philip the Fair granted Flanders its independence. However, the aristocracy, still loyal to the French, gradually reasserted their power, and by 1329 Flanders was under French rule once more.

Events in Brussels followed a similar pattern. Lying on the main trade route between Cologne and Bruges, it too had prospered, and it developed its own flourishing industries, particularly weaving and goldsmithing. In 1225 work on the **Cathédrale Saint-Michel** was begun. A massive new city wall was built in the early 14th century and completed in 1379. (Its course is now marked by the inner perimeter ring road called 'la Petite Ceinture'. The shape of the space within the city walls gave rise to the name for the city centre: 'le Pentagone'.)

Brussels also had its share of unrest, as workers rose up against the merchants. The Guild of Weavers, Dyers and Fullers won some political power after the Battle of the Golden Spurs, but in 1306, after continuing turmoil, the rebels were defeated by Duke Jean II of Brabant at the **Battle of Vilvoorde**. To show he meant business, Duke Jean had the leaders buried alive outside the city gates.

The Hundred Years' War (1337–1453)

English claims to French territory, plus their trading interests in Flanders, led to a protracted series of military confrontations with France known as the Hundred Years' War. The trigger was the death of the last French Capetian king, who died in 1328. The English king **Edward III** (r.1327–77), the maternal grandson of Philip the Fair of France, reckoned he had a good claim to the French throne—as least as valid as Philip's nephew, Philip de Valois, who became Philip VI.

The aristocracy of Flanders naturally sided with the French—so England responded with sanctions: all wool exports to Flanders ceased. Since English wool was the foundation stone of the Flemish textile trade, this had a rapid and profound effect and the wealthy Flemish wool merchants were faced with ruin. In 1338 a brewer from Ghent called **Jacob van Artevelde** led a successful rebellion against the French authorities, and invited Edward the Black Prince (1330–76), son of Edward III, to become Count of Flanders. Edward III arrived in Flanders with an army, and was proclaimed king of France in Ghent in 1340.

The weavers (as opposed to the wool merchants) had other views. They murdered Jacob van Artevelde in 1345 and seized control of the Flemish cities. It was a unilateral move guaranteed to antagonize other craftsmen. The result was civil war, which ended with the reassertion of the power of the (real) Count of Flanders, with the support of France.

Events in Brabant, further south, now brought the people of Brussels into conflict with Flanders. In 1355 Duke Jean II of Brabant died without a male heir, and the succession fell to his daughter **Jeanne**, who was married to Wenceslas of Luxembourg. In 1356 **Louis de Male**, Count of Flanders, seized the opportunity to invade and took Brabant for himself, although the Flemish were driven out of Brussels by rebels led by the leader of the guilds, **Everard 't Serclaes**. So matters rested until 1381–2, when **Philip van Artevelde** (son of Jacob) led an uprising, defeating Louis de Male before himself coming to grief in a battle against the French. Meanwhile Jeanne and Wenceslas transferred their centre of power from Leuven to Brussels.

In 1384 the throne of Flanders passed to **Philip the Bold of Burgundy** by virtue of his marriage to Louis de Male's daughter, Margaret. Bit by bit, the Burgundians took control of most of what is Belgium today: in 1406 the Duchy of Brabant also passed into their hands through marriage, when Jeanne (the last of the Leuven line) died and inheritance passed through the line of her sister.

The Dukes of Burgundy were part of the Valois family (Philip the Bold was the brother of Charles V of France), and so were directly connected to the French throne. They ruled over one of the wealthiest regions in Europe, now magnified by the acquisition of these northern territories.

Meanwhile the Hundred Years' War rumbled on. Charles VI (r.1380–1422) succeeded his father to the French throne: known as Charles the Mad, he was of unsound mind, and power in France seemed up for grabs. The Dukes of Orleans and Burgundy entered into bitter rivalry to take control. In 1407 the Duke of Burgundy, **John the Fearless**, had Louis Duke of Orleans murdered, plunging France into civil war. John then negotiated with the English, offering to support **Henry V**'s claim to the French throne. Henry thereupon opened up a new campaign with his famous victory over the French at Agincourt in 1415.

As the English laid siege to Paris, John the Fearless got cold feet. He attempted to negotiate with the new Duke of Orleans, but was himself murdered. In revenge John the Fearless's son, **Philip the Good** (r.1419–67), now gave his open support to the English, and had soon forced Charles VI to sign the Treaty of Troyes, in which Henry V was named as Charles's successor to the French throne.

But it was not to be. Henry V died just two months before Charles, and the throne went to Charles' son, Charles VII (1422–61). The French then launched a new campaign, inspired by Joan of Arc (1412–31), and eventually pushed the English out of their lands.

The Burgundian Period (15th century)

Philip the Good's Burgundian empire covered two distinct areas: the Burgundy region of central eastern France and the area covering most of modern Belgium plus the Netherlands—the 'Low Countries'. Philip adopted Brussels for his main residence, and by 1430 it had stolen the limelight from Dijon, the former capital of Burgundy. The **Grand' Place** began to take shape as guild houses were constructed around the old market square, and the monumental **Hôtel de Ville** was erected during the first half of the 15th century. Philip was the richest man in Europe and his court was the height of European fashion, attracting some of the greatest men of the times—including composers, writers and painters, the most notable of whom were the brothers **Van Eyck**. French became the language of government and of the nobility in Brussels. Philip also created the **Order of the Golden Fleece** in Bruges in 1430, its name acknowledging the continuing importance of the wool trade.

Philip's son, **Charles the Bold** (r.1467–77), attempted to extend his territory by conquering the rest of Lorraine, but was killed at the Battle of Nancy. Louis XI of France (r.1461–83) then seized the French part of Burgundy for France. Charles's only heir was his daughter, **Mary**, who was thus left with only the Burgundian lands of the Low Countries. Arriving in Ghent, she faced all kinds of opposition and subversion orchestrated by agents of Louis XI. Louis' plan was to coerce Mary into marriage with his own son, but Mary's mother, Margaret of York (sister to Edward IV of England) had a scheme to thwart the French: in 1477 she arranged a marriage between Mary and **Maximilian I**, a member of the ruling German-Austrian **Habsburg** family, and future Holy Roman Emperor—as the heirs to the eastern Frankish kingdom liked to call themselves, in the style of Charlemagne.

When Mary died in 1482 after a fall from a horse, Maximilian assumed sovereignty over the Burgundian Low Countries, and in 1494 he passed them on to his son, **Philip the Handsome**. Two years later, Philip married **Joanna of Castile**, and they ruled Castile (effectively Spain) together for just one year (1506) before Philip died. This was enough, however, to assure the succession of their son, Charles V, to an unprecentedly vast kingdom.

Emperor Charles V (1500–58)

Charles V (Charles Quint in French) was by far the most powerful ruler of Europe in his day. Born in Ghent, he grew up in Mechelen and always regarded the Low Countries as his homeland. However, events and his restless energy took him much further afield, and for most of his reign the home countries were governed by his sister, **Mary of Hungary**.

In 1517 Charles took over the Spanish throne on the death of his grandfather. Then in 1520 he assumed the crown of Holy Roman Emperor after the death of Maximilian—ruling Austria and Germany, Burgundy and the Low Countries, as well as the kingdoms of Naples and Sicily. He put down rebellions in Spain, and in Italy he fought the French under François I (r.1515–47), his long-term rival, whom he succeeded in capturing at the Battle of Pavia (1525). He also defeated the Turks under Suleiman the Magnificent in 1532.

Meanwhile Hernán Cortés conquered Mexico (1521) and Francisco Pizarro conquered Peru (1532) in the name of Spain, bringing in not only vast new territories but also huge quantities of gold. The Age of Exploration was also an age of extravagance, fostering a get-rich-quick mentality in which huge sums were speculated on trading expeditions—to the Americas or the Far East—and the gains were spent lavishly on fancy buildings, paintings, banquets and feasting.

At home, land reclamation schemes, using dykes and windmills, began to push back the sea from the flat lands of the north, while the gardens of the Low Countries became the envy of Europe. Tapestry, pottery and glass were produced and exported, and the linen industry also took off, notably in Ghent and Kortrijk.

Charles's reign coincided with the remarkable advances of Renaissance learning and art in northern Europe. The great Humanist **Desiderius Erasmus** (*see* pp.206–208) acted as adviser to Charles and went on to play a leading role in the development of Leuven/Louvain University. **Christopher Plantin** set up his famous printing workshop in Antwerp in the 1570s. Charles's own physician, **Andreas Vesalius** (1514–64) is now regarded as the father of modern anatomy. By carrying out a controversial programme of the dissection of corpses he identified many of the organs, as illustrated in his *De Humani Corporis Fabrica* (1543).

The new thinking promoted by the Renaissance, however, smacked to some of subversion, and its most feared and controversial manifestation was **Protestantism**. Martin Luther posted his 95 theses to the church door of Wittenberg in 1517, and thereafter the course was set: the Reformation rapidly spread among the dissident German states and in the northern Netherlands. It was the one challenge that Charles was not equal to.

Meanwhile the people of the Low Countries were taxed heavily for the privilege of being part of Charles's mighty empire. It was, after all, expensive to run. When Ghent rebelled in 1540, Charles personally saw to a crushing suppression—a rude shock from their favourite son.

In 1555, exhausted by his struggles, Charles announced from his palace in Brussels that he was abdicating: he gave his Spanish crown to his son Philip and the crown of the Holy Roman Empire to his brother Ferdinand.

Suppression in the Spanish Low Countries (late 16th century)

Brussels and the rest of the Low Countries did not take kindly to the fact that, shortly after the beginning of his reign, Philip II decided to rule at arm's length, from Spain. 'I would prefer to lose all my domains and die 100 times than rule over heretics,' Philip, a fanatical Catholic, is quoted as saying. He meant it. The Inquisition was sent to the Low Countries in order to apply its ruthless answer to Protestantism. All unconventional thinking came under the Inquisition's scrutiny.

When heavy taxes were imposed to finance Philip's extravagant wars, resentment in the Low Countries boiled over into rebellion. Good citizens and Catholics were caught up in this mood, as well as the Protestants. The Low Countries had been placed under the governorship of **Margaret of Parma** (daughter of Charles V), who bore the brunt of increasingly vociferous criticism. The opposition found a champion in **William of Orange** ('the Silent'), whose forebear had been rewarded for his loyalty to Charles V with substantial estates in the Netherlands. William formed a League of Nobility, which appealed for moderation in the treatment of Protestants. Their petition, however, was roundly rejected by Margaret's advisers, one of whom was the Walloon councillor **Baron Berlaymont**, who labelled the League as '*ces gueux*' ('those beggars'). The riposte of the opposition's supporters was to go around dressed as beggars, waving their begging bowls and shouting, '*Vivent les gueux!*'

In 1566 the resentment of Calvinist Protestants turned to violence. Throughout the Low Countries they vented their pious wrath on the churches, vandalizing the interiors in an orgy of **iconoclasm**. More moderate forces recoiled in horror and swung back in favour of Margaret. William of Orange and the Governor of Flanders, Count Egmont, tried to find a compromise, but as events slipped out of control William withdrew to Germany.

Philip's answer was to send the **Duke of Alva** with 10,000 troops to restore order. He was assisted by the Inquisition, which set up the **'Council of Disorders'** (also known as the 'Council of Blood') and handed out 8000 death sentences. Among those executed were **Counts Egmont** and **Hornes**: left to carry the can in William's absence, they were beheaded in Brussels in 1568.

From this year on, William began a military campaign against Spanish rule, aided by a navy of privateers called Sea Beggars. After several false starts, William gained the upper hand, and took the towns of the Low Countries one by one. Facing mutinous troops and angry creditors, the Duke of Alva fled in 1573. William entered Brussels in triumph in 1576 and won Amsterdam in 1578.

However, not everyone in the Low Countries was overjoyed. The problem was that the south—essentially modern Belgium—was primarily Catholic, and did not believe it shared a destiny with the Protestant provinces of the north—the modern Netherlands. Indeed, Catholics were now being persecuted in the north.

In 1578 Philip of Spain sent Alexander Farnese, **Duke of Parma**, into the south at the head of a large army, and he was rewarded by a series of capitulations in the French-speaking provinces. Many of these then signed the Union of Arras in 1579, declaring their allegiance to Spain. In response, the Protestant northern provinces—called the **United Provinces**—declared their independence and appointed William of Orange as their *stadhouder* (governor). The Duke of Parma pressed on north, taking Antwerp after a bitter year-long siege and Brussels in 1585. Most of Flanders and the French-speaking provinces were now back in Spanish hands, and these lands became known as the **Spanish Netherlands**, with Brussels as the capital.

Just before his death in 1598 Philip II handed the Spanish Netherlands over to his daughter, the **Infanta Isabella** (1566–1633), and her husband, **Albert, Archduke of Austria** (1559–1621). The news was received with great joy in Brussels, and Isabella entered the city amid celebrations, sumptuously dressed and riding on a saddle studded with diamonds and rubies. The Spanish, however, still aspired to regain the United Provinces—but they insisted that only Catholicism would be tolerated. Isabella refused (in 1601) to change her shirt for the duration of her husband's siege of Ostende; the siege lasted three years—and *isabelle* is now a colour, a sort of yellowy brown. The Twelve Years' Truce of 1609 sealed independence for the United Provinces, at which point 100,000 Protestants from Flanders emigrated across the border.

Europe's Battleground: the Spanish Netherlands (1579–1713)

For a while the Spanish Netherlands, and Brussels in particular, enjoyed a period of peace and prosperity. The mood is caught by the ebullient paintings of **Rubens**, who was court painter to Isabella and Albert. But Europe was overshadowed by the Thirty Years' War (1618–48), in which Protestants contested the power of the Catholic Habsburgs. Isabella and Albert took the opportunity to take up the cudgels once more against the United Provinces, who entered an alliance with the French in 1633. The lasting result was that Philip IV of Spain (r.1605–65), desperate to be able to turn all his military strength on France, signed the **Peace of Münster**, which gave formal recognition to the independence of the United Provinces. The terms of the treaty allowed the United Provinces to stop all traffic through the mouth of the River Scheldt, which ran through territory now controlled by them. Antwerp's access to the sea was sealed off and its fortunes doomed until Napoleon lifted the ban 150 years later.

Spain's conflict with France was a running sore throughout the 17th century, and inevitably the Spanish Netherlands were drawn into it. When William III of

Orange, *stadhouder* of the United Provinces, became king of England in 1689 by virtue of his marriage to Mary, Protestant daughter of James II, the stage was set for a major bust-up.

The first phase was the **War of the Grand Alliance** (1690–7), designed to put an end to the expansionist exploits of Louis XIV of France. Louis took Namur in 1692. This was then besieged by forces under William. When **Marshal de Villeroy**, commanding 70,000 French troops, failed to lift the siege, he marched on Brussels in a fit of pique. After issuing an ultimatum, he turned his cannon on the city, which was bombarded from Anderlecht throughout the night of 13 August 1695. The city centre—including the Grand' Place and many of the old churches—was flattened and some 4000 houses were burned to the ground. The French then dusted their hands and withdrew.

It is a credit to the determination of the citizens of Brussels that they immediately set about re-erecting what Villeroy's cannons had knocked down. Most of today's Grand' Place was built within five years of the bombardment.

Louis' antics were not over yet. In 1700 Charles II of Spain died—the last of the Spanish Habsburgs. Charles had no direct heir, so he passed the crown of Spain to Philip, Duke of Anjou, the grandson of Louis XIV. Louis leaned upon Philip to hand over the Spanish Netherlands to France, but such a solution was unacceptable to either England or the United Provinces of the Netherlands, who greatly feared the French domination of Europe. The result was the **War of the Spanish Succession** (1701–13). England, the Netherlands, Austria and many German states formed an alliance against France, and the brilliant generalship of the Duke of Marlborough and Prince Eugene of Savoy drove the French out of the Spanish Netherlands, but not before the armies had raged across Flanders. Ghent and Bruges changed hands twice, while the allies won two victories on Belgian soil: at **Ramillies** (1706), near Namur and **Oudenaarde** (1708), southwest of Ghent.

At the end of the war France was left in ruins. In the **Treaty of Utrecht** it renounced its claims to the Spanish Netherlands, which passed into the hands of **Charles VI**, the Habsburg Emperor of Austria and became the Austrian Netherlands. This high-handed reassignment of ownership was bitterly resented in some quarters. In Brussels the leader of the guilds, **François Anneessens**, led a revolt, but it was short-lived, and he was beheaded in 1719.

The Austrian Netherlands (1713–94) and the Age of Napoleon

Charles VI of Austria had no male heir, so in 1713 he announced a '**pragmatic sanction**'—eventually accepted by most of the European powers—that the succession would pass into the female line through his daughter **Maria Theresa**.

However, when Charles died in 1740, the European powers disregarded this arrangement and Maria Theresa had to contend with the **War of the Austrian Succession** (1740–8), a complex conflict that was fought across most of Europe as well as in North America. Maria Theresa emerged from it with her succession affirmed, and a period of prosperity followed in the Austrian Netherlands.

In 1741 Maria Theresa put these provinces in the hands of her enlightened brother-in-law, **Charles of Lorraine** (1712–80), who set up a dazzling court in Brussels, famed for its generous and elegant hospitality and its ceaseless round of masked balls and merry-making. The sedate neoclassical style was adopted for ambitious building projects, notably at what is now the Place des Martyrs. The Place Royale and the adjoining royal palace rose on the site of the old Coudenberg palace, which had been destroyed by fire in 1731. Industry was transformed by investment; new roads connected the cities and linked Brussels to Vienna. But while the aristocracy partied, draped in voluminous lace and eating off the finest European porcelain, the poor faced crowded, insanitary conditions exacerbated by high levels of unemployment. With the Age of Enlightenment came also the rumblings of intellectual discontent.

Charles of Lorraine died in 1780 and Maria Theresa died five months later. She was succeeded by her son, **Joseph II**. He was in many ways a child of the Enlightenment, and introduced various reforms–in education and administration, as well as freedom of worship–which allowed Protestants to build churches, to become full citizens, and to take up public office. He also wanted to streamline Austrian government by centralizing power in Vienna; and in 1784 it was announced that German was to be the official language of the empire.

For all Joseph's good intentions, such reforms were interpreted in Belgium as the unwelcome meddling of a despot. A vociferous opposition arose, composed of two quite different tendencies: on the one hand there were the liberals who wanted to expel the Habsburgs in favour of a democratic, modern state; on the other there were the Catholic conservatives and aristocracy, who looked back nostalgically to the *ancien régime* of Maria Theresa. The latter were led by **Henri van der Noot**, who, following an insurrection in 1788, became the main voice of the opposition. This was in stark contrast to the fervently radical political atmosphere which carried the French Revolution the following year.

Nonetheless, the Revolution in France inspired an uprising in Belgium, and when this was crushed by the Austrians at Turnhout, the whole country rose to the call in what has become known as the **Brabançon Revolt**. In January 1790 the provinces agreed to form their own Congress, with Van der Noot as its prime minister, and they unilaterally proclaimed an independent **United States of Belgium**. This was readily recognized by England, Holland and Prussia.

But events were about to overtake this first attempt at Belgian nationhood. In February 1790 Joseph II died, to be replaced by **Leopold II** (r.1790–2). He immediately despatched troops to crush the revolution and returned Belgium to the Austrian fold. However, in 1792 the French went to war against Austria and quickly scored a success at Jemappes (near Tournai). Austria expelled the French in 1793, but the following year the **French Revolutionary Army** under Marshal Jourdan finally scored the decisive victory at Fleurus (near Charleroi), thus ending Austrian rule in Belgium.

The French were welcomed by many Belgians as an army of liberation—one that heralded the advent of a modern state in which merit, not family connections and wealth, would be rewarded. Initially the French proceeded carefully, wisely respecting the power of the Church and Belgian autonomy. But to many of the more radical French revolutionaries Belgian Catholicism was anachronistic and a hindrance to change. In October 1795 Belgium was absorbed into France and religion was suppressed. The churches were closed, many were vandalized and appropriated as stables, warehouses and factories. Brussels was in uproar as the old revolutionaries of bluish hue tried to come to terms with the *sans-culottes* and Jacobins. A **Peasants' Revolt** in 1798, led by **Emmanuel Rollier**, was brutally crushed.

Despite his charisma as leader of the young French state, Napoleon failed to win over the Belgians. In 1815, when he was finally defeated by the allies (Britain, Prussia, Austria and Russia) at **Waterloo**, just south of Brussels, the majority of Belgians celebrated his downfall too. They thought their hour had come.

The United Kingdom of the Netherlands (1815–31) and the 1830 Revolution

It hadn't. The Congress of Vienna in 1815 decided instead to create the United Kingdom of the Netherlands, tacking Belgium on to the Netherlands and entrusting it to the care of **William of Orange** (called William I).

It was an insensitive decision: all the historic resentments about big-power carve-ups and about Protestant Netherlands, all the aspirations to Belgian nationhood gave William I an impossible task. He was not exactly a master of diplomacy: he tried to impose Dutch as the national language and he failed to grant the south fair representation in the States General (the Netherlands parliament).

In 1830 the July Revolution in France removed the revisionist King Charles X (r.1824–30) and put the more egalitarian Louis Philippe (r.1830–48) in his place. In Brussels too revolt was in the air. The birthday of King William was to be celebrated on 24 August with a great display of public festivity. However, posters appeared with the following announcement: '*Le 23, feux d'artifice* [fireworks]*; le 24, illuminations; le 25, Révolution.*' The festivities were abandoned on the pretext of a bad weather forecast.

On 25 August a new opera called *La Muette de Portici* (The Dumb Girl of Portici) by the contemporary French composer Daniel-François-Esprit Auber, was performed at the Théâtre de la Monnaie in Brussels. The story concerns a revolutionary called Masaniello who led an uprising in Naples against the Spanish in 1647. Such sentiments as, 'Far better to die than to live a wretched life in slavery and shame! Away with the yoke before which we tremble; away with the foreigner who laughs at our torment!' incited the audience to a ferment. They ran out to join a workers' demonstration already taking place in the Place de la Monnaie, stormed the Palais de Justice, drove out the Dutch garrison and raised the flag of Brabant over the Hôtel de Ville. Barricades were erected and uprisings spread throughout the provinces. William of Orange responded by sending in the troops, which defeated the rebels at **Hasselt**.

On 23 September the Dutch troops advanced on Brussels and four days of street fighting ensued. Gradually the Dutch were confined to what is now the Parc de Bruxelles, surrounded by revolutionaries. From there, during the night of 27 September, the Dutch simply melted away. Brussels was free. On 4 October the Provisional Government declared Belgium independent.

The fighting was not quite over yet. In the northeast of the country volunteers (dressed in their distinctive indigo-blue tunics) took on Dutch troops and battled to free Ghent and Antwerp, which finally fell to them in 1832, with the support of the French.

The New Nation Flourishes

Largely because Belgium's Revolution was widely supported by the nobility and was not simply the work of an unruly rabble, independence was accepted by the international community at the **London Conference** of 1831. The European powers also insisted on Belgian neutrality.

Since constitutional monarchy was in vogue, the Belgians then looked for a king, and Prince Leopold of Saxe-Coburg, an uncle of Queen Victoria, agreed to take the throne as **King Leopold I** (r.1831–65). William of Orange eventually accepted the division of his nation in 1839. In 1832 Leopold married **Louise-Marie**, daughter of King Louis Philippe of France, thus sealing the friendship between the two nations.

Brussels looked to its future as the new nation's capital with enthusiasm. Continental Europe's **first public railway line**, connecting Brussels to Mechelen, was inaugurated in 1834, and **Brussels University** was founded that same year. The decaying medieval city walls were knocked down and replaced by wide, tree-lined boulevards. The **Galeries Royales de Saint-Hubert** opened in 1847, the first grand covered shopping arcade of its kind in Europe.

Belgium's 1830 constitution embodied numerous jealously guarded liberties, such as freedom of speech, of the press, and of association. As a result it became a refuge for numerous writers and intellectuals, such as Karl Marx and Victor Hugo, and something of a cultural and artistic melting pot.

Leopold I was succeeded by his son **Leopold II** (r.1865–1909), a man with great ambitions for his nation. During his reign Belgium was transformed into a modern industrial state, drawing on its great reserves of coal to fuel its new factories, pro-ducing iron and steel, textiles and pottery. The population of Brussels more than doubled, from 250,000 at Leopold's coronation to 600,000 at his death.

Leopold II personally oversaw numerous grand building projects, most of them in a retrospective neoclassical style, such as the huge **Palais de Justice**. The River Senne in Brussels was covered over in the 1860s and 1870s as part of a major sewer and drainage scheme that cleaned up the crumbling slums overlooking the sluggish river. Parks were laid out and adorned with statues of famous national figures of the past. In 1880 the fiftieth anniversary of Belgium's independence was celebrated by an International Exhibition at the specially constructed **Parc du Cinquantenaire** in Brussels. The overall effect was to reinforce Belgium's sense of nationhood and identity.

Leopold II wanted to place Belgium among the big league of European nations, and that meant acquiring colonies. In the 1880s with the help of the British-American explorer **Henry Morton Stanley**, Leopold personally took charge of a vast slice of Central Africa, the **Belgian Congo** (*see* **Topics**, pp.34–6). This brought not only status but also considerable wealth through the exploitation of the Congo's raw materials—copper, tin, diamonds, rubber and cotton.

Leopold II may be seen as Belgium's equivalent of Queen Victoria: both presided over what in retrospect appears to be an age of rapid progress and modernization accompanied by a sense of national pride and dignity. But it was also a period in which the French-speaking south prospered at the expense of the Flemish north. The Walloons tended to be the pit owners, the industrialists, the magnates. French was the language of success; indeed Flemish was not recognized as an offi-cial language of equal value until 1898. For many of the Flemish, cast as the workforce of the nation, life was a Dickensian nightmare of drudgery and squalor. Women and children worked in the mines until the 1890s, half a century after this practice had been outlawed in Britain.

The Two World Wars

By the early 20th century the European nations were again jostling dangerously with each other for pre-eminence, both within Europe and across the continents that they had carved up between them. In June 1914 the assassination in Sarajevo of the Archduke Ferdinand, heir to the Austro-Hungarian throne, triggered off a complicated system of alliances that dragged all the great powers of Europe into war. Germany invaded Belgium, breaching its neutrality, and came to a grinding halt close to the Belgian border with France. Three years of devastatingly costly trench warfare ensued. The beautiful Renaissance trading city of **Ypres** found itself at the heart of the conflict, and was flattened. The nearby region around **Passchendaele** was the scene of further carnage in 1917–18, in which 245,000 British troops died.

The German occupying powers treated the Belgians harshly, brutally suppressing opposition, confiscating property, and commandeering labour to work in Germany. Meanwhile the King of Belgium, **Albert I** (r.1909–34), nephew of Leopold II, led the Belgian army in a spirited defence from the polders (reclaimed land) around the River Yser in northwest Belgium, causing havoc to the Germans by opening the sluice gates to flood the land. His persistence and fortitude endeared this 'Soldier King' to his nation.

After the First World War Belgium was left to pick up the pieces. Like the rest of Europe it faced the huge task of reconstruction against the background of the Depression. Tragically, Albert I died when rock climbing near Namur in 1934. He was succeeded by his son, **Leopold III** (r.1934–51), but fortune soon struck a second cruel blow when the new king's wife, the beautiful **Princess Astrid** of Sweden, was killed in a motoring accident in Switzerland the following year.

Belgium had acquired the German-speaking provinces of **Moresnet**, **Eupen** and **Malmédy** as compensation after the war. It had also renounced its neutrality, but in the early 1930s the rise of Adolf Hitler in Germany began to send shudders through the nation. Belgium reasserted its neutrality in 1936, but to little avail. On 10 May 1940 Germany invaded the Netherlands and Belgium, and Leopold III surrendered.

The Belgian government found exile in England, but Leopold III stayed on. The German army of occupation gradually turned the screws on the Belgian people, transporting workers to factories in Germany, rounding up the Jews (25,000 Belgian Jews died in the war), meeting any activity of the **Belgian Resistance** movement with harsh reprisals. It was a time of immense bravery: Jews were concealed by non-Jewish families for years, and downed Allied pilots were spirited back across the Channel by clandestine Resistance networks at incalculable personal risk. Belgium also had its share of Nazi sympathizers and home-grown Fascists, particularly—but certainly not exclusively—among the Flemish population, who were already disenchanted with Belgian nationhood and the traditional dominance of the French-speaking south. The Nazis were happy to exploit these tensions, and accorded Flanders a special status. There were even two Flemish units of the SS (the dreaded German security forces) which helped to run Belgium's own concentration camp at Breendonk.

Belgium was liberated in September 1944, but Allied progress very nearly came unstuck in December. As the nation settled down to enjoy its first Christmas in freedom for five years, German tank divisions under Field-Marshal von Rundstedt launched a last-ditch counter-offensive across the Ardennes (the **Battle of the Bulge**), and bombed Antwerp and Liège. American troops under General MacAuliffe were trapped at Bastogne. Invited to surrender, MacAuliffe came up with the famous response: 'Nuts!' Eventually the Germans were pushed back. The offensive had cost them a total of 120,000 men and contributed to the rapid conclusion of the war.

Post-War Prosperity and Federalization

Belgium was free again, but immediately encountered a constitutional crisis about the controversial role of Leopold III during the war. Some argued that he had spared the nation a calamity by surrendering; and that he had suffered as an effective prisoner of the Germans, who had confined him to his palace at Laeken then deported him to Germany in 1944. Many British military analysts argue that, by holding out against massive odds for 18 days, Leopold's 60,000 troops had permitted the Allied evacuation at Dunkirk. (Churchill had deliberately avoided informing Leopold of the evacuation, and sent a cable to Lord Gort, Commander-in-Chief of the British Expeditionary forces saying: 'We are asking the Belgians to sacrifice themselves for us.' His vilification of Leopold after the war was considered quite shameful by many, including George VI.)

In Belgium, however, Leopold's performance was compared unfavourably with that of his father, Albert I, in the First World War, and many hinted darkly at collaboration. His wartime marriage to a commoner, Mary Lilian Baels, in 1941 didn't help.

Leopold's brother Charles stood in as regent from 1944 to 1950, and during this period Socialists and Communists (mainly from Wallonia) campaigned actively to form a republic. While Leopold III remained in self-imposed exile in Switzerland, a referendum showed that 57 per cent of the nation favoured his return—but the fact that 58 per cent of Walloons voted against it was effectively a thumbs-down. He returned to Belgium nonetheless, but the mood soon turned ugly. Violent clashes resulted in three deaths, and Belgium seemed on the brink of civil war. In 1951, under pressure from Walloon socialists, Leopold III abdicated in favour of his son (by Queen Astrid), **Baudouin I** (r.1951–93), hoping thereby to restore unity. These hopes were justified: Baudouin, although only 21 years old, demonstrated an exceptional ability to heal the rifts in the nation.

Since the war Belgium has once again found its historic form as a major industrial and trading nation. Like other European countries, it had to give up its colonial economy, and it granted independence to the Congo (now Zaire) in 1960—although it was much criticized for its haste (*see* **Topics**, pp.34–6). It also had to go through the painful transition from heavy industry towards the light and service industries. This effectively removed the trump cards from the hands of the French-speaking south in favour of the Flemish north. The language divide, exploited successfully by politicians from both communities, has resulted in an increasingly devolved, federal system of government, with an undercurrent of tension that arcs sporadically across Brussels. Under the 'Saint-Michel Accords' of 1993, Belgian federalization was further reinforced, with the result that Belgium is now effectively ruled by three regional governments (Wallonia, Flanders and Brussels), overseen by a national government (*see* **Topics**, pp.30–31).

In its post-war history, the **European Community** has proved a godsend to Belgium in two ways. Belgium was a founder member of the EEC, and Brussels, geographically at the heart, became its headquarters in the 1960s, with all the attention, status and income that that entails. In addition, Belgium's view of itself within the political framework of Europe—a Europe seen as a confederation of nations—has allowed it to accommodate a confederation within its own boundaries. By defining itself in terms of Europe, there is less pressure to define itself as a nation.

Throughout so much of its history Belgium has stood between competing nations, earning itself the sobriquet 'the cockpit of Europe'. History has taught it to be flexible and agile, and given it the ability to accept with grace what has become respectfully known as the 'Belgian Compromise'. It remains an essential characteristic of the nation.

Art and Architecture

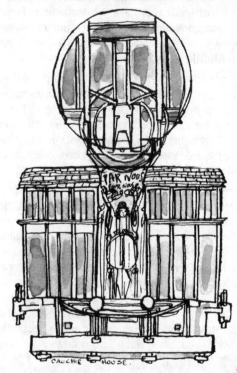

CAUCHIE HOUSE.

Belgian Art? Because this concept does not fit a convenient slot in the history of European art—in the same way as French or Italian Art—it may invite the conclusion that it is somehow second-rate. Nothing could be further from the truth. Belgian Art is simply the victim of categorization. The fact that Belgium has only existed as a nation since 1830 obscures a much longer history of great Flemish Art to which it can legitimately lay claim. The European tradition of oil painting was born on Belgian soil, perfected by Jan van Eyck and later applied with unique charm by Pieter Bruegel. Antwerp produced Rubens, one of the great geniuses of 17th-century art. After independence, the liberal atmosphere in Belgium fostered a keen interest in the avant-garde, out of which the Symbolists developed, as well as the feverishly eccentric talents of James Ensor. Belgium was also home to two of the leading Surrealists of the 20th century, René Magritte and Paul Delvaux.

As a result, Brussels, Bruges, Ghent and Antwerp contain some of the most rewarding art galleries in Europe—rich with surprises. In particular they have the distinction of containing collections that are not only of high quality, but almost entirely home-grown.

The Middle Ages

For over 700 years until the Renaissance the main inspiration for European art and architecture was the Church. When Charlemagne set up his court in Aachen in the late 8th century, it attracted some of the leading manuscript illustrators of the day. Illuminated books remained one of the chief fields of artistic endeavour in the Low Countries for five centuries. One of the best-known series of illuminations, the *Très Riches Heures du Duc de Berry*, was produced by friars from the province of Limburg in around 1411.

Manuscript illuminations were highly detailed, brightly coloured and demonstrated great technical skills in portraiture and the depiction of textiles and artefacts. These same talents were put to work when oil painting was developed in the 15th century. Previously any large-scale paintings had had to be done on the walls, but although fresco painting might have been appropriate in Italy, where it had been used since Roman times, it was not a suitable technique for the damp conditions of northern Europe. Oil paints, however, provided the ideal solution: a broad range of rich colours could be manufactured and applied to wooden panels with great control to give the kind of detail and intense coloration that were achieved in illuminated manuscripts. Furthermore, the paintings were now easily portable, which helped to create a new kind of art market.

Jan van Eyck (1390–1441), who was based in Bruges, was the first artist to demonstrate the full potential of oil painting, and he produced some of the most dazzling work of the late medieval period. *The Adoration of the Mystic Lamb* (painted with his brother Hubert in 1426–32) in Ghent Cathedral is one of the great treasures of European art, full of saintliness and sensuality and luminescent detail. Jan van Eyck is one of the earliest Flemish painters known to us by name, as he signed his work. At that time painters worked in guilds, usually remaining anonymous, hence speculative titles such as the Master of Hoogstraaten.

Jan van Eyck was official painter to Philip the Good, Duke of Burgundy, who presided over an economic boom in the Low Countries. Paintings of this era are primarily religious, but they also offer a fascinating insight into the quality of life of the well-to-do at that time, from their sumptuous textiles and encrustations of jewellery, to the ornately carved choir stalls and the glazed floor tiles.

Another speciality of this period was the retable, a large, screen-like altarpiece which contained a mixture of elaborate high-relief woodcarving (usually gilded) and painting. Retables are usually divided up as folding triptychs, depicting complex religious scenes enacted by dozens of carved characters, often within a framework of miniaturized Gothic church architecture. There were celebrated workshops producing retables in Brussels, Mechelen and Antwerp.

The achievements of architecture during the Middle Ages were likewise principally ecclesiastical. The chief influences came from France, and for about 150 years after the 11th century the **Romanesque** style predominated. Romanesque churches were robust and solid, with massive supporting columns and semicircular arches. (They were supposedly influenced by Roman architecture, hence the name.)

If you look at the cross-section of two intersecting rounded arches, you will see a pointed arch. This became the leading motif of the next phase of architecture, which evolved in the mid-12th century and was later dubbed **Gothic** by Renaissance architects, who considered it a barbarian perversion of the classical ideal. Architects now attempted to create magical illusions of space and light, filling walls with huge, elongated windows held in place by delicate columns and supported by external buttresses. During the 15th century the increasingly flamboyant Gothic style was adopted by secular architecture. The Hôtel de Ville in Brussels was rebuilt after 1402, with its towering spire a potent symbol of the growing strength and confidence of the merchant classes. But perhaps the most stunning secular manifestation of Gothic architecture is the town hall of Leuven (built 1439–69), a wedding-cake building in cream-white stone (*see* pp.278–9).

Jan van Eyck's place at Philip the Good's court was later taken by his pupil, **Rogier van der Weyden**, called Rogier de la Pasture in French (c.1400–64). His religious paintings are emotionally charged and full of stress, as in his great triptych, *The Seven Sacraments*. He was closely involved in the decoration of the new Hôtel de Ville in Brussels, but his paintings for it were destroyed in the French bombardment of 1695. Like many other painters over the next 300 years, he also designed for the famous tapestry workshops of Brussels (*see* pp.36–8). Other major names of this late medieval period include **Hugo van der Goes** (?1435–82); **Hans Memling** (?1430–94); and **Dirk Bouts** (1415–75), perhaps best known for his *The Justice of Otto* (1471–3). As with Van Eyck, a distinctive mark of the work of these artists was a limited understanding of space: perspective is not rendered with complete confidence, landscapes are often naive, and groups of people are packed slightly too close together. These problems were addressed by the next great phase of painting in the Low Countries.

The Renaissance

The Renaissance was a watershed between the medieval and the modern world, a long and gradual phenomenon which began in Italy in the 13th century and lasted for some 300 years. It was triggered by the rediscovery of classical learning and literature—and the gradual realization that not only had the Greeks and Romans achieved rather more than the medieval world in terms of science, medicine, architecture and philosophy but that they had done so without the assistance of Christianity. The Renaissance, therefore, effectively freed people from the straightjacket of purely Christian teaching and encouraged them to approach all questions with an open mind.

Italian art and architecture were the leaders of fashion during the Renaissance, and accomplished artists from northern Europe travelled to Italy to admire and learn from the likes of Leonardo da Vinci, Michelangelo, Titian and Tintoretto. The Italian Renaissance, however, was only partially assimilated in the Low Countries. Although architects were happy to borrow Renaissance motifs, such as classical columns and garlands of flowers, their application of these was mainly cosmetic: Renaissance façades were essentially adaptations of the traditional step-gable (which had been around since the 11th century) tacked on to traditional Flemish houses. Ecclesiastical architecture, meanwhile, remained Gothic.

Flemish painting now followed two main courses. One set of artists was directly influenced by Italian painting. **Quentin Metsys** (1466–1530) represents the link between the medieval world and the Renaissance, as well as the shift from Bruges to Antwerp as the main centre of art in the southern Low Countries. Metsys' *The Lineage of St Anne* (c. 1508) shows a real understanding of architectural perspective, and also uses the kind of hazy, distant blue landscape so beloved of Leonardo da Vinci. **Bernard van Orley** (c. 1499–1541) brought the Renaissance to Brussels, in painting and in his designs for tapestry and stained glass. Other 'Romanists' include Van Orley's pupil **Michiel Coxie** (1499–1592), who lived in Rome in the 1530s, and **Jan Gossaert** of Mauberge (1478–1532) (also known as Mabuse), who painted the first classically inspired nudes in Flemish art.

Other painters, however, developed a more independent Flemish style of painting, reflecting the distinctive outlook and heritage of the Low Countries. Supreme among them was **Pieter Bruegel the Elder** (c.1525–69). He trained in Antwerp and made a trip to Italy in about 1551, but this appears to have left him unmoved. His interest lay in the people and landscape of his homeland, so even when painting a classical subject such as his famous *Fall of Icarus* (1567) his main focus is on rural life, leaving poor Icarus's plight virtually incidental. Bruegel was particularly successful in translating religious scenes into Flemish village life, breathing into them a new poignancy and relevance. Another line of work took him into the realms of bizarre fantasy associated with the Dutch painter Hieronymus Bosch (1450–1516)—as in his *The Fall of Rebel Angels* (1562).

In 1563 Pieter Bruegel moved to Brussels and married. He had two sons late in life, who became painters in their own right well after their father's death. Pieter Bruegel the Younger (1564–1638) painted numerous versions of his father's work; he used a more polished style that somehow lacks the naive spontaneity of his father's paintings (of which only some 40 examples have survived). His younger brother Jan 'Velvet' Bruegel (1568–1625) is celebrated for his landscapes and his delicate flower paintings.

Another artist in the Flemish tradition is **Joachim Beuckelaer** (1530–74), who produced richly packed market scenes, full of vivid and affectionate details, in a confident, flowing style somewhat in advance of his times.

During the Renaissance, painters found extra outlets for their work among the newly rich middle classes. The full flowering of the Renaissance, however, was cut short by the religious troubles that swept through northern Europe in the second half of the 16th century, disrupting patronage. There was no stability until the following century, when the Counter-Reformation brought its own remarkable flourish in both arts and architecture.

The Age of Rubens

It was largely because of **Pieter Paul Rubens** (1577–1640) that Antwerp remained a cultural centre in the Low Countries during the 17th century. Born of well-to-do Flemish parents, he started training as an artist when just thirteen years old. In his twenties, he lived and worked in Italy for eight years, and was strongly influenced by the work of Michelangelo, Titian and his contemporary Caravaggio. Rubens returned to Antwerp in 1608 with a glittering reputation; the following year he became court painter to Archduke Albert and the Infanta Isabella, married Isabella Brant and bought his fine house in the city (now a museum, *see* p.353). His *Raising of the Cross* (1610–11) and *Descent from the Cross* (1611–14) for Antwerp Cathedral caused a sensation, and commissions rolled in. Rubens' ability to handle vast paintings on dramatic subjects was unsurpassed. His compositions carry the eye through the paintings with a unique vigour, assisted by his deft, virtuoso touch, often applied in thin, almost sketchy layers of paint. Throughout almost all his work there is a lusty, life-enhancing quality, very Flemish in nature. This is typified by his predilection for the sensuous, buxom nudes which are virtually his trademark.

After his wife died in 1625, Rubens entered the diplomatic service. He travelled to Spain and England in an effort to broker peace, for which he was rewarded in England by a knighthood. He also won several major commissions in both countries (including the ceilings of the Banqueting House in Whitehall, London). In 1630, at the age of 53, he married Hélène Fourment, the 17-year-old daughter of a wealthy tapestry merchant. He painted her in a series of charming portraits, full of life and flirtatiousness. He also maintained a flow of work right up to the end of his life, bringing his total *œuvre* to over 2000 major paintings.

The other two great Antwerp painters of this era were both closely associated with Rubens. **Antoon (Anthony) van Dyck** (1599–1641) was celebrated for his sedate portraits which capture the solemnity and dignity of the affluent—notably after he became court artist to Charles I of England in 1632. **Jacob Jordaens** (1593–1678) painted in a vigorous, expressive style in the manner of Rubens and specialized in joyous, bacchanalian scenes.

During this period Flemish 'genre' painting also thrived—portraits of ordinary rural and town life in inns, markets and kitchens, often spiced with gentle humour. Two of the leading genre painters of the period were **David Teniers the Younger** (1610–90) and **Adriaen Brouwer** (1605–38).

The fecund, flowing style of Rubens and his followers is typical of the Baroque period, which can be most readily identified in architecture. Baroque architecture was essentially a lavish, curvaceous interpretation of classical style: pediments became broken pediments, columns became barley-sugar twists, façades became embellished with *œil de bœuf* windows. The principal Flemish architects were also sculptors, such as Rubens' pupil **Luc Fayd'Herbe** (1617–97), who may have been responsible for Brussels' most successful Baroque church, Saint-Jean-

Baptiste au Béguinage (see p.154). Baroque can become overbearing, but with the right balance it is joyous and delicate, elegant and swanky, befitting the osten-tatious lifestyles of the wealthy merchant classes of the 17th century. Nowhere is the Flemish version of the Baroque better expressed than in Brussels' Grand' Place, a festival of individualistic design and gilded ornamentation.

The religious troubles of the 16th century had left numerous churches stripped or in ruins, their statues shattered by the iconoclasts. During the 17th century they were restored, and the statues of the saints were replaced by new works in the Baroque style of Bernini—vigorously moulded and expressive, but often out of keeping with the Gothic architecture on to which they were grafted. Among the most noted sculptors in this line were **Jérôme Duquesnoy the Younger** (1602–54), son of the original sculptor of the Manneken-Pis (see p.97), and Luc Fayd'Herbe. This was also the era of the fantastically elaborate wooden pulpits, as seen for example in the Cathédrale Saint-Michel in Brussels.

Classical Revival

During the 18th century fashions imitated the French once more, and in partic-ular the styles associated with Louis XV. During this period architects reassessed the lessons of classical architecture and pressed for more stringent, sober adher-ence to these models, with emphasis on well-modulated proportions and symmetry. Both churches and mansions took on the outward appearance of Greek temples. In the Brussels of Charles of Lorraine several major building pro-jects were undertaken in this new mould, notably the Place Royale and the Palais de la Nation, designed by **Barnabé Guimard** (fl.1765–92), and what is now the Place des Martyrs, designed by **Claude Fisco** (1736–1825). The sculptor **Gilles-Lambert Godecharle** (1750–1835) worked in corresponding neoclassical style, but this mood was not as successfully translated to painting.

The end of the 18th century was marked by the turbulence of the Brabançon Revolt and the French occupation, and the prevailing style was again neoclassical. The French neoclassical painter Jacques-Louis David (1748–1825) spent the last years of his life in Brussels and had a number of disciples in Belgium, but—with the possible exception of **François-Joseph Navez** (1787–1869)—they lacked David's ability to inject a sense of noble drama into their classical scenes.

Truly Belgian Art

Belgian independence in 1830 gave fresh impetus to artists, sculptors and archi-tects. The new nation needed to make its own statements about its role in the world and to glamorize its heritage. Sculptors such as **Willem Geefs** (1805–85) were called in to evoke the Belgian past through historical sculptures. In painting, a wave of Romanticism—passionate, vigorous and poetic—swept neoclassicism before it. **Gustave Wappers** (1803–74) painted his huge *Day in September 1830* to the glory of the Belgian Revolution in the style of Delacroix; while the morbid works of **Antoine Wiertz** (1806–65, *see* p.169) attempted to convey profound messages through erotic and macabre images. After the 1850s a Realist school evolved in the fashion of the French painter Gustave Courbet (1819–77), in which ordinary scenes such as peasants at work and cowbyres were depicted with the Romantics' eye, but unprettified and (in principle) devoid of interpretation. **Hippolyte Boulenger** (1837–74), **Jan Stobbaerts** (1838–1914) and **Henri de Braekeleer** (1840–88) are the best-known exponents of this trend. The social implications of Realism were taken up with greater vigour by the painter and sculptor **Constantin Meunier** (1831–1905, *see* p.191), who focused on both the misery and the dignity of industrial labour.

In the latter part of the century, architecture took on all shapes and forms, ranging from the Neo-Gothic to the neoclassical, which were seen as complementary rather than contradictory. The most famous architect of the day, **Joseph Poelaert** (1817–79), produced Neo-Gothic churches, such as Notre-Dame de Laeken, as well as the mighty neoclassical Palais de Justice. For such public projects, stately grandeur based on well-tried principles was the essential criterion.

However, Belgium was also noted as a liberal country, a refuge for artists from more repressive regimes, notably France, and this fuelled a taste for the avant-garde. Various societies were formed to discuss and promote contemporary work. One of these was Le Cercle des Vingt (**Les XX**), founded by Octave Maus in 1883. It held controversial exhibitions of invited artists, many of whom were unknown at the time. Paul Cézanne, for example, who was later dubbed the 'father of modern art', was exhibited by Les XX long before he was recognized in his own country.

Despite the influence of innovative groups such as these, Belgian art essentially followed the patterns of French painting during the late 19th century. Artists such as **Théo van Rysselberghe** (1862–1926) adopted a form of pointillist impressionism; **Emile Claus** (1849–1924) created a kind of late impressionism which he called 'Luminism', depicting rural scenes with famously fetching charm.

Belgium also produced more individualistic talents, notably the decidedly bizarre **James Ensor** (1860–1949). He began his painting career with well-made post-impressionist paintings of interiors and portraits. In the mid-1880s, however, his palette suddenly became charged with intense, clashing colours, which he applied with aggressive vigour to increasingly oddball subject matter, such as dead fish, animated skeletons and Punch-and-Judy-like caricatures. His great masterpiece is the carnival-like *Entry of Christ into Brussels* (1888).

At the same time a very loosely defined group of painters called the **Symbolists** began to explore the world of suggestion, mystery and dreams. Many of their works are fascinating for their sheer idiosyncrasy, such as the visionary fantasy world of **Jean Delville** (1867–1953). By contrast **Léon Frédéric** (1856–1940) painted large triptyches of social realism infused with the kind of saintly clarity found in the works of the medieval Flemish masters. Perhaps the most haunting Symbolist is **Fernand Khnopff** (1858–1921), who used a soft, polished style to bring a dreamlike quality even to his group of tennis players (*Memories*, 1889).

Another highly individual painter associated with Symbolism is **Léon Spilliaert** (1881–1946), who brought a strong sense of design to his stylized interiors and unmistakable landscapes—often brooding silhouettes set against empty twilight coastlines, filled with the abstract shapes of cloud and reflected patches of water.

Les XX was superseded by **La Libre Esthétique** (1894–1914) as Brussels' leading artistic circle. This group encouraged cooperation between artists, architects and craftsmen, creating an atmosphere that fostered the emerging decorative style, Art Nouveau. Belgium was at the forefront of Art Nouveau, with leading figures such as **Victor Horta** (1861–1947, *see* pp.187–9), **Gustave Serrurier-Bovy** (1858–1910) and **Henri van de Velde** (1863–1957), who became director of the Art and Crafts School in Weimar in 1901, which in 1919 evolved into the Bauhaus. Art Nouveau remained fashionable until the First World War.

The 20th Century

Out of Impressionism and postimpressionism grew Fauvism, whose name was based on a term of abuse meaning 'wild beast', applied by a critic, and reflected an unbridled use of colour. Belgium's most successful exponent was **Rik Wouters** (1882–1916), also a gifted sculptor, who used bright but carefully modulated colours to produce work of great charm and subtlety, usually featuring his wife Nel.

Meanwhile a school of painters developed in the village of Sint-Martens-Latem, near Ghent (*see* p.333). The first wave, founded in around 1904, included mystic, symbolist-style painters such as **Valerius de Saedeleer** (1867–1941) and **Albert Servaes** (1883–1966). The second wave developed in around 1909 and in the post-war period; it was centred upon **Constant Permeke** (1886–1952), who painted emotionally charged, blocky portraits with thick dingy colours—a unique combination of social realism, Cubism and Expressionism.

Two of Belgium's best-known 20th-century painters are Surrealists. Surrealism developed in Paris in the 1920s as an effort to unveil a reality in the subconscious through spontaneous, automatic behaviour and events, usually of a highly unconventional nature. By extension the term was applied to the dreamworld evoked by painters such as Salvador Dali. **René Magritte** (1898–1967) lived in Paris in the 1920s then returned to Belgium to begin producing his inimitable small-scale paintings of witty absurdities and visual puns, such as floating men in bowler hats, paintings within paintings, trains emerging from fireplaces and nude female torsos which become faces. Meanwhile, **Paul Delvaux** (1897–1994), over his long life time, painted countless versions of his primary obsessions: trams and stations by night, peopled by sleepwalkers, skeletons and reclining nudes, all suffused with a haunting, dreamlike quality and latent eroticism.

During most of the 20th century, architecture in Belgium has followed the same course as in the rest of the Western world. The angular, machine-age style of Art Deco was in vogue during the early interwar years, then was gradually superseded by the clean lines and functionalism of the International Style. This led to the soulless highrise urban developments of the post-war years, sad perversions of the Bauhaus ideals, and then the prettified eclecticism of the post-modern architects over the last 20 years.

In art, too, recent Belgian work has reflected movements elsewhere in the world. In the immediate post-war years, a group called **La Jeune Peinture Belge** (1945–48) attempted to gather together the various strains of contemporary art. Its members produced primarily abstract work, influenced particularly by the mechanistic abstractions of **Victor Sevranckx** (1897–1965). **Anne Bonnet** (1908–60), **Louis van Lint** (1909–89) and **Gaston Bertrand** (b.1910) are probably the best known of these today. In 1948 an international group called **Cobra** (an acronym from Copenhagen, Brussels, Amsterdam) formed around a common interest in children's painting and primitive art, free of the encumbrance of Western painting traditions. Belgium's most famous participant in Cobra is Pierre Alechinsky (b.1927), whose poetic, semi-figurative works (particularly in inks) have reached the international stage. The more recent trend towards non-gallery art and installations has left the Belgian art world in a state of some confusion, and generally it looks to the USA and the past for guidance.

Brussels is a compact city. It takes no more than half an hour to walk across the Pentagon—the historic central zone delineated by the course of the (now demolished) medieval city walls. This zone contains virtually all the main museums, churches and other attractions of Brussels and, although it is spanned by a web of public transport systems, the best way to travel about is on foot. Brussels has been designed with the walker in mind, with numerous traffic-free streets and covered shopping galleries, and plenty of pavement cafés where the weary pedestrian can rest and watch the world go by.

The essential layout of Brussels was established in medieval times, and since then all developments in the city centre have been grafted on to the original groundplan. It was only in the 19th century that the city expanded into the surrounding countryside, absorbing neighbouring townships and villages such as Anderlecht.

The Walks

As a result, the centre of Brussels cannot be divided into convenient historical areas: it's a historical jumble where Renaissance, Baroque, neoclassical and post-modern buildings jostle with one another on a street plan half a millennium old.

It would be artificial to try to sort this complex mosaic into themes. The six walks that follow, therefore, are not so much thematic as geographical, covering Brussels area by area and linking the main sites by the most interesting routes. The sole exception is Walk VI, which explores the Art Nouveau architecture of a residential district just outside the city centre.

Most of these walks will take half a day or more. Below is a list of highlights for visitors with less time to spare.

ST MICHAEL,
HOTEL DE VILLE

Indispensable:	The Grand' Place (Walk I); Manneken-Pis (Walk I)
Art:	The Musées Royaux des Beaux-Arts (national gallery) (Walk II)
Museums:	Musée Horta (Art Nouveau) (Walk VI)
Churches:	Notre-Dame du Sablon (Walk III); Saint-Jean-Baptiste au Béguinage (Walk IV); Notre-Dame de la Chapelle (under restoration) (Walk III); Cathédrale Saint-Michel (Walk II)
Historic houses:	Musée de l'Hôtel Charlier (Walk II)
Characteristic districts:	Sablon (Walk III); also Place Sainte-Catherine (Walk IV)
Unusual:	Centre Belge de la Bande Dessinée (comic-strip museum); studio of Antoine Wiertz (Walk V); Musée Boyadjian du Cœur (Walk II); Palais de Justice (Walk III)
Worth seeking out:	Café Falstaff (Art Nouveau) (Walk I); Café Métropole (plush) (Walk IV); Galeries Royales de Saint-Hubert (19th-century shopping arcade) (Walk I)

Start: *the Grand' Place (Flemish: Grote Markt), which is a short walk from* Ⓜ *Bourse, or a slightly longer walk from* Ⓜ *Gare Centrale.*

I: The Grand' Place: Heart of Brussels

Walking Time: *about 3 hours. Allow a further 2–3 hours to visit the four museums.*

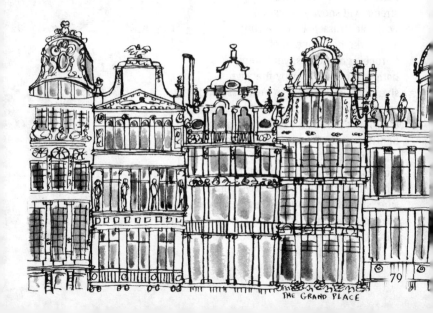

THE GRAND PLACE

I: The Grand' Place and the Heart of Brussels

The Grand' Place is the jewel in Brussels' crown—and such a splendid jewel that the rest of the crown might just as well be made of iron. Of course, it is on just about every postcard, brochure, poster—and guidebook cover—of the city. But nothing can quite prepare you for the sense of elation you feel when you emerge from the warren of surrounding streets into this spacious, gilded arena. The French dramatist Jean Cocteau described the Grand' Place as 'un riche théâtre', and that is what it is: a splendid stage for the public, for the individual—for you.

This gentle amble around the Grand' Place and its surrounding streets will show you just how walkable Brussels is. Here you are, at the heart of one of Europe's great cities, yet barely bothered by traffic or by the aggressive intrusion of modern business and its architecture. The Grand' Place is Brussels' top tourist attraction, so it is almost permanently overrun by tourists and the neighbouring streets are tacky with tourist tat; despite all this it glows with an atmosphere of infectious, easy-going pleasure, suggesting the more sedate pace of bygone eras and providing as convincing a link with the past as its medieval street plan.

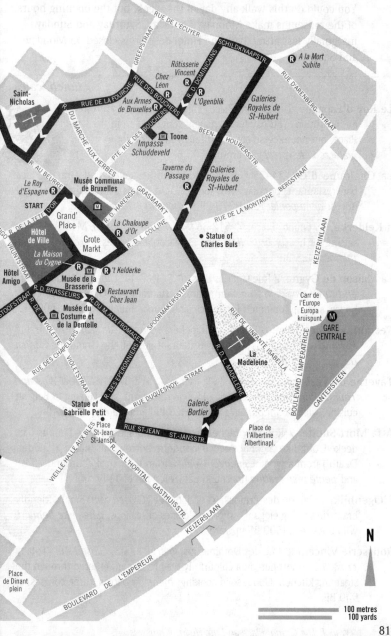

RUE DE L'ECUYER

GREEPSTRAAT

SCHILDKNAAPSTR.

Rötisserie Vincent (R)

Chez Léon (R)

RUE DES BOUCHERS

R-D. DOMINICAINS (R)(R)

L'Ogenblik

(R) *A la Mort Subite*

RUE D'ARENBERG STRAAT

Saint-Nicholas

RUE DE LA FOURCHE

R DU MARCHE AUX HERBES

Aux Armes de Bruxelles (R)

PTE. RUE DES BOUCHERS

(M) **Toone**

Impasse Schuddeveld

Galeries Royales de St-Hubert

BEEN-

HOUWERSSTR.

BERGSTRAAT

R AU BEURRE

Musée Communal de Bruxelles

GRASMARKT

Taverne du Passage (R)

Galeries Royales de St-Hubert

Le Roy d'Espagne (R)

R-D. HARENGS

RUE DE LA MONTAGNE

START

R. DE LA TETE D'OR

(M)

Grand' Place

La Chaloupe d'Or

R. D. L. COLLINE

● **Statue of Charles Buls**

KEIZERINLAAN

Hôtel de Ville

Grote Markt

La Maison du Cygne

MIGO VIRUINSTRAAT

(R) (M) (R) *'t Kelderke*

Hôtel Amigo

Musée de la Brasserie

R. D. BRASSEURS

Restaurant Chez Jean

Carr de l'Europe Europa kruispunt (M)

STOOFSTRAAT

R. DE LA VIOLETTE

R. DU M. AUX FROMAGES

SPOORMAKERSSTRAAT

RUE DE L'INFANTE ISABELLA

GARE CENTRALE

Musée du Costume et de la Dentelle (M)

RUE DES CHAPELIERS

VIOLETSTRAAT

R. DES EPERONNIERS

R. D. L. MADELEINE

La Madeleine

BOULEVARD L'IMPERATRICE

CANTERSTEEN

RUE DES CHAPELIERS

RUE DUQUESNOY STRAAT

Statue of Gabrielle Petit

Galerie Bortier

Place de l'Albertine Albertinapl.

VIEILLE HALLE AUX BLES

Place St-Jean St-Jansplein

RUE ST-JEAN ST-JANSSTR.

R. DE L'HOPITAL GASTHUISSTR.

KEIZERSLAAN

N

Place de Dinant plein

BOULEVARD DE L'EMPEREUR

100 metres
100 yards

81

You could do this walk any day of the week, but the opening hours of the museums make Monday, Thursday, Saturday and Sunday marginally less attractive. The Hôtel de Ville is closed on Monday and Saturday.

Le Roy d'Espagne, 1–2 Grand' Place. This atmospheric bar/restaurant is an institution. You pay for its magnificent position in the Grand' Place, but not excessively. Light lunch menu of, for example, *waterzooi de volaille* for around 500 BF.

La Chaloupe d'Or, 24–25 Grand' Place. Another celebrated Grand' Place bar/restaurant, popular with locals. Light meals at marginally inflated prices: *demi-poulet garni* (370 BF); *croque-monsieur* (220 BF).

't Kelderke, 15 Grand' Place, © 512 36 94. *Closed Sat lunch.* Medieval cellar setting for hearty *bruxellois* food at reasonable prices: *carbonnades flamandes* (425 BF).

La Maison du Cygne, 2 Rue Charles Buls, © 511 82 44. *Closed Sat lunch, Sun and three weeks in Aug.* Sumptuous restaurant in a Grand' Place guildhouse, serving top-notch French cuisine. Lunch menu at 1300–1600 BF.

Restaurant Chez Jean, 6 Rue des Chapeliers. *Closed Sun, Mon.* Admirably down-to-earth Brussels-style bar/restaurant, just off the Grand' Place. *Plat du jour* at 285 BF.

Taverne du Passage, 30 Galerie de la Reine, © 512 37 31. *Closed Wed and Thurs in June and July.* Classic old-style restaurant, specializing in Belgian cuisine, such as *andouillette grillée* (425 BF) and *waterzooi* (485 BF).

A la Mort Subite, 7 Rue Montagne aux Herbes Potagères. This famous bar, decked out like a large rococo boudoir, borrows its name ('Sudden Death') from a type of *gueuze*. *Gueuze* from the barrel at around 75 BF and *petite restauration* (toast and pâté, etc.) for 110 BF.

L'Ogenblik, 1 Galerie des Princes, © 511 61 51. *Closed Sun.* Small, friendly brasserie serving elegant—if pricy—dishes of scallops, *gâteau de homard*, wild duck, etc. (500 BF upwards).

Rôtisserie Vincent, 8 Rue des Dominicains, © 511 23 03. *Closed Aug.* Totally *bruxellois* atmosphere in a colourfully tiled restaurant entered through the steaming kitchen. Good, solid cooking; *menu du patron* (three courses) at 940 BF.

Aux Armes de Bruxelles, 13 Rue des Bouchers ✆ 511 21 18. *12 noon –11pm, closed Mon.* Sophisticated restaurant, always busy, with impeccable service. French and Belgian cooking at around 1500 BF per head. .

Chez Léon, 18 Rue des Bouchers, ✆ 511 14 15. *12 noon–11pm.* The jam-packed, multi-storeyed original (founded in 1893) of the famous chain, specializing in *moules-frites* (550 BF).

Falstaff, 19 Rue Henri Maus. Large, classic Art Nouveau café serving light meals of Belgian cuisine; lunch menus at 325 BF.

La Fleur en Papier Doré, 55 Rue des Alexiens. Splendid old *estaminet* (*see* p.98). Good beers from the barrel, plus light snacks.

Quite what Brussels would be without the Grand' Place does not bear thinking about. The good burghers of Brussels looked this prospect in the face in 1695. Having failed to raise the siege of Namur by William III of England, Marshal de Villeroy, leading the French troops of Louis XIV, issued an ultimatum: Brussels would be bombed unless the English and Dutch lifted their blockade of the French ports. He gave the authorities just six hours to consult all parties, then on the night of 13 August his troops opened up a great barrage, demolishing the Grand' Place along with nearly 4000 houses and 16 churches. The splendid tower of the Hôtel de Ville was practically the sole survivor—something of an irony, since this was what the artillery had used as their principal target.

What you see, then, is not quite what it seems. The Grand' Place looks like a perfect Flemish Renaissance-Baroque square, but much of it was built at the very end of the 17th century, within five years of the bombardment, in a style that was already outmoded and retrospective. The Grand' Place was Brussels' main marketplace from the very beginnings of the city's history. The names of the streets that lead into the Grand' Place today bear witness to this past: Rue au Beurre (butter street), Rue Chair et Pain (meat and bread), Rue des Harengs (herrings), and so on. These streets once threaded past various halls and covered markets occupied by butchers, bakers, cheesemongers, fishmongers and other traders.

The rising stars of civic power in medieval times were the *échevins*, assistants to the burgomaster. In the 1390s they permitted the formation of *corporations*, guilds of craftsmen and traders which became the backbone of the economy. Then during the 15th century the *échevins* organized the building of a grand Hôtel de Ville—a bold statement of the city's wealth and pride which confirmed the Grand' Place's central role in the public life of Brussels. This was where all important public decrees would be announced; it was the setting for colourful pageants and jousting tournaments—and also the scene of public executions. The guilds wanted to be near the seat of civic authority, and during the 16th century the borders of the old market square started to fill up with their guildhouses, first in wood, then in stone.

The Grand' Place was now less a market, more the city's gathering place, busy with ladies and gentlemen parading in their finery, gilded carriages, carts, stray dogs, mobile theatres, hawkers, quacks and charlatans. The centre of Brussels earned a reputation for lively taverns, reckless spending and licentiousness—and the *échevins* were soon struggling to formulate legislation to curb this behaviour.

The role of the Grand' Place as the city centre survived even after the guilds were disbanded in the 1790s by French Revolutionaries. With the large-scale renovations to the Hôtel de Ville and the Maison du Roi during the 19th century and in recent decades, the Grand' Place could have become a museum piece, but it hasn't: today the old guildhouses are occupied by cafés, banks, hotels, lace shops—even a pet supply store. Now that all traffic has been outlawed, a daily plant and flower 'market' (actually just a couple of stallholders) occupies the centre stage, and every Sunday morning (8–12.30) this is joined by a bird market.

The Grand' Place is still the focal point of Brussels' grand civic traditions, too. In early July it is taken over by the Ommegang (*see* p.19), a spectacular costumed pageant which dates back over at least four centuries. During one weekend in mid-August it is filled with the '*Tapis de Fleurs*'—a carpet of flowers. On 31 December it is the traditional gathering place for thousands of revellers who come to this great floodlit stage to welcome in the New Year.

> *Our tour of the Grand' Place starts in the northwest corner, where the Rue du Marché au Charbon (coal-market street) enters the square. Brussels' main tourist office (see p.27) is close at hand, housed beneath the arcade of the Hôtel de Ville.*

Like most of the buildings lining the Grand' Place, **No. 7** has a picturesque name, Le Renard (The Fox). Many of the guildhouses' names date back to the earliest building occupying the site and have no link with the guilds themselves. The name Le Renard (Flemish: *De Vos*) predates the acquisition of the building by the haberdashers' guild in the 15th century; it was later elaborated by the carving of the fox over the doorway. A statue of St Nicholas, patron saint of haberdashers as well as of merchants generally, stands on the crest of the gable. As with almost all the guildhouses, each storey is decorated by a different style of classical column or pilaster: Doric, Ionian (topped by a scroll) and Corinthian (with an ornate capital incorporating foliage, such as acanthus leaves).

No. 6 is Le Cornet (The Horn), the most successful of the buildings designed by one of the main architects of the Grand' Place, Antoon Pastorana. This was the boatmen's guildhouse and is encrusted with marine symbols. The gable resembles the stern of a galleon, and the horn that gives the building its name can be seen over the central window.

No. 5 is La Louve (The She-Wolf), so named because there is a statue over the entrance of Romulus and Remus suckling the wolf. This was the house of the archers, a kind of city militia raised to the rank of a corporation. This connection made the house the target of assault in 1793 by *sans-culottes* inspired by the French Revolution, who pulled down the statues on the third storey. Since restored to their plinths, these represent Truth, Falsehood, Peace and Discord; the medallions set high on the façade show Emperors Trajan, Tiberius, Caesar Augustus and Julius Caesar, who are held to be symbols of each of these properties. The gable is topped by a phoenix rising out of the ashes.

La Louve is now occupied by a branch of the Crédit Général bank. The interior has been transformed by plate-glass and brickwork into a large open-plan office—modern and totally incongruous.

No. 4 is Le Sac (The Sack). Over the door two jolly-looking characters are standing with an open sack, one with his head in it. This became the guildhouse of the cabinet-makers and coopers in 1444, and the lower two storeys, constructed in 1644, survived the bombardment of 1695. The later upper storeys—richly adorned with cherubs, barley-sugar balustrades, cornucopias, garlands and urns—are another example of the work of Antoon Pastorana, who was by training a cabinet-maker.

No. 3 is La Brouette (The Wheelbarrow), with the forerunners of the modern wheelbarrow pictured over the door. This belonged to the tallow merchants—demonstrating their power in the days before petrol-based lubricants and electric lighting. A statue (1912) of their patron saint, St Gilles, stands over the gable. Although the building is dated 1697, in fact this refers to restoration work carried out by the architect-sculptor Jan Cosyns, although much of the façade survived the bombing of 1695.

Jan Cosyns is also thought to be the designer of **Nos. 1 and 2**, which form La Maison des Boulangers (The Bakers' House), the grandest of the guildhouses, and distinguished by its elegant domed lantern in place of a gable. The golden head over the door is St Lambert, patron saint of bakers. The six figures lining the balustrade represent the elements needed to make bread: energy, grain, wind, fire, water and prudence. The bust in the middle of the upper storey is the King of Spain ('Den Coninck van Spaignien'), Charles II (r.1661–1700). The kings of

Spain were effectively rulers of this country from 1517 to 1713, during which Spain was one of the most powerful lands on earth. Their reputation as imperial rulers is given a somewhat backhanded compliment by the two figures flanking the bust of the king, an American Indian and a Moor in a turban, both looking dejected with their hands tied behind their backs. The canons and flags are rather misplaced symbols of imperial glory: Charles II was both mentally and physically handicapped and furthermore had no direct heir. During his reign the Spanish empire began to falter. Medallions of the Roman Emperors were used for both decorative effect and to imply a moral message: here Antoninus Pius and Trajan represent long and just rule; Nerva and Decius, by contrast, had dubious claims to power and ruled for only a couple of years. The gilded figure of Fame, perched on the top of the dome, is one of the most delightful statues in the Grand' Place.

This building now houses one of the most celebrated bars in Brussels, called Le Roy d'Espagne (The King of Spain) (*see* listings above), famous for its authentic atmosphere, its waiters dressed in traditional aprons, and the inflated pigs' bladders that decorate the central chimney on the ground floor.

> *The Rue au Beurre enters the Grand' Place at the northern corner. To the right there is a series of less elaborate houses, dated 1696–7 and now occupied by cafés and lace shops. No. 37, Le Chêne (The Oak), was once the guildhouse of the weavers, the most powerful guild of the medieval period. Moving clockwise, you come to the Rue Chair et Pain and the **Maison du Roi**. For over a century now the Maison du Roi has housed the city museum, the **Musée Communal de Bruxelles**. Open Mon–Fri 10–12.30, 1.30–5, closes at 4pm Oct–Mar; Sat, Sun, public holidays 10–1 only; adm 80 BF.*

The **Maison du Roi** is a bizarre construction, a confection of arches and loggias, finials, crestings, crockets and steep-pitched roofs topped by statues of knights waving banners and swords. This is 19th-century Gothic run riot, now blackened by city grime to look like something from the House of Horrors. It should not belong, but somehow it does.

This building has changed its skin at least five times. It was first of all a centre for the bakery trade, the Brodhuis; then in the 15th century a new building was erected on this site to house the Duke of Brabant's high court, hence it became known as the Duke's House. The high court was supplanted in the 16th century by the Royal Assizes, so it became known as the King's House. (The loaf and crown on the weathervane refer to this history.) The Counts Egmont and Hornes (*see* p.57) were held here before their execution in the Grand' Place in 1568. This first King's House was replaced by another in the 17th century and yet another after the bombing of 1695. Lastly, in the 1870s, the present building was constructed, its design modelled on etchings of the 16th-century building.

The Musée Communal de Bruxelles is a rather oddball collection of painting, pottery, tapestry, historical documents, models showing the evolution of Brussels, and—its most famous possession—the vast wardrobe of clothes tailormade around the world for the Manneken-Pis. Its sombre, neo-medieval halls will prove rewarding for anyone who is seriously interested in Brussels' history, and there are also a number of treasures to delight the more casual visitor. On the ground floor are some superb retables (the ornate, sculpted and painted altar-pieces for which Brussels was renowned) dating from 1480 to 1510. In the same room is a rare painting by Pieter Bruegel the Elder, who lived in Brussels from 1563 to 1569: *Le Cortège de Noces* (The Wedding Procession) is an affectionate caricature of peasant life. Neighbouring rooms contain fine examples of Brussels' tapestries from the 16th and 17th centuries, and porcelain, which was produced in Brussels (at Tervuren, Schaerbeek, Etterbeek and Ixelles) from 1767 to 1953.

The historical models on the first floor show how Brussels has developed through the ages. In the model of the old walled city, for instance, you can see the old path of the River Senne, the Ile Saint-Géry (the site of the original settlement), the Grand' Place, the city walls, and the Coudenberg. A good collection of paintings serve to illustrate notable historical landmarks, such as the magnificent Coudenberg Palace, destroyed by fire in 1731.

The second floor includes a series of displays relating to the traditional crafts of Brussels—lacemaking, printing, weaving and so forth. A further, large room has been devoted to the costumes of the Manneken-Pis, where about 100 of his 500 or so outfits are on display. The earliest here dates from the 1920s, but most are modern. They include regimental uniforms, the costume of the Gilles de Binche (*see* p.18), sporting kits (including a sub-aqua outfit), tradesmen's working clothes (plumber, beekeeper, etc.) and samurai armour—all carefully designed so the little chap can continue the activity for which he is so well known.

As you leave the Maison du Roi you might picture the dejection of the great French poet Charles Baudelaire (1821–67) as he too left the building in 1863, after a literary disaster. In one of his meet-the-poet seminars here, he addressed a large and enthusiastic audience, including a contingent from a highly respected girls' school. Seeking to thank his audience for helping him to overcome his nerves, he said: '*Votre grâce m'a bien vite fait connaître que cette virginité de parole n'est, en somme, pas plus difficile à perdre que toute autre.*' ('Your kindness has quickly made me realize that this virginity of words is in fact no more difficult to lose than any other.') The schoolgirls were hastily ushered out, followed by the rest of the audience. Baudelaire's standing as a celebrity had been eradicated in a single phrase, and he became increasingly embittered towards the Belgians thereafter.

Turn left to continue round the Grand' Place.

Next to the Rue des Harengs is **No. 28**, La Chambrette de L'Amman (The 'Little Room' of the Amman). The Amman was the Duke of Brabant's representative to the council of *échevins*, and also a senior legal officer. His main office was over the other side of the square, at L'Etoile (*see* below). **No. 27** shares a frontage with **No. 26** and is known as Le Pigeon (The Pigeon), acquired by the Guild of Painters in 1510 and reconstructed after 1695.

Plaques on either side of the door of No. 26 announce the fact that Victor Hugo lived here in 1852. A bitter critic of Louis Napoleon, who had just declared himself Emperor Napoleon III, Victor Hugo had been forced to flee from France. He stayed in this house for several months, protected from the intrusions of an admiring public by his landlady, Madame Sébert, who owned the tobacconist's on the ground floor. When Victor Hugo, by his continued vitriolic outpourings against Napoleon III, became a security risk and embarrassment to the Belgian government, he went to live in the British Channel Islands, but returned frequently to Brussels. His long-suffering wife, Adèle, took up residence in the Place des Barricades, while his unhappy mistress of the past 18 years, Juliette Drouet, found lodgings nearer at hand in the Galeries Royales de Saint-Hubert. Hugo himself, however, directed his formidable amorous energies towards a string of servant girls and prostitutes.

Next door is another double-fronted house, **Nos. 24 and 25**, designed by another of the great architects of the Grand' Place, Willem de Bruyn. Called La Maison des Tailleurs (The Tailors' House), it has a bust of the patron saint of tailors, St Barbara, over the entrance, and St Boniface on the gable, beneath whom you can see a plaque bearing tailor's shears. This pair of houses is now another celebrated bar/restaurant called La Chaloupe d'Or (The Golden Boat) (*see* listings above).

Nos. 22 and 21 form another pair, the ground floor of which is a shop selling Godiva chocolates (*see* **Food and Drink**, pp.226–7). The two houses are known as Anna-Joseph from the inscription over the lower windows. (The reference is to Joseph, husband of the Virgin Mary, and Anne, her mother.) The iron pulley on the gable is a survivor from the days when stores and furniture were raised to the upper storeys on ropes, rather than up the internal stairs. **No. 20** is known as Le

Cerf (The Stag); the stag in question can be seen sculpted in relief around the corner in the Rue de la Colline.

Cross the Rue de la Colline, the street entering the Grand' Place from the east.

The entire south of the Grand' Place is occupied by **La Maison des Ducs de Brabant**—in fact a series of six houses unified by a single façade and designed as a whole in 1698 by Willem de Bruyn. The building was conceived in palatial style, and is decorated by the busts of the dukes of Brabant (which gave the building its grand name). Recently restored and cleaned, it glistens with scrubbed-up stonework and newly painted gilding.

> *You now reach the southernmost corner of the Grand' Place, and the Rue des Chapeliers (hatmakers).*

The last stretch of gabled buildings begins with **Nos. 12 and 11**, dating from 1699 and 1702 respectively and called Le Mont Thabor (Mount Thabor) and La Rose (The Rose)—so named because it belonged to the Van der Rosen family and was used as a private house. Both of these are now occupied by a restaurant.

> ***No. 10*** *is La Maison des Brasseurs (The Brewers' House), for this was the headquarters of the brewers' guild, and is the only house in the Grand' Place still occupied by the guild which built it, now called the Confédération des Brasseries de Belgique. It houses a small museum of brewing, the* **Musée de la Brasserie**. *Open 10–5; adm 100 BF, which includes a free glass of beer.*

This is one of the most striking buildings of the Grand' Place—a reflection of the wealth and standing of brewers since medieval times. Beer was the most common drink in Europe before the development of safe piped water in the late 19th century. The crew of a man-of-war in Napoleonic times, for example, were given 4.5 litres of the stuff as part of their daily rations. Statistics for the Belgian brewing industry today are no less impressive: the industry's total annual output is 14,000 million litres, more than 1000 litres per head of population.

Designed by Willem de Bruyn, the Maison des Brasseurs is unusual in that the columns rise right through the second and third floors to a simple but effective semi-circular pediment. Note the hop vines and grain stalks entwined around the lower sections of the columns. The brewing museum in the basement consists of two rooms: the first contains a variety of traditional paraphernalia from the old days of brewing, while the second gives a flavour of the hi-tech, squeaky-clean world of modern brewing. Touch-screen computers offer a breakdown of statistics about the Belgian brewing industry. Although brewing is one of Belgium's great art-forms (*see* **Food and Drink**, pp.227–30), this museum is not essential viewing: if you want to visit only one brewing museum during your visit to Brussels, the unique Musée de la Gueuze (*see* p.196) is a more interesting option.

No. 9 is Le Cygne (The Swan), so named after the sculpture of a swan, wings outstretched, over the door. This elegant, classical-style house was rebuilt as a private dwelling in 1698 but became the butchers' guildhouse in 1720. It differs from others in the Grand' Place by having a dome-shaped roof pierced by dormer windows in place of a gable. Le Cygne is now an expensive restaurant, an ironic twist of fate given that Karl Marx used to hold meetings of the Deutscher Arbeitverein (German Workers' Union) in a café on this site during the period that he was writing the *Communist Manifesto* with Friedrich Engels.

Marx's antagonism to the Prussian government, expressed in a series of articles in a German paper produced in Brussels, made the authorities nervous, and his meetings were regularly infiltrated by spies. Matters came to a head on 24 February 1848 following the revolution in France. Like most European capitals, Brussels was alive with revolutionary fervour, and the Grand' Place filled with an excited crowd fuelled by rumours of the abdication of Leopold I. The police intervened, with sabres drawn, and made a number of arrests. Following this, the authorities thought it prudent to expel all foreign subversives, and so on 2 March Marx was given 24 hours to leave the country (he eventually took refuge in England).

No. 8 is L'Etoile (The Star), built over the arched arcade that leads into the Rue Charles Buls. This was the main office and residence of the Amman, one of whose duties was to oversee executions as the king's representative. It is said that his balcony gave him a good view of executions taking place in the Grand' Place. The original building was demolished in 1850 to given better road access to the Grand' Place, and the present building was erected over an arcade in the 1890s, to redress the lost sense of architectural balance.

> *Turn left into the arcade beneath L'Etoile. Stand for a moment and observe passers-by rubbing their hands along the bronze statue fixed to the wall. Over the years his limbs have been polished to a shine.*

This is the 19th-century monument to Everard 't Serclaes, the alderman and leader of the guilds who, in 1356, led a rebellion that repulsed the Flemish occupation of Brussels. The Duke of Flanders, Louis de Male, had invaded the city while laying claim to the vacant Duchy of Brabant. In 1388 Everard 't Serclaes was captured during an attack by troops from Gaasbeek loyal to Flanders, and his tongue was cut out. He was brought to the building on this site, L'Etoile, where he died. In revenge the furious citizens of Brussels attacked and demolished the castle of Gaarbeek—during which they fed robustly on chickens and so, according to some theories, earnt the Bruxellois their nickname *kiekerfretters* (chicken eaters). Stroking his limbs is said to bring good fortune. However, some Flemish activists see this tradition as provocative and have made equally provocative calls for the monument's removal.

The Art Nouveau monument to its left is rather more endearing. It is dedicated to Charles Buls, burgomaster of Brussels from 1891 to 1899. A goldsmith by training, but also an artist, reformer and man of letters, Buls was the political force behind the restoration of much of old Brussels, including the Grand' Place.

Go back into the Grand' Place and turn left.

You are now standing beneath the imposing **Hôtel de Ville**, or Town Hall. Although it was originally built in the early 15th century, what you see now is really what 19th-century romantics thought a medieval town hall should look like—for almost all the arches, statues, crocketed spires, turrets and balustrades date from a restoration programme that was begun in 1821. Its real glory, however, is the vast tower, which stood alone amid the rubble after the French bombardment of 1695. (Renovation likely to continue until 1996.)

Buildings on this site were used as a town hall as early as 1327, but after 1380 the area was cleared to make way for a grand new building. Work proceeded on an ever more ambitious scale during the 15th century, culminating in the tower, by Jan van Ruysbroeck. It rises 96m and is topped by the splendid, primitive 15th-century statue of St Michael (the patron saint of Brussels) killing the devil.

Enter the inner courtyard of the Hôtel de Ville through the arched gateway at the base of the tower.

After the destruction of 1695, a new town hall was built around a central courtyard in the neoclassical style associated (ironically) with Louis XIV of France. The star in the cobbles in the middle of this courtyard marks the official centre of Brussels, from which all measurements are made. The 18th-century marble statues set against the west wall represent the two main rivers of Belgium, the Meuse (by Jean de Kinder), and the Scheldt (by Pierre-Denis Plumier).

*Although mostly 19th century, the **interior of the Hôtel de Ville** is worth a visit if you can manage to slot into the limited and rather complex schedule of guided tours on offer. Tours, in English, German, Dutch or French, last about 45 min; Tues–Fri April–Sept: 9.30–12.15 and 1.45–5; Oct–March 9.30–12.15 and 1.45–4; English tours Tues 11.30 and 3.15, Wed 3.15 and Apr–Sept Sun 3.15; adm 80 BF.*

The tour takes you through just one level of the building, which consists mainly of grand public rooms. The 18th-century Council Room is a dazzling confection of tapestries, gilt mirrors and ceiling paintings, and seems like a cross between a royal bedchamber and a funfair roundabout. In the Antechamber of the Burgomaster there is a series of interesting oil paintings by Jean-Baptiste van Moer, dated around 1874. They were based on his earlier watercolours depicting the River Senne flowing through Brussels before it was covered over. Most of the remaining rooms are grandiose examples of municipal Neo-Gothic.

*Leave the Grand' Place by the Rue Charles Buls. The shop on the left is a young branch of the **Biscuiterie Dandoy**, a company founded in 1829 and famous for its delicious, crumbly biscuits and other specialities. To your right, at the junction with Rue de l'Amigo, is the **Hôtel Amigo**.*

'*Il va se retrouver à l'Amigo*' is still a common expression, meaning something like, 'He'll end up in the clink [if he doesn't watch out].' Every police station has its 'Amigo'—its cells where prisoners are temporarily held. The term derives from a building on this site which was acquired by the state in 1522 to serve as a prison for criminals awaiting trial, as well as for tramps and drunks. The name is believed to have been a mistranslation: in Flemish it was known as *vrunte*, meaning an enclosure, but the Spanish authorities confused this with *vriend*, meaning friend: hence *amigo*. It was rebuilt in 1792 to hold political prisoners and subsequently became a police station. It was here that Karl Marx and his wife, Baroness Jenny von Westphalen, were brought the night of their expulsion; Jenny was scandalized to be held in the same cells as common prostitutes.

Across the street is Rose's Lace Boutique. There's a rather funereal plaque on the wall here which recounts that this is the site of a hotel called A la Ville de Courtrai.

It was here, on 10 July 1873, that the French poet Paul Verlaine, drunk and impassioned, shot and wounded his young fellow poet and lover Arthur Rimbaud, who had threatened to leave him. Rimbaud was only wounded on the wrist, and after receiving treatment he reiterated that he wanted to leave Brussels. On the way to the railway station another row blew up. Verlaine drew his revolver again, and Rimbaud had to seek refuge with a police officer. Verlaine paid for the incident with two years' imprisonment at Mons.

*Walk around to the other side of Rose's Lace Boutique and turn left into Rue de la Violette. A short way up this street is the **Musée du Costume et de la Dentelle**. Open Tues, Thurs, Fri 10–12.30, 1.30–5, closed 4pm Oct–March; Sat, Sun and public holidays 2–4.30; adm 80 BF.*

This small museum, housed in an 18th-century building, contains a rich collection of lace and clothing accessories from the 17th century to the present day. It shows how traditional lace is made and traces the history of lace-making in Belgium and its importance in the economy of Brussels (*see* **Topics**, pp.36–8). If you want to make some sense of all the lace that fills so many of the shops in the surrounding streets, this a good place to start. The museum's extensive costume collection forms the basis of a rolling series of temporary exhibitions.

> *Now retrace your steps to the Verlaine-Rimbaud plaque and walk up this street (Rue des Brasseurs, but there is no street name here.) Continue over the crossroads with the Rue des Chapeliers into a street called Marché aux Fromages (cheese market—for this is what it once was).*

Close your eyes and you might be in Greece—or somewhere vaguely Mediterranean. Today the cobbled roadway of the Marché aux Fromages is lined with tavernas and doner-kebab shops. As in all the streets around the Grand' Place, there is a pleasantly animated atmosphere—like the foyer of a theatre during the interval, to extend Cocteau's metaphor. Many buildings have preserved their 17th-century gables, and the street plan has changed little since medieval times.

> *At the top of the Marché aux Fromages, turn right into the Rue des Eperonniers (spur-makers). This comes out into Place Saint-Jean, at the centre of which is a statue of **Gabrielle Petit**.*

Gabrielle Petit (1893–1916) was a resistance worker during the First World War, who helped to conceal Allied soldiers and usher them across the border to the Netherlands. She was arrested in 1916 and sentenced to death. The Germans were sensitive to the international outcry over the execution of Edith Cavell in 1915 (*see* pp.42–3), and made it clear to Gabrielle Petit that her sentence would probably be commuted if she appealed. She refused, and faced the firing squad on 1 April 1916 after making the declaration inscribed (in French) on this monument: 'I have just been condemned to death. I shall be shot tomorrow. Long live the King, long live Belgium...and I shall show them that a Belgian woman knows how to die.'

> *Take the second exit on the left out of Place Saint-Jean. This is Rue Saint-Jean, a street of printsellers and booksellers. Walk up to Nos. 17–19, the entrance to the **Galerie Bortier**.*

This cavernous 19th-century shopping arcade was designed (like the far more glamorous Galeries Royales de Saint-Hubert) by J.P. Cluysenaar. Beneath a canopy of glass and ornate ironwork, it is now a dimly lit shrine for bibliophiles, lined with shops selling second-hand books (mainly in French), prints and postcards.

Walk through the Galerie Bortier and turn left at the other end to descend the Rue de la Madeleine, which is lined with an attractive jumble of art galleries, bookshops and antique shops. On the right is the **Eglise de la Madeleine**. *Mon–Fri 7am–7pm, Sat 8.30–12.30 and 4–8; Sun 7–12.30 and 5–8.*

This pretty, 15th-century brick church had a Baroque chapel, the chapel of Sainte-Anne, tacked on to its northern side in 1957, when it was transferred from the nearby Rue de la Montagne to make room for a car park. Radical modern restoration has made the interior rather soulless—but beggars encountered in the dim entrance lobby during Mass restore some of its lost medieval mood.

Follow the Rue de la Madeleine down into the broad, triangular junction at its foot. In the central reservation is a striking bronze monument to Charles Buls, dated 1886.

This is the junction with the busy thoroughfare called the Rue du Marché aux Herbes (herb market). Brussels was once on a major trade route that linked Bruges to Cologne, and in the days before ringroads and bypasses cities thrived on through traffic. For centuries heavy carts, accompanied by men on horseback or walking in clogs, would have come trundling down the Rue du Marché aux Herbes, laden with grain, wool, meat, ironware, pottery and textiles.

The Rue de la Montagne, behind the statue of Charles Buls, is lined with gabled houses. Between 1864 and 1866 Baudelaire lived at No. 26.

He occupied a cheap, dingy room, which he shared with a pet bat fed on milk sops. In March 1866 he became ill during a visit to Namur then went into morbid decline, emerging from his room only to take short walks. He was eventually bailed out by his mother who took him back to Paris, where he died in 1867.

Walk past the statue of Charles Buls into Rue du Marché aux Herbes. Almost immediately on your right is the entrance to the **Galeries Royales de Saint-Hubert**.

This beautiful, marbled shopping arcade, designed by J.P. Cluysenaar and built in 1847, was the first of its kind in mainland Europe, and is in two halves, the Galerie de la Reine and the Galerie du Roi (with a further spur called the Galerie des Princes), intersected by the Rue des Bouchers. It is a celebrated shopping precinct, with ostentatiously expensive clothes shops, dainty *chocolatiers*, and elegant cafés providing excellent coffee and the day's newspapers. With their air of 19th-century elegance, the Galeries Saint-Hubert are the picture of established calm. Yet their construction was highly controversial. It involved the destruction of a considerable swathe of traditional housing, leading to the eviction of both inhabitants and businesses. A famous barber called Pameel was driven to kill himself in protest by slitting his throat in his own salon.

*Walk the length of the Galeries Saint-Hubert, then turn left into the Rue de l'Ecuyer, then left again down the Rue des Dominicains. At the end of this, turn right into the **Rue des Bouchers** (butchers' street).*

The Rue des Bouchers is a visual feast: wall-to-wall restaurants with gaily painted awnings, fronted by spectacular displays of fish, shellfish and fruit laid out on ice-strewn trestles—and patrolled by importuning waiters. Pretty, it may be, but no self-respecting Bruxellois would dream of eating in such places: the displays, in their view, are in inverse proportion to the quality of the cooking.

Take the first left, the Petite Rue des Bouchers. Stop for a moment and look up. From here you have an excellent view of the statue of St Michael on the top of the tower of the Hôtel de Ville. Walk past more restaurants and look for a tiny alleyway halfway down the Petite Rue des Bouchers, on the left-hand side: the Impasse Schuddeveld.

At the bottom of this atmospheric little alleyway is the remarkable Toone puppet theatre (*see* pp.249–50) in a house built in 1696. Shows take place only in the evening at 8.30pm, but you can make reservations after 12 noon in the bar. There is also a Toone Theatre Museum, with a collection of the distinctive, elongated puppets used in the show, but this is only open in the intervals during performances. It is nonetheless worth coming down this alley, if only to glimpse this famous Brussels institution and its medieval surroundings.

*Retrace your steps to the Rue des Bouchers. Turn left, and continue until you reach the Rue de la Fourche. Turn left here and continue down the Rue de la Fourche to return to the Rue du Marché aux Herbes. Turn right, then almost immediately left into the Petite Rue au Beurre. When you reach the Rue au Beurre at the end of this short street, turn right. At 31 Rue au Beurre is the older, more celebrated of the **Dandoy** biscuit shops. Facing you at the end of the street is the grand façade of the Bourse. Ignore this for the moment. Turn to the church immediately to your right, the **Eglise Saint-Nicholas**. Usually open 9–6.30.*

This is one of the oldest and most atmospheric churches in Brussels, with its dim, candlelit interior and quaintly crooked aisle. A church has been on this site virtually since Brussels' foundation, closely linked to the market activities on the Grand' Place. St Nicholas, said to be a 4th-century bishop of Myra in Turkey, is the patron saint of merchants—although he is better known as Santa Claus. Most of the present structure dates from the 14th and 15th centuries. The church suffered from vandalism at the hands of Protestant iconoclasts during the 1570s and was damaged in the 1695 bombardment. Restoration gave it its Baroque flourishes. The impressive reliquary of the Martyrs of Gorcum dates from 1868; the martyrs were tortured to death by the Protestant '*gueux*' (rebels) in 1572.

Turn right as you come out of the church.

Immediately facing you is **La Bourse**, the former stock exchange, an impressive rectangle in neoclassical style but with little sense of neoclassical restraint. Decked with garlands of stone flowers and cherubs playing at horticulture, it is typical of the retrospective style used for many of the grand buildings in the Brussels of Leopold II. Though it looks much earlier, the Bourse dates from 1873.

*Walk along the right-hand side of the Bourse, along the Rue de la Bourse, to the grand neoclassical front of the building. To your left the excavations of a 13th-century Franciscan convent, destroyed in the religious wars of the 16th century, have been made into the **Musée Bruxella** (guided tours only, see p.197).*

The Bourse is now used to mount temporary exhibitions. Even when no exhibition is taking place, you can glimpse the interior and its ornate stucco ceiling by going through the entrance into a glass-canopied walkway.

*Follow round the front of the Bourse, and turn left into Rue Henri Maus. On the right-hand side is the **Café Falstaff** (see listings above).*

This is a famous and classic Art Nouveau bar. Push on through the maze of tables beneath the awnings (heated in winter) into the interior: it is like walking into the turn of the century, or 1903 to be precise. The sweeping curves of Art Nouveau woodwork (by Victor Horta's cabinet maker and decorator), the lamps and the stained glass, lie beneath a dingy but comforting patina of time and cigar smoke.

*Walk to the end of Rue Henri Maus, then turn right into the Rue du Midi, a street dominated by philatelist's shops. The second right takes you into the curving Rue du Marché au Charbon. At about No. 91, with the coat of arms of Charles of Lorraine over the door, is **Eglise Notre-Dame de Bon Secours**. Open 9–6, closed Sun afternoon Oct–June.*

This modest little gem was built between 1664 and 1694 in Flemish Baroque style. The body of the church is based on an octagonal plan soaring to a domed ceiling, made all the more impressive by a nave that has been compressed to virtual non-existence. As in many Brussels churches, recorded sacred music is played here during visiting hours, demonstrating the church's remarkable acoustics.

Backtrack a short way to the Café au Soleil and turn right into the Rue des Grands-Carmes, named after the old Carmelite convent that was destroyed in the 1790s by Revolutionary zealots during the French *occupation (a common Brussels tale). At No. 7 is the workshop of Jean-Pierre Forton, **master pipe-maker**.*

On display in this mecca for pipe-smokers are Monsieur Forton's fanciful creations in wood and meerschaum depicting animals and famous people, such as John F. Kennedy. A world tour of tobacco mixtures includes home-grown Belgian tobacco from the valley of the River Semois.

*Continue along the Rue des Grands-Carmes, crossing over the Rue du Midi. You will soon come to the intersection with the Rue de l'Etuve. This is the site of Brussels' most famous statue, the **Manneken-Pis**.*

Manneken is *bruxellois* for little man; Pis speaks for itself. This bronze statue of a little naked boy peeing with happy abandon has long been held in great affection by the people of Brussels and has become a symbol of their city. No one can quite explain why—which must be part of his charm.

Endless legends have evolved to fill this gap in human knowledge. One is that the statue celebrates a little boy who prevented a great fire during the time of the Burgundian dukes by extinguishing a firebomb in this manner. Another relates how a wealthy citizen lost his son in the carnival crowds. When the child was found, his grateful father decided to have a statue made of the boy in the pose—and erected in the place—in which he was discovered. In another version, relating back to the 12th century, the infant Godfrey, future Duke of Brabant, was taken to the battlefield where Brussels was fighting against Mechelen. He was placed in the branches of an oak tree to watch the battle, where he was discovered by one of the enemy. Godfrey's response was to piss in his face, a gesture of scorn that so demoralized the whole Mechelen army that they fled.

MANNEKIN-PIS

Here's another idea. One day the infant son of Duke John III of Brabant exposed himself to a company of women in the Rue de l'Etuve. This coincided with a period during which the 14th-century mystic philosopher Jean de Ruysbroeck was having a great public debate with another Brussels mystic called Bloemaerdinne. Bloemaerdinne argued that there was no sin involved in fulfilling the natural impulses of love—an idea that appealed to the hedonistic Bruxellois. A statue of the child served as an apt symbol of Bloemaerdinne's cause.

Perhaps, more prosaically, it was just a rather apt and charming adornment for a public fountain in a district where there were public baths during medieval times (*étuve* means 'steam-bath').

Whatever, when the first bronze statue was cast by Jérôme Duquesnoy the Elder in 1619, it was probably based on an earlier model. Duquesnoy's version was already held in great affection when French soldiers tried to carry it off in 1747. The citizens of Brussels were furious, and to make amends Louis XV had a brocaded suit made for the Manneken-Pis—the first in his splendid collection of costumes. In 1793 he was given a Revolutionary bonnet by the Paris Convention.

When an ex-convict stole the Manneken-Pis in 1817 the town was distraught; the culprit was caught and branded in the Grand' Place, then sentenced to eleven lifetimes' hard labour. But the statue was in ruins and had to be recast. This, then, is the statue you see today. It is much smaller than you expect, perched on his plinth behind high railings. A programme listing which costume he will be wearing over the current period is posted on the railings.

> You can return to the Grand' Place from here by walking down the Rue de l'Etuve. Tourist shops line the street, selling lace, postcards, Delftware and knick-knacks—and rank upon rank of diminutive copies of the Manneken-Pis. The poor child has been put to countless debased uses, such as corkscrews and drinks dispensers. Alternatively you can take a short excursion to see a remnant of the old city wall. Walk up the Rue du Chêne (the continuation of the Rue des Grands-Carmes) and take the first right, the Rue de Villers. In a derelict wasteland, next to a broken-down garage, stands the **Tour de Villers**.

This semi-circular bastion is one of the few surviving pieces of the first set of city walls, dating from the 12th century. There is not much to see and there is no real access to it, but it provides a useful yardstick by which to measure the massive scale of the second city walls, constructed 200 years later.

> A short walk around the corner into the Rue des Alexiens brings you to **La Fleur en Papier Doré**, one of the most charming of Brussels' few surviving estaminets (pubs). Originally founded by the Soeurs de Charité in 1846, it was owned by the actor/artist/Dadaist Gérard (Geert van Bruaene) in the 1920s, and the nicotine-brown walls of its three tiny rooms are encrusted with paintings, prints, inscriptions and a tantalizing collection of oddities. It's an excellent place to refresh yourself with a cool blanche, straight from the barrel.

II: Coudenberg & Parc de Bruxelles

Start: *the Mont des Arts, which is a short walk from Ⓜ Gare Centrale.*

Walking Time: *it would not take you more than about 45 minutes to cover the full circuit of this walk, but to see all the museums you should start early and allow at least 5 hours, if not the whole day.*

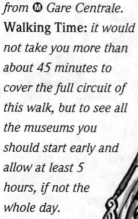

LOUIS XV MARQUETRY BOMBÉ CHES

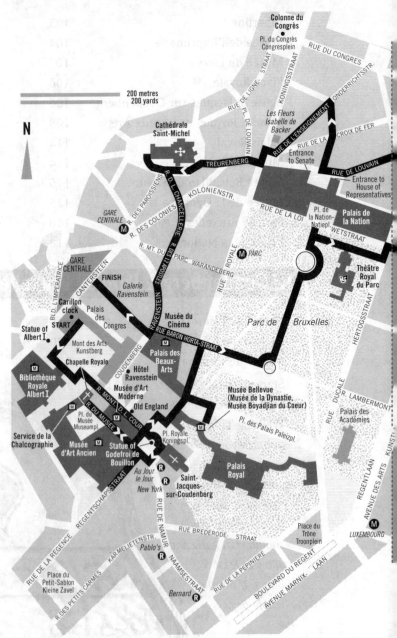

No visit to Brussels would be complete without paying a call on the national art collection at the Musées Royaux des Beaux-Arts, which consist of the Musée d'Art Ancien and the Musée d'Art Moderne. These museums contain work by numerous big names in European art—Bruegel, Rubens, Van Dyck, Magritte—and several classic pieces reproduced in all the art history books. But best of all, they show the true strength of Belgian art across the board, and provide excellent introductions to lesser-known movements and individuals, such as the Symbolists and James Ensor.

The Musées Royaux des Beaux-Arts sit on the summit of the Coudenberg, the high ground south of the city centre which was once an enclave for the ruling classes and the aristocracy. It is still a very grand, breezy part of town, with long vistas, stately architecture and a large, formally planned park overlooked by the royal palace. A handful of small museums reflect this noble past—rich collections of furniture, paintings, costume accessories. Here you can see how 18th-century ladies clipped their nails, and where the arty crowd of the late 19th century lounged and clinked their Art Nouveau glasses, surrounded by chinoiserie and the bright colours of Belgian post-impressionism.

A short walk back towards the city centre leads to Brussels' cathedral, St Michael's. Its calm, echoing interior provides a suitably meditative finish to a kaleidoscopic walk. If you reach here in the early evening, however, you could end the day at the Musée du Cinéma, which runs a daily programme—unique in Europe—of classic silent movies performed to live piano accompaniment (at 7pm and 9pm; for details of the complex system for guaranteeing a seat in advance, *see* p.122.)

This walk is not long in terms of distance covered, but demands a fair degree of museum stamina. The Musées Royaux des Beaux-Arts really deserve a day to themselves, and you cannot hope to do them justice in such a short time. Regard this as a flying visit in preparation for a fuller visit, and reserve your energies for the other museums on the walk. (You pass close to the Musées Royaux des Beaux-Arts on Walk III, so could visit them again then.)

The best day to do this walk is Wednesday; Tuesday and Thursday are slightly less good (the Musée du Livre is closed). On Friday the Musée Bellevue is closed; the Hôtel Charlier closes over the weekend, and the Musée du Livre closes on Sunday. The Musées Royaux des Beaux-Arts are closed on Monday.

---

lunch/cafés

Unusually for Brussels, this area is not well served by lunch-stops. Here are a few suggestions, some slightly off the path of the walk. Note also that the Musées Royaux des Beaux-Arts are not far from the Place du Grand-Sablon (see listings for Walk III).

Musée d'Art Ancien. Stylish museum cafeteria serving light refreshments at rather inflated prices.

Au Jour le Jour, 4 Rue de Namur, ✆ 502 80 00. *Closed Sat.* Low lights, friendly service and a faithful following of habitués for dishes such as *carpaccio* and *cuisse de canard à l'Ardennes*; lunch menu at 390 BF.

New York, 8 Rue de Namur. A *snack*, offering sandwiches, pizza and basic lunch dishes for around 200 BF.

Pablo's, 51 Rue de Namur. Upbeat Mexican restaurant with a bar the size of a bowling alley. *Tacos, enchiladas, arroz con pollo* etc., with lunchtime specials for around 395 BF.

Bernard, 93 Rue de Namur, ✆ 512 88 21. *Closed Mon evening and Sun.* Entered through the marbled hallway of an upper-crust delicatessen, this is a hallowed shrine to fish cookery. *Filet de saumon frais aux chicons* for 1450 BF, and the like.

Resto-Snack Cordon-Bleu, 15a Rue Joseph II. Modest restaurant catering for hungry but discriminating office workers. Sandwiches, and dishes of the day like *saltimbocca alla Romana* (240 BF); *moules marinière* (450 BF).

The Cambridge, corner of Rue Louvain and Rue Nord. Large modern tavern greets the lunchtime invasion with a no-nonsense 230 BF *menu du jour*.

---

*The starting point of this walk is the foot of the street called Mont des Arts, which leads up past the Palais des Congrès. Try to reach it just before the hour and walk under the modern rectangular arch that spans the street: on the other side is a modern **carillon clock**.*

The clock has 24 bells and a cast of 12 characters, one for each hour. Just before the hour a figure emerges from its niche and shuffles about while the bells sing out their tunes—one Walloon, the other Flemish at alternate hours—before the top-hatted burgher on the parapet above strikes the hour. The sculptures represent various key figures from Belgian history, such as a Gaul, Godefroi de Bouillon, Philip the Good, Charles V, Count Egmont (holding his severed head under one arm), and the tam-tam player, representng the Belgian Congo.

Carillon clocks are found throughout the Low Countries. They were developed around 1500, when sets of small bells, designed to play simple tunes, were attached to town clocks in order to alert the citizens to the coming hour. The carillon on the Mont des Arts is a modern version, erected in the early 1960s.

Facing up the Mont des Arts once more, turn right to cross the formal garden of gravel avenues, parterres and fountains.

The focal point of this garden is the large equestrian statue of **Albert I**, the popular king who led the Belgian army against the Germans throughout the First World War (*see* **History**, p.64). Dubbed 'Le Roi Chevalier', he was in fact a modest man and had to overcome a natural shyness to promote his particular interests, notably scientific research, social justice and an improvement of the lot of Africans in the Congo. A diminutive modern statue of his wife, Elisabeth, stands in front of him on the other side of the road. Albert died in a climbing accident in 1934, and Elisabeth outlived him by 31 years.

The surrounding complex of buildings is known collectively as the **Albertine**, originally planned as a memorial to Albert, but not constructed until 1954–69. Turn to face up the hill. To the right is the Bibliothèque Royale Albert I, and to the left is a large congress centre, the Palais des Congrès.

*Climb the stone steps on the right-hand side of the garden. These lead to the main entrance of the **Bibliothèque Royale Albert I**.*

This is Belgium's national library, with a collection that began in the 15th century with the illuminated manuscripts of the Dukes of Burgundy. The library itself is open only to registered cardholders, but within the same building you may visit the Musée de l'Imprimerie, the Musée du Livre and the Chapelle de Nassau.

> The **Musée de l'Imprimerie** *(Printing Museum) (open Mon–Sat 9–5, closed last week in Aug; adm free) is spread out along the marbled corridors of the floor below the entrance to the library.*

It consists of a collection of old printing presses and equipment, from massive hand-pulled presses and compositors' trays to hot-metal casting machines, bewilderingly complex monotype keyboards and a vast camera on a wooden frame for making early photographic plates. It offers a brief glimpse of the world of printing, which computer technology has rendered archaic in less than two decades.

> *On the same floor is the **Musée du Livre** (Museum of the Book) (Open Mon, Wed and Sat only, 2–4.45pm, closed last week of Aug; adm free.) This is a little gem, but with frustratingly restricted visiting hours. You may have to come back here after visiting the Musées Royaux des Beaux-Arts, which are a stone's throw away.*

The museum occupies just one small room—a womb-like interior of dark carpeting and softly lit display cases, containing books of up to 1200 years old. The 12th- and 13th-century exhibits date from the heyday of the illuminated manuscript, while a printed text from Japan of AD 770 is a salutary reminder that Gutenberg's breakthrough in around 1430 was not so much printing itself but the development of movable type. The earliest European printed book on display, dating from 1474, is so immaculately preserved that it might have been printed 50 years ago, not 500. There are also 16th-century books from Christopher Plantin's famous workshop in Antwerp (*see* pp.350–52), and a priceless manuscript by Matisse illustrating a work by the 15th-century poet Charles d'Orléans.

The short entrance passageway to the museum is lined with a series of reconstructed rooms which show donated collections of books displayed in their original settings. They include a stylish Art Nouveau library with furniture by Henri van de Velde (*see* p.47), the theatrically decorated study of the celebrated Belgian playwright Michel de Ghelderode (*see* p.45), and the study of the Belgian poet Emile Verhaeren (*see* p.47) from his house at Saint-Cloud.

> *The **Chapelle de Nassau** (Nassau Chapel) is on the floor above the Musée du Livre and is the setting for a range of temporary exhibitions on any subject to do with books and the written word. (Access to the chapel is restricted to the opening times of these exhibitions.)*

The Chapelle de Nassau is only really of interest as the last remnant of the magnificent Hôtel de Nassau. The Nassau family rose to prominence in the Low

Countries when Philip the Good, Duke of Burgundy (r.1419–67) appointed Engelbert II of Nassau as Governor General. Engelbert transformed an earlier palace on this site in Flemish Renaissance style and began renovations on the chapel which were completed in 1520. Later that century the Nassau estates in the Low Countries were awarded to the House of Orange by Charles V. In 1731 the Coudenberg Palace (further up the hill) was burned to the ground, and after 1756 Charles of Lorraine converted the whole site into a grand new palace in neoclassical style (*see* 'Place du Musée' below). The chapel survived this new scheme, and the construction of the Albertine in the 1960s. After deconsecration during the Napoleonic era, it had a chequered career as a brewery warehouse and then, in the 1880s, as a workshop for pioneer palaeontologists assembling some of the first complete dinosaur skeletons. Today the chapel's bare architectural bones are all that remain to be seen—a rather strange hybrid of early Gothic and late Gothic, and the flat-topped arch associated with the Tudor period.

Leaving the Royal Library, turn right and follow the walkway around the garden of the Mont des Arts. Mount the stairs at the head of the garden which lead to a broad sweep of road called the Coudenberg.

To your left, on the other side of the street, stands an attractive red-brick building with a stepped gable. This is the **Hôtel Ravenstein**, the only substantial survivor of the old Coudenberg quarter, dating from the 15th century. It formed part of the palace of the Princes of Cleves-Ravenstein and was the birthplace of Anne of Cleves (1515–57), fourth wife of Henry VIII of England. This was a disastrous political marriage: Henry found her not to his taste and declared that he could 'never in her company be provoked and steered to know her carnally'. Dubbing her the 'Flemish Mare', he divorced her the same year as he married her, 1540.

*Cross the road and continue up the Rue Mont de la Cour. On the left, on the corner of Rue Villa Hermosa, is the site of a former department store called **Old England**—a throwback to the late 19th century when the British Arts and Crafts movement and Liberty style were all the rage.*

This classic Art Nouveau building was designed by Paul Saintenoy (1862–1952) and completed in 1899. It is now being restored as part of the new home for the Musée Instrumental (Musical Instrument Museum), which is currently situated in the Rue de la Régence (*see* **Walk III**). To achieve this it has been stripped to its essentials—cast-iron pillars with characteristic swirling Art Nouveau motifs, and steel joists painted with floral decoration.

Continue up the Rue Mont de la Cour. As you do so, turn around and look back down the Mont des Arts.

For centuries the city centre below—*le Bas de la Ville*—was prone to flooding from the sluggish River Senne, while the ridge of higher ground on which you are standing—*le Haut de la Ville*—was spared. For this reason *le Haut de la Ville* became popular with the ruling classes and well-to-do, particularly the part you are now approaching, the Coudenberg, which was first adopted by the counts of Leuven for their fortress-residence in the 11th century.

*At the top of the Rue Mont de la Cour is the **Place Royale**.*

This busy yet intimate neoclassical square was laid out on the site of the splendid 15th-century Coudenberg palace, built by Philip the Good as a successor to the original fortress. Contemporary paintings (notably in the Musée Communal de Bruxelles, *see* **Walk I**) indicate that this palace was the crowning glory of Brussels' architecture—until 1731, when it was completely destroyed in just six hours by a fire which apparently started in the kitchens. Charles of Lorraine commissioned the French architect Barnabé Guimard to create a new square over the 'Cour Brûlée', and it was built between 1772 and 1785. For the sake of economy the foundations were laid on top of the cellars and underground passageways of the old palace, which still run beneath the cobbles of the square.

An equestrian statue, erected by Leopold I in 1848, now dominates the centre of the Place Royale. This is **Godefroi de Bouillon** (1061–1100), a medieval hero and the subject of numerous legends and *chansons de geste*.

Born in Brabant, he became Duke of Lower Lorraine, and was one of the leaders of the First Crusade (1096–9). This succeeded in wresting Jerusalem from the Muslims, after which Godefroi was asked by the crusading kingdoms to take the title of King of Jerusalem. Contrary to the inscription on this statue, he refused, preferring the more modest title 'Avoué du Saint-Sépulcre' (Defender of the Holy Sepulchre). He died the following year during a typhoid epidemic, and Jerusalem was subsequently ruled by a series of European kings for almost a hundred years until it was recaptured by Saladin in 1187.

*The church behind Godefroi de Bouillon is the **Eglise Saint-Jacques-sur-Coudenberg** (open Mon–Sat 2.30–6, Sun 9–12 and 2.30–5). Again, the opening hours may mean you have to return here after visiting the Musées Royaux des Beaux-Arts.*

The original 18th-century façade of this church was an uncompromising reconstruction of a Graeco-Roman temple. Perhaps it was too pagan a concept for 19th-century sensibilities, for on to this was grafted an incongruous, squat, octagonal bell-tower. You have to block this out in your imagination to visualize the restrained elegance of the original conception.

Despite this mongrel exterior, Saint-Jacques-sur-Coudenberg is one of the loveliest 18th-century churches in Brussels, with a barrel-vaulted nave leading up to the half-domed apse dotted with floral cartouches. There has been a church on this site since the 12th century, when it served as a stopping-off point for pilgrims on their way to Santiago de Compostela in Spain, hence its connection with St James (Iago, Jacques).

Saint-Jacques-sur-Coudenberg is directly connected to the Royal Palace next door. Members of the royal entourage can cross the palace gardens, take a seat in the royal box on the left-hand side of the choir and peer at the service from behind glass, rather like looking through a railway carriage window.

SAINT- JACQUES- SUR- COUDENBERG

During the funeral of King Baudouin I on 7 August 1993, which took place in the Cathédrale Saint-Michel, the service was relayed on to a screen at this church, which was packed with 600 men all called Baudouin (or Boudwijn). This somewhat surreal situation arose from a tradition founded by Leopold I whereby the seventh consecutive son in any family is automatically the godson of the monarch, and takes the monarch's name. (The seventh successive daughter takes the name of the queen, but this occurrence is statistically far rarer.)

Two monumental paintings by Jan Frans Portaels (1818–85) hang on either side of the nave. The one on the right depicts people of all nations gathering around the Cross, while the *Crucifixion and Transfiguration of the Heart* on the left centres upon precisely the image celebrated in the Musée Boyadjian du Cœur (*see* below). The beautiful white and gold statue of the Virgin to the right of this painting, surrounded by a gilded filigree tree, was brought here from s' Hertogenbosch in the Netherlands in 1629 as a gift from Archduchess Isabella. It survived both the fire of 1731 and the deconsecration of the church during the Napoleonic era (when the building served as a 'Temple of Reason' and a 'Temple of Law'), and was restored to its place in 1853.

Turn left as you come out of the church and walk a short distance down the Rue de la Régence. The massive neoclassical pile that looms up in *the hazy distance at the western end of the road is the Palais de Justice (see **Walk III**). Cross the Rue de la Régence to the conglomeration of grimy pillars and statues of angels and muses. This is the entrance to the Musée d'Art Ancien (open Tues–Sun 10–12 and 1–5, closed Mon and public holidays; adm free, but see p.195). It also provides access to the Musée d'Art Moderne (open Tues–Sun 10–1 and 2–5, closed Mon and public holidays; adm free), although the museum also has its own entrance in the Place Royale. These two together are known as the* **Musées Royaux des Beaux-Arts***.*

By the standards of most major national art collections, the Musées Royaux des Beaux-Arts are refreshingly single-minded. The main focus is squarely on Belgian art—or at least the art of the Low Countries for those centuries before Belgium came into existence. Italy and Spain, even France, barely get a look in, but nonetheless the collection is a ravishing *tour de force* and a monument to the technical virtuosity and distinctive mood of North European art.

The Musée d'Art Ancien alone contains over 90 rooms, so it is worth stopping for a moment to plan your visit. At the reception desk you can pick up a schematized map, which lays out the colour-coded chronological paths leading from room to room. Note that the Musée d'Art Ancien closes for lunch at 12, and reopens at 1pm; during this time the Musée d'Art Moderne remains open, closing for its lunch hour at 1pm. You can pass freely between the two.

An excellent way to start your visit is with the 35-minute **audiovisual**, which is effectively an introduction to the history of Belgian art from the 15th to 17th century, focusing on selected works in the collection. (*See* also **Art and Architecture**, pp.67–76) The audiovisual is presented more or less continuously (including over the lunch hour) in Auditorium B on the ground floor, and you can pick up a set of radioactivated headphones in the language of your choice at the reception desk beforehand, if you leave some form of identity as security.

Start with the blue section on the first floor, rooms 10 to 45.

This contains the collection of 15th- and 16th-century paintings. The earliest 'Flemish primitive' work concentrates primarily on religious subjects, since the Church was the main patron of the arts up to and during the Renaissance. Early Flemish artists depicted these with intense colour and detail, reminiscent of the illuminated manuscripts that were a major influence on their style. The settings, however, are usually contemporary, as in the *Annunciation* (Room 11) by the **Master of Flémalle** (first half of the 15th century), set in an interior with tiled floors and shutters. The *Sforza Triptych* (Room 12) by **Rogier van der Weyden** (*c.*1400–64), a celebrated resident of Brussels, depicts the Crucifixion attended by figures in contemporary dress, with a medieval city in the background.

One of the most celebrated paintings of this section is *La Justice d'Othon* (The Justice of Otto) (Room 13), a huge narrative diptych by **Dirk Bouts** (1415–75), which tells the tragic story of the German Holy Roman Emperor Otto II (r.973–83). Left-hand panel: Otto's malicious wife tells him that a certain count has adulterous designs on her, so Otto has the count beheaded and delivers the head to the count's wife. Right-hand panel: the count's wife goes to Otto to protest her husband's innocence. She volunteers to undergo trial by ordeal to prove it, holding a rod of hot iron in one hand and her husband's head in the other. Otto realizes the error of his judgement, and so has his own wife burned at the stake. So much for medieval justice.

Secular art, particularly portraiture, becomes increasingly prominent as the decades progress, and there are some vivid contemporary portraits that make the faces of history come alive, such as the *Portrait of Guillaume Moreel and his Wife* (Room 14) by **Hans Memling** (1430/5–94), and the *Portrait of Dr J. Sheyring* (Room 18), a rough-looking burgher in a fur-lined coat, by the German painter **Lucas Cranach** (1472–1553).

The influence of the Italian Renaissance can be detected in the growing prevalence of classical architectural settings, meticulously rendered in perspective, and the introduction of subjects from Roman mythology. *The Virtue of Patience* (Room 26) is an extraordinarily ambitious work by the Brussels painter **Bernard van Orley** (c.1499–1541), in which debauched diners dash and stumble with foreshortened perspective towards the viewer through an ornate classical hall, while devils fill the ceiling space like some foul black gas.

Pride of place in this section is given to **Pieter Bruegel the Elder** (c.1525–69) (Room 31), who lived in Brussels during the later part of his life (*see* **Walk III**, p.140). What this collection lacks in quantity it makes up for with quality. Bruegel's sideways view of the world is well represented by his famous *Fall of Icarus*, in which poor Icarus is banished to a mere detail in the backdrop, completely ignored by the farmer in the foreground tilling his field. *The Census in Bethlehem* is one of Bruegel's most endearing works, a Flemish winter scene full of villagers working and playing in the snow and on the ice. The census itself seems quite incidental, but the effect is very powerful: it implies not only that momentous historical and religious events had their own, ordinary contexts but also that our ordinary lives can be invested with monumental significance.

This same effect was used by Bruegel's son, **Pieter Bruegel the Younger** (1564–1638), whose subjects, often copied from works by his father, are equally powerful but whose more polished style lacks the immediacy of his father's painting. There are numerous examples of his work to test this judgement (Room

34), including the heart-breaking *Massacre of the Innocents*, depicting villagers pleading for the lives of their children.

> *Follow the brown arrows on the next floor around the section devoted to 17th- and 18th-century painting.*

The star of this section is **Pieter Paul Rubens** (1577–1640) (Rooms 51, 52, 62). For anyone who knows him mainly for his well-fed, rose-pink nudes, this large collection is a revealing insight into his versatility. The *Portrait of Hélène Fourment*, his second wife, demonstrates the great sense of verve and confidence of this new age of painting. The paintings in Room 62 are vast, full of drama, and painted with a swift, dynamic touch. *La Montée au Calvaire* (The Ascent to Calvary) and *Le Martyre de Saint Liévin* (The Martyrdom of St Livincus) are extraordinarily stirring works—depictions of the relentless forces of history, in which even the most savage detail (such as St Livincus's severed tongue being fed to a dog) has a logical place.

More representative images of the times are provided by the portraits of the well-to-do by **Antoon (Anthony) van Dyck** (1599–1641) (Room 53) and **Cornelis de Vos** (1584–1651), full of solid burgher virtues and gravitas. The paintings of **Jacob Jordaens** (1593–1678), by contrast, are brimming with ebullience and *joie de vivre*. He is the painter *par excellence* of the sensuality of women past their prime, as seen in the fleshy folds of his *Allégorie de la Fécondité*, which centres on a well-endowed woman bearing a bust-load of ripe grapes.

> *For 19th-century painting, return to the ground floor and follow the yellow arrows, first around the entrance hall, or Forum, then in the adjacent modernized galleries.*

In this section there are some notable exceptions to the Belgian-Flemish focus of the museum. The first are two works—startling in both content and execution—by the French neoclassical painter **Jacques-Louis David** (1748–1825), who died in exile in Brussels (*see* **Walk IV**, p.148). The famous *Marat Assassiné* (Room 68) portrays the French Revolutionary Jean-Paul Marat (1743–93), slumped dead in his bath. Suffering from a painful skin complaint, Marat could only find relief by spending long periods in his bath, providing an easy target for his young assassin, Charlotte Corday, who stabbed him to death. *Mars Désarmé par Venus* (Mars Disarmed by Venus) is a complete contrast, full of ethereal blue light and naked, hairless, idealized bodies—an inspiration, perhaps, to late 19th-century soap advertisements.

The large painting by **Gustave Wappers** (1803–74) in Room 70, entitled *Épisode des Journées de Septembre 1830 sur la Place de l'Hôtel de Ville de*

Bruxelles, is a finely executed tribute to the Belgian Revolution, if in a rather anachronistic, idealized style that evokes the French Revolution rather than 1830.

The Forum contains a number of provocatively sensual 19th-century statues and an odd selection of paintings—none odder than *Le Ruisseau* (The Stream) by the Symbolist **Léon Frédéric** (1856–1940), painted right at the end of the century. This large triptych depicts hordes of naked babies and children frolicking and sleeping in watery settings, the older ones awakening to their sensuality.

Chronology is restored in Rooms 72–91. These include some rather gloomy land-scapes, typical of the celebrated Brussels-based artist **Hippolyte Boulenger** (1837–74), and strong social-realist work such as *A l'Aube* (Dawn) (Room 78) by **Charles Hermans** (1839–1924) in which young and flushed gentlemen spill out on to the street with their women in the early hours under the pious gaze of a family of labourers on their way to do an honest day's work. This section contains good examples of work by the Brussels sculptor **Constantin Meunier** (1831–1905), including one of his famous social-realist studies of a foundry-worker, or *puddleur* (*see* also **Walk VI**, p.191). Another large triptych by Léon Frédéric enti-tled *Les Marchands de Craie* (The Chalksellers) (Room 79) is equally mordant. Here wearing his realist colours, Frédéric portrays an impoverished family, ground down by their labours, eating a simple meal at the margins of a semi-industrial landscape. It is a powerful, desolate and touching work.

Room 80 includes work by **Henri Evenpoel** (1872–99), a young painter with a highly distinctive post-impressionist style; he used thickly plastered paint in a mosaic-like style to produce slightly mocking portraits, interiors and street scenes.

Room 85 contains one of the great collections of Symbolist painters in Europe. There are several classics here, including *Des Caresses/L'Art/Les Caresses* or *The Sphinx* by **Fernand Khnopff** (1858–1921), in which, in a mood of dreamy sensuality set vaguely in antiquity, a male/female figure stands cheek to cheek with a similarly ill-defined personage, whose head is attached to the body of a cheetah. His *Memories/Lawn Tennis* portrays seven women tennis players in an empty green landscape, calm, silent but filled with unspoken thought and pent-up emotion. By contrast, the unrestrained, psychedelic side of Symbolism can be seen in *Les Trésors de Satan* (Satan's Treasures) by **Jean Delville** (1867–1953), in which a demonic figure with octopus tentacles for wings steps over a sub-aqua stream of naked damsels and youths lying in sleepy abandon.

Rooms 87, 88 and 90 contain a scattering of late 19th-century French paintings by **Renoir**, **Monet**, **Seurat**, **Signac**, **Gauguin**, **Vuillard** and **Bonnard**. Pause, however, to look at the work of the Belgian painter **Emile Claus** (1849–1924), who was a founder of a post-impressionist movement called Luminism, and who has few rivals in his ability to evoke the sweetness of the rural idyll.

Room 89 is devoted to the Belgian **James Ensor** (1860–1949), a fascinating and enigmatic precursor of Expressionism. His early paintings, such as the portraits of his mother and father (1881 and 1882) are well executed in a rapid, grainy, impressionistic style, but comparatively controlled and conformist. Within ten years, however, he had taken the imaginative leap into the bizarre personal world for which he is renowned—a world of masks, skeletons and Punch-and-Judy characters painted in bright, feverish slabs of paint. *Squelettes se disputant un hareng-saur* (Skeletons arguing over a pickled herring) shows the drift.

*Return to the Forum and follow the 'circuit' signs to the **Musée d'Art Moderne**.*

The building is an ingenious solution to the problem of finding space to house this collection of 20th-century art while preserving the integrity of the 18th-century Place du Musée. The answer (subsequently adopted by the Louvre): bury it. The Musée d'Art Moderne, completed in the 1980s, drops downwards from street level through a series of gently spiralling ramps and stairs, illuminated on one side by a lighting well and a vast, angled, curving window.

The collection is laid out chronologically, descending to the 1990s. It includes a spattering of big names such as **Dufy**, **Rouault**, **Picasso**, **Braque**, **Matisse**, **Nolde**, **Kokoschka**, **Chagall**, **Ernst**, **Chirico** and **Dali**. But take this opportunity rather to study the Belgians. **Rik Wouters** (1882–1916) was both a sculptor and painter. His paintings are reminiscent of Cézanne, but have a quite distinct voice: bright, cheering, and with a deft sense of finish. See, for example, *Dame en Bleu devant une Glace* (Woman in Blue before a Mirror).

Léon Spilliaert (1881–1946) produced sombre, melancholic works, implying a remote and inward-looking world yet shot through with a unique sense of design. His work has a haunting, emblematic quality, as in his *Baigneuse* (Swimmer), featuring a twilight figure set against patterned, rippling water.

The extensive selection devoted to work by the Sint-Martens-Latem school (*see* p.75) includes most notably the earth-toned, thickly pasted Expressionist work of **Constant Permeke** (1886–1952).

Belgium produced two major Surrealist painters. **Paul Delvaux** (1897–1994) is well represented here, with several large paintings of tram and railway stations peopled by nudes with body hair, and skeletons. Silent non-communication and eroticism help to evoke a faintly disturbing dreamlike quality. The collection of work by **René Magritte** (1898–1967), mainly the legacy of his wife, Georgette, is a little disappointing, given his huge output. Nonetheless it includes plenty of the usual visual puns and incongruities, in sketches, sculptures and paintings—among which is the famous *L'Empire des Lumières*.

Descending further, you come to the collection of post-war work from the 1940s group **La Jeune Peinture Belge**—a highly disparate movement which included the lyrical abstraction of **Louis van Lint** (1909–89), the geometric abstraction of **Anne Bonnet** (1908–60) and **Gaston Bertrand** (b.1910). The influential group **Cobra**, founded in 1948, is best represented by the abstract expressionism of **Pierre Alechinsky** (b.1927).

> *On leaving the Musée d'Art Moderne, turn right, then right again into the little cobbled street called the Rue du Musée. This leads into the* **Place du Musée**.

During your visit to the Musées Royaux des Beaux-Arts you will probably have been completely unaware that they are housed in the elegant palace built after 1756 by Charles of Lorraine around this vast, sloping courtyard. The sober, white-painted façades, topped with neoclassical sculptures, urns and cavorting cherubs, now look down on to a virtually redundant square of empty, echoing cobbles.

Look over the elegant stone parapet in the middle of the courtyard. Lurking beneath the cobbles is the Musée d'Art Moderne, sitting in its glazed well. A large bronze statue of Charles of Lorraine used to stand on this spot but has since been shifted to its present position at the lower right-hand side of the courtyard.

> *Close to the statue, at 2 Place du Musée, is the* **Chapelle Royale** *(open June–Sept, Thurs only, 11–5).*

This small chapel has only limited opening hours but it is worth seeing if you are in the right place at the right time. It is a pearl: a white-painted, ornate neoclassical sanctuary, full of light. It was built in the 1760s by Charles of Lorraine (you can see the double Cross of Lorraine on the capitals and balustrades), but in the 1790s it was turned into a stable by the French revolutionary army. In 1802, under a decree issued by Napoleon, Protestants were given freedom of worship in Belgium, and the chapel was restored as a Protestant church in 1804. The interior was then pasted with copious layers of whitewash, which preserved the delicate plasterwork until its renovation to pristine condition in 1987.

In 1831 it became the private chapel of King Leopold I, who was a Protestant. (The uncomfortable situation of a Protestant king in a Catholic country was soon put right when Leopold married a Catholic, and hence his offspring were Catholic.) Charlotte Brontë, a fervent Protestant, also came to worship here during her stay at the nearby Pensionnat Héger in the 1840s (*see* below).

Next door, at 1 Place du Musée, is the **Service de Chalcographie** *(open Mon–Fri 9–12.45, 2–4.45, closed Sat, Sun, public holidays and last week in Aug). Press the bell to gain access, and follow signs that lead down several storeys.*

Chalcography is a fancy name for the art of engraving using copper plates. This department of the Bibliothèque Royale Albert I owns a collection of 5400 engraving plates which include everything from old views of Brussels to abstract art. You can buy prints over the counter or select others from their catalogue, which will then be printed using traditional presses.

Returning to the Place Royale, turn left into the Rue Royale then turn right, into the Place des Palais. To its left is the Parc de Bruxelles and to its right the **Palais Royal**. *(The state rooms are open to the public only in August, depending on the royal agenda; apply to the tourist office for details.)*

The Palais Royal is a grand if rather cold-looking building, set too close to the road for comfort and with only a sunken formal parterre garden to relieve the weight of its deadening architecture. The interior is spacious, glittering with chandeliers, brocade curtains and polished marble, but rather soulless. It is no surprise that the royal family prefer to live at their other palace at Laeken (*see* pp.214–5). The two wings date from the 18th century, but the central section was rebuilt in the French 18th-century neoclassical style of Louis XVI—in 1904–12, no less. It looks more impressive at night, under its soft pink floodlights.

On special occasions the royal family presents itself on the balcony to crowds assembled in the Place des Palais. This was the scene of a moving demonstration in support of the royal family—and for a united Belgium—after King Baudouin I's death in 1993. On 5 and 6 August 125,000 people queued in the rain for seven hours or more to pay their last respects to the king, who lay in state in the palace. A few days later, the Place des Palais was thronged with people who had come to greet the new king, Albert II, as he performed the ancient tradition of *La Joyeuse Entrée* (*see* pp.173–4), after swearing his oaths at the Palais de la Nation.

The first wing of the palace that you reach is the Hôtel de Bellevue, designed by Barnabé Guimard, who was also responsible for the Place Royale. It was incorporated into the Palais Royal by Leopold II, and now houses the **Musée Bellevue** *(open Sat–Thurs, 10–4.45, closed Fri and public holidays; adm free). This also includes the Musée Boyadjian du Coeur and the Musée de la Dynastie.*

The Musée Bellevue consists of a small collection of furniture, accessories, ceramics and tableware that might have belonged to the rich and famous who once graced these elegant halls in the 18th and 19th centuries. The accessories in the first room are particularly exquisite: jewel-encrusted enamel watch cases; soap dishes and shaving bowls; fans, slim cases for dance cards; delicate *nécessaires* for the lady of the house, containing scissors, needles and scent bottles. The chandelier in this room is an outstanding example of Empire style.

> The **Musée Boyadjian du Cœur** *(Boyadjian Heart Museum) occupies two small rooms in the same building.*

The tourist office's description of this museum sounds alarming: 'Dr Boyadjian, a cardiologist with a passion for everything concerning the heart, was fascinated by the charm of these interesting, unusual and very varied hearts.' Images spring to mind of deformed hearts removed in the mortuary and pickled in alcohol. Of course it is nothing of the sort. Dr Boyadjian, a leading contemporary heart surgeon, has always been interested in the way that the heart is used as a symbol, and this interest led to the acquisition of an extensive private collection which he has donated to the Musées Royaux d'Art et d'Histoire. An explanatory panel claims that the role of the heart in Christian symbolism can be traced to the piercing of Christ's side by the soldier at Calvary; the flaming heart denotes fervent devotion and is the symbol of charity. The collection includes reliquaries, silver *ex-voto* offerings given in thanks for relief of ailments of the heart (both physical and emotional, no doubt), and church treasures of fabulous vulgarity.

> The **Musée de la Dynastie** *(open 10–4; adm free) is on the top floor.*

This small museum tells the history of the Belgian royal family through a collection of paintings, prints, photographs, furniture, clothing and other mementoes. Even if you are not an avid royal-watcher, it's worth at least a quick visit, if only to be able to put faces to the names of the Belgian royals through their short history and see them in their historical context. (*See* **Topics**, p.33).

> The next part of the walk takes you through the Parc de Bruxelles, which lies in front of the Palais Royal. First cross the Rue Royale by the pedestrian crossing to your left. The view right, down the Rue Royale, takes the eye all the way to the Eglise Sainte-Marie, 2km away (see **Walk IV**). On the opposite side of the road, totally obscured behind a wall topped by urns and neoclassical military hardware, is the **Palais des Beaux-Arts.**

This was designed in Art Deco style by Victor Horta (*see* pp.187–9) and completed in 1928. It is now a cultural centre, where major temporary exhibitions and concerts are staged, and home to the Philharmonique de Bruxelles. Horta had to contend with a highly restrictive brief: in order to preserve the view from the Palais Royal he was not allowed to build above the level of the parapet.

You can gain a better idea of this building by walking a short distance up the Rue Royale then taking the first left, the Rue Baron Horta (he was made a Baron in 1932). Walk to the top of the stone steps.

The Palais des Beaux-Arts stretches down the left-hand side of the street—a bold, angular exterior, very different from those of Horta's Art Nouveau heyday. The Palais des Beaux-Arts was to be part of a grand urban redevelopment plan referred to as the Quartier Ravenstein, stretching from here to the Gare Centrale, but it remained unfinished at Horta's death in 1947. (Note that the Musée du Cinema is in the Palais des Beaux-Arts, but we come to that later.)

The statue at the top of Rue Baron Horta commemorates General Augustin Daniel, Comte de Belliard (1769–1832). He took part in all the major campaigns of the Napoleonic Empire, but was rehabilitated by Louis XVIII of France after 1819 and sent as envoy to Brussels. This statue, dated 1836, is a good example of the work of Willem Geefs (1805–85), who created several major public monuments for the new nation.

Until the first decade of this century there was a large house and garden where the Palais des Beaux-Arts now stands. This had once been the Pensionnat Héger, a girls' boarding school which Charlotte Brontë attended in 1842–3, and where she developed an unrequited passion for the husband of the principal (*see* **Topics**, pp.40–42). Despite all the changes, the surroundings are still recognizably the setting for her novels *The Professor* and *Villette*. The narrator of *The Professor* recalls arriving at this spot:

> *I remember, before entering the park, I stood awhile to contemplate the statue of Count Belliard and then advanced to the top of the great staircase just beyond and I looked down into a narrow back-street which, I afterwards learnt, was called the Rue d'Isabelle [this used to connect the Coudenberg Palace with what is now the Cathédrale Saint-Michel]. I well recollect that my eye rested on the green door of a rather large house opposite, where, on a brass plate, was inscribed 'Pensionnat de demoiselles'.*

Cross back over the Rue Royale and walk into the **Parc de Bruxelles**. *Follow one of the paths to the central avenue.*

This is Brussels' most attractive formal park. Ranks of mature trees stand over the broad avenues, which lead past statues, ornate cast-iron benches and fountains to vistas of the palaces at either end. The Dukes of Brabant once owned a famous Renaissance pleasure park on this site, known as the Warande, or warren. It is said that its ingenious fountains inspired the architects of the gardens of Versailles. Following the fire of 1731 the park fell into ruin until it was renovated in French style after 1778. The unusual layout has invited speculation that it represents the symbols of freemasonry. Certainly from a map or aerial view it is possible to trace out the shapes of several of the masonic symbols, such as the compass, set-square and the bricklayer's trowel. The park was designed during the heyday of freemasonry and, like many of his contemporaries, Charles of Lorraine belonged to a freemason's lodge, so such speculation may have some basis in fact.

The park witnessed a series of dramatic events in the early 19th century. On the eve of the Battle of Waterloo, it was used as an assembly point for Allied troops, who were summoned by bugles ringing out over the city throughout the night. (Wellington was staying at the corner of the Rue Montagne du Parc and the Rue Royale.) Their departure was recorded in Mrs Eaton's *Waterloo Days*:

> As dawn broke, the soldiers were seen assembling from
> all parts of town, in marching order, with their knapsacks
> on their backs, loaded with three days' provisions.
> Unconcerned in the midst of the din of war, many a sol-
> dier laid himself down on a truss of straw and soundly
> slept, with his hands still grasping his firelock; others
> were sitting contentedly on the pavement, waiting the
> arrival of their comrades. Numbers were taking leave of
> their wives and children, perhaps for the last time, and
> many a veteran's rough cheek was wet with the tears of
> sorrow. One poor fellow, immediately under our win-
> dows, turned back again and again to bid his wife
> farewell, and take his baby once more in his arms; and I
> saw him hastily brush away a tear with the sleeve of his
> coat, as he gave her back the child for the last time, wrung
> her hand, and ran off to join his company, which was
> drawn up on the other side of the Place Royale. Many of
> the soldiers' wives marched out with their husbands to
> the field, and I saw one English lady mounted on horse-
> back slowly riding out of town along with an officer, who,
> no doubt, was her husband. Soon afterwards the 42nd
> and 92nd Highland regiments marched through the Place
> Royale and the Parc, with their bagpipes playing before

> *them, while the bright beams of the rising sun shone full
> on their polished muskets and on the dark waving plumes
> of their tartan bonnets. Alas! We little thought that even
> before the fall of night these brave men whom we now
> gazed at with so much interest and admiration would be
> laid low.*

In September 1830, during the Belgian Revolution, troops from the Dutch garrison holed up in the park, surrounded by revolutionary barricades and sniped at by insurgents from the windows of houses in the Rue Royale. On the morning of 27 September, however, a party of revolutionaries crept into the park to find it deserted: the Dutch had fled. A joyous mob assembled and invaded the royal palace, where they inspected the royal wardrobe and destroyed portraits of King William of Orange. They also brought out a marble bust of the king, crowned it with a Dutch cheese, and chanted, 'Down with the first and last King of the Netherlands.' Moderation is a Belgian virtue, even in a revolution.

> *The avenues of the park converge on the huge round pond and fountain
> at its northern end. Continue to the Rue de la Loi. Facing you is the
> **Palais de la Nation**. (Public access to the interior is from the other side
> of the building only, from the Rue de Louvain, see below.)*

This neoclassical building was designed by Barnabé Guimard in 1783 as the seat of the ruling council of the Austrian Netherlands. The sculptured pediment, representing Victory and Justice, is the most notable work of Gilles-Lambert Godecharle (1750–1835), sculptor to Napoleon and then to William of Orange. Since 1830 it has been the main parliament building of Belgium.

> *Turn to your right. On the edge of the park, overlooking the Rue de la
> Loi, is the **Théâtre Royal du Parc**.*

This late 18th-century theatre still contains its original tiered auditorium. This can only be visited on a group tour, but there is a model of it in the foyer, to help theatre-goers to select their seats. The theatre stages well-respected seasons of French plays, both classical and modern.

> *Walk eastwards down the Rue de la Loi. At the far end you can see
> L'Arche du Cinquantenaire, crowned by its quadriga (see **Walk V**).
> Cross the Rue Ducale and then also the broad Boulevard du Régent.*

This is part of the busy ring road called the 'Petite Ceinture', which takes traffic around the edge of the city centre along the course of the 14th-century city walls, demolished in the 19th century. This has proved a perfect route along which to channel Brussels' thundering traffic, preserving the middle of town from the congestion that blights so many great city centres.

*Turn left when you reach the other side of the road. This is the Avenue des Arts. Some 150m up this street, at No. 16, is the **Musée de l'Hôtel Charlier**. Open Mon–Fri 2–5, closed Sat, Sun and public holidays; adm 100 BF; ring on the brass doorbell to gain entry.*

The Hôtel Charlier is a grand *maison de maître*, built in the 19th century in neo-classical style. In 1890 it was bought by the wealthy and cultivated Henri van Curtsem, who commissioned Victor Horta to replan the interior. A great patron of the arts, Van Curtsem effectively adopted a poor young sculptor called Guillaume Charlier, and gave the house to him when he retired to the country. Charlier maintained Van Curtsem's tradition that had made the house a cultural meeting point, and he left the house to the surrounding commune, Saint-Josse-ten-Noode, when he died in 1925. Preserved as a museum since 1928, it offers an exceptional insight into the décor of a house where the well-to-do of the late 19th century entertained their friends.

This was a period in which interest in antique furniture was growing, and the house includes a series of rooms in period style, such as the Salon Louis XV, with its fine marquetry bombé chests, and the Salon Chinois, with coromandel lacquer furniture. The Empire-style bedroom contains an excellent collection of furniture and accessories, decorated with ormolu plaques, sphinxes and caryatids. Contemporary late 19th-century taste is represented by paintings by James Ensor, Fernand Khnopff, Léon Frédéric and others, and sculpture by Rik Wouters and Charlier himself. Look out for the glass display case by Victor Horta, an ingenious and typically elegant solution to a design problem.

A room at the top of the house provides a historical perspective on the commune of Saint-Josse: old prints show the city walls that once ran along the street below.

Turn right as you come out of the Hôtel Charlier and cross the Avenue des Arts and Boulevard du Régent at the next crossing (over the raging underpass) to Place Madou.

In the middle of this square is a statue to *La Brabançonne*, the song which was the battle cry of the 1830 Revolution and thereafter became the national anthem. This monument, erected on the centenary in 1930, bears the first four lines (the only four that most Belgians know) in French and Flemish.

From Place Madou there is a fine view down the Rue du Congrès to the Colonne du Congrès (*see* **Walk IV**).

*Walk back down the Boulevard du Régent and turn right into the Rue de Louvain. This leads along the back of a series of elegant buildings to the courtyard on this side of Guimard's **Palais de la Nation**. Doors on*

*either side of this courtyard give access to the interior, which contains
the Senate (door No. 7b) and the House of Representatives (door
No. 11). The public is permitted to watch proceedings from the public
galleries while the houses are sitting (mid-Oct to end June); identity documents must be presented at the entrance. Outside parliamentary
sessions you may join a guided tour; between 10am and 4pm, duration
1 hour; adm free; telephone reservation is recommended, © 519 81 11
(House of Representatives) or 515 82 11 (Senate).*

The central government legislature is divided into two houses, along the lines of
most Western governments. The Representatives (*députés*) and over half the
Senate are elected for a four-year term of office. In recent years, however, the role
of these houses has been gradually eroded as increased power has been devolved
to the regional governments. Nonetheless, they still have responsibility for legislation that affects Belgium as a whole, in fields such as finance, defence and
foreign affairs.

*Turn right off the Rue de Louvain into Rue du Parlement, which leads
into Rue de la Tribune. Turn left down Rue de l'Enseignement, a
pleasant Victorian-style street with cast-iron balustrades lining the balconies. This leads to a statue of Henri-Alexis Brialmont (1821–1903), a
military engineer and statesman, and the Rue Royale. Turn right. About
three doors down in the Rue Royale is a florist's called* **Les Fleurs
Isabelle de Backer**.

This shop has a celebrated Art Nouveau frontage, designed by Paul Hankar
(1859–1901) in 1899: the glass is held by a curvaceous web of woodwork.

*Cross the road at the pedestrian crossing. Walk down Rue de
Treurenberg, which leads to the eastern end of the* **Cathédrale Saint-
Michel**. *Open summer 7–7, winter 7–6.*

Brussels' cathedral is currently undergoing a massive programme of restoration,
which is bringing its creamy-grey stone back to life, but unfortunately this means
that large portions of the interior will be closed off for the foreseeable future.

It may seem unfair to criticize a building in the midst of restoration, but sadly this
is not Brussels' greatest church. Its twin towers struggle to be noticed among the
modern buildings that surround it, and it seems isolated from the real centre of
the city. (The spire of the Hôtel de Ville can be seen from the parapet.)

If it seems disappointing as Brussels' cathedral, that may be explained by the fact
that it was ravaged twice—by Protestant iconoclasts in 1579 and French revolutionaries in 1793. Furthermore, it only became a cathedral in 1962, when the

archbishopric of Mechelen-Brussels was created. In the past it was a collegiate church dedicated to St Michael (the patron saint of Brussels) and Ste Gudule.

Ste Gudule, an 8th-century lady of royal blood, was celebrated for her piety. She is often portrayed holding a lamp, since the most famous tale about her concerns her battle with the devil, who kept on blowing out her light when she attempted to reach her isolated chapel in the marshes to pray. Through the power of prayer, however, she was able to rekindle the flame. Her venerated remains were brought to this church from the chapel on Ile Saint-Géry in the 11th century. When the church became a cathedral, however, it was named after St Michael alone because Ste Gudule was not on the official papal register, but the people of Brussels still obstinately refer to the cathedral as 'Sainte-Gudule'.

The original Romanesque church was replaced after 1226 by the present Gothic one, which then took three centuries to complete. The towers were designed by Jan van Ruysbroeck, the 15th-century architect of the Hôtel de Ville; they contain a 50-bell carillon, most of which was installed in 1975.

The interior is light and airy, with some spectacularly delicate stone tracery in the clerestory. A series of 17th-century statues of the apostles attached to the columns of the nave seem incongruous—albeit that they were commissioned from notable sculptors such as Luc Fayd'herbe and Jérôme Duquesnoy the Younger (son of the creator of the Manneken-Pis). For Baroque ponderousness, however, the monumental oak pulpit is supreme: it is a riot of figures and foliage. Adam and Eve stand beneath the Tree of Knowledge, berated by St Michael and a skeleton; the serpent snakes upwards to the firmament, where its head is crushed with a cross held by the Infant Jesus under the protective arms of the Virgin Mary. Baroque pulpits such as this are found throughout Belgium, and this is one of the most celebrated, created by the sculptor Hendrik Verbruggen (c. 1655–1724) in 1699.

The stained glass windows in the transepts date from 1537 and 1538 and were designed by the gifted painter Bernard van Orley. They depict (north) the king of the day, Charles V (1500–58), and his wife, Isabella of Portugal; and (south) Mary of Hungary, sister of Charles V, and her husband. Stairs in the nave lead down to what appears to be a crypt, but in fact simply shows the recently excavated foundations of the Romanesque church *(open 10–5pm, except during Mass on Sun; adm 30 BF)*.

> *From the cathedral you can return to the Gare Centrale by walking along the Rue des Paroissiens and then Cantersteen. However, the **Musée du Cinéma**, underneath the Palais des Beaux-Arts, has unusually late hours for a museum (daily, 5.30pm–10.30pm; adm 80 BF, or 50 BF if prebooked). To reach it from the cathedral, walk down the Rue de la*

Chancellerie to Ravenstein, then turn left up the Rue Baron Horta. The museum is on the right, just below the steps.

The Musée du Cinéma has two auditoriums, one screening a programme of three 'art films' every evening starting at 6.15pm (most shown in their original language with French subtitles), the other showing old silent films at 7pm and 9pm every evening, accompanied by live piano music. The museum publishes a leaflet each month (20 BF) giving details of its programme. Tickets are valid for 2 hours and include entrance to the auditoriums. However, possession of a ticket is no guarantee that you will get a seat: the auditorium for silent films has only 30 seats, so for a popular movie you have to hover near the entrance for some time before the film starts to be sure of a place. Alternatively you can reserve a seat by telephoning, © 507 83 70, after 9.30am on the day itself (or on Friday for the weekend). Reserved seats have to be taken up at least 15 minutes before the start, otherwise they are offered to waiting hopefuls in the foyer.

Laid out in the restful, dimly lit foyer are numerous ingenious exhibits to demonstrate the early history of the moving image, including such early wonders as the Phénakisticope (1832) and Zoetrope (1834), in which series of images pasted to spinning drums and discs appear to move. Eadweard Muybridge's experiments of the 1870s, using multiple cameras triggered by people or animals in motion, demonstrated the potential of photography to show movement, a concept pursued in conjunction with the magic lantern by Emile Reynaud in 1881. But the breakthrough was made ten years later by Thomas Edison with his Kinetograph using celluloid film. This history is succinctly explained through working models and various historic exhibits, many of them set up to operate at the push of a button.

To return to the Gare Centrale, descend the Rue Baron Horta. Immediately opposite, across Rue Ravenstein, is the entrance to the Galerie Ravenstein, a covered walkway lined with shops and restaurants. Opened in 1958, it is decorated with rectangular panels in dusty blue shades and with folksy brave-new-world sculpture and murals—all very 1950s. The Galerie Ravenstein leads directly to Cantersteen and the Gare Centrale.

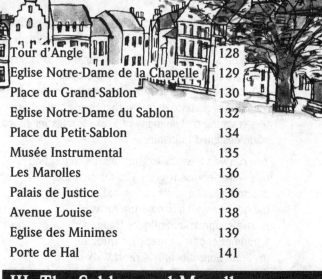

III: The Sablon and Marolles

Start: *Tour d'Angle. To reach it, go to Gare Centrale, then walk down Boulevard de l'Empereur.*

Walking Time: *about 3 hours minimum, but allow a further 2 hours for dawdling in the (small) museums, and browsing around the markets and shops.*

ANTIQUE MARKET, GRAND SABLON

III: The Sablon and Marolles

'*Faire du lèche-vitrines*' ('window-licking') is an activity indulged in with much relish by the Bruxellois. 'Window-shopping' sounds much more prosaic, and quite inadequate to describe that pleasurable, hopeless yearning that so many of Brussels' classier shops seem designed to inspire.

You can window-lick to your heart's content on this walk because it takes you through the charming Sablon district—an old residential quarter which is now the focus of Brussels' upmarket antiques trade, with a number of chic art galleries thrown in. From here it is only a short walk to the area called Porte Louise (around Place Louise), which is Brussels' answer to the Champs-Elysées, a showpiece of Euro-commerce with a roll call of the world's most revered designer names.

This walk is not entirely dedicated to Mammon, however. It includes Brussels' loveliest Gothic church, and the gargantuan Palais de Justice—the ultimate neoclassical pile. In the shadow of the Palais de Justice lies the Marolles district. This is the old artisans' quarter, with a long and ragged history, its own dialect,

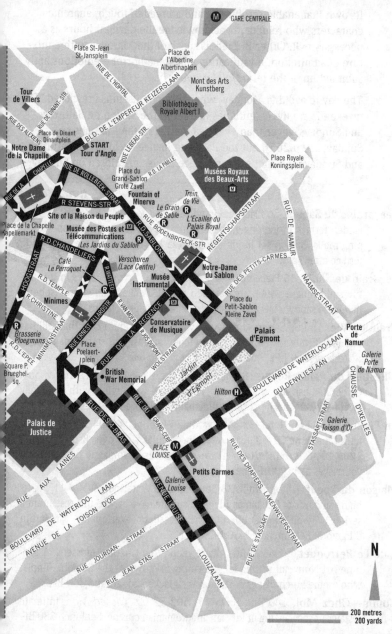

M GARE CENTRALE

Place St-Jean
St-Jansplein

Place de
l'Albertine
Albertinaplein

Mont des Arts
Kunstberg

Tour
de Villers

Bibliothèque
Royale Albert I

RUE DE DINANT STR.

RUE DES ALEXENS

Place de Dinant
Dinantplein

Notre Dame
de la Chapelle

BLD. DE L'EMPEREUR KEIZERSLAAN

RUE DE L'HOPITAL

RUE LEBEAU STR.

START
Tour d'Angle

RUE DE LA CHAPELLE

RUE DE ROLLEBEEK-STRAAT

Place du
Grand-Sablon
Grote Zavel

R.D. LA PAILLE

Place Royale
Koningsplein

Musées Royaux
des Beaux-Arts
M

REGENTSCHAPSSTRAAT

Fountain of
Minerva

Trein
de Vie R

Le Grain
de Sable R

L'Ecailler du
Palais Royal R

RUE DE LA

R STEVENS-STR.

RUE DE BODENBROECK-STR.

Site of la Maison du Peuple

Place de la Chapelle
Kapellemarkt

Musée des Postes et
Télécommunications M R
Les Jardins du Sablon

R.D. CHANDELIERS

R.D. SABLONS

Notre-Dame
du Sablon

RUE DE NAMUR

NAAMSESTRAAT

HOOGSTRAAT

Café
Le Perroquet

R.D. TEMPLE

R.WATTEU

Verschuren
(Lace Centre)

Musée
Instrumental

M

Place du
Petit-Sablon
Kleine Zavel

RUE DES PETITS-CARMES

R.CHRISTINE

Minimes

MININENSTRAAT

RUE ERNEST ALLARD STR.

R.VAN MOER

RUE DE LA REGENCE

RUE JOS DUPONT STR.

Conservatoire
de Musique

Palais
d'Egmont

Porte
de
Namur

Brasserie
Ploegmans R

R.D.L'EPEE

X

Square P.
Brueghel-
sq.

Place
Poelaert-
plein

British
War Memorial

WOLSTRAAT

Jardin
d'Egmont

Hilton H

BOULEVARD DE WATERLOO-LAAN

GULDENVLIESLAAN

Galerie
Porte
de Namur

CHAUSSEE D'IXELLES

STASSARTSTRAAT

Galerie
Toison d'Or

Palais de
Justice

RUE AUX LAINES

RUE DES 4-BRAS

RUE DU GRAND-CERF

PLACE
LOUISE

M

Petits Carmes

RUE DES DRAPIERS LAKENWEVERSSTRAAT

RUE DE STASSART

BOULEVARD DE WATERLOO- LAAN

AVENUE DE LA TOISON D'OR

Galerie
Louise

AVENUE LOUISE

RUE JOURDAN- STRAAT

RUE JEAN STAS- STRAAT

LOUIZALAN

N

200 metres
200 yards

125

its own inalienable scruffiness, and a breed of rough, anarchic characters who reluctantly acknowledge the daylight hours as a necessary evil. Other Bruxellois speak of the Marolles with a mixture of admiration, mystification and some horror—emotions aptly summed up in the term '*folklorique*'.

The day to avoid is Monday, when all the museums are closed. The weekends are lively (antiques market in the Sablon on Saturday and Sunday; bigger than ever flea market in the Marolles on Sunday, *see* p.265), but the Palais de Justice is closed on Saturday and Sunday, and shops around Place Louise are closed on Sunday.

---

lunch/cafés

Les Jardins du Sablon, 36 Place du Grand-Sablon. *Closed Mon.* An ersatz garden terrace inside one of the Sablon's most chic antiques shopping malls. Stylish set lunch at 425–495 BF; becomes a tea terrace after 3pm.

Le Grain de Sable, 15 Place du Grand-Sablon. One of several cafés in this picturesque square which are part and parcel of its animated atmosphere. Inventive sandwiches and salads served at pavement tables.

Trein de Vie, 18 Rue Sainte-Anne. An invigorating, modern café that still has one foot firmly in tradition. Sandwiches, salads, and standards such as *waterzooi* (260 BF). Small open terrace to the rear.

L'Ecailler du Palais Royal, 18 Rue Bodenbroeck, ℐ 512 87 51. *Closed Sun.* Celebrated fish restaurant: classy, elegant and welcoming, with absolutely *comme il faut* cuisine. The set lunch at 950 BF is a bargain.

En Plein Ciel, Hilton Hotel, 38 Boulevard de Waterloo, ℐ 504 11 11. Elegant buffet lunch on 27th floor, with a spectacular view over Brussels, 600–1200 BF. *Sun only, 10am–2pm*: sumptuous champagne brunch Spoil yourselves at 1190 BF a head.

Maison du Boeuf, Hilton Hotel, 38 Boulevard de Waterloo, ℐ 504 11 11. Its high standards of Belgian and French cuisine have earned this restaurant a seriously good reputation. On the first floor overlooking the Jardin d'Egmont. Set lunch at 1450 BF.

Café Le Perroquet, corner of Rue Watteeu and Rue Charles Hanssens. A genuine Art Nouveau setting for the young in-crowd of the Sablon. Simple, wholesome lunch dishes posted on the blackboard, around 300 BF.

Comme Chez Moi, 140 Rue Haute, ℐ 502 52 09. *Closed Mon.* Intimate restaurant specializing in Russian and Romanian cuisine. Set lunch 380 BF.

Brasserie Ploegmans, 148 Rue Haute. Dingy 1930s wood panelling, gravel-voiced card players and their dogs, pinball machines, and cellar-cool *kriek* and *faro* served from the barrel. You could probably find a more *marollien* dive than this—but would you want to?

Indigo, 160 Rue Blaes. *Open 9–3, closed Mon.* Busy, arty café decorated with miscellaneous *brocante* (junk), which is for sale along with well-crafted salads (avocado, Roquefort and bacon, 220 BF), wine and mouthwatering slabs of cake (95–120 BF). Open terrace to the rear.

De Skieven Architek, 50 Place du Jeu de Balle. Welcoming modern bar-café with a sense of history (*see* p.136) Sandwiches and pastries.

Les Chevaliers, 137 Boulevard de Waterloo. *Closed Sun lunch and Sat.* Above-average pizzas (around 200 BF) cooked in a wood-fired oven: a good place to stop off at if you are feeling peckish at the end of this walk.

Brussels first became a walled city in around 1100, when a modest curtain of stone was erected around today's city centre and the palace quarter on the Coudenberg hill. Some 250 years later a vast new wall was constructed about 1km further out, gathering into its protective embrace a motley collection of religious foundations, hospices, market gardens, water meadows, and the homes of thousands of the merchants, artisans and labourers who were the key to the city's burgeoning wealth.

A ridge of higher ground lay on the southern perimeter of the city, between the Coudenberg (where the Place Royale now is) and the Galgenberg ('Gallows Hill'), the place of public execution—on which the Palais de Justice now stands, appropriately enough. On the slopes between these hills was an open space called the Zavelpoel, or sandy marsh, traditionally used as a horse market. It became known in French as the Sablon (*sablon* means fine sand). Around the skirt of the Galgenberg lay a teeming artisans' quarter, the powerhouse of Brussels' textile trade. Here weavers, dyers and bleachers lived with their families, close to the markets in the centre of town and to the river on whose banks much of the industry was conducted. During the 17th century a religious foundation called Les Sœurs Marolles was set up at the southern end of the city, near to the present Rue de Montserrat, and gradually this area took on their name—the Marolles. (Some claim, however, that the term is derived from the Spanish *marrullero*, meaning cunning or wily, a description of its inhabitants.)

In the 17th century the Sablon marsh was drained and merchants and the nobility began to build their homes here, strategically placed between the palaces on the

Coudenberg and the Marolles, whose numbers now swelled with an influx of carpenters and builders. The church for the people of the Marolles remained Notre-Dame de la Chapelle, while the daintier folk of the Sablon attended Notre-Dame du Sablon.

The distinction between the two quarters is just as real today . The Sablon, with its spacious ease, its beguiling step-gabled houses, antiques shops, restaurants and cafés, is clearly where the money is. The Marolles is rough and ready, with over-crowded housing, overtaxed mothers, knots of idle youths and a permanent car-boot-sale atmosphere which emanates from the *marché aux puces* in the Place du Jeu de Balle and pervades the dingy, alcoholic bars.

The Bruxellois are proud of the Marolles traditions, but quite what these are today is hard to pin down. This area went into a tailspin after the River Senne was vaulted over in the 1860s, when many of the old industries on its banks closed down or relocated. Once the Marolles had been the home of proud artisans, who spoke their own distinct version of *bruxellois* called *marollien*, incomprehensible to all but themselves. Now it became a marginalized refuge for casualties of the Industrial Revolution, with its own subculture and ready violence, its lively bars and Sunday dance halls. It still had a certain appeal. The late 19th-century *Guide des Plaisirs à Bruxelles* speaks admiringly of '*les jeunes apaches et leurs fidèles amies*' ('young tearaways and their faithful girlfriends'); however, it warns its readers to be discreet in their admiration of these pretty Marolliennes, '*car les compagnons de ces dames boxent avec entrain les admirateurs trop excessifs—en dehors des heures de travail*' ('for these ladies' companions will readily box with any overzealous admirers—outside working hours').

The Marolles is now undergoing a phase of redevelopment, encouraging a flourish of arty bric-a-brac shops, small galleries and design studios which bring a new touch of colour and vitality to the area. However, plenty of detractors deplore this development at the expense, as they see it, of the real character of the Marolles. This is an argument that has run for at least 100 years. In the 1890s Verlaine lamented the disappearance of characteristic watering holes '*où la moule et le café au lait, alternant avec ce bon faro aigre et soûlant, nourrissent et désaltèrent le Marollien habitueux et le touriste vraiment sérieux*' ('where mussels and white coffee, alternating with good, sour, heady faro, nourish and quench the thirst of both the Marollien habitué and the serious tourist'). Undoubtedly such places that have survived are under threat from a changing world, but they are far from extinct.

> *The walk begins at the* **Tour d'Angle** *('Corner Tower'), on the southern side of the Boulevard de l'Empereur.*

This half-ruined, circular tower is a rare survivor of the first set of city walls, and was once connected to the Tour de Villers nearby (*see* **Walk I**) and the Tour Noire (*see* **Walk IV**). It may look a solid enough piece of defensive walling, but it is modest compared to the huge city walls built two centuries later. Note the arrow slits, whose French title *meurtrières* (literally, 'killers') graphically describes their function.

This corner tower stood close to the Steenpoort gate (demolished in 1760), around which clustered the community that was to become the Marolles. Both the tower and the gate were used as prisons. During the 15th century the Tour d'Angle became known as the *pyntorre*, because it housed a torture chamber. François Anneessens, a leader of the guilds who led a rebellion against Austrian rule, was thought to have been held in the tower before his execution in 1719, and hence the Tour d'Angle is sometimes referred to as the Tour d'Anneessens.

> *Continue westwards along the Boulevard de l'Empereur, which leads up to the northern flank of the **Eglise Notre-Dame de la Chapelle**. While under restoration, it is open only around the hours of Mass at weekends (Sat 4pm, Sun 11am).*

The fortress-like grandeur of this church, with its orbed and black-shingled clock tower and its massive creamy-white stone walls, has made it one of the great landmarks of Brussels. However, it has been off-limits for many years because of a huge, on-going restoration programme. Built originally in the 13th century, the church belongs to that transitional period when the pointed Gothic arch was beginning to emerge from the intersection of rounded Romanesque arches. The choir and transept are essentially Romanesque and transitional, whereas the nave and aisles are Gothic, added in the 15th century. The curious clock tower was a later addition by Antoon Pastorana, one of the main architects of the Grand' Place, after the church was damaged by the French bombardment of 1695.

The interior is a bright, elevating space of arching stone vaults, lit by Gothic windows of clear glass set between delicate stone tracery. Much of the church was decorated in the 15th century with polychrome paintings, and remains of these served to guide restorers during the 19th century, notably in the choir (currently undergoing restoration). The statues of the apostles attached to the columns of the nave are a typical 17th-century device, less discordant here than elsewhere. The sculptors include Jan Cosyns (later noted as a major architect of the Grand' Place), Luc Fayd'Herbe (designer of Notre-Dame des Riches Claires), and Jérôme Duquesnoy the Younger, son of the original sculptor of the Manneken-Pis. The wooden pulpit, topped by palm trees and cherubs, is another example of exuberant Baroque carving. This one, dating from 1721, is by Pierre-Denis Plumier, who also sculpted the statue representing the River Scheldt at the Hôtel de Ville.

Notre-Dame de la Chapelle is noted most of all as the burial place of Pieter Bruegel the Elder (*see* p.45), and the third side-chapel of the south aisle is dedicated to his memory. Born in Flanders, he trained in the studio of Pieter Coecke in Antwerp, but moved to Brussels in 1563. That same year he married Maria Coecke, the daughter of his old master, in this church. They lived on the Rue Haute in the Marolles district (*see* below), and she bore him two sons before his death in Brussels in 1569, at the age of 44.

> *Walk to the northwestern corner of the Place de la Chapelle, which surrounds the church. From here you can look down the Rue des Brigittines to the red-brick and stone façade of the **Eglise des Brigittines**.*

You need walk no further, because this is as much as you can see of this pretty little Italo-Flemish church, built in the 1660s for a religious order named after the 14th-century Swedish mystic and saint, St Brigitte. The church was damaged in the 1695 bombardment, and the convent was suppressed in 1784, after which the building had a varied career as a prison (1792), a poorhouse (after 1794) then, after the 1850s, a butcher's shop with a dance hall overhead. Still surviving, but in a sorry state of neglect, it is now used for periodic cultural events: its crumbling, dilapidated interior provides an intense and dramatic setting for performances on an impromptu scaffolding stage.

> *Now walk around the Place de la Chapelle, crossing first the Rue Blaes, then the Rue Haute, which leads down through the Marolles district. Cross Rue Joseph Stevens, and walk a little way up Rue Haute to the next right, **Rue de Rollebeek**.*

This sloping, cobbled street—lined with step-gabled houses, restaurants, cafés and tasteful furnishing shops—provides a suitable entry to the Place du Grand-Sablon above. Its slightly crooked course is due to the fact that it was built over a stream that once flowed out of the marsh. The houses on the left used to back on to the old city walls.

> *When you reach the top of Rue de Rollebeek you are at the foot of the **Place du Grand-Sablon**, a large, triangular square fronted by enough quaint old step-gabled façades to illustrate how it looked when it was first laid out in the late 17th century. At the top of the square is the Eglise Notre-Dame du Sablon. At weekends a superior antiques market (see p.256), set out beneath boldly striped awnings, clusters around the foot of the church, making the square look like an encampment for a medieval jousting tournament. We shall come to this church later; first of all, turn right and walk to the top of Rue Joseph Stevens. This gives a fine view of Notre-Dame de la Chapelle. In a small circus halfway down Rue*

*Joseph Stevens, on the left-hand side at No.11, is a faceless modern building. This is the scene of a modern architectural tragedy, for on this site once stood **La Maison du Peuple**, one of the chefs-d'oeuvre of Art Nouveau supremo, Victor Horta.*

La Maison du Peuple was built in 1898–9 for the Société Coopérative and consisted of a large café, an auditorium, and a number of shops and offices. It was an innovative project, particularly as the main load-bearing internal structure consisted only of cast-iron joists and columns. Arising from the most intensely Art Nouveau period of Horta's long career, every detail—from the balustrades and lamps to the furniture—was given an Art Nouveau flourish. As others have pointed out, it was a work of art to which nothing could be added or taken away without compromising the whole: and this was its downfall. By the 1960s it no longer corresponded to the needs of the Société Coopérative, who, in the face of protests from the architectural world, demolished it in 1965.

*Take the pedestrian crossings over Rue Joseph Stevens and the Rue des Minimes. Looking right along the Rue des Minimes you can see the dome of the Palais de Justice. From this distance, and with this narrowed perspective, it looks misleadingly dainty. Argus, the antique shop on the corner of the Rue des Minimes and the Place du Grand-Sablon, specializes in Art Nouveau and Art Deco, and provides a foretaste of the numerous stylish antique shops in and around the Sablon. Walk up the right-hand side of the Place du Grand-Sablon. Halfway up, in the centre of the square, is the **Fountain of Minerva**.*

This weatherbeaten statue of Minerva, the Roman goddess of war, was built on the site of an earlier fountain, whose very practical function was to drain the water from the Sablon marshes. The new fountain was endowed by the will of an Englishman, Thomas Bruce, third Earl of Elgin and second Earl of Aylesbury. He spent 45 years in exile in Brussels, from 1696 to 1741—the price of being a supporter and friend of James II, who had been forced to flee the English throne in 1688 in favour of the Protestant William of Orange. Married twice to continental noblewomen, the Earl of Aylesbury lived comfortably in a *hôtel* on the square (at Nos. 23–6) and was buried in the Eglise des Brigittines. The fountain was his way of thanking the city and its Austrian overlords.

Facing the fountain on the left-hand side of the Place du Grand-Sablon, at Nos. 6 and 12, are two shops belonging to Wittamer, celebrated chocolatier and pâtissier—expensive but supreme. Opposite them on the *other side of square, at No. 40, is the **Musée des Postes et Télé-communications**. Open Tues–Sat 10–4, Sun and public holidays 10–12.30, closed Mon; adm free.*

In 1500 the head of the Turn and Taxis family was made Master of the Posts by Philip the Handsome, a job which was assiduously cultivated during the reign of Charles V so that within half a century the family controlled the most effective post and messenger service in Europe, stretching right across the Habsburg empire. Four centuries later, Turn and Taxis is still a society name to be reckoned with, and the family owns a vast palace in Regensburg, Germany. The last prince, Johannes von Thurn und Taxis, died in 1990 aged 64, leaving a young widow who gained notoriety after her marriage when the Press dubbed her the Punk Princess. Since her husband's death, however, she has been struggling to pay off millions of Deutschmarks in death duties.

In the 16th century, the Turn and Taxis family lived in a palace up the hill from here, off what is now the Rue de la Régence, and so it is appropriate to find this small museum on their own postal round. It may not sound too thrilling, but it's free, and worth visiting if only to admire the huge boots—like plaster casts—worn by postillions to ward off the weather and passing traffic. Other artefacts from postal history include post-horns, uniforms, historic letterboxes (dating from their introduction in 1800), models of post coaches and long forks carried by rural postmen to keep dogs and geese at bay. Exhibits in the telecommunications section explain various communications systems that led from the 'visual telegraph' set on hilltops—which linked Brussels to Paris in 1803—to the first electrical telegraph networks introduced with the railways, and from thence to successive generations of telephones and the fax. There is also a philately department.

*A little further up the right-hand side of the Place du Grand-Sablon is the **Antiques Fair Centre** (No. 37), a dusty warren of dealers' boutiques selling good-quality furniture—notably elegant Biedermeier pieces of the mid-19th century. Next door (at No. 36) is the contrasting **Les Jardins du Sablon**, a sleek, modern mall lined with upper-crust antiques shops and fine-art galleries. When you have had your fill of these, continue along the same pavement to the Rue de la Régence. Look right, and behold the gigantic silhouette of the Palais de Justice. Then turn left to reach the entrance (through the south transept) of the **Eglise Notre-Dame du Sablon**. Open 9–6, but not accessible during church services.*

Notre-Dame du Sablon (also known as Notre-Dame des Victoires) is Brussels' most beautiful Gothic church. Unfortunately the grime-blackened external masonry is in such a decrepit state that an unsightly, semi-permanent metal canopy has had to be erected around it to protect passers-by from any stray bits of falling stonework. The interior, however, is like a magic lantern. Soft light filters through the stained glass to settle on the delicate, cream-coloured flagstones. The semi-circular choir is particularly lovely, lit by 11 towering lancet windows.

The Guild of Crossbowmen (*arbalétriers*) built a chapel on this site in 1304. In 1348 Baet (Béatrice) Soetken, a hemp weaver from Antwerp, heard celestial voices instructing her to steal a wooden statue of the Madonna at which she worshipped and take it to Brussels. She set off on the mission with her husband, bringing the statue to Brussels in a boat via the Rivers Scheldt and Senne. The statue was set up in the crossbowmen's chapel and became the focus of fervent devotion. Margaret of Austria (Regent to Charles V) added her name to the cult, bringing the church into the ambit of the royal quarter nearby. The Sablon thereafter became the starting-point for the city's grand processions, notably the Ommegang (*see* p.19), which still sets out from here.

The Gothic church of today was built in the 15th and 16th centuries to accommodate the cult surrounding Baet's Madonna. The statue itself, however, was destroyed by iconoclasts in 1580. A large model of the boat, complete with Baet Soetken, her husband and the statue, was given to the church in around 1600 by an Italian doctor at the court of Archduke Albert and the Infanta Isabella, and this has been placed on top of the entrance porch (south transept) inside the church.

The wealth and standing of the church's congregation can be judged by the elegant family tombs and the coats of arms in the stained glass. Two marbled Baroque chapels were erected in the 17th century by the Turn and Taxis family, one in the south transept (which now contains the church shop), the other in the north transept *(open daily at 1pm only, June–Sept)*. The latter, the Chapel of St Ursula, also contains the family vault and a sculpture of St Ursula by Jérôme Duquesnoy the Younger.

Various valuable altarpieces that used to adorn this church have since been removed to the safety of the Musée Communal in the Grand' Place (*see* **Walk I**) and the Musée d'Art Ancien (*see* **Walk II**). However, next to the Chapel of St Ursula is a triptych of *The Resurrection (and donors)* by Michiel Coxie (1499–1592), who trained in Rome then returned to Brussels to become painter to the court of King Philip II.

> *The Musées Royaux des Beaux-Arts (see* **Walk II**) *are just 100m or so from here, should you wish to pay them a quick visit before resuming this walk. Otherwise turn right as you come out of the church and then cross*

*the Rue de la Régence. This grand thoroughfare was laid out in two stages—in 1827 (connecting the Place Royale to Notre-Dame du Sablon) and in 1872 (cutting through a chaotic expanse of old housing to the Palais de Justice). This development also opened up the view to the green space facing you, now occupied by the **Place du Petit-Sablon**. Walk into the formal gardens that occupy the middle of this square.*

These gardens were laid out in 1890 by Henri Beyaert (1823–94)—the architect whose face graces the 100-franc note. They are dedicated to the memory of Counts Egmont and Hornes, and to the spirit of the struggle for liberty and enlightenment that marked the medieval and Renaissance periods. During the reign of Charles V both Egmont and Hornes had distinguished military records and they were respected establishment figures in their late forties by the time that William of Orange led a rebellion of nobles against the repressive régime of Philip II. Although they sided with the rebels, they were moderates. Notwithstanding, they were singled out by the Duke of Alva, who had them arrested, found guilty of treason, and beheaded in front of the Maison du Roi in the Grand' Place in 1568. This made them heroes to a nation which saw them as unjustly punished for defending the legitimate rights of the people.

Statues of the counts stand over the fountain in the centre of the garden. These same statues, cast in 1864, originally stood in front of the Maison du Roi in the Grand' Place, but—as photos show—this was not a happy arrangement. In this garden they are joined by sculptures of other luminaries from the same epoch of Belgian history. Most of these have since returned to obscurity, but they include the Flemish geographer and mathematician Gérard Mercator (1512–94), who is credited with the projection on which most school maps of the world are still based. Such historical statues crop up all over Brussels, reflecting the concerted bid of the Belgian authorities in the 19th century to establish the cultural heritage of their new nation.

The most endearing feature of these gardens is the series of 48 small statues depicting representatives of the various medieval guilds of Brussels—also noted defenders of their liberties—each standing on his individual pillar around the perimeter. Here you'll find an armourer, bleacher, wood-turner, hatter, leather chairmaker, shoemaker, dyer, blacksmith, locksmith, barber-surgeon, cutler and so on—all easily identifiable by the distinctive tools or products of their trade.

Walk up the steps to the rear of the gardens and cross the Rue aux Laines to the large wrought-iron gates on the other side of the street.

The palace behind this gateway is known as the **Palais d'Egmont**, for this was the site of a mansion built in the 16th century by the parents of the unfortunate

Count Egmont. In the 18th century it was replaced by the neoclassical palace of the Duke of Arenberg, who had married the Egmont heiress and was one of the leading socialites in the elegant court of Charles of Lorraine. Louis XV of France numbered among his guests here. After being destroyed by fire in 1891, the palace was rebuilt in the same style, and now belongs to Belgium's Ministry of Foreign Affairs. This was where, in 1972, Great Britain, Ireland and Denmark signed the treaty that brought them into the European Community.

> *This is as close as you can get to the Palais d'Egmont from this side, but its gardens, the Jardin d'Egmont, are accessible from the south (see p.138). For now, cross back over the Rue aux Laines, which was once the site of a number of glamorous palaces and hôtels and still retains a noble air. Walk back towards the Rue de la Régence, along the west side of the Place du Petit-Sablon. At No. 17, at the corner with the Rue de la Régence, is the* **Musée Instrumental** *(Musical Instrument Museum). Open 2.30–4.30, closed Mon; adm free.*

At some date in the future (not yet fixed at the time of writing) this museum is due to move into a magnificent new home in a restored Art Nouveau department store called Old England, just off the Place Royale (*see* **Walk II**). For the time being, a small but select number of its 6000 historical instruments is on display, sparsely laid out in glass cases over three floors. The collection is mainly European, dating from the Renaissance onwards, and it includes numerous interesting oddities, such as the 18th-century kits or *pochettes*—tiny violins which dancemasters could carry about in their pockets. The vast tromba marina, dated 1680, is a single-stringed cello-like instrument that can only produce harmonics—amplified by 20 sympathetic strings inside the triangular body—creating the unearthly sound that gave it its misleading name, 'marine trumpet'. The glass harmonica designed by the American statesman and inventor Benjamin Franklin (1706–90) produces a similarly eerie humming sound by employing the same principle as running a wet finger around the rim of a wine glass. Beethoven and Mozart both wrote music for it.

> *Turn left into the Rue de la Régence as you come out of the museum and walk towards the Palais de Justice. On the left, attached to the Musée Instrumental, is the* **Conservatoire Royal de Musique***.*

This handsome red-brick and stone building stands on the site of the palace of the Turn and Taxis family and was designed by J.P. Cluysenaar in 1875, nearly 30 years after his innovative Galeries Royales de Saint-Hubert (*see* **Walk I**). The statue in the courtyard depicts François Auguste Gevaert (1828–1908), director of the Conservatoire from 1871 until his death, and a composer of operas that were performed to acclaim in the 1850s and 1860s.

Now walk on to Place Poelaert, which stands before the Palais de Justice. The monument on the corner of Place Poelaert is a tribute from the British people to the Belgians who helped wounded British soldiers and prisoners during the First World War. Use the pedestrian subway to cross to the north side of the Rue de la Régence. Walk across the open space of Place Poelaert to the vantage point on your right.

You are now standing on the Galgenberg, the hilltop used as a place of execution until the beginning of the 16th century. The view north across Brussels should be wonderful, but has been sadly blighted by the intrusion of the ugly rooftops of the Athénée Robert Catteau. (Many of the old-established state secondary schools in Belgium are called *Athénée*, from the Greek Athenaeum.) Nonetheless, you can still look across western Brussels to the green copper dome of the 20th-century Basilique Nationale du Sacré Cœur (better known as the Basilique de Koekelberg, *see* p.201). Straight ahead is Notre-Dame de la Chapelle, and to the right is the distinctive spire, topped by St Michael, of the Hôtel de Ville.

Immediately below you stand the unappetizing modern tenements of the **Marolles**. The term Marolles is often used loosely to describe the area around the Rue Haute and Rue Blaes, but the true Bruxellois will put you right: the Marolles lies strictly around the foot of this hill, to the west of the Palais de Justice and eastwards to Notre-Dame de la Chapelle. It used to occupy a larger part of the Galgenberg, but some 1000 houses were forcibly cleared to make way for the huge plinth on which the Palais de Justice was built. This caused great outrage, and the architect, Joseph Poelaert (1817–79), became the object of hatred. The expression *de skieven architek* ('filthy architect') soon became a term of serious abuse in the Marolles, over which brawls would be fought.

*Now walk to the entrance in the northwestern flank of the **Palais de Justice**. Officially open Mon–Fri 9–4, but may also be open at other hours; adm free.*

The Palais de Justice is a monumental hulk of a building—dream architecture for a megalomaniac. The area that it covers, 180m by 170m, made it the largest construction in continental Europe in the 19th century. Its dome—an elaborate confection of copper and gilt, that is dwarfed like a pincushion on an overstuffed sofa—rises to 105m. It cost 50 million francs to build, a huge sum in its day, contested as sheer folly by many of the citizens of Brussels. The plan was initiated under Leopold I in 1833 but was not undertaken until the reign of Leopold II. It was the crowning achievement of Joseph Poelaert, a distinguished architect, who paid for it with his sanity. Building started in earnest in 1866 and was not completed until 1883, by which time Poelaert had died in a mental asylum.

You are free to wander the public hallways, staircases and galleries of this extraordinary building at your leisure. The entrances alone show that subtlety was not Poelaert's strong card. Using just about every trick in the neoclassical book, the ranks of giant columns that line the portico seem specially designed to belittle anyone who passes between them. But this is nothing compared to the interior, which consists mainly of one colossal, marbled atrium, with broad marble stairs rising on either side to the galleries and lit from windows somewhere close to the firmament. Two typically bizarre and sensuous allegorical canvases by the visionary Symbolist Jean Delville, painted in 1914, hang at either end of the first-floor gallery, serving only to enhance the surreal atmosphere. The main waiting hall of a building like this is known as the *Salle des Pas Perdus* ('Hall of Lost Footsteps'), particularly appropriate here in the face of its disorienting scale, but if you were standing trial you might think it was an oblique reference to your cause.

Almost as an afterthought, there are 25 courtrooms tucked away in the walls of this building, including the *Cour de Cassation*, the highest court in the land. Groups of lawyers and their anxious clients pepper the floor, speaking in hushed, staccato tones; waiting jurors gaze vacantly into the mid-distance from scattered benches or hang about outside the courtrooms, reading scruffy handwritten instructions attached to the oak doors with sticky tape. All around them, and over the city outside, the architecture booms imperiously: 'Justice Shall Be Done!'

At this point you can make a short excursion which loops around the shops near the Place Louise and returns via the Jardin d'Egmont. If it is a Sunday, however, the area will be fairly dead—although a surprising number of people will be out gazing at the window displays of firmly closed shops. From Place Poelaert turn right and walk along the Rue des Quatre Bras. This leads to the Boulevard de Waterloo and Place Louise. *(If you don't wish to take this excursion, turn to p.139.)*

The **Boulevard de Waterloo** and its twin, the **Avenue de la Toison d'Or** (Golden Fleece) form part of the busy thoroughfare called the 'Petite Ceinture', which rings the city centre along the course of the ancient city walls. The area between the former sites of two city gates—the Porte Louise (in Place Louise) and the Porte de Namur to its left—forms one of Brussels' most impressive shopping zones, not so much for the shops on the streets but for the covered modern *galeries* that lead off the Avenue de la Toison d'Or to the south—the Galerie Louise, the Galerie de la Toison d'Or and the Galerie Porte de Namur. This is where Eurocrats in blazers and snappy tweeds come in their shiny cars to spend Euromoney. Smart cafés spill out over the pavements, where bejewelled friends hail each other across the throngs of shoppers and the constant hubbub of traffic.

Cross the Place Louise and enter the **Avenue Louise**.

Around the top of the Avenue Louise the concentration of famous names thickens: Chanel, Gianni Versace, Gucci, Nina Ricci, Bally, Cartier. Avenue Louise—a grand boulevard shaded by chestnut trees—is considered to be the smartest street in Brussels. Lining the pavements are modern picture and sculpture galleries, showrooms for exclusive furniture designers, and the kind of couturiers' boutiques where you wonder if the decimal point has been left out of the prices.

Once, the central lane of the avenue was an *allée des cavaliers*, a sandy strip reserved for people out exercising on horseback. Now it is a tramline, with impatient traffic roaring up and down on either side. Before long the shops peter out and the road degenerates into a noisy eight-lane racetrack.

Before you reach that point, however, turn left opposite Rue Jean Stas and enter the **Galerie Louise**.

This 20th-century Aladdin's Cave occupies the ground floor of a 1960s office block, but it has been through ceaseless facelifts and does not show a wrinkle of age. It is a showcase of elegant style, packed with shops selling mainly *haute couture*, jewellery, and shoes that smell sweetly of fine leather—all of which will be delicately giftwrapped and emblazoned with prestigious shop names to make you feel especially good about parting with your money.

Take the first left inside the galerie, *turn right, then left. Turn right as you approach the exit on the Avenue de la Toison d'Or and take the escalator to the upper level of the* **Espace Louise**, *an extension of the mall opened in 1989. As you emerge on the Avenue de la Toison d'Or, turn right. Walk past the Eglise des Petits-Carmes—a modernized church stripped of all distractions from serious worship—to the corner with the Rue des Drapiers. Cross the Avenue de la Toison d'Or and Boulevard de Waterloo to the foot of the Hilton, a shameless modern monolith. Turn right to reach a coach-sized archway at No. 31 Boulevard de Waterloo, marked 'Institut supérieur pour l'étude du langage plastique'—another way of saying 'art appreciation'. An alleyway leads to this institute, and to the* **Jardin d'Egmont**.

This alleyway is in fact a kind of coaching yard, attractively draped with creeper. At the end of it lies the old garden of the Palais d'Egmont, now a shady public park which wears a slightly forlorn air, with a derelict orangery and threadbare lawns scuffed up by dogs and footballers. But it affords a good view of the palace, albeit now rather over-restored in kitsch shades of pink and grey. The park has a 1924 copy of the statue of Peter Pan that stands in Kensington Palace Gardens in

London, and also a statue of Charles-Joseph, Prince de Ligne (1735–1814). Diplomat, statesman, writer and friend of both Charles of Lorraine and the unpopular Joseph II, the Prince de Ligne was the personification of the cosmopolitan ruling class of the Austrian Netherlands. His family seat was the splendid château of Beloeil in western Belgium, and he was dubbed the 'Prince Charming of Europe'. He is remembered for his epigram: '*Chaque homme a deux patries: la sienne et puis la France*' ('Every man has two fatherlands: his own and France').

> *Leave the Jardin d'Egmont by the path that leads out behind the classical folly to the Rue du Grand-Cerf. Turn right, then left into the Rue aux Laines. This brings you back to the Palais de Justice. Cross the Rue de la Régence again, walk towards the parapet overlooking the city, and then turn right down Rue Ernest Allard. Pass Le Perroquet, an Art Nouveau café on the corner of Rue Charles Hanssens and turn left down Rue Watteeu. At No. 16 is **Verschuren**, a commercial enterprise which serves as a centre for the Belgian lace industry. Open 9–6.*

Here you can see a lace-maker at work, a video which explains the art of lace-making and its survival as a cottage industry, and hundreds of samples of real Belgian lace. All these are for sale, at prices ranging from 600 BF to 40,000 BF.

> *Continue down Rue Watteeu to the Rue des Minimes, then turn left. Just beyond the junction with Rue Charles Hanssens is the **Eglise des Minimes**. Open Mon–Sat 10–2.*

The Eglise des Saints-Jean-et-Etienne des Minimes was built between 1700 and 1715 in a period when the neoclassical style was taking over from Flemish Baroque. Hiding behind an unpromising façade is a church of elegant, cool simplicity, as befitted the Minimes, a mendicant order of monks. Founded in Cosenza, southern Italy, in the 15th century, the order came to Brussels in 1616 and built a convent on this site—a site which was formerly occupied by the house of the great anatomist Andreas Vesalius (1514–64). The convent was closed down in 1796 during the French occupation and the buildings were used as an artillery store, workhouse and a tobacco-processing factory. The church was restored to use in 1819.

The small chapel of Notre-Dame de Lorette to the right of the nave reveals a more surprising Italian connection. In wild contrast to the rest of the church, the walls are painted with naïve murals bright with Mediterranean colour. The chapel was built as a reconstruction of the *Santa Casa*, Christ's family home in Nazareth, which according to legend was brought to Loreto, near Ancona in eastern Italy, by angels in 1294. By association, Our Lady of Loreto is patron saint of aviators and air-travellers. The earlier murals fell into decay and were replaced in 1987 by scenes depicting Christ at different ages in his house at Nazareth, which evidently looked very similar to a Greek taverna. The black Madonna over the altar is said to date from 1621 and to be made out of wood from the oak tree that grew from a stick planted by Saint Guidon at Anderlecht (*see* p.209).

> *Now retrace your steps along the Rue des Minimes until you reach the Rue des Chandeliers, opposite Rue Watteeu. This narrow alleyway drops down to the Rue Haute, crossing the Rue de la Samaritaine. You might say this area was picturesque if it wasn't so clearly poor. This is archetypal Marolles—not much to look at, but its unique character becomes more apparent in the bars and cafés after 10pm. Continue to Rue Haute. At No. 132, on the corner with the Rue de la Porte Rouge, is the house where **Pieter Bruegel the Elder** apparently lived from 1563 until his death in 1569. (Open only to groups on written request.)*

This red-brick step-gabled house, much restored, gives a flavour of how this district might have looked in the 16th century when it was a prosperous suburb. So little is known about Bruegel's life that it is not certain that he did live here. However, it does seem that the house belonged to Anne Bruegel, Bruegel's granddaughter (and wife of the painter David Teniers the Younger), who probably inherited it through her father, Jan ('Velvet') Bruegel.

> *Continue down the Rue Haute and take the third right, the Rue des Capucins, named after the Capuchin monastery that had an extensive property and garden here from 1587 until 1803, when it too became a victim of the French occupation. This leads to the Rue Blaes, a street that was forged through this district during the late 19th century. Turn left, and walk down Rue Blaes to the **Place du Jeu de Balle**.*

This large square—where a ball-game similar to pelota used to be played, and known to all older Bruxellois for its black market during the war—is now the scene of a daily flea market *(7–11am)*, which augments considerably on Sunday mornings. This is definitely the opposite end of the antiques trade from the Sablon, where hopeful stall-holders try to shift not-so-old typewriters, bits of carpet, brass odds and ends, second-hand tools, shop mannequins and execrable oil paintings. But you may also find interesting craftwork among the dross, and—who knows?—a real bargain.

Facing the square, on Rue Blaes, is the **Caserne des Pompiers**, the old red-brick fire station, designed by Joseph Poelaert and built in 1863 to provide one of the most advanced fire stations of its day. In recent years it has been imaginatively renovated by the City of Brussels and now houses a series of junk shops, small art galleries and book shops. A modern art gallery occupies the glassed-in arch of the gateway through which horse-drawn fire engines would once have charged.

*Turn left at the southern end of the Place du Jeu de Balle and walk up Rue de la Rasière. This passes the **Cité de la Rasière**.*

This public housing complex is divided into a series of lateral streets named after various guilds: Orfèvres (goldsmiths), Brodeurs (embroiderers), Chaisiers (chair-makers) and so on. In fact these are just folksy names applied when the complex was built in 1912. This could be just another depressing backwater of shabby tenements were it not for the inventive use of polychromatic brick, balconies and interconnecting arches, which betrays an enlightened approach and gives it some claim to lasting appeal.

*Continue up the Rue de la Rasière to the Rue Haute. At the unpromising address of 298a Rue Haute, on an upper floor of a 1930s office block for the social services, is the **Musée du Centre Public d'Aide Sociale de Bruxelles (Hôpital Saint-Pierre)**. Open Wed only, 2–5—worth visiting only if you happen to pass by at this time.*

The Hôpital Saint-Pierre was founded here in the 12th century as a leprosy hospital, at a time when this site was surrounded by countryside and considered sufficiently remote from the city. Leprosy was a scourge of the Middle Ages: victims were shunned by society and could find solace only in such rare charitable institutions as this. By the 17th century leprosy had more or less died out in Europe, but the hospital continued in name, and survives today in the 20th-century complex behind this building. Over time, the hospital received gifts through various legacies, and its small, oddball but valuable collection of treasures can be seen displayed in a corridor and series of conference rooms. The collection includes 17th-century furniture, Roman coins, tapestries, church treasures and several notable paintings, including the curious *Christ Surrounded by the Sponsors of the Hospital* by Gaspard de Crayer (1584–1669). The gem of the collection, however, is a small folding altarpiece by Bernard van Orley, dated 1520. Entitled *La Dormition de la Vierge*, it is a beautiful early-Renaissance depiction of the deathbed of the Virgin, with accompanying scenes from the beginning of Christ's story, from the Annunciation to the Circumcision, all painted with loving detail and tenderness.

*Continue to the southern end of the Rue Haute. The street snakes around a bend, and suddenly the isolated, impressively bold shape of the **Porte de Hal** stands before you. It now houses what is grandly called the **Musée du Folklore**, a branch of the Musées Royaux d'Art et d'Histoire. Open 10–5, closed Mon; adm 80 BF.*

The sheer scale of this bastion gives some idea of the ambitious size of the second perimeter wall that was built around Brussels over about three decades after

1357. The wall was 7km long in all, with 72 defensive towers and seven fortified gates. This one, built over the road that led to Hal (or Halle), is the sole surviving remnant. In 1782 the modernizing Austrian monarch Joseph II decreed the dismantling of all city walls in his empire, as weapons technology had rendered them redundant. The Porte de Hal, however, was retained because it served as a prison. In the 1840s it was once again reprieved, and began its career as a museum. When there was widespread rebuilding in Brussels during the 1860s, it was radically restored and embellished by Henri Beyaert, the architect who later designed the Petit-Sablon. As a result, what you see today is partly a truncated city gate and partly a Neo-Gothic fantasy castle.

THE
PORTE
DE HAL
ONE OF THE
OLD CITY GATES

Much of the original interior has been preserved, and in the echoing vaulted hall on the first floor you can look down through glass plates to the place where a huge portcullis was once lowered. The robust military tone is curiously disarmed by a temporary display of 'folklore' items on two floors—in reality a modest collection of Toone puppets and toys. Among these is an exceptional doll's house dating from the late 19th century, which is a miniature replica of a real *maison de maître*, complete down to the newspapers on the table.

A spiral staircase added by Beyaert, and decorated with sculptures of medieval figures, leads to the upper storey, from where you may be allowed to walk around the parapet. Views from here extend over the Marolles to the Palais de Justice and across the city to the Atomium. Shut out the roar of traffic, let your imagination roll, and see if you can conjure up an image of what might have lain around you if you had stood on this spot at the southernmost tip of the medieval city of Brussels 500 years ago.

To return to the centre of town, you can go by métro (Porte de Hal), or take Bus 48, which leads past the Sablon to the Bourse; or you could walk back up the Rue Haute or Rue Blaes (about 20 min).

IV: Origins to the Ultimate Hallucination

Start: *Place de la Monnaie (close to the Grand' Place)* Ⓜ *de Brouckère.*

Walking time: *about 4 hours minimum; but add a further 1½ hours if you want to visit the waxwork museum.*

IV: Origins to the Ultimate Hallucination

This walk peels back some of the layers of history across the northern sector of the 'Pentagon'—the heart of Brussels. The starting point is the opera house where the modern state of Belgium was born; it then takes you to the spot where the very first settlement of Brussels was founded over a thousand years ago. It leads through narrow medieval passageways, over the worn flagstones of peaceful churches and into the bustle of some of Brussels' most hectic shopping streets. It passes through the elegant old administrative

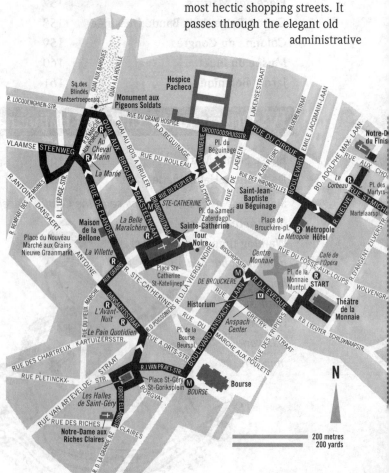

district created in the 19th century in the first élan of independence, and ends at one of Brussels' most celebrated Art Nouveau bar-restaurants: the Ultimate Hallucination.

The Pentagon of Brussels was first created when its great city walls were erected around it in the 14th century.

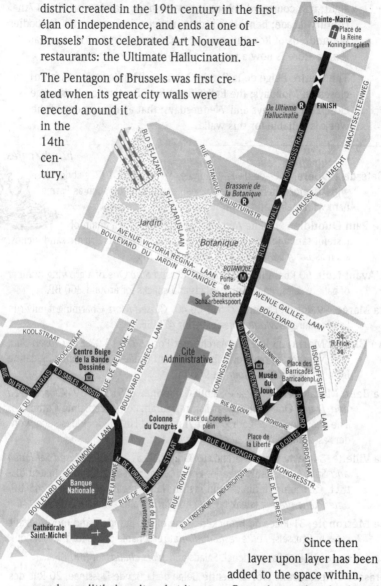

Since then layer upon layer has been added to the space within, and very little is quite what it seems. Beneath a modern boulevard flows the river on which the city was founded, buried and out of sight; in a courtyard behind a row of shops stands a pristine 17th-century façade; beneath a sedate, neoclassical square lie the bodies of hundreds of Revolutionaries; what was once an Art Nouveau textile store is now a museum devoted to comic strips.

The Centre Belge de la Bande Dessinée (Comic-Strip Museum) closes on Mondays; the Eglise Saint-Jean-Baptiste au Béguinage is closed on Mondays and Wednesdays; that apart, any day of the week is suitable for this walk.

---

lunch/cafés

Café de l'Opéra, 4 Place de la Monnaie. Welcoming 1920s-style café, with pavement terrace, offering *petite restauration* such as Parma ham with melon at 425 BF.

Le Pain Quotidien, 16 Rue Antoine Dansaert. One of a chain of tasteful sandwich bars. Minimal décor and inventive rustic sandwiches, such as *bœuf au basilique* for around 175 BF.

L'Avant-Nuit, 50 Rue Antoine Dansaert. *Closed Sun.* One of a growing number of gallery-cafés. Imaginative salads and snacks for around 300 BF.

La Marée, 99 Rue de Flandre, ✆ 511 00 40. *Closed Mon.* Charming family-run fish restaurant. *Moules marinière* for 475 BF.

Au Cheval Marin, 25 Rue du Marché aux Porcs, ✆ 513 02 87. *Closed Sun.* Highly respected old-world fish restaurant inside a gabled building dating from 1680. *Menu du jour* for 900 BF.

La Belle Maraîchère, 11 Place Sainte-Catherine, ✆ 512 97 59. *Closed Wed and Thurs.* One of the great fish restaurants of Place Sainte-Catherine. The changing three-course menu for 900–1100 BF includes such wonders as *saumon braisé au champagne*.

La Villette, 3 Rue du Vieux Marché aux Grains, ✆ 512 75 50. *Closed Sat lunch and Sun.* A decidedly meat-oriented restaurant in a fish-dominated district. Charming, intimate and stylish. Light meals of salads at 245 BF, *américaine maison* (steak tartare) at 425 BF, plus serious steaks.

Le Métropole, 31 Place de Brouckère. One of the grandest and most elegant cafés in Brussels. *Petite restauration* at reasonable prices for the location.

Le Corbeau, 18 Rue Saint-Michel. Salads and *plats chauds* for 200 BF.

Brasserie-Restaurant Horta, Centre Belge de la Bande Dessinée, 20 Rue des Sables. Stylish lunch-spot in the Comic-Strip Museum, a popular venue for the design world. Menus at 500–1000 BF, and children's menus.

Brasserie de la Botanique, in the glasshouse of the Jardin Botanique. Pleasant rendezvous spot with *plats du jours* at 300–375 BF.

De Ultieme Hallucinatie, 316 Rue Royale, ✆ 217 06 14. *Closed Sat lunch and Sun.* Drinks and bar food (*plat du jour* 250 BF) in the stylish bar; full and adventurous menu (*magret de canard aux figues* 825 BF) in the ultimate Art Nouveau restaurant.

In the Place de la Monnaie old and new Brussels come squarely face to face, confronting each other across a cobbled square. In the Red Corner is the vast Centre Monnaie, a huge X-shaped block of curving glass and concrete that houses various municipal offices and the headquarters of the banking giant, the CGER. It stands on the site of the old mint, built in 1420, which has given the square its name. Dwarfed in the Blue Corner is the **Théâtre de la Monnaie**, built in 1819 to resemble a robust Greek temple. But this contender has form. On 25 August 1830 an excitable audience was stirred into a frenzy by the provocative text of the opera *La Muette de Portici* (*see* p.62). Dressed in their opera finery, they burst out of the theatre, rushed to the Grand' Place and raised the flag of Brabant over the Hôtel de Ville, yelling defiance at the Dutch authorities. It was the start of the Belgian Revolution and—after a scrappy, sometimes bloody, conflict—led directly to the declaration of Belgian independence just one month later.

There has been a theatre on this site since 1698. After struggling for decades in a moral climate that denigrated all theatre as immoral, this 'Hôtel des Spectacles' began to flourish during the era of Charles of Lorraine (1741–80). In 1766 a company called the Théâtre de la Monnaie was set up, modelled on the Comédie Française in Paris—i.e. with no star system. The theatre was soon all the rage with members of the court: it had gambling tables, and furthermore the cast-list provided the nobility with a string of beautiful and much contested mistresses.

The old building was demolished in 1810 to make way for a new version. The interior of this, however, was gutted by a fire in 1855 and then remodelled to designs by Joseph Poelaert, just before he began his *magnum opus*, the Palais de Justice (*see* p.136). With only 1200 seats, this is a small opera house. It has a deliberate policy of not contracting the megastars of the opera world, preferring instead to nurture rising stars and to concentrate on the staging and theatrical qualities of opera, for which it has earned a high reputation. The theatre also maintains a resident ballet company, separate from the opera. For three decades until the late 1980s it was the home of the Twentieth Century Ballet of Maurice Béjart, king of the big spectacle in modern dance. When Béjart left after a series of disagreements, he was replaced for a brief but mercurial spell by the troupe formed by the celebrated American dancer Mark Morris; his effusively camp antics and risqué comments succeeded in ruffling the feathers of crustier season-ticket holders while delighting the avant-garde. The slot has now been filled by Anne Teresa De Keersmaeker, who has successfully held the middle ground.

Like any great theatre, the Monnaie has a wingful of theatrical tales. In 1973, so the story goes, W. H. Auden and Chester Kallman were invited as honoured guests to the première of Nicolas Nabokov's opera *Love's Labour's Lost*, for which they had written the libretto. Auden had lived in Brussels in the late 1930s and knew the city well—perhaps too well. Their seats remained empty until well after the opera was due to begin. The audience became restive, and so the conductor decided to start without them. Barely had he got underway, however, when two tramp-like figures shambled into the auditorium, their coat pockets bulging with bottles of whisky: the celebrated librettists had arrived. Proceedings were halted for their benefit and restarted. As the music altered pace and softened, the audience again became aware of their honoured guests—this time because of their loud snoring.

> *The Rue Léopold runs along the back of the opera house. The great French neoclassical painter **Jacques-Louis David** (1748–1825) lived and died at No. 5.*

Having been First Painter to Napoleon, David feared reprisals in Paris after the final defeat of his master in 1815, and so came to live in Brussels. The house he chose is suitably neoclassical, with Empire-style Grecian harp motifs on the balcony, but is now in a state of semi-dereliction.

> *The street running into the Place de la Monnaie from the direction of the Grand' Place is the **Rue des Fripiers** ('second-hand clothes sellers').*

Picture a snow-covered Brussels in February 1814, and this street filled with exhausted Cossacks huddled around camp fires. The Cossacks had pursued Napoleon's troops in their catastrophic retreat all the way from Moscow, but they missed the French rearguard in Brussels by just one hour.

> *Walk up Rue de l'Evêque. To the right is the covered shopping mall of the Centre Monnaie, to the left the shopping mall of the Anspach Center, the two connected by a pedestrian bridge. Go into the Anspach Center and walk through the corridor of boutiques and shops to the escalators. On the first floor is **Historium**, the Historical Waxwork Museum. Open 10–6, last entry 5pm; adm adults 190 BF, children 150 BF. Entry includes the loan of radio-triggered headphones with a commentary in English; the tour takes about 1½ hours.*

This museum attempts to sum up Belgian history in a series of tableaux depicting great historical moments. It is not easy to make waxworks look convincing at the best of times, especially when trying to recreate historical scenes—and this wax museum is not among those that has triumphed. The tableaux are comically wooden, but the commentary is very informative. If you come armed with a basic knowledge of Belgian history and want to learn more, this will prove a rewarding kind of audiovisual lesson; and children (of seven or over) seem to enjoy it.

Leave the Anspach Center by the exit on **Boulevard Anspach.**

Many a great city has its own splendid river or harbour front; Brussels has the River Senne. Unfortunately this was never a great river. Instead, it was small and sluggish, wending its way through marshland punctuated by low, damp islands, prone to flooding, contamination and stench. Maps of the 1860s mark its course, entering the city near the Gare du Midi and leaving it close to the Gare du Nord. Contemporary paintings show picturesque, lopsided houses and workshops cramming the river's edge, gently sinking into the sludge.

After repeated outbreaks of cholera, the Senne was identified as a health hazard, and in 1867 the city fathers decided that it had to go. A vast building project was initiated in which the Senne was channelled underground, vaulted over and linked into a new city sewage system. There are few places where it can be seen today: one occurs later on in this walk, another is at the Musée des Egouts (Sewer Museum, *see* p.198). Over the top of the river a new throughfare was built, running straight through the city, of which Boulevard Anspach forms the central section. It was inaugurated in 1871 and named after Jules Anspach, burgomaster from 1863 to 1879.

> *Turn left and walk down Boulevard Anspach. On your left at No.46 is a large outlet for the fresh-cream chocolates made by Leonidas: its counter opens directly on to the street. When you reach the Bourse Métro station, take the steps down to the entrance foyer.*

Over the escalators is a large painting by Paul Delvaux (*see* p.45). *Nos Vieux Trams Bruxellois* (1978) covers familiar Delvaux territory—trams set in a silent, surreal world.

> *Exit from the Métro station on the north side of Boulevard Anspach, and turn left. The stately neoclassical building on the other side of the road is the Bourse (the old stock exchange, see **Walk I**). Cross Rue Auguste Orts and turn right into Rue Jules van Praet—a mini-Chinatown of restaurants and oriental food suppliers. Continue to **Place Saint-Géry**.*

This square once stood in the middle of the Ile Saint-Géry, one of a cluster of islands formed by the River Senne. Some time in the late 6th century, as tradition has it, St Géry (Bishop of Cambrai) founded a chapel here. This became the focus of a small settlement which remained obscure for 400 years until AD 977, when Charles, Duke of Lorraine, built a castle on the island, and the history of Brussels began. St Géry's original chapel was destroyed in about AD 800, but a succession of churches stood on this spot until 1798, when the last became a victim of French Revolutionary zealots. The red-brick covered market, Les Halles de Saint-Géry, which now occupies the middle of the square, was built in 1881 as a meat market. It was recently restored as a shopping arcade, but the venture failed.

Ile Saint-Géry has now become fashionable, and the developers have moved in to subject the area to what is jocularly referred to as '*façadisme*': the façade of an old building is propped up and preserved while everything behind it is demolished to make way for rebuilding.

> *Walk to the west side of Place Saint-Géry. At No. 23 there is an iron gate, which is often open, leading to a courtyard of tastefully refurbished apartment blocks. In this courtyard a small segment of the River Senne can be seen. Leave Place Saint-Géry by the Rue de la Grande Ile. At the next junction, on the right-hand side, is* **Notre-Dame aux Riches Claires** *(currently closed for renovation).*

This small, red-brick church once stood on the northern tip of one of the larger islands, overlooking the bridge that connected it to the Ile Saint-Géry. This is one of Brussels' finest Baroque churches, designed by Luc Fayd'Herbe (1617–97)—a pupil of Rubens and a noted sculptor—and built in 1665.

> *Return to Place Saint-Géry and take the exit at the northeast of the square. This is called the Rue Pont de la Carpe ('carp bridge'), for until the 1860s there was a bridge over the River Senne here. At the next junction take the third left, Rue Antoine Dansaert, which has recently been colonized by avant-garde fashion shops. Walk down this street and take the first right, the Rue du Vieux Marché aux Grains, which becomes a pretty, tree-lined square filled with small café terraces and their candy-striped awnings. At the far end is the Eglise Sainte-Catherine: we come back to this later. For now, turn left up the* **Rue de Flandre**.

Modest though this street now looks, it was once one of Brussels' main thoroughfares, linking the Rue du Marché aux Herbes and the Grand' Place (*see* **Walk I**) to the Flanders Gate and the road to Ghent. Today it is a pleasantly quiet backwater. No. 17 is a butcher's specializing in tripe and other offal—the base ingredients of some famous Bruxellois dishes such as *choesels* (*see* p.224). No. 28, La Maison de la Casquette, is a hatmaker's, specializing in headgear for the clergy, traditional berets and long-peaked student caps, which are displayed in the window. Each university has its own design.

Continue up the Rue de Flandre to No. 46. This is the **Maison du Spectacle** *(often misleadingly referred to as the theatre museum). Open 10–5; adm free, though admission is charged for temporary exhibitions. It is really a theatre centre, with an archive and library, where rehearsals and workshops, as well as public concerts, small-scale performances and exhibitions, are held. Go through the glass door and along the passage. At the end of this, through another glass door is a courtyard, overlooked by the* **Maison de la Bellone** *(open only during temporary exhibitions).*

This beautifully proportioned, honey-coloured façade is all the more delightful for the surprise of finding it here, tucked away behind a row of shops. The house was built in 1697 to designs by Jan Cosyns, a sculptor-cum-architect who was also engaged in the restoration of the Grand' Place. His signature can be seen over the door, on the plinth of his bust of Bellona, a Roman goddess of war. Stone reliefs of various war trophies and weapons of imperial Rome, and medallion portraits of four emperors at the height of Rome's power (Hadrian, Trajan, Antoninus Pius and Marcus Aurelius), take up the theme of power and war; these strike a dissonant but satisfying chord against the mellow rhythms of the Renaissance-Baroque architecture. The gable is crowned by a pelican plucking her breast (to nourish her young on her own blood), an old symbol for the sacrifice of Christ.

When it was built, the Maison de la Bellone backed on to orchards and was separated from the Rue de Flandre by a long garden and another house fronting the busy street—as can be seen in the print displayed just inside the glass door to the courtyard. The house had a chequered history, with a series of residents. In 1913 Charles Buls, the burgomaster celebrated for his determined efforts to save the historic face of Brussels, persuaded the city to purchase it. It has been a gallery since 1980.

Continue up the Rue de Flandre, cross Rue Lepage and turn left into Rue Rempart des Moines. At No. 15 is a Boucherie Chevaline, a horsemeat butcher: horsemeat is still eaten in Belgium but it is now a rarity. On the *right-hand side of Rue Rempart des Moines is a grey stone arch, dated 1760. This is the entrance to the **Rue de la Cigogne**.*

'Stork Street' is a tiny, crooked passage between cottages, a rare survivor of a network of alleyways that threaded through the city in medieval times.

*Walk through the passage, which leads to the Rue de Flandre. Turn right and then second left into the Rue du Marché aux Porcs. At the end of this is the **Square des Blindés** ('armoured vehicles').*

This square lies on the edge of a poor district of Brussels, a glum area of soulless tenement blocks mainly inhabited by immigrants. The square is named after its monolithic monument to armoured cars in the two World Wars. Opposite it is one of Brussels' most charming and unusual public monuments: a bronze statue of a woman holding a pigeon. It is dedicated 'aux pigeons soldats'—the messenger pigeons used by the military, notably in the First World War.

Walk a little further into the broad open space between the Quai aux Briques and the Quai au Bois à Brûler.

You are now standing on the dogleg corner of the final stretch of the old **Willebroeck Canal**, which, from its inauguration in 1561, brought goods from Antwerp and the North Sea to the city centre—a vital element in Brussels' burgeoning prosperity. The treelined strip of grass in the centre of the avenue to the north and the cobbled area running south were once filled with water and packed with barges, sailing ships, rowing boats and, latterly, small steamships. On either side were the quays lined with warehouses, an antheap of activity as dockers in their wooden clogs loaded and unloaded shipments of salt, barrels of herrings, sacks of grain, timber, cases of Chinese porcelain, and squealing pigs.

The canal, however, suffered from repeated flooding, and by the 1850s the railways had begun to usurp its role. So in 1853 it was closed and covered over. The quays retained their old titles from the days when merchants of a kind clubbed together: Quai à la Houille (coal), Quai au Bois de Construction (building timber), Quai au Bois à Brûler (firewood), Quai aux Briques (bricks). The newly created square was occupied by a fishmarket, moved from its old site by the River Senne. This was demolished in 1955, but there is still a tang of fish in the air, emanating from the few surviving fishmongers' warehouses and from the many restaurants that now line the old quays. This area, referred to loosely as Place Sainte-Catherine or the Marché aux Poissons, is still *the* place to eat fish in Brussels.

*Walk south down the Quai aux Briques. The large fountain here is a **monument to Jules Anspach** erected in recognition of his role in redesigning the city centre in the 1860s.*

This splendid piece of late 19th-century medievalism depicts a naked St Michael slaying a devil, towards which four fanciful, spitting crocodiles and jaguar-like beasts aim their jets of water. It was originally erected in 1897 in Place de Brouckère (over the River Senne), but had to be moved to accommodate a Métro station during the extension of the Métro system in the 1970s. Another Métro station, Sainte-Catherine, was built into the site of the old canal just south of here.

Walk on to the large church which fills the end of the old canal strip. This is the **Eglise Sainte-Catherine** *(open 9–6), which sits in the middle of what is strictly the real Place Sainte-Catherine. Walk round to the entrance at the west door, which is to the right.*

You might be forgiven for thinking that this grime-coated church has been here longer than the canal. In fact it is a piece of 19th-century Neo-Gothic designed in 1854 by Joseph Poelaert. Formerly the canal ended in a T-shape, the top of the T being formed by the Bassin Saint-Catherine. After this was covered over in 1853 a new church was built over it. An earlier Eglise Sainte-Catherine, dating from the 13th century, was pulled down in 1893, but its ruined belfry can still be seen close to the west door of the new church, on the other side of the street.

The interior of the Eglise Sainte-Catherine Mark II now has the air of a neglected greenhouse, with peeling paint, the whiff of decay and the odd pigeon flitting about the vast vacant spaces beneath the roofing vaults. On a grey winter's day it looks decidedly down-at-heel, in tune with the pious gloom of the wooden statues of suffering saints. In contrast it comes to life in bright weather, when light streams in through the pale yellow and blue windows: perhaps there simply aren't enough such days in Brussels to make this church much loved.

At the top end of the north aisle there is a famous 'Black Virgin', a 15th-century limestone statue depicting the Virgin in a beautifully observed pose, holding her child on her hip. The statue was dumped into the River Senne by Protestants in 1744, and by the time it was recovered the stone had turned black.

In the south aisle there is a painted wooden statue of St Catherine, a 4th-century Christian from Alexandria. Although they ended up beheading her, the Romans first attempted to martyr her on a wheel, from which she was miraculously saved—hence the name of the firework called the Catherine wheel. In this statue her wheel can be seen beneath the folds of her dress.

Leaving the church, walk around its south side to the square called Place du Samedi. On a patch of wasteground surrounded by metal grille fencing, is the **Tour Noire** *(Black Tower).*

This is the best-preserved remnant of the first major set of city walls, built in the 12th century. The other surviving segments are the Tour de Villers (*see* **Walk I**) and the Tour d'Angle (*see* **Walk III**). The Tour Noire was a D-shaped bastion built out from the wall so that archers, hiding behind narrow slits, could pick off any enemy trying to mine the wall.

> *Now walk back around the eastern end of the Eglise Sainte-Catherine and up the other side of the old canal, the Quai au Bois à Brûler. Take the first right, the Rue du Peuplier, which leads to the semi-circular Place du Béguinage and the Baroque façade of the **Eglise Saint-Jean-Baptiste au Béguinage**, one of Brussels' loveliest churches. Open Tues, Thurs–Sat 9–5, Sun 10–5, closed Mon and Wed.*

This church was once the hub of Brussels' largest béguinage (*see* pp.208–9)—one of many semi-religious, charitable communities for single women in the Low Countries. This Béguinage dates from 1250, when it was established by four wealthy sisters with the blessing of the Bishop of Cambrai. In its heyday it possessed most of the land in the northwestern corner of Brussels, up to the outer city walls—a self-contained area filled with orchards and fields and dotted with the houses of some 1200 Béguines. Some of these lived in style, in large houses with servants; the less well-off lived in communal houses. They ran a laundry, a windmill and a hospital serving the community at large. By the 14th century the Béguinage was rich enough to build a large Gothic church on this site.

In 1579 marauding Calvinists laid waste this peaceful community, returning to flatten the church in 1584. The Béguines were dispersed, but drifted back over the following years. It took over half a century to rebuild the Béguinage, and only in 1657 were they able to begin work on the present church. But the Béguinage was already in decline. Members now had to pay high entrance fees and maintenance and were also expected to build their own house and donate it to the community. These conditions made it the preserve of the rich, and it soon became out of kilter with contemporary life and values. The number of Béguines declined, and in the early 19th century the Conseil des Hospices had to intervene, handing empty houses out to aged people who had fallen on hard times. The last Béguine of this community died in 1833. Little of the Béguinage has survived, except the streetplan and their church.

No one knows who designed this church, although Luc Fayd'Herbe has been suggested, mainly for the church's similarities to Notre-Dame aux Riches Claires. The façade is a crescendo of twirls, curls, finials, pediments and *œils de bœuf*—a triumph of the Italian-influenced Flemish Baroque. Over the door is a statue of Saint Begga, who is thought by some to have founded the first Béguinages in the 7th century. The great bronze doors were installed during renovation in the 1850s.

The interior is a model of cool, grey tranquillity, a delicate mixture of massive architectural force and deft stone-carving, seen for example in the winged cherubs' heads that fill the intervals between the Romanesque-style semi-circular arches. The grey and black stone floor recalls the calm church interiors painted by Dutch masters such as Saenredam. Many of the flagstones are redeployed tombstones from the earlier church and the surrounding cemetery, commemorating Béguines and their chaplains. The Béguines could be buried in the cemetery, nave or choir according to an established structure of fees—an important source of income for the Béguinage.

The pulpit is a supreme piece of Baroque woodcarving. It was sculpted in 1757 for a Dominican church in Mechelen, and St Dominic can be seen with his foot on a prostrate heretic. The four apostles are represented by their old medieval symbols: the ox for St Luke, the lion for St Mark, the angel for St Matthew and the eagle for St John.

> Turn right as you leave the church and take the Rue de l'Infirmerie. Before you leave the square, however, turn round and look at the Italianate belfry tacked on to the eastern end of the Eglise du Béguinage, almost as an afterthought. From the west this is quite overwhelmed by the façade. The short Rue de l'Infirmerie leads to a narrow, tree-lined square which fronts the imposing **Hospice Pacheco**.

This massive building, set around two leafy courtyards, was built in 1824, during the declining years of the Béguinage. In 1835 it became the new home of the Hospice Pacheco, founded in 1713 through generous funds willed by the widow of Don Augustin Pacheco, a governor during the last years of the Spanish Netherlands. Still very much in use today, the Hospice Pacheco maintains a tradition of caring for the old and infirm that has been a feature of this quarter of Brussels for seven centuries.

> Turn right and walk along the Rue du Grand-Hospice to the busy Rue de Laeken. Turn left, cross the street and take the first right, the Rue du Cirque. Here you pass through the lower reaches of the red-light district. In recent years sleazy bars, peepshows and brothels have spread south from their traditional base around the Gare du Nord. As elsewhere in Belgium, brothels often display their living wares in the window.

> When you reach the Boulevard Emile Jacqmain, pause and look left. Further north lies the immense modern business city of glass and steel called the Quartier Nord. Turn right, however, and walk towards the Centre Monnaie. The street opens out into **Place de Brouckère**, a busy thoroughfare lined by some grand 19th-century commercial buildings.

This is the continuation of the Boulevard Anspach, and is also built over the vaulted River Senne. The name commemorates Charles de Brouckère (1796–1860), a leading political figure of his day, a member of the Provisional Government that was set up in the immediate aftermath of the Revolution, and burgomaster from 1848 to 1860.

Turn left in Place de Brouckère and cross **Boulevard Adolphe Max.**

This street is named after the burgomaster who held the post for a total of three decades, from 1909 to 1939. He is fondly remembered for his dignified and spirited resistance to the oppressive policies of the Germans in occupation during the First World War—for which he was deported and imprisoned—and as an advocate of universal suffrage, including votes for women.

On the south side of Place de Brouckère is the **Métropole Hôtel**, *one of the great hotels of Brussels, and famously grand. If you adopt the persona of a prospective guest you can glimpse the lavish, gilded interior, designed in around 1900. Alternatively you can stop for a coffee at the equally ornate Café Métropole next door, which dates from 1890. To continue the walk, return to where the Boulevard Adolphe Max joins Place de Brouckère. Close by is the entrance to the* **Passage du Nord**.

This shopping arcade was built in 1882, and still retains the flavour of the late 19th century, with its curving iron-work lamps, towering glass vaulting and lines of Grecian ladies propping up the architecture.

Walk through the Passage du Nord and turn left into **Rue Neuve**. *This is one of the Brussels' busiest shopping streets, with many of the capital's more upmarket chainstores, such as Sarma and Marks & Spencer. The narrow thoroughfare is often so packed that it is hard to cross the flow—even though it has been pedestrianized. The shops, bars and boutiques resound to the patter of countless footfalls and the steady throb of imported music: small wonder that it looks a little ragged at the edges.*

Continue down the Rue Neuve, crossing Rue Saint-Michel. The next right is called Rue aux Choux ('Cabbage Street'). Many of the street names in this area recall the fact that there were market gardens here until the 15th century. Opposite Rue aux Choux is the Italian Renaissance-style façade of **Notre-Dame du Finistère** *(at the time of writing, closed for renovation).*

Most of this church was built between 1708 and 1730, although the upper portion of the façade was added in 1828. The Baroque interior includes another example of the extraordinarily lavish pulpits of the period—featuring a grotto, the

Tree of Life and the Tree of Death—as well as a revered Madonna, the Notre-Dame du Bon Succès, which was brought from Aberdeen in 1625. During renovation this pretty statue—Madonna and Child in azure robes with gilded crowns—can be seen in the side-chapel to the east of the main door (*open 8–5*).

> *Walk back to Rue Saint-Michel and turn left into it. Continue to the* **Place des Martyrs.**

After the brash hurly-burly of the Rue Neuve this charming neoclassical square comes as a refreshing surprise. Designed by Claude Fisco (1736–1825), it was built in 1775 and preserves the stylish, genteel air that characterized the rule of Charles of Lorraine. However, having fallen into almost total disrepair the square is currently undergoing radical renovation of the *façadisme* kind.

Its original character was transformed between 1830 and 1840 when it was dedicated to the memory of the 445 'martyrs' killed in the critical days (23–26 September 1830) of the Belgian Revolution. The centre of the square was turned into their mausoleum, a kind of subterranean cloister faced with commemorative marble slabs. The white marble statue rising above this depicts 'Belga', and is one of many notable public monuments by Willem Geefs (1805–85). The combination of the location and the architectural understatement of this mass grave makes it a curiously powerful memorial.

The renovation of the Place des Martyrs has become the subject of heated contention. The Flemish regional government has been buying up property with the intention of making this their headquarters, and indeed the *Kabinet van de Minister-President* of the Flemish government now occupies the restored northern end of the square, draped in Flemish flags. The effect could hardly be more inflammatory to the majority of Bruxellois, who see themselves as increasingly under threat from Flemish nationalism.

> *Leave the Place des Martyrs by the street opposite the one you came in on. This is Rue du Persil ('Parsley Street'), which follows a dogleg between two huge modern office blocks in contrasting styles, both belonging to the CGER bank. Walk left down the Rue du Marais and take the first right into Rue des Sables.*

In early August this corner is the scene of the planting of the may tree (Meiboom), a ceremony that has taken place for close on 700 years. A large, deracinated may tree is paraded joyously from the Place Sainte-Catherine to the Grand' Place, then erected on this spot.

> *Walk up the Rue des Sables. On the left-hand side at No. 20 is an old Art Nouveau textile megastore designed in 1903 for Les Magasins*

Waucquez by Victor Horta. Stylishly renovated in the 1980s, it was opened in 1989 as the **Centre Belge de la Bande Dessinée** *(Comic-Strip Museum). Open 10–6, closed Mon; adm 150 BF.*

This shrine to the comic strip consists mainly of a large collection of original drawings. The comic strip is an art form which is far better developed—and far more popular and widely appreciated—in Belgium, France and Italy than in any English-speaking nation. However, the Belgians credit an American cartoonist, Winsor McCay, with the origins of the European comic-strip tradition. He created 'Little Nemo in Slumberland' for the *New York Herald* in 1905, and when *Les Adventures du Petit Nemo au Pays des Songes* appeared in French in 1908 it proved a wild success. Belgian artists soon became leaders of this new field, and as their characters became better known, their escapades became more ambitious and the magazines more substantial. By far the most famous of these characters is Tintin (*see* **Topics**, pp.38–9), whose creator, Hergé, began producing novel-type adventures in book form after the Second World War.

Tintin, naturally enough, is accorded a special place in this museum, with original drawings, historical notes and some 3-D models of famous Tintin scenes. Other characters, such as Lucky Luke the lackadaisical cowboy (by Morris), are only vaguely recognized by the English-speaking public, but are known to every Belgian. There are hundreds more: Gaston Lagaffe (by André Franquin), Petit Biniou (by Dupa), Boule et Bill and the Ribambelle gang (by Jean Roba), the wily Brussels kids Quick et Flupke (by Hergé), and numerous other characters from the hugely popular magazine *Spirou*. Asterix, by the way, is French. More recently comic-strip artists and their publishers have created a new genre of more adult works. The museum bookshop contains thousands of comic-strip books, almost all in French or Flemish, and is a measure of the scale of this industry: 850 new titles are published every year in Belgium alone.

This spacious museum is beautifully presented, with pristine Art Nouveau stairways, a superb Art Nouveau lamp in the entrance hall and cantilevered glass roofs; yet it has a strangely serious air, given its subject. The people poring over the comic strips are not children but adults. It is a window on the extraordinary talents of comic-strip artists, and rewarding for devotees of Tintin and Victor Horta (the museum includes a section devoted to his work, with an audiovisual on Art Nouveau design)—but others may find that the cultural gap is just too wide to justify the admission charge. (Annotation is in French and Flemish only.)

Turn left as you come out of the museum and walk up the Rue des Sables. Cross the Rue du Meiboom and climb the stone steps to the point where Boulevard Pacheco runs into Boulevard de Berlaimont. You now pass through a slice of the modern world, filled with monumental architecture which, by its abrupt contrast, serves as a reminder that much of the charm of central Brussels lies in its human scale. The huge marble-clad building to your left is the Ministry of Finance and Royal Mint. Cross the street and climb the Rue de la Banque to the junction with Mont de l'Oratoire. The old stone building which can be glimpsed at the end of the Rue de la Banque is the Cathédrale Saint-Michel (see **Walk II***). Turn up Mont de l'Oratoire. To your left is a faceless building covered by acres of green glass, part of the huge civil service complex called the Cité Administrative de l'Etat. Turn left into the Rue de Ligne, named after Charles-Joseph, Prince de Ligne (see p.139).*

Walk a little way up the Rue de Ligne, but stop when the **Colonne du Congrès** *(Congress Column) comes into view. This is the best place to see it from afar. Then continue to the Place du Congrès where it stands.*

Designed by Joseph Poelaert and built in 1850–9, the handsome 47m-high Colonne du Congrès celebrates the foundation of Belgium's constitutional monarchy after the Revolution of 1830. The statue of Leopold I on the top is by Willem Geefs. Strangely, he has his back to the city—but turned the other way round he would have his back to the administrative district, including the Palais de la Nation (*see* **Walk II**), which might have been even less diplomatic. The inscriptions at the base of the column include extracts from the constitution and lists of the members of the Provisional Government (September 1830–February 1831) and the first National Congress (November 1830–July 1831). Between the outsized bronze lions is the flame to the Unknown Soldier of both World Wars.

You have now reached another part of the ridge that forms 'le Haut de la Ville', *linked by the Rue Royale which runs all the way to the Place Royale (see* **Walk II***). The huge paved open space of the Cité Administrative de l'Etat to your west promises a fine view over* 'le Bas de la Ville', *but it is disappointing. Instead, walk up the steps to the Rue Royale, noting the superb cast-iron street lamps around the Place du Congrès, adorned with prim cherubs, lions and garlands and topped by St Michael slaying the dragon.*

Turn right, and cross the Rue Royale at the pedestrian crossing. To your right you can see the Palais Royal on the other side of the Parc de Bruxelles (see **Walk II***); to your left, at the far end of the Rue Royale, is the Eglise Sainte-Marie. Take the road opposite the Colonne du Congrès, the Rue du Congrès, and walk up to the* **Place de la Liberté***.*

You are now entering a district constructed for the administrators of the new nation. As they left their homes in their top hats and spats, the street names would remind them of the pillars of their constitution. At the Place de la Liberté the Rue du Congrès is intersected by the Rue de l'Association (freedom of association), the Rue des Cultes (freedom of religion), the Rue de la Presse (freedom of the press), and the Rue de l'Enseignement (freedom of education). In the centre of the tree-shaded Place de la Liberté is a statue of Charles Rogier (1800–85), erected in 1897. He was a member of the Provisional Government of 1830, and subsequently remained a prominent statesman for the rest of his long life.

*Take the Rue des Cultes and turn left into the Rue du Nord. At the end of this street is an elegant Regency-style circus, the **Place des Barricades**.*

The name of this square commemorates the barricades erected in September 1830 by Belgian Revolutionaries around the Parc de Bruxelles, trapping the Dutch garrison and enforcing their retreat.

In the 1850s Victor Hugo rented the house at No. 4, where he installed his wife Adèle. While her husband lived mainly in Jersey, she held regular soirées at this house, entertaining other French exiles such as Charles Baudelaire and Alexandre Dumas, bon viveur and best-selling author of *The Count of Monte-Cristo* and *The Three Musketeers*. Adèle died here in 1868. When Hugo was staying here in 1871, a riotous mob of students caused a commotion at his door, drawing the attention of the authorities to Hugo's support for the Paris Commune. Sensing dangerous subversion, the government forced Hugo to leave Belgium once and for all.

The statue in the centre of the circus is a 19th-century portrait of the Brussels-born doctor Andreas Vesalius (1514–64), one of the great pioneers of modern anatomical studies, who fell foul of the Spanish Inquisition for his dissection of cadavers. In lieu of the death penalty, he was sentenced to a pilgrimage to the Holy Land, during which he died.

*Leave the Place des Barricades by the Rue de la Révolution (no less), and turn right when you reach the Rue de l'Association. At No. 24 is the **Musée du Jouet** (Toy Museum). Open 10–6; adm adults 100 BF, children 60 BF, children under 5 free.*

This museum has the one ingredient that the Musée de la Bande Dessinée lacks: joy. Housed on three floors in a grand but rather dilapidated 19th-century *maison de maître* (gentleman's residence), it is crammed with toys of all kinds and all ages: dolls, teddy bears, cars, trains, farm animals, magic lanterns, puppets. It is run on a shoestring, but the improvised display cases, higgledy-piggledy arrangement of the exhibits, handwritten labels and histories (French and Flemish only) help to create a magical world—a kind of walk-in toy box. Children are genuinely welcome: there is an area where they can play with numerous larger toys, the display cases have steps so that smaller children can see into them, and the top floor can be hired for children's parties. Grown-ups will be assailed by nostalgia; and there are some unusual curiosities, such as the set of model figures depicting King Baudouin I's visit to the Congo in 1955.

Turn right as you leave the museum and walk down the Rue de l'Association to join the Rue Royale once more. Cross the Rue Royale, turn right and walk to the **Boulevard du Jardin Botanique**.

This wide boulevard is another part of the 'Petite Ceinture', the rim of the 'Pentagon' which follows the course of the 14th-century city walls. At this junction between the Rue Royale and the Boulevard du Jardin Botanique there once stood one of the great city gates, the Porte de Schaerbeek, which led to the outlying community of Schaerbeek, now part of the city sprawl.

It was from here that the charismatic early photographer 'Nadar' (Félix Tournachon, 1820–1910) launched his Montgolfier balloon in a series of flights in the mid 1860s, during which he took aerial photographs of the city. On one occasion the wretched Baudelaire was due to join him, delighting in the opportunity to '*fuir ce sale peuple en ballon, aller tomber en Autriche, en Turquie peut-être, toutes les folies me plaisent, pourvu qu'elles me désennuient*' ('to flee from these filthy people, go and land in Austria, or in Turkey maybe, any mad idea would please me, provided that it relieved my boredom'). However, the balloon was not able to take off with his extra weight, so he had to disembark before the large crowd, which included King Leopold I—another humiliation.

Cross the Boulevard du Jardin Botanique, and walk to the beautiful domed glasshouse that stands in the **Jardin Botanique**. *The botanical gardens themselves have been transferred to the medieval estate of Meise (see p.202); the glasshouse now serves as the* **Centre Culturel de la Communauté Française Wallonie-Bruxelles** *(Cultural Centre of the French Community of Wallonia and Brussels). Open 11–6; adm free. There is an entrance on the Rue Royale.*

This glasshouse was built for the Brussels Horticultural Society in 1826–9 following drawings by a painter and theatre designer called Pierre-François Gineste (1769–1850). Although the exterior was cleverly preserved, the glasshouse was converted into a cultural centre in the early 1980s, and now contains a series of spaces for temporary exhibitions, concerts and plays, as well as a cinema and brasserie. Only the main corridor retains its hothouse atmosphere, with its small fishponds, ferns and papyrus plants. In the huge hollow in front of the glasshouse is a formal garden with box hedges and statuary, some of which is by Constantin Meunier. (Note that the Jardin Botanique has a sinister—and, alas, well-founded—reputation for muggers, but this really refers to the part to the west of here, now cut off from the formal garden by the Boulevard Saint-Lazare.)

> *Turn left as you leave the 'Botanique' and walk 500m up Rue Royale (or catch Tram 92 or 93). You are now in the quarter called Saint-Josse-ten-Noode, a rather rundown area which has a large immigrant popula-tion. At the head of the Rue Royale is the Place de la Reine, in the middle of which stands the* **Eglise Sainte-Marie** *(at the time of writing, closed for renovation).*

This is the most beautiful 19th-century church in Brussels, worth the visit even if you can only see the exterior. It was designed by a 25-year-old architect from Ghent, Louis van Overstraeten (1818–49), who died of cholera just four years after building work commenced in 1845. Its style is best described as Neo-Byzantine: the octagonal ground plan is topped by a star-spangled copper dome and offset by semicircular side-chapels, buttresses, pepperpot spires, rose windows and fretted, receding arches. The builders have used a traditional Brussels mix of stone, cream-coloured for the body of the church and grey for the detailing—the beauty of which has now been restored by cleaning.

> *Retrace your steps a short way down Rue Royale. No. 316 is the cele-brated Art Nouveau bar and restaurant* **De Ultieme Hallucinatie**.

The building dates from 1856, but it was transformed at the turn of the century by Paul Hamesse (1877–1956), a pupil of Paul Hankar (*see* pp.186–7). Even the umbrella stand and piano in the hall have had the Art Nouveau wand waved over them, but the real triumph is the small restaurant (which you can poke your head into from the more spartan bar). Nothing has been left to chance: the chandeliers, stencilled wall-hangings, fireplace, side cabinets, ceiling mouldings, stained-glass partitions—all have been rethought and redefined with the graceful curves and oriental surprise of Art Nouveau. With its dimmed lighting and soft, brooding tones, this restaurant speaks eloquently of the twilight years that preceded the First World War.

> *To return to the city centre you can catch Tram 92, 93 or 94 to* Ⓜ *Parc or Botanique; or go to the stop in front of the Colonne du Congrès and take Bus 29 or 63.*

LE SPHINX MYSTÉRIEUX
(MUSÉES ROYAUX D'ART ET D'HISTOIRE)

V: Quartier Léopold: Heart of Europe

Start: Ⓜ *Luxembourg.*

Walking time: *about 1½ hours to cover the ground, but allow another 3–4 hours to visit the museums.*

V: Quartier Léopold & the Heart of Europe

Belgium burst upon the economic and world stage in the latter part of the 19th century when it began to reap the rewards of its new, coal-driven industries, its reawakened trading links across Europe, and its wholesale pillage of raw materials from the Belgian Congo.

No one stamped this era more decisively than the king, Leopold II (r.1865–1909), who on ascending the throne promised to create '*une Belgique plus grande et plus belle*'. Brussels boomed, and a swathe of wealthy suburbs began to spread out from the old centre, notably in the area just south of the Palais Royal, named after Léopold I. In 1880 Belgium celebrated 50 years of independence with an International Exhibition in the newly laid out Parc du

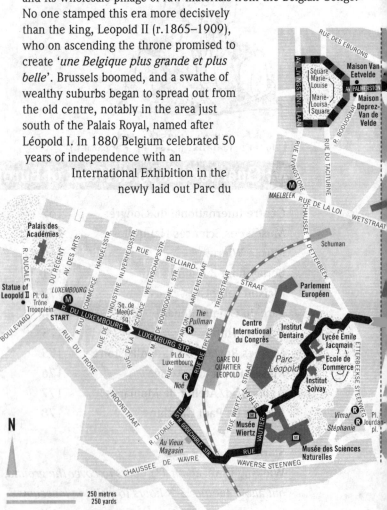

Cinquantenaire. This now forms a grand setting for a series of museums—so grand, in fact, that these major collections rattle about in acres of space and are not quite able to fill the hollows.

This very same part of town was adopted by the headquarters of the European Community (EC)—now more properly called the European Union (EU)—and an unexpected sense of hollowness hangs over that too. At the time of writing, while the EU itself is adrift in the wake of the Maastricht Treaty, the centre of its operations is a building site. In place of grey-suited Eurocrats stepping out of limos, you find burly builders in hard hats charging about in dumper trucks.

This walk includes an optional excursion to Brussels' most floridly Art Nouveau building,

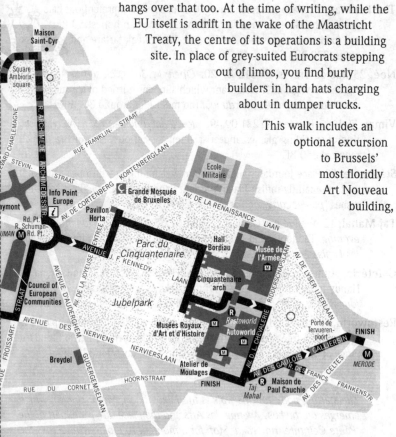

as well as two decidedly zany little museums. The first is the studio of Antoine Wiertz, archetypal artist of 'le Romantisme macabre'—a man who overreached his limited talents so spectacularly that it is almost touching. The second is the Atelier de Moulages, where time stands still among rooms of silent, pristine-white plaster casts, freshly minted from a treasure-house of over 4000 historic moulds.

This walk is suitable for any day except Monday, when all the museums except Autoworld are closed.

lunch/cafés

The Pullman, 12 Place du Luxembourg. One of a set of unpretentious bars around the Gare du Quartier Léopold. Beer at an honest 50 BF; bar food such as *assiette Américaine-frites* (steak tartare and chips, 230 BF.)

Noé, 25 Rue de Trèves, ✆ 512 85 20. *Open 11.30–3, closed Sat and Sun.* Agreeable vegetarian restaurant which supplies hurried office staff with a wholesome, balanced *plat du jour* (no menu) for around 300 BF.

Vimar, 70 Place Jourdan, ✆ 231 09 49. *Closed Sat lunch and Sun.* A stylish setting of sparkling glasses and crisp linen for serious fish cuisine. Lunch menu at 850 BF.

Stéphanie, 52 Place Jourdan. One of several welcoming lunch-stops spilling out on to the faintly raffish Place Jourdan. Sandwiches at 65–85 BF and hot dishes (*poulet curry*, etc.) at around 280 BF.

Taj Mahal, 12 Avenue des Gaulois, ✆ 734 51 55. *Closed Sat lunch and Mon evening.* Tandooris and tikkas served in the Raj-like splendour of a *tous-les-Louis* salon in a *maison de maître*. Set lunch at 580 BF.

Cafétéria, at the Musées Royaux d'Art et d'Histoire, Parc du Cinquantenaire. Handy museum restaurant, serving snacks as well as a range of *plats du jour* such as *scampi à l'ail* (320 BF) and *brochettes d'agneau* (350 BF).

Restoworld, at Autoworld, Parc du Cinquantenaire. Modern, glass-canopied balcony with a free view over the collection of historic vehicles. Standard range of sandwiches and salads; two-course set lunch for 320 BF.

*The starting point for this walk is the Luxembourg Métro station, which emerges on the busy Avenue des Arts and the Place du Trône, part of the 'Petite Ceinture' ring road. Stop for a moment to look north, across the Avenue des Arts. To your right is the **Palais des Académies**.*

This grandiose neoclassical building stands at the foot of the Place des Palais, next to the Palais Royal (*see* **Walk II**). It was built in 1823–6 for the Dutch King, William of Orange, during his brief reign over Belgium prior to independence. It then served as a picture gallery before becoming the seat of the Académie Royale de Belgique, an august society of established figures from the arts and sciences.

*Now look to the left, to the **equestrian statue of Leopold II** on the far side of the Place du Trône.*

It's a solemn, dignified portrait of this powerful, determined and obstinate monarch, who is always immediately recognizable by his voluminous beard, square-cut like a bib. Belgium's second king was driven by the ambition to raise Belgium to the status of a great nation. He was dismissive of the Belgians' natural inclination to modest ambitions—'*Petit pays, petites gens*' ('small country, small people'), he grumbled. Before ascending the throne he embarked on a series of voyages to India, China and North Africa which ignited his growing desire to acquire colonies—a dream eventually realized when he established the Belgian Congo as a personal fiefdom (*see* pp.34–6). Meanwhile he instigated an ambitious building programme, notably in Brussels and Ostend.

The one cloud in Leopold's life was the fact that he had no male heir. His only son died aged ten. He had three daughters, whom he treated coldly and married off unsuitably, and he finally barred succession through them in favour of his nephew, Albert I. If he was capable of affection it was directed not to his family but to a string of mistresses, including the dancer Cléo de Mérode, whom he met in 1894. After this, his famous beard became the leitmotiv for a deluge of scurrilous cartoons. In 1899 he became enamoured of 17-year-old Blanche-Caroline Delacroix, la Baronne de Vaughan, and his liaison with her continued after the death of his long-suffering wife in 1902. Caroline gave Leopold two children, and it is still a mystery whether or not he made an honest woman of her on his deathbed, when he was 74.

*Turn immediately to your right down the Rue du Luxembourg, which leads through the Square de Meeûs, an attractive patch of green dotted with sculpture and shaded by mature trees. Continue to the **Place du Luxembourg**.*

This picturesque if rather rundown square was laid out in the mid-19th century beside the mainline railway station, then called the Gare de Luxembourg but since renamed the Gare du Quartier Léopold. Today the neoclassical façade of the station is dwarfed by the huge, glass-fronted, barrel-vaulted **Centre International du Congrès**, which rises up from the other side of the tracks. This will be the new Brussels headquarters of the European Parliament. The European Parliament, of course, usually meets in Strasbourg, but from time to time it ups sticks and heads for Brussels *en masse*; meanwhile a number of parliamentary committees have their base in Brussels, close to the two other main EU institutions, the Council of Ministers and the European Commission.

The Centre International du Congrès will not be completed until 1996, by which time visitors will be able to reach the building by a concourse leading from the Place du Luxembourg and the station. This development will completely change the character of the Place du Luxembourg, which at present is an agreeably sleepy backwater, lined with a series of small restaurants and bars catering for people with time to spare on their way to and from the station. The Pullman at No. 12 is a bar where '*il n'y a pas de clef*' ('there is no key'). In other words, it is always open to serve a cast of characters in a twenty-four-hour slice-of-life drama. These include overalled city workers dropping by at 7am for *un petit coup*, usually a small beer, to start the day on a good note (a dying tradition), and youthful party-goers returning home after late-night revels. Het Ketje at No. 4, on the opposite side of the square, is another such bar. (*Ketje* is a cherished *bruxellois* term for a young lad.)

The statue in the middle of the square depicts the British entrepreneur John Cockerill (1790–1840), who brought British steel-manufacturing techniques to Belgium and built an industrial empire upon them. Whether he deserves the inscription '*Au père des ouvriers*' ('To the father of the workers') is debatable.

> Pending completion of the concourse through the station to the Centre International du Congrès, you have to walk to a bridge over the railway line, a little to the south of here, to reach the other side. Turn right in front of the station and leave the Place du Luxembourg by the Rue de Trèves. Take the first left, Rue Godecharle. The whole of this quarter is currently undergoing massive renovation. A rare survivor is an antique shop at 39–41 Rue Godecharle, called **'Au Vieux Magasin'**. This Aladdin's cave of miscellaneous bibelots (knick-knacks) has been here since 1908. When you reach the Chaussée de Wavre, turn left, then take the second left, the Rue Vautier. A short way along, on the right-hand side, is a large modern façade studded like a chocolate box with gold crowns, with a statue of a dinosaur in front. This is the **Musée de l'Institut Royal des Sciences Naturelles**. Open 9.30–4.45, Sun 9.30–6, closed Mon; adm 120 BF, children 6–17 years old 90 BF.

Its modern shell incorporates a 19th-century museum inaugurated by Leopold II in 1891. The original halls, with their tiled floors and ornate, painted, cast-iron structure, were built to house a major find of iguanodon skeletons at Bernissart (near Mons) in 1870. These have now been joined by a dozen or so life-size, moving, roaring models—the survivors of a temporary exhibition called

Dinosaurs & Co. This section is still the highlight, and your life really would not be much the poorer if you gave the museum a miss. (Children, however, seem to enjoy it.) The main body of the museum consists of hundreds of stuffed animals and skeletons displayed in a maze of long rooms, floors and corridors, which are interconnected by lifts and spiral staircases. It is in a constant state of flux, and even if you invest in a plan of the layout you are likely to find your progress unexpectedly barred by sections that have been cordoned off. There are some redeeming features besides the dinosaurs, however, such as the rooms of glittering, gem-like minerals, and an impressive collection of shells. The only living representatives of the animal world are a set of scorpions and some large, forlorn-looking, hairy spiders.

> Turn right as you leave the museum and continue down Rue Vautier. The street takes a turn to the left, and on this corner, on the left-hand side is the **Musée Wiertz**. Open April–Oct 10–12 and 1–5, Nov–Mar 10–12 and 1–4, closed Mon; adm free.

This is one of the truly original sights of Brussels. For one thing, it offers the rare possibility of seeing inside a 19th-century artist's studio. But this was not just any 19th-century artist—this was Antoine Wiertz, who from an early age liked to compare himself to Rubens and Michelangelo. His ambitions and delusions were on a truly epic scale.

Antoine Wiertz (1806–65) had the misfortune to win the Prix de Rome in 1832, after which he felt he was on course for true greatness. He set about painting a series of vast canvases (11m tall, 8m wide) depicting melodramatic biblical or classical scenes and using ambitious perspectives in the style of Rubens—but unfortunately without his genius. Notwithstanding, Wiertz had his admirers in Brussels, and he hatched a grand plan to enable him to make the most of his talents. In 1850 he approached the government with a proposal: if the state would build a studio large enough for him to carry out his projects, he would bequeath the studio and his works to the nation as a museum. The state agreed—a measure of Wiertz's standing in Brussels in his day—and here you see the consequences.

The main part of the studio is an aircraft-hangar of a room, just high enough to hang several immense canvases. These are rather crudely executed (supposedly in imitation of fresco) and instantly forgettable. Wiertz's more remarkable works are on a smaller scale, technically very uneven, but stamped with his own peculiar vision. Some are a bizarre combination of the macabre and erotic; others are loaded with a crushingly blunt moral message. (If you are being charitable, you can say he prefigured the Symbolists and Surrealists.) His famous *La Belle Rosine* depicts a sensuous nude woman gazing at a skeleton which has a label on the skull bearing the former owner's name: 'La Belle Rosine'. (Oh, the fickleness of life!) *Le Suicide* graphically illustrates a young man blasting his brains out with a pistol under the covetous gaze of good and bad angels. In *Une Scène d'Enfer* (A Scene from Hell) distraught men and women present severed limbs to a smouldering (literally) figure of Napoleon.

There are some real gems in the smaller rooms to one side of the studio. The criminal laxity of doctors is paraded in *L'Inhumation Precipitée* (The Overhasty Burial), in which a body is seen emerging from a coffin in a crypt—despite an inscription scribbled on the coffin affirming that doctors had certified the victim well and truly dead. *La Liseuse de Romans* (The Reader of Novels) shows what happens if you have the wrong kind of bedtime reading: a woman lies reading in naked abandon, while a horned devil pushes corrupting literature towards her.

Antoine Wiertz saw himself as a visionary, a socialist, a breaker of taboos. He was ruled by obsessive ideas, one of which was inspired by the rejection of a painting by the Paris Salon of 1839. Stung by this, he launched a campaign calling for the development of Brussels as a giant metropolis—a vast, glittering city of magnificent buildings, industry and commerce, arts and literature, which would render Paris a mere *ville de province* by comparison. He wrote a tract entitled 'Bruxelles Capitale et Paris Province' (his hand-written version hangs in the passageway outside the studio). Amongst the ravings of his overwrought mind, one reads this impassioned address to the city of Brussels: '*Vous vous appelez capitale de la Belgique; votre position géographique est belle; celle que vous occupez dans l'industrie et les arts est plus belle encore; osez dire ceci et sans trembler: je veux être capitale de l'Europe.*' ('You call yourself the capital of Belgium; you have a fine geographical position; your position in industry and the arts is even better; dare to say without hesitation: I want to be the capital of Europe.') Crackpot or visionary? Antoine Wiertz would have been deeply gratified to see the capital of Europe now blossoming on his very doorstep.

> *Cross Rue Vautier as you leave the museum and turn left. A few metres down the hill, on the right-hand side, is a gap in an ivy-covered wall. This leads into* **Parc Léopold**, *which runs along the back of the Centre International du Congrès. Follow the paths to the left as you walk into the park, keeping a set of elegant 19th-century buildings to your right. These include the recently restored Institut Solvay (one of the Solvay family's noble public works, see p.184), a former Ecole de Commerce of the Université Libre de Bruxelles, and the Lycée Emile Jacqmain, a hand-*

some mixture of cast-iron and stone, where neoclassical collided with Art Nouveau in 1895. Walk down the hill, past the Institut Dentaire (dental school) built in 1935, and follow the path around the back of the lake to the gate at the northeastern corner of the park. As you leave the park, look left along Rue Belliard to the modern bridge supported by glinting steel spans and crowned by a pair of naked female statues waving ribbons. This is part of the **Parlement Européen**, *the current headquarters of the European Parliament in Brussels.*

The bridge in fact links the old European parliament building to its modern extension on the right-hand side of the road. Built in 1988–90, the extension has a squat, muscular shape, and is rather more challenging and satisfying than the new Centre International du Congrès, which is something of an architectural cliché.

Now look straight ahead to the huge brown-marble, plate-glass sprawl on the other side of Rue Belliard. This is the new headquarters for the **Council of the European Union**.

This unappealing hulk has been built to house the offices of the Council of Ministers, a forum at which ministers from member states gather to discuss EU policy—backed by some 2500 officials. The Council is the main decision-making body of the EU, although the European Parliament is gradually edging into its sphere of action. (Note, by the way, that the term European Community still exists—this is the formal legal entity of the European Union.) The President of the Council changes every six months so each country can have a turn in rotation.

Use the crossing to your right, over the Chaussée d'Etterbeek, and walk up Rue Belliard, which is boarded up and dilapidated, awaiting complete refurbishment. Turn left up Rue Froissart, which runs alongside the Council of European Communities. At the top of Rue Froissart you come to a rather desolate roundabout, the **Rond-Point Schuman**.

This whole area is now a patchwork of buildings under construction, vacant properties held together by a peeling skin of posters, temporary wire barriers, piles of steel joists, and broken pavements. Welcome to the heart of Europe.

In front of you, across the Rond-Point Schuman, is the curving, dark-ened, plate-glass façade of the **Berlaymont Building**, *the former home of the European Commission.*

For two decades after its completion in 1970, the Berlaymont Building with its twelve flags fluttering before it was the very symbol of the European Community. Then in 1991 disaster struck: it was found to be riddled with asbestos, and was thus in breach of the very regulations overseen by the thousands of Eurocrats within it. The Berlaymont Building was vacated, and the offices of the Commission scattered about the district. The asbestos is now being removed at vast cost, and the building is due to reopen for business in 1999.

> *Turn right as you enter Rond-Point Schuman, and cross the Avenue d'Auderghem. Look to your right as you do so. On the right-hand side is a row of flags. These stand in front of the* **Breydel** *building, which currently serves as the headquarters of the European Commission.*

The Commission is another key EU institution, an autonomous body designed to see that the European Union functions correctly. It is led by 17 commissioners who are appointed by member states but do not take instructions from their governments: their loyalties—in principle at least—are to the Community itself.

> *Continue walking around the Rond-Point Schuman to the next road that enters it, the Rue de la Loi. This offers a fine view of the huge triumphal arch—topped by a chariot drawn by four horses—that dominates the Parc du Cinquantenaire. We shall come to this later. For now, continue your journey by crossing the Avenue de Cortenberg. On the next corner is* **Info Point Europe** *(Open Mon–Fri, 9–4).*

This information centre—spattered with EU flags, with the ring of stars on a field of sky blue—has been set up by the Commission to disseminate literature about the workings of the European Union. Here you can get up to date with European health and safety regulations, or the latest edict of the Common Agricultural Policy. Alternatively, if the EU is still a complete mystery to you, you can pick up one of their beginner's guides, such as the handy *Europe in Ten Lessons*. It's also a good place to gauge something of the supra-national idealism that was the original inspiration of the EU and still informs its activities.

> *From here you have the option of taking a half-hour excursion to see the façades of one of Brussels' most flamboyant Art Nouveau houses and a celebrated house by Victor Horta. (If you would rather head straight for the Parc Cinquantenaire, go to p.174.) Turn right by Info Point Europe and walk down Rue Archimède to Square Ambiorix, a large, scrappy patch of greenery, named after the rebel chieftain who wiped out a Roman garrison in 54 BC. Go straight across the square. A short distance to your right, at 11 Square Ambiorix, is the* **Maison Saint-Cyr***.*

This extraordinary building takes the Art Nouveau idiom to its ultimate conclusion: the façade is a veritable cascade of looping carved stone, swirling wrought iron and entwined woodwork. Glass occupies almost the entire width of its narrow groundplan, veiled by the web of intricate balustrades lining the curving balconies. There is barely a straight line in sight.

One would not call the Maison Saint-Cyr beautiful: in fact the overall effect is almost unsettling. Here Art Nouveau drifts towards the sickly, degenerative art deplored by the more functionalist designers of the Arts and Crafts movement and the Vienna Secession. Such elaborate fantasies, however, were the hallmark of the architect of the Maison Saint-Cyr, Gustave Strauven (1878–1919). This is his most famous work, all the more remarkable considering that he was just 20 years old when he designed it. (Art Nouveau is dealt with in greater detail in Walk VI.)

> Turn left and follow the pavement around the edge of Square Ambiorix to Avenue Palmerston, named after the British Prime Minister, Lord Palmerston (1784–1865), who had been foreign secretary at the time of Belgian independence. At the foot of this sloping road, at No. 4 on the right-hand side, is the **Maison Van Eetvelde**, a house designed by the father of Art Nouveau architecture, Victor Horta, in 1895–7.

Compared with the Maison Saint-Cyr, this façade is very strait-laced. However, it is typical of Horta, who applied Art Nouveau sparingly and with rigid discipline (for more about Victor Horta see pp.187–9.) The very restraint of this design, with its cast-iron columns and pronounced horizontals, was novel for the time. Art Nouveau embellishments can be seen in the curved brackets beneath the first-floor projection and the decorative panels between the windows. Horta was particularly renowned for his interiors—in this case an ingenious design arranged around an octagonal well and lit by an overhead glass canopy.

> On the opposite side of Avenue Palmerston, at No. 3, is the **Maison Deprez-Van de Velde**, also by Horta. It was built at the same time as the Maison Van Eetvelde, and its exterior is even more conventional.

> Avenue Palmerston leads down to the **Square Marie-Louise**, effectively a semi-circular park, filled by a large duck pond with a soaring water jet in the middle. If you have time, you can extend this excursion a further quarter of an hour by walking around the Square Marie-Louise.

The view across the pond and up the sloping Avenue Palmerston to Square Ambiorix shows what the planners had in mind whan they laid out this area: green and spacious, it is one of Brussels' most surprising and elegant vistas.

> Now retrace your steps to the Rond-Point Schuman, and take the Avenue de la Loi towards the Parc du Cinquantenaire. Cross the **Avenue de la Joyeuse Entrée**.

From earliest times the rulers of Brabant were acclaimed by their subjects in a procession known as the *Joyeuse Entrée* (*Blijde Inkompst*), during which representatives of the people offered their assent to their new ruler in exchange for his undertaking to protect their liberty and privileges. It served as a kind of charter and constitution, and remained a valid benchmark of government until the end of the 18th century. The tradition is still maintained today, albeit in a watered-down form: after making his vows to parliament—to defend the constitution and the integrity of Belgium's borders—the new king performs the *Joyeuse Entrée* by greeting the public throngs gathered before the Palais Royal in a prolonged bout of hand-shaking.

On the other side of the **Avenue de la Joyeuse Entrée** *is a bust of* **Robert Schuman***.*

This statue, and Rond-Point Schuman, honour the memory of Robert Schuman (1886–1963), the French statesman whose Schuman Plan led to the formation of the European Coal and Steel Community in 1952. This was the embryo, based on a vision of European integration, from which the EC/EU was to develop.

Now enter the **Parc du Cinquantenaire***.*

During the late 19th century there was a succession of great international exhibitions, beginning with the Great Exhibition of 1851 in the Crystal Palace built in Hyde Park, London. These fairs were designed to promote industry and trade, and above all to trumpet the prestige of the host nation. Huge halls were built to house comprehensive displays of the latest and best manufactured products, from porcelain to steam engines, as well as all manner of gadgets and inventions to delight the public, who thronged to the fairs in their thousands. Brussels played its part. The year 1880 marked the *Cinquantenaire* (the 50-year jubilee) of the Belgian nation. At Leopold II's insistence, an area reserved for military manoeuvres was transformed into a park in which the exhibition halls were built. The original plan was designed by the architect Gédéon Bordiau (1832–1904), who adapted it over the remainder of his career for further exhibitions in 1888 and 1897. In the 1880s Bordiau's complex consisted of a pair of large, barrel-vaulted exhibition halls linked by a semicircular colonnade which met at a triumphal arch. The rudiments of this concept have survived, although today's triumphal arch was added in 1905 to mark Belgium's 75th anniversary. The copper-green quadriga on the top of the arch is by Thomas Vinçotte (1850–1925), official sculptor to Leopold II: if it looks familiar, no doubt it reminds you of the more famous Brandenburg Gate in Berlin, created over a hundred years earlier. In Leopold's Brussels, originality was not a criterion.

Since 1880 these buildings have had a varied history as exhibition halls and museums. Today they house three major museums: the Musées Royaux d'Art et d'Histoire, the Musée Royal de l'Armée, and Autoworld.

*First of all, however, turn left and walk down the shady sand avenue to a temple-like building in the northeast corner of the park. This is the **Pavillon Horta**.*

Also known as the Edicule Lambeaux, this was designed by the young Victor Horta in 1889, during the period when he was working closely with his neoclassically oriented master, Alphonse Balat. It is, in effect, a straightforward neoclassical temple, with a few streamlined refinements, and was built to house a series of remarkable relief sculptures called *Les Passions Humaines* by Jef Lambeaux (1852–1908). Lambeaux set about his subject with the same graphic realism as his contemporary, Rodin—with the result that the contents of his pavilion earnt a reputation for being shocking. Today they are not easy to see, but for reasons of economy rather than morality—the Musées Royaux d'Art et d'Histoire run occasional tours during the summer months.

Just beyond the Pavillon Horta is the Grande Mosquée de Bruxelles, one of the few purpose-built mosques serving Brussels' large Muslim population.

*Now walk along the avenue leading toward the main Cinquantenaire buildings. This is a pleasing park of sandy walkways shaded by mature trees. Sadly, however, it has never been quite the same since the Avenue J.F. Kennedy surfaced in its midst to give its thundering lanes of traffic a breath of fresh air before plunging them back into a tunnel beneath the Cinquantenaire arch. The first building you come to is the Hall Bordiau. This is the sole survivor of the pair of exhibition halls designed by Bordiau—a huge canopy of glass and blue-painted cast-iron, and a monument to 19th-century industrial ingenuity. Its twin stood on the other side of the Cinquantenaire arch but was destroyed by fire in 1946; rebuilt in a different, but sympathetic style, it now forms part of the **Musées Royaux d'Art et d'Histoire** (the entrance is marked with a large green arrow). Open Tues–Fri 9.30–5, Sat and Sun 10–5, closed Mon; adm free, but see p.195.*

Since its foundation in 1835, this collection has accumulated a wealth of historical artefacts, in the tradition of the great European capitals—from Phoenician glass and Hoplite helmets to medieval tankards and Renaissance armillary spheres, from *netsuke* and Chinese Buddhas to Brazilian Indian headdresses and erotic Art Nouveau sculptures. In early 1993 a further 30 newly refurbished rooms were opened up, focusing on pre-Columbian art and artefacts from Central and South America.

The museum is set out in a series of palatial halls and corridors and clusters of smaller rooms, separated by sweeping marble staircases and domed lobbies topped by glass lanterns. (Bordiau, it might be noted, was also the architect of the sumptuous Métropole Hôtel, *see* **Walk IV**.) Vast though the whole collection is, however, it is barely large enough to fill the huge space assigned to it.

You cannot hope to see everything, partly because of the scale of the place, partly because many of the sections are frequently closed off. The best policy is to decide what you want to see, then use the colour-coded map of the museum's three levels, displayed in the foyer (with lights to indicate which sections are open and closed), to plan your route.

Particularly worth seeking out are the 'Sculptures et Arts Décoratifs' of the Middle Ages and Renaissance (Level 1, red section). This includes superb Brussels tapestries designed by Bernard van Orley (*c.* 1499–1541), a remarkable collection of carved, painted and gilded retables (altarpieces) for which Brussels was famous, as well as church treasures and reliquaries, and fragments of medieval houses.

Level 1 also includes a series of rooms (light blue section) displaying 19th-century furniture, one of which contains some superb examples of the Empire style—the form of neoclassicism favoured by Napoleon, ornamented by ormolu sphinxes, lion's feet and palmette motifs. Also in this group is 'La Salle Wolfers', in which Art Nouveau and Art Deco artefacts are displayed in glass-fronted cases from the Magasins Wolfers, designed by Victor Horta in 1909. Art Nouveau had a special line in sensuous female statues for the mantelpiece, made of ivory, silver and bronze—a theme later given a more overtly erotic twist by Art Deco designers. *Le Sphinx Mystérieux*, a helmeted female bust made of ivory and cupro-silver, might be seen as a kind of icon of the age.

> *Turn right as you leave the museum and walk under the Cinquantenaire arch. Immediately to your left you will see the* **Musée Royal de l'Armée et d'Histoire Militaire***. Open 9–12 and 1–4.45, closed Mon; adm free.*

This is another huge collection, but rather easier to assimilate in a quick visit, mainly because the core is packed into a series of rooms close to the entrance. The oldest part of the exhibition (installed in 1923) contains ranks of antique, glass-fronted cabinets stuffed with uniforms, weapons, flags and assorted military mementoes, mainly from the 19th century. Portraits of mustachioed generals, tattered regimental colours and neatly arranged sunbursts of rifles, swords and lances on the walls create the cheery atmosphere of a baronial hall. Running parallel to this hall is an impressive armour collection, including a complete set of horse armour. Outlying rooms contain heavy weapons from the 19th and 20th centuries, but are often closed because of staff shortages.

Follow signs to the 'Section Air et Espace'. In a vast hall built for the 1910 International Exhibition, big enough to house a Zeppelin, is a jumble of antique and not-so-antique aircraft—from fragile, canvas-winged biplanes of the First World War, which have you reaching for your leather helmet and goggles, to Russian MiGs and a sleek Starfighter. It's a rough and ready display, where children are free to scamper around and rows of worn airliner seats are provided for you to slump into whenever your feet grow weary. Outside, open to the skies, is the 'Section Blindés', a kind of graveyard of tanks and armoured cars.

> As you leave the Musée de l'Armée, cross the large, rather soulless courtyard to reach the opposite side. Housed in a building which is the mirror-image of the air museum is **Autoworld**. Open April–Sept 10–6, Oct–Mar 10–5; adm 150 BF, children 5–13 years old 80 BF.

Filling a vast space beneath the towering cast-iron arches of this trimly restored exhibition hall is a formidable array of over 300 glistening motor vehicles, dating back to the dawn of the combustion engine. There are rickety old horseless carriages, dashing early sports cars, prewar breadvans, tail-finned American gas-guzzlers of the 1950s, and various huge limousines which once transported the rich and famous. The core of the collection was put together by a single private enthusiast, Ghislain Mahy, but the museum is run as a joint-venture project assisted by state funds.

If you are not sure you want to see this, you can get a free sneak preview by going directly to the museum cafeteria, Restoworld, which overlooks the hall.

> In the vaults beneath Autoworld is one of the Parc Cinquantenaire's most extraordinary institutions. To reach it, turn right as you leave Autoworld, then right again along a tree-lined road leading south. (Take care: because there is no pavement, drivers seem to think pedestrians are fair game.) Turn right at the foot of this road, into a car park. Here you will find a notice announcing the **Atelier de Moulages** (Casting and Moulding Workshop). Open Mon–Fri 9–12 and 1.30–4; adm free.

During the 1880s an exhibition of some 5000 plaster casts of famous statues filled the Hall Bordiau, and was greeted with rapturous enthusiasm. A workshop attached to the exhibition could supply copies from the moulds—so members of the public, government institutions and schools were able to order fine art on demand. The Atelier de Moulages has survived since that time, and still has about 4000 moulds, many taken from originals in great art collections around the world. Some are newly created, but others date back to the 19th century. (Their Venus de Milo mould was made in 1893.) In cases where the original has been lost or destroyed, the moulds represent a unique archive.

Over the years, demand has tapered off, but the workshop has been preserved by the state—though now in this less prominent position beneath Autoworld. You are free to wander the workshops and watch a small number of craftsmen produce their pristine-white casts. Behind them are deep, cavernous storerooms where the shapeless moulds lie piled high on wooden racks. Another storeroom contains a jumble of miscellaneous casts: here cultures and historical ages collide in a surreal encounter between nude Greek athletes, Egyptian cats, busts of 19th-century royalty, Madonnas and saints, Roman friezes, horses' heads, Dante and Voltaire, dismembered limbs, Buddhas and death masks.

You can buy casts from the small showroom or order them from the catalogue (allow 3–4 months). Prices vary according to the size and complexity of the piece: they start at 1800 BF; you would need 180,000 BF for a Victory of Samothrace.

Here the walk ends. You can return to the city centre by Métro, which you can take from ⓜ Schuman—reached by a pleasant walk back across the southwestern corner of the Parc du Cinquantenaire. Art Nouveau fans, however, might like to take a short detour to another celebrated house front. Cross the road as you leave the Atelier de Moulages and turn left to walk along the Avenue des Nerviens and the Avenue des Gaulois. Turn right into the Rue des Francs. (These street names celebrate tribes of early Belgian history: the Nervii, Celts and Franks.) At 5 Rue des Francs is the **Maison de Paul Cauchie***.*

This is one of the most spectacular Art Nouveau façades in the city, brought to life by a large, gilded mural of togaed maidens painted in a style reminiscent of Alphonse Mucha and Paul Klimt. The design of the house shows the clear progression towards sterner, more angular shapes that took place after the turn of the century under the influence of the Vienna Secession. The emphasis is on strident verticals and horizontals and clean-cut geometric shapes—far removed from the effusion of curves on the Maison Saint-Cyr.

This was the private house—and the only architectural work—of its creator, Paul Cauchie, a little-known neo-impressionist and Symbolist painter. It was also his studio and workplace, as the painted inscriptions by the door imply: '*M. et Mme Cauchie décorateurs: cours privé d'art appliqué*'. They could hardly have made a more convincing advertisement for their skills.

From here the closest Métro stop is ⓜ Mérode, reached by continuing a short distance up the Avenue des Gaulois.

Start: *intersection of Avenue Louise and Rue Lesbroussart. To reach here from the centre of town go to* ⓜ *Place Louise, then take Tram 93 or 94 down Avenue Louise to tram stop Lesbroussart.*

VI: Art Nouveau: Ixelles, Saint-Gilles

Walking time: *about 2½ hours; allow a further 2 hours to visit the three museums. (Note that most of the Art Nouveau buildings described are not open to the public.)*

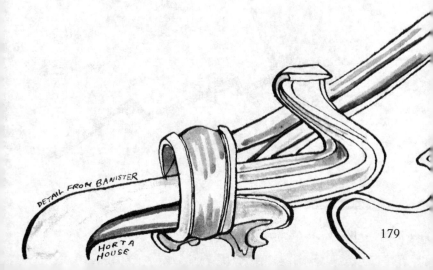

DETAIL FROM BANISTER

HORTA HOUSE

VI: Art Nouveau in Ixelles and Saint-Gilles

Brussels is an Art Nouveau city *par excellence*. In the 1890s this novel decorative style swept through the recently built suburbs like a new religion: no progressive house owner would consider anything else. Art Nouveau peppers just about every street dating from this era—sometimes in the form of full-blown Art Nouveau *hôtels* (large private houses), but more often in countless small details, such as swirling ironwork railings, curvaceous door handles and hinges, or plaques featuring dreamy maidens with blonde, flowing hair. Even after decades in the doldrums of fashion—

PLACE LOUISE
600 metres

CHARLEROISESTWG.

RUE FAIDER

R. DE LIVOURNE

AVENUE LOUISE

STR.

LIVORNOSTR.

Hôtel Tassel

START

R. P. E. JANSON-

STRAAT

STRAAT

La Tsampa

Hôtel Solvay

LOUIZ

RUE DEFACQZ

RUE SIMONIS

BALJUWSTR.

R. DE AMAZONE

R. DU BAILLI STR.

R. DE L'AQUEDUC

Trinité

STR.

WATERLEIDINGSSTRAAT

CH. DE CHARLEROI

AFRIKASTR.

Musée Horta

RUE AFRICAINE

RUE AMERICAINE

STRAAT

TENBOSSTRAAT

AVENUE DUCPETIAUX- LAAN

La Quincaillerie

RUE DU PAGE

Pl. A. Leemans-pl.

AMERIKAANSESTR.

CHAUSEE DE STR. WATERLOO

BRUGMANN- LAAN

Hôtel Hannon

AV. D. L. JONCTION VERBINDINGSLN.

AVENUE

AV. DU HAUT- PT.

STRAAT

RUE FRANZ MERJAY-

NEURAK STR.

R.F.

RUE DE LA REFORME

RUE DE LA REFORME

La Canne en Ville

RUE TENBOSCH

RUE WASHINGTON-

Le Pain Quotidien

AVENUE LOUIS LEPOUTRE

WATERLOOSE-STEENWEG

R. DE L'ABBAYE

N

250 metres
250 yards

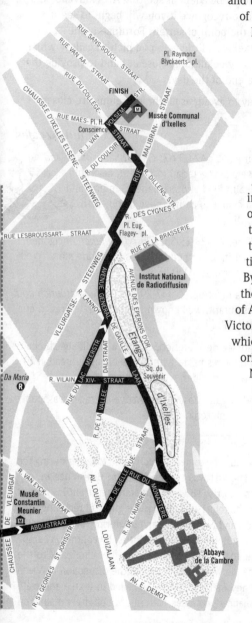

and the widespread destruction of much of Brussels' Art Nouveau heritage—there is plenty of it about.

There are famously extravagant Art Nouveau houses scattered all over Brussels (such as the Maison Saint-Cyr and Paul Cauchie's house—*see* **Walk V**), so it's impossible to encompass all of them in a single walk. But this itinerary takes you through an area with a particularly high concentration. By no accident, this was also the quarter where the doyen of Art Nouveau architecture, Victor Horta, lived. His house, which is the embodiment of the originality and felicity of Art Nouveau style, is now one of Brussels' most celebrated museums, and a focus of pilgrimage. Do not expect to be alone when you visit it. Art Nouveau has become a popular passion, fuelled by tourist-office leaflets and numerous publications—some of which were timed to coincide with Art Nouveau's declared centenary in 1993.

After this walk you should be adept at spotting Art Nouveau, and once you have learned to recognize it you will begin to see it everywhere—even to the point of surfeit. Fortunately the Musée Communal d'Ixelles, a little gem of a picture gallery which stays open until 7pm on weekdays, is close at hand to provide the perfect antidote at the end of the day.

Monday is the only day to avoid, as all the museums are closed.

---

lunch/cafés

La Tsampa, 109 Rue de Livourne, ✆ 647 03 67. *Closed Sat evening and Sun.* A cut above the average vegetarian restaurant, beautifully set out at the back of a health-food shop. Japanese, Indian and Vietnamese touches add colour to an inventive menu, with main dishes at 350–430 BF.

La Quincaillerie, 45 Rue du Page, ✆ 538 25 53. *Closed Sat lunch.* Invigorating restaurant newly installed in an authentic 1900s hardware store. Well-prepared French cuisine at around 1000 BF.

La Canne en Ville, 22 Rue de la Réforme, ✆ 347 29 26. *Closed Sat lunch and Sun.* Charming small restaurant, well-known for its first-rate French cuisine. Bargain lunch at 380 BF.

Le Pain Quotidien, 515 Chaussée de Waterloo. One of a small, stylish chain offering imaginative sandwiches made with hunks of rustic bread (120–300 BF) and washed down with cider, wine or coffee.

Da Maria, 153 Chaussée de Vleurgat. *Closed Sun.* Above-average, reasonably priced Italian restaurant and pizzeria.

Art Nouveau was the result of four phenomena which came together during the latter half of the 19th century. The first was the revolution in British design, pioneered in the 1860s by William Morris (1834–96). It stemmed from his disgust with industrial design, which in the mid-19th century was guilty of recycling tired old styles, such as the neoclassical and Neo-Gothic, and plastering them willy-nilly on mass-produced goods of all descriptions. William Morris, by contrast, championed the beauty of hand-made goods and craftsmanship. Looking back to the guilds of pre-Renaissance Europe, he wanted to eliminate the distinction between craftsman, artist, architect and designer. He himself excelled in textile and wallpaper designs; his beautifully balanced, complex patterns, which drew mainly on the organic shapes of plants, were hugely influential in Europe. His ideas were adopted by several design movements in Britain, notably the one that, after 1888, was referred to as Arts and Crafts.

After the 1860s Japan began to emerge from a 200-year hibernation and Europe was seized with a fascination for all things Japanese: fans, prints, kimonos, ceramic vases. Japanese design seemed remarkably inventive and original—in its colour combinations, its unexpected compositions, and its confident use of asymmetry. For European artists and designers this was hugely emancipating. Shops such as Liberty's in London (founded in 1874) bought large stocks of Japanese goods, which were sold side by side with their own lines of the latest Arts and Crafts products—jewellery, candlesticks, lamps, ceramics and pewterware.

Meanwhile, the development of new building materials, notably cast iron, meant that architects could now create structures in any shape they fancied, and light them with picture windows, glass canopies and decorative screens of leaded glass.

The final phenomenon affecting Art Nouveau was urban development. With the expansion of suburban transport systems—notably the trams and the railways in the case of Brussels—new suburbs mushroomed. Some 30,000 houses were built in Brussels during the last four decades of the 19th century.

In Belgium this combination of factors led to a search for a brand new style which would appeal to the acquisitive, newly wealthy middle classes, who were well informed about current trends and had no particular nostalgia for the patrician styles of old. During the 1880s and early 1890s, architects and designers were stimulated by a rash of architectural competitions, and by high-profile art forums, notably Les XX (*see* pp.74–5) and its subsequent manifestation La Libre Esthétique, which directly encouraged dialogue between thinkers, artists, craftsmen and decorators. At first they drew on a broad variety of models ranging from Tuscan villas to Moghul palaces, producing what has subsequently become known as the 'eclectic style'. Then, in 1893, a 32-year-old architect called Victor Horta (1861–1947) designed a house for an engineer and professor called Tassel. The Hôtel Tassel, with its organic, flowing shapes in ironwork, stained glass and carved stone, caused a sensation. Many saw it as a monstrosity, others championed it as a masterpiece. Soon Horta was inundated with commissions. Meanwhile the message was spread by other architects and designers, such as Henri van de Velde, Paul Hankar, Gustave Serrurier-Bovy, Ernest Blérot, Octave van Rysselberghe, and a host of lesser names eager to jump on the bandwagon.

In the early 1890s this newfound passion for curvaceous, swirling design went by various names, including 'Modern Style' and 'Style Anglais'. In 1894 Henri van de Velde referred to '*un art nouveau*', a term picked up the following year in the name of a new shop in Paris, La Maison de l'Art Nouveau. Art Nouveau was adopted as a label in both French and English, but it had different names elsewhere: Jugendstil in German and Dutch (after a journal named *Jugend*), and Stile Liberty in Italy. It was a truly international style, occurring also in the USA, where Louis Comfort Tiffany (1848–1933) became a leading proponent—remembered mostly for his stained-glass lamps.

One of the few countries in Europe that did not get caught up in Art Nouveau fervour was Britain, still soldiering on with the ideals of more stolid Arts and Crafts design well into the 20th century. Here Art Nouveau was restricted to details such as fireplaces and the stained glass in doors. Home-grown talents, such as Arthur Mackmurdo (who had a direct influence on Belgian Art Nouveau) and Charles Rennie Mackintosh (who was much appreciated by the Vienna Secession, led by Gustav Klimt, among others) were largely ignored in their own country.

By the time of the Paris International Exhibition of 1900, Art Nouveau was all the rage on the Continent. That same year Hector Guimard began designing his famous métro entrances in Paris. Art Nouveau remained a major stylistic force up until the First World War, albeit in an increasingly popularized and watered-down form. After the war, however, it was regarded with some distaste, not simply for being old-fashioned, but because it somehow spoke of the *fin de siècle* decadence that was held responsible for the war. It was ousted by the more strident, angular, Machine-Age style of Art Deco.

Only in the hazy, flower-power romanticism of the late 1960s did Art Nouveau become popular again. By this time many of Brussels' Art Nouveau landmarks had been demolished, or had decayed beyond recovery. Once there had been some 2000 Art Nouveau houses in Brussels; only about half of these have survived.

> From the tram stop at Lesbroussart, cross the busy Avenue Louise and walk a short distance southwards to No. 224 Avenue Louise. This is the **Hôtel Solvay**, designed by Victor Horta.

Ernest Solvay (1838–1922) was a chemist who discovered a way of making soda (still called the Solvay process), which hitherto had only been found naturally in modest quantities as sodium carbonate. As soda was used in the manufacture of a wide variety of industrial products, such as washing soda, soap, paper, glass, ceramics and aluminium, Solvay was on his way to a fortune. He went on to create one of Belgium's great industrial empires, and also became a leading liberal politician, a patron of the arts and a noted philanthropist. In 1894 he commissioned Victor Horta to build and furnish this large private house, which was completed four years later.

Compared to some Art Nouveau buildings, Horta's façades were restrained, but you can detect the spirit of Art Nouveau in the gently curving stonework and in the sinuous ironwork of the balcony railings. Note the cast-iron columns that run up the two storeys of the projecting bays, complete with projecting rivets. No attempt has been made to disguise these. On the contrary, Horta has made a virtue of their industrial connotations—a provocative gesture at the time.

Horta was noted above all for his interiors, with their cunning use of light, ingenious configuration of space, and—despite the emphasis on decorative effect—a rigorous functionalism. He liked to design everything down to the door handles and light bulbs. He was given *carte blanche* by Solvay, and so here he worked in marble, teak and mahogany. You can get a sense of what might lie inside by peering through the glass front door into the spacious hallway, which is lit by Art Nouveau lamps.

> *Retrace your steps, crossing back over Avenue Louise to the Rue du Bailli. At the end of the Rue du Bailli you can see the Baroque façade of the Eglise de la Trinité, which we shall come to later. For now, walk down the Rue du Bailli and take the first right into the Rue de Livourne, which gives you a distant view of the green dome of the Palais de Justice (see **Walk III**). Take the first right again into Rue Paul-Emile Janson. No. 6 is the **Hôtel Tassel**.*

This *hôtel*, designed and built by Victor Horta in 1893–5, is generally acknowledged as the first building in the world in which Art Nouveau was applied to architecture. It has one of Horta's more exuberant façades, with swirling stonework counterbalanced by the stained glass on the first floor. Here cast iron, exploited for both its structural and its sculptural properties, was left exposed for the first time.

Victor Horta believed that a house '*devait être non seulement à l'image de la vie de l'occupant, mais qu'elle devait en être le portrait*' ('should not just correspond to the lifestyle of the occupant, but should be a portrait of it'). Tassel was a bachelor who liked to entertain; an engineer who belonged to the coterie of the new, liberal and artistically minded industrial class; an enthusiastic amateur photographer; and someone who, as a professor at the Université Libre de Bruxelles, needed a quiet space for his studies. Horta had to work all these elements into this building, and succeeded triumphantly.

However, in the long term these highly individualistic specifications were the downfall of such buildings, because it was difficult to adapt them to other uses. When the architect Jean Delhaye, the great modern champion of Victor Horta's work, bought this house in 1980, he found the murals painted over, other

L'HÔTEL TASSEL

decorative features concealed behind false ceilings and panels, and the rooms crudely partitioned to provide student accommodation. Now the house has been beautifully restored, its potential for letting has to be limited to clients who can be trusted to treat it gently. At the time of writing, the Hôtel Tassel is available to rent again—at a comparatively modest annual sum of 4.5 million BF. Only careful clients need apply.

Walk back up Rue P.E. Janson, crossing the Rue de Livourne. No. 23 Rue P.E. Janson has Art Nouveau doors and ironwork. At the top of the street, at **No. 83 Rue Faider,** *is one of the most delightful Art Nouveau façades in Brussels.*

Its undulating stone and ironwork carry the eye upwards from its glass and wooden doors, through the floral motifs in the first floor windows, to the sensual murals on the upper storey featuring a Mucha-style woman, children, poppies and stars. Every detail has been carefully rethought in the Art Nouveau idiom—even the boot scraper and the perversely curved letterbox. Like many Art Nouveau buildings it has been signed and dated like a painting: A. Roosenboom, 1906. Albert Roosenboom (1871–1943) was one of Victor Horta's draughtsmen, but apart from this house he did very little work of his own in the Art Nouveau style.

Turn right up Rue Faider, then right into Rue Defacqz. **No. 48 Rue Defacqz** *is by Paul Hankar.*

Paul Hankar (1859–1901), the son of a stonemason, worked for the architect Henri Beyaert (who designed the Place du Petit-Sablon, *see* **Walk III**), before emerging in the 1890s as one of the most prolific architects of the Art Nouveau style. No. 48 Rue Defacqz was built in 1897 as the house and studio of the Symbolist painter Albert Ciamberlani (1864–1956), who is best known for the huge, semi-circular mural on the Cinquantenaire (*see* **Walk V**). This building demonstrates the new-found freedoms which Art Nouveau offered, with its huge round windows on the first floor and its extravagant fish-bone ironwork on the balcony. Although now peeling, the murals on the upper storey—depicting peacocks, fanciful trees and a lightly draped, idealized family—are typical of the soft-focus mood of Art Nouveau figurative painting.

Next door, No. 50, was also designed by Paul Hankar, in 1898; although radically altered in 1905, it still shows Hankar's imaginative treatment of window space.

It is interesting to compare these with **No. 71 Rue Defacqz**, *reached by retracing your steps a short way and continuing along the street.*

This was the house that Paul Hankar built for himself in 1893–4, right on the cusp between his eclectic period—heavily influenced by Beyaert's medieval and Renaissance styles—and Art Nouveau (note the ironwork in the uppermost arches). It has all the imaginative panache of the architecture of the 1890s but lacks the curvaceous and cohesive vision that developed with Art Nouveau.

For a brief change of mood and epoch, take the second left, down Rue de l'Amazone (no street sign) to a small square called the Parvis de la Trinité. Occupying most of this square is the **Eglise de la Trinité** *(open at irregular hours).*

The gable-like façade of this church is a fine example of the transitional period between the Flemish Renaissance and Baroque—a confection of neoclassical pediments, *oeil-de-boeuf* windows and barley-sugar columns. It was built in 1620, but did not arrive here until 1895. It used to belong to a church on Place de Brouckère in the city centre, but when this was condemned to make room for the new boulevard that was built over the River Senne in the 1870s, members of this parish raised funds to have the façade rebuilt on this site, where it now seems perfectly at home. The interior of the church, however, is bland and disappointing.

There are several Art Nouveau details in the Parvis de la Trinité. At No. 1, the apartments above a butcher's shop are decorated with Art Nouveau murals, while No. 6 has Art Nouveau ironwork on the balconies and tilework featuring swallows and a female head in profile.

Walk around the church into the Rue de l'Aqueduc and turn right. You are now crossing from the Commune d'Ixelles into the Commune de Saint-Gilles, both boroughs created during the late 19th-century building boom. Take the first left into the Rue Africaine. No. 5 has Art Nouveau ironwork at basement level and faded murals on the upper storeys. Take the first right into the Rue Américaine. At 25 Rue Américaine is the **Musée Horta**. *Open Tues–Sun 2–5.30, closed Mon; adm 100 BF on weekdays, 200 BF at weekends.*

Victor Horta built this as his home and studio in 1899–1901, when he was at the pinnacle of his powers. He later wrote wistfully: '*Pourquoi avais-je eu l'impression en cours d'achèvement que j'atteignais au sommet de mon bonheur... et que la courbe descendante s'ouvrait pour moi?*' ('Why did I get the impression as

I put the finishing touches to it that I was reaching the peak of my happiness… and that the downward curve now opened up before me?')

Victor Horta, the son of a Ghent shoemaker, had been something of a child prodigy. He attended architecture courses at the Académie des Beaux-Arts in Ghent from the age of 13, and won a gold medal for his work two years later. He spent three influential years as an apprentice in Paris (1878–81) before returning to study at the Académie des Beaux-Arts in Brussels. Here he joined the practice of Alphonse Balat (1818–95), Leopold II's favourite architect, who is best remembered for the huge royal glasshouses, the Serres de Laeken (see p.214). These were exceptional not only for their scale but for the novel way in which the external cast-iron structure was turned into a decorative feature.

In 1884 Horta won the Prix Godecharle for architecture (established in memory of the sculptor Gilles-Lambert Godecharle), and the following year he began to design houses on his own account. In 1889 he created the Edicule Lambeaux (now called the Pavillon Horta), a temple-like pavilion in the Parc du Cinquantenaire which was built to house relief sculptures by Jef Lambeaux (see **Walk V**). It demonstrates Horta's strong feeling for neoclassical proportion, which he never totally rejected.

The Hôtel Tassel, built in 1893, was his breakthrough, and for a decade or so Horta reigned supreme in the world of fashionable house-design. He was an *'ensemblier'*—an architect who conceptualized not only the building but everything within it. It was an exacting task, requiring great imaginative and practical energy from himself and his team of draughtsmen. After 1898 he was working simultaneously on both his home and the Maison du Peuple (built 1898–9), an ambitious complex near the Sablon, demolished in 1965 (see **Walk IV**).

In the early 1900s, however, a new vogue began to take over, led by the architects and painters of the Vienna Secession. Like Mackintosh in Scotland, they adopted a more symmetrical, angular, upright look, prefiguring Art Deco. The Palais Stoclet (see p.219) is the outstanding example of this in Brussels. The sensuous, organic lines of Art Nouveau began to look outmoded to private clients, and from now on Horta did little domestic architecture. Instead, he concentrated on a number of new department stores, to which he applied his usual attention to detail. These included L'Innovation (1900–03), in the Rue Neuve, which was destroyed in 1967 by a horrific fire that killed 251 people; the Magasins Waucquez (1903–06), now the home of the Centre Belge de la Bande Dessinée (see **Walk IV**); and the Magasins Wolfers (1909), Rue d'Arenberg, whose salvaged display cases can be seen in the Musées Royaux d'Art et d'Histoire (*see* **Walk V**).

During the First World War Horta travelled to London to take part in a conference on the reconstruction of Belgium. When the Germans discovered this, he was unable to return, and spent the rest of the war in Britain and the USA. When he came back to Brussels in 1919 he decided to sell his house in Rue Américaine, partly because the studio was too small for his practice, and partly because its style was now considered old-fashioned. Horta's new style was more akin to Art Deco, and his major projects of the postwar period were the Palais des Beaux-Arts and the Halte-Centrale in the Quartier Ravenstein (*see* **Walk II**). As a widely respected figure in the architectural world, holding eminent positions at various institutes, he was made a baron in 1932. He died in 1947.

Horta's former home was bought by the Commune de Saint-Gilles in 1961, and opened as the Musée Horta in 1969. The interior, which had remained more or less intact, has been carefully restored and is now furnished with pieces Horta designed for the house, as well as others from his buildings elsewhere. As soon as you walk through the front door, the Art Nouveau motifs in the mosaic flooring and the flowing shapes of the coathooks, hatstand and door furniture tell you that you are entering a manicured environment. As in the jewellery of René Lalique, the glassware of Emile Gallé, or the furniture of Louis Majorelle, the genius of good Art Nouveau design is not just in the grace of these sensuous shapes but in the element of surprise. Look out, for instance, for the ribbed, angular shapes of some of Horta's details, as in the brass, columned pier of the entrance lobby and the supports for the arches in the dining room—a room which, with a stroke of inventive daring, he lined with white-enamelled industrial brick. Much of the furniture is in American ash, a pale, matt-surfaced wood far removed from the typically sombre and heavy furniture of the late Victorian period.

One of the distinctive features of a Horta house is his use of light, particularly in stairwells lit by an overhead canopy of glass. Here the stairs rise to a crescendo of gold, white and copper beneath the glass canopy, enhanced by pond-shaped mirrors, abstracted floral designs on the walls, and the ribbon-like wrought-iron of the light fittings (originally gas) and banisters. The overall effect is one of elegance, comfort and uplifting joyousness.

> *Turn left as you leave the museum and walk to the Chaussée de Charleroi. Straight ahead of you is a branch of Brico, a chain of DIY stores, housed in a 1938 Modernist building that was originally designed as a Mercedes-Benz showroom. Try and picture the vehicles of the*

*1930s set against this architecture. The building looks part of the modern world, while the cars belong to the remote past. Turn left and walk down the Chaussée de Charleroi to the intersection with the Chaussée de Waterloo. Cross straight over into Avenue Brugmann, which is named after Georges Brugmann (1829–1900), a leading banker of the late 19th century and a generous philanthropist. Continue down Avenue Brugmann to the Avenue de la Jonction. At **Nos. 53 and 55 Avenue Brugmann** are two Art Nouveau houses.*

These were built in 1898 and 1899 respectively, by a little-known architect called E. Pelseneer. No. 55 is called Les Hiboux, and has murals, round windows and, on the false chimney tops, sculptures of two owls, which give the house its name.

*However, the main reason for coming here is next door, at the corner of the Avenue de la Jonction. This is the **Hôtel Hannon**, which is now a gallery for temporary photographic exhibitions called **L'Espace Photographique Contretype**. Open 1–6, closed Mon; adm 50 BF.*

Compared to the Musée Horta, this corner house has a spacious ground plan. It was designed for the engineer Edouard Hannon (1853–1931), who worked his way up the Solvay soda empire to become one of its big wheels. He spent part of his career at a Solvay factory near Nancy, in eastern France, where he saw the work of the great Art Nouveau glass, ceramics and furniture designer Emile Gallé (1853–1904). When Hannon decided to build his *hôtel* in 1902, he persuaded his friend the architect Jules Brunfaut (1852–1942) to abandon his usual eclectic style and create a wholly Art Nouveau house, and he commissioned Emile Gallé to design the furniture and other accessories. Following Gallé's death in 1904, Hannon asked Louis Majorelle (1859–1926), also from Nancy, to take his place. In other words, this was once one of the great Art Nouveau houses of Europe.

Hannon was a major art collector, and was a patron to James Ensor and Emile Claus, among others. He was also a gifted photographer, and during the 1870s he helped to pioneer the art of landscape photography. Unfortunately, all the original contents of the house have now been dispersed; the house itself was only saved from destruction by the intervention of the Commune de Saint-Gilles in 1976, and remained a vandalized wreck until renovation in 1984–8. The architectural rudiments of the house remain, together with the Tiffany-influenced stained glass in the large bow window and the striking set of murals by Paul-Albert Baudouin, a French artist who passionately wanted to revive traditional techniques of fresco painting. The murals in the stairwell and main living room, therefore, are genuine frescoes, painted, like early Renaissance works, directly on to wet plaster.

Leaving the Hôtel Hannon, cross the Avenue Brugmann and walk down the street almost opposite, the Avenue du Haut Pont. Turn left into the Rue Franz Merjay, then first right into the Rue de la Réforme.

This is a typical late 19th-century street built for the well-to-do. Its cobbled pavements are overlooked by tall, terraced houses, whose front doors open directly on to the street. The narrow façades created an ideal canvas upon which to apply Art Nouveau style—as can be seen at No. 79 (murals under the eaves) and No. 74 (ironwork and murals).

*Turn left when you reach Avenue Louis Lepoutre, then right into the Chaussée de Waterloo. Take the third left, the Rue de l'Abbaye, walk up the hill, and cross the Chaussée de Vleurgat. At 59 Rue de l'Abbaye is the **Musée Constantin Meunier**, the house where Meunier lived towards the end of his career. Open 10–12 and 1–5, closed Mon; adm free. Ring the bell for admittance.*

The painter and sculptor Constantin Meunier (1831–1905) is best remembered for his bronzes of industrial workers—notably the gaunt forge-workers called *puddleurs* ('puddlers'), with their round leather hats to protect them from sparks. In his early career, Meunier painted only monastic and religious scenes, but between 1879 and 1881 his visits to the industrial regions around Liège and the coal-mining Borinage district (which also so impressed the young Van Gogh at about the same time) left a deep mark. Meunier thereafter became a social realist in the mould of Gustave Courbet and Jean-François Millet. Although he played with impressionism and pointillism, generally he stuck to his guns throughout a period when other painters were using ever more luminous colours and challenging the very basis of figurative painting. Barring the odd lapse into sentimentality, Meunier's work has a deep sense of conviction, and the power to evoke the hardships of physical labour and the misery of industrial society through which pride and dignity burn like embers.

The museum consists of a collection of Meunier's paintings, drawings and sculpture set out on the ground floor and in his large, north-facing studio to the rear. It includes sketches and trial work on the theme of fecundity for his monument to Emile Zola, which was erected in Paris but destroyed by the Germans during the Second World War. One of his most famous paintings, *Le Retour des Mineurs*, is on show here; look out also for the dramatic preparatory sketch (in the passage to the studio), in which the miners are rendered in skeletal cross-hatching and set against a dismal industrial landscape.

*Continue along the Rue de l'Abbaye, then cross the Avenue Louise once more. Take the road that leads to the Avenue Louise at an angle, Rue de Bellevue. **Nos. 46, 44 and 42 Rue de Bellevue** were designed by the prolific Art Nouveau architect Ernest Blérot.*

Ernest Blérot (1870–1957) was both a property developer and an architect. It is reckoned that in just eight years after 1897 he created some 200 houses—of which only 50 have survived. Like many of the Art Nouveau architects he was something of an idealist, believing that everyone should have access to practical and stylish living accommodation. His interiors were left deliberately uncluttered, with the emphasis on light and space. This group of three is typical. The exteriors are all variations on the same theme: brick, curving stonework and murals.

***Nos. 32 and 30 Rue de Bellevue** are also by Blérot, and were built at about the same time. Here he has applied the Art Nouveau style to the traditional terraced house. Take the next right, which leads to **No. 30 Rue du Monastère**.*

This is the earliest house attributed to Blérot, dating from 1897. The ironwork is its most striking Art Nouveau feature on an otherwise subdued building. Note, however, the amount of window space, designed to fill the house with light.

*Now for a time warp. Follow the Rue du Monastère down to the arch at its foot. Walk through the arch into the large courtyard beyond. This is the **Abbaye de la Cambre**.*

This tranquil, elegantly proportioned quadrangle is formed by a set of 18th-century buildings which once belonged to the Abbaye de la Cambre. They are now home to various government offices, including Belgium's National Geographical Institute. The property, which extends to the south, nestles in a wooded hollow and provides a haven of peace for dog-walkers and strollers. It includes a series of duck ponds and a raised formal garden that was originally laid out in the 1720s. By virtue of the contrast, you suddenly become aware of the constant throb of city traffic beyond.

Founded in 1201 as a Cistercian nunnery, the abbey thrived in this valley of the River Maelbeek until the religious disturbances of the 16th century. It was renovated during the 18th century, but was then closed by the French in 1796.

*Walk to the **abbey church** at the bottom left of the quadrangle. Open Mon–Fri 9–12 and 3–6, Sat 3–6, Sun 9–12.30. During restoration of the western front, enter via the green door to the left of the main west door.*

This is the sole survivor of the medieval monastery, a simple but pretty Gothic church, with a bare stone nave leading up to a semicircular apse decorated with harmonious modern stained glass. The nave has an unusual vaulted ceiling lined with wood. To the south, in the nook formed by the cruciform ground plan of the church, is the abbey cloister, which dates from the 14th century.

> *Leave the abbey by the Rue du Monastère, take the first right, then the first left, along the road that borders the western side of a park. This becomes the Avenue Général de Gaulle, which runs alongside the two narrow ponds called the* **Etangs d'Ixelles**.

There was once a string of ponds that lined the course of the River Maelbeek. The surviving two were bought by the Commune d'Ixelles in 1871 and became the focus of a small park, while the land on either side was developed as a fashionable residential district. Today the ponds have a calming effect, where mothers push out prams and infants feed the ducks, and lovers sprawl on the grassy banks behind the stooped figures of fishermen.

> *Continue up the Avenue Général de Gaulle beyond the Square du Souvenir, which separates the two ponds, to* **Nos. 38 and 39 Avenue Général de Gaulle**.

These are two more houses by Blérot, dating from 1902 and distinguished by the flamboyant ironwork banisters which lead up to the front doors. Blérot frequently worked on pairs of houses, which together form a unity, but each house nonetheless has been treated individually.

> *Retrace your steps a short way and turn right up Rue Vilain XIIII (sometimes written XIV). This street was named after the statesman Charles Vilain XIIII (1803–78), who as Foreign Minister (1855–7) resisted external pressure to bridle the Belgian press with the famous retort, 'Jamais!'* **Nos. 9 and 11 Rue Vilain XIIII** *are another pair by Blérot, again dating from 1902, but here the composition includes stained glass and murals. Continue up Rue Vilain XIIII, and take the first left.* **No. 40 Rue de la Vallée** *is yet another Blérot, this time a large, individual maison de maître, again 1902. Backtrack to Rue Vilain XIIII, walk up it to the next right, the Rue du Lac. Walk down this to find* **No. 6 Rue du Lac**.

This is something rather different: an extravagant Art Nouveau façade consisting of sweeping circles of stained glass and a stepped, lit stairway that runs diagonally up to a projecting upper floor. It was designed by an architect called Léon Delune in 1904. Note how the top right-hand corner of the front door cleverly forms a quadrant of one of the circular windows.

*Continue down the Rue du Lac to the Avenue Général de Gaulle, turn
left and walk up to Place Eugène Flagey. The unmistakable, tiered round
tower on your right was built as the* **Institut National de Radio-
diffusion***, and now belongs to Radio-Télévision Belge (RTB).*

Although one might not call it attractive, this is something of a classic 1930s
building, designed by Joseph Diongre (1878–1963), who is noted as a pioneer in
the use of reinforced concrete. Its strong emphasis on elongated horizontals
reflects the influence of cruise-ship design on the architecture of this period.

*Walk up Rue Malibran and take what is effectively the third left, the Rue
du Collège. Turn right at the pretty little circus formed by Place Hendrik
Conscience. At 71 Rue Jean van Volsem is the* **Musée Communal
d'Ixelles***. Open Tues–Fri 1–7, Sat and Sun 10–5, closed Mon; adm free.*

This museum is a delight—a small, informal gallery with all kinds of unusual surprises. The collection was founded in 1892 and includes numerous interesting
minor works by great artists, such as sketches by Rembrandt, Boucher, Fragonard
and Delacroix, a tiny self-portrait by Jongkind, 15 original posters by Toulouse-
Lautrec, a small Cubist painting in acrylic by Picasso, a watercolour of Cannes by
Raoul Dufy, and a painted metal work by Frank Stella. Belgian artists are particularly well represented, with paintings by Léon Frédéric, Magritte and Spilliaert.
Two works by Rik Wouters (1882–1916) may help to convince you that he was
one of Belgium's most endearing artists: one a painting of his wife Nel in a red
hat, the other called *La Vierge Folle* (The Mad Virgin, 1912)—a bronze statue of
a nude dancing with energetic abandon, stepping out, arms akimbo. This sculpture is full of the *joie de vivre* for which Wouters' work is celebrated.

*It takes about 40 minutes to return to the city centre on foot. You can
reach the Porte de Namur by following the series of streets leading off
from Rue van Aa opposite the museum entrance, then follow the Rue de
Namur to the Place Royale (see* **Walk I***). Alternatively, Buses 95 and 96
go all the way to the Bourse, near the Grand' Place. They stop at Place
Raymond Blyckaerts, a minute's walk from the museum. To reach it, turn
right as you leave the museum. Turn right into Rue Sans-Souci, then left
into Rue Malibran. Place Raymond Blyckaerts lies at the top of Rue
Malibran.*

Brussels boasts 70 museums in all. Many of these, it has to be said, are tiny, specialist museums of limited interest, open only by appointment or to groups, while others are downright cranky, and disappointing to boot. That still leaves a wealth of hugely varied museums to visit. What follows is a selected list of the best known or more interesting among them.

The admission charges shown are for adults; there are usually discounts for children under 16, and most museums admit children under 4 for free.

You should perhaps be aware that recently there has been discussion about charging an entrance fee for some of the

Museums and Monuments

public museums that are currently free—notably the Musés Royaux des Beaux Arts, the Musées Royaux d'Art et d'Histoire and the Musée Royal de l'Armée. The situation may change while this guide book is in print.

Atelier de Moulages, Parc du Cinquantenaire (on Avenue des Nerviens), © 741 72 94. *Open Mon–Fri 9–12 and 1.30–4; adm free.* Historic workshop producing plaster casts of sculptures; *see* pp.177–8.

Autoworld, Parc du Cinquantenaire, © 736 41 65. *Open April–Sept 10–6, Oct–March 10–5; adm 150 BF.* A gleaming collection of antique and classic cars; *see* p.177.

Centre Belge de la Bande Dessinée, 20 Rue des Sables, © 219 19 80. *Open 10–6, closed Mon; adm 150 BF.* A rather erudite monument to Belgium's major contribution to the comic strip (Tintin, plus many others), housed in a restored department store designed by Victor Horta; *see* p.158.

Historium, Anspach Center (1st Floor), 36 Boulevard Anspach, © 217 60 23. *Open 10–6; adm 190 BF.* The history of Belgium in wax tableaux, with audio commentary; *see* p.148.

Hôtel de Ville de Bruxelles, Grand' Place, © 512 75 54. *Guided tours only, in English, German, Dutch or French: Tues–Fri April–Sept 9.30–12.15 and 1.45–5; Oct–March 9.30–12.15 and 1.45–4; English tours Tues 11.30 and 3.15, Wed 3.15 and April–Sept. Sun 3.15; adm 80 BF* A tour through the halls and audience chambers of the town hall; although the building dates from the 15th century, the interior is 18th-century and 19th-century Neo-Gothic; *see* pp.91–2.

Koninklijk Museum voor Middenafrika, *see* Musée Royal de l'Afrique Centrale.

Musée d'Art Ancien, 3 Rue de la Régence, © 508 32 11. *Open 10–12 and 1–5, closed Mon.* Excellent national collection of art from medieval to 19th century: Bruegel, Rubens, Jordaens, Ensor, Symbolists and many others; *see* pp.108–112.

Musée d'Art Moderne, 1–2 Place Royale, © 508 32 11. *Open 10–1 and 2–5, closed Mon; adm free.* National collection of 20th-century art, particularly strong on Spilliaert, Wouters, Delvaux and the Sint-Martens-Latem school, with a fair number of Magrittes; *see* pp.112–3.

Musée du Béguinage d'Anderlecht, 8 Rue du Chapelain (Anderlecht), © 521 13 83. *Open 10–12 and 2–5, closed Tues and Fri; adm 20 BF.* A charming *béguinage* with reconstructed, furnished interiors; *see* pp.208–9.

Musée Boyadjian du Cœur, *see* Musée de l'Hôtel de Bellevue.

Musée de la Brasserie, Maison des Brasseurs, 10 Grand' Place, © 511 49 87. *Open 10–5; adm 100 BF.* Disappointing beer museum; *see* pp.89–90.

Musée Bruegel, 132 Rue Haute. *Group tours only, by written request*. The house where the Bruegel family probably lived.

Musée Bruxella 1238, Société Royale d'Archéologie de Bruxelles, Rue de la Bourse, ✆ 512 75 54. *Guided tours only, from Hôtel de Ville; adm 80 BF* Visit to excavations of a Franciscan convent, a feature of Brussels for five centuries.

Musée Bruxellois de la Gueuze, 56 Rue Gheude, ✆ 521 49 28. *Open Mon–Fri 8.30–4.30; Sat Jan–May and 15 Oct–31 Dec 10–6; Sat 1 June–14 Oct 9.30–1; adm 70 BF; guided tour on request, 90 BF*. The atmospheric old brewery where Cantillon, one of the great *gueuze* beers, is made in the traditional way from *lambic* (*see* pp.227–30 for an introduction to these unique beers). The beer is brewed only in the winter months (approximately 15 Oct–15 May), but there is still plenty to see outside this period. A must for all beer lovers.

Musée du Centre Public d'Aide Sociale de Bruxelles, Hôpital Saint-Pierre, 298a Rue Haute, ✆ 535 30 28. *Open Wed only 2–5; adm free*. A small collection of bequests, which contains antique furniture and paintings, including an excellent altar piece by Bernard van Orley; *see* p.141.

Musée du Chemin de Fer Belge, Gare du Nord (off the central hall), ✆ 224 62 79. *Open 9–4.30 (upper floor open only 1st Sat of month); closed Sat (except 1st Sat of month) and Sun; adm free*. A small collection of engines and detailed models of trains and carriages; photographs and railway equipment: for railway buffs.

Musée du Cinéma, Palais des Beaux-Arts, 9 Rue Baron Horta, ✆ 507 83 70. *Open 5.30–10.30pm; adm 80 BF*. Extensive collection of mechanisms and cameras explaining the history of the moving image, set in the foyer of two cinemas; silent films to live piano accompaniment included in entry ticket; *see* pp.121–2.

Musée de Cire, *see* Historium.

Musée Communal d'Ixelles, 71 Rue J. van Volsem, ✆ 511 90 84 (ext. 1158). *Open Tues–Fri 1–7, Sat and Sun 10–5, closed Mon; adm free*. Excellent small public gallery with paintings and drawings by Rembrandt, Delacroix, Toulouse-Lautrec, Picasso, Magritte, Spilliaert, Wouters and more; *see* p.194.

Musée Communal de la Ville de Bruxelles, Maison du Roi, Grand' Place, ✆ 511 27 42. *Open Mon–Fri 10–12.30 and 1.30–5, closes at 4pm Oct–Mar; Sat and Sun 10–1; adm 80 BF*. A mixed bag of paintings, porcelain, tapestry, historical models and odds and ends illustrating the history of the city: most famous for its collection of costumes for the Manneken-Pis; *see* pp.86–7.

Musée Constantin Meunier, 59 Rue de l'Abbaye, ✆ 648 44 49. *Open 10–12 and 1–5, closed Mon.* Paintings and sculpture by this noted social-realist artist (1831–1905), housed in his former home and studio; *see* p.191.

Musée du Costume et de la Dentelle, 6 Rue de la Violette, ✆ 512 77 09. *Open Tues, Thurs and Fri 10–12.30 and 1.30–5, open until 4pm Oct–Mar; Sat and Sun 2–4.30; adm 80 BF.* Major collection of lace, as well as 17th–20th-century costumes and textiles; *see* pp.92–3.

Musée David et Alice van Buuren, 41 Avenue Léo Errera (Uccle), ✆ 343 48 51. *Open Mon at 2pm only, guided tour; adm 200 BF.* Dutch banker's elegant private house, with gardens, built and furnished in Art Deco style in the 1930s. It contains a remarkable collection of paintings, including works by Bruegel (a version of the *Fall of Icarus*), Wouters, Van Gogh, and the Sint-Martens-Latem School.

Musée de la Dynastie, 7 Place des Palais (same building as Musée de l'Hôtel de Bellevue), ✆ 511 55 78. *Open 10–4, closed Fri.* A small, well-presented museum for royal-watchers, illustrating the history of the Belgian royals with artefacts, paintings and mementoes; *see* p.115.

Musée des Egouts, Pavillon d'Octroi, Porte d'Anderlecht (on Boulevard du Midi), ✆ 513 09 64. *Open Wed only, 9am, 11am, 1am and 3pm (you may need to ring bell at door on southeast side); adm 80 BF.* An exhibition with video explaining the history of the Brussels sewer system and the fate of the River Senne, which was covered over in the 1860s. Visit includes a descent to see the Senne and a short walk along a main sewer.

Musée d'Erasme, 31 Rue du Chapitre (Anderlecht), ✆ 521 13 83. *Open 10–12 and 2–5, closed Tues and Fri; adm 50 BF.* A collection of books, prints, paintings and furniture focusing on the life and times of the great Humanist Erasmus, who lived in this gabled brick house in 1521; *see* pp.206–8.

Musée du Folklore, Porte de Hal, Boulevard du Midi, ✆ 534 15 18. *Open 10–5, closed Mon; adm 80 BF.* Awaiting completion, this is just a small, temporary collection of toys and puppets, but offers an opportunity to see inside the only surviving city gate, built in the 14th century and restored in the 19th; *see* p.142.

Musée Horta, 25 Rue Américaine, ✆ 537 16 92. *Open 2–5.30, closed Mon; adm 100 BF on weekdays, 200 BF at weekends.* The home and studio of Victor Horta, founding father of Art Nouveau architecture; an Art Nouveau dream, and probably the most memorable of all of Brussels' museums; *see* pp.187–9.

Musée de l'Hôtel de Bellevue, 7 Place des Palais, ✆ 511 44 25. *Open 10–4.45, closed Fri; adm free.* A small but good-quality collection of 18th- and 19th-century furniture, ceramics, knick-knacks and accessories housed in a wing of the royal palace; also includes the Musée Boyadjian du Cœur, a collection of artefacts with the heart as the main motif; *see* pp.114–15.

Musée de l'Hôtel Charlier, 16 Avenue des Arts, ✆ 218 53 82. *Open Mon–Fri 2–5, closed Sat and Sun; adm 100 BF.* Fine private house furnished in the late 19th century with numerous antiques and a collection of contemporary paintings; *see* p.119.

Musée de l'Imprimerie, Bibliothèque Royale Albert 1er, 4 Boulevard de l'Empereur, ✆ 519 53 11. *Open Mon–Sat 9–5, closed Sun; adm free.* Historic printing machines; *see* p.104.

Musée de l'Institut Royal des Sciences Naturelles de Belgique, 29 Rue Vautier, ✆ 627 42 33. *Open Tues–Sat 9.30–4.45, Sun 9.30–6, closed Mon; adm 120 BF.* Dinosaurs (skeletons and working models), stuffed wildlife and glittering minerals; *see* pp.168–9.

Musée Instrumental du Conservatoire Royal de Musique, 17 Petit-Sablon, ✆ 511 35 95 (due to move to 2 Montagne de la Cour). *Open 2.30–4.30, closed Mon; adm free.* A selection of some of the 6000 antique musical instruments in the Conservatory's collection; *see* pp.135–6.

Musée du Jouet, 24 Rue de l'Association, ✆ 219 61 68. *Open 10–6; adm 100 BF.* Charming, child-friendly toy museum in a large old private house; *see* pp.160–61.

Musée Lilliput Belgium ('Centre de la Miniature'), 59 Rue Colonel van Gele, ✆ 732 24 71. *Open Tues–Sat 10–5, closed Sun and Mon; adm 60 BF.* A small exhibition of doll's houses and furniture and other tiny interiors, run by a pair of craftworkers who specialize in miniaturization.

Musée du Livre, Bibliothèque Royale Albert Ier, 4 Boulevard de l'Empereur, ✆ 519 53 11. *Open Mon, Wed, Sat 2–4.45; adm free.* Tiny but well-presented collection of valuable historical books, *see* p.104.

Musée Numismatique et Historique de la Banque Nationale de Belgique, 9 Rue du Bois Sauvage, ✆ 221 22 06. *Open Mon 10–5; July–Aug Mon 10–5, Tues–Fri 2–4; adm free.* Coins and banknotes.

Musée des Postes et Télécommunications, 40 Place du Grand Sablon, ✆ 511 77 40. *Open Tues–Sat 10–4, Sun 10–12.30; adm free.* Small but interesting museum devoted to postal history and the evolution of telecommunications, *see* p.132.

Musée Royal de l'Afrique Centrale, 13 Leuvensesteenweg, Tervuren, ✆ 769 52 11. *Open 16 Mar–15 Oct 9–5.30; 16 Oct–15 Mar 10–4.30; adm 50 BF.* Palatial monument to Leopold II's Africa, containing a large anthropological collection, stuffed animals and explorers' memorabilia; *see* p.221.

Musée Royal de l'Armée et d'Histoire Militaire, Parc du Cinquantenaire, ✆ 733 44 93. *Open 9–12, 1–4.45, closed Mon; adm free.* Vast and impressive collection of arms and armour; includes a collection of historic aircraft; *see* pp.176–7.

Musées Royaux d'Art et d'Histoire, Parc du Cinquantenaire, ✆ 741 72 11. *Open Tues–Fri 9.30–5, Sat and Sun 10–5, closed Mon; adm free.* The national collection of cultural booty from the ancient world, plus Belgian tapestry, glass, clocks, antique furniture and Art Nouveau; *see* pp.175–6.

Musées Royaux des Beaux-Arts, *see* Musée d'Art Ancien, Musée d'Art Moderne.

Musée du Théâtre de Toone VII, 6 Impasse Schuddeveld, ✆ 511 71 37. *Open only in the intervals during performances; adm free.* Exhibition of the puppets used in this unique Brussels intitition; *see* pp.255–6.

Musée du Transport Urbain Bruxellois, 364b Avenue de Tervuren, ✆ 515 31 08. *Open weekends and public holidays only, 1st Sat of April–1st Sun of Oct, 1.30–7; adm free, or 125 BF with return trip on historic tram to Tervuren.* Tram sheds full of the old trams and buses that once ruled the streets of Brussels; *see* p.219.

Musée Wiertz, 62 Rue Vautier, ✆ 648 17 18. *Open 10–12 and 1–5, closes at 4pm Nov–Mar; closed Mon; adm free.* The immense studio of Antoine Wiertz, the ambitious 19th-century creator of famously bizarre paintings, many of which are displayed here; *see* pp.169–70.

Pavillon Chinois, 44 Avenue van Praet (Laeken), ✆ 268 16 08. *Closed for restoration until end 1994.* Dazzlingly ornate Chinese pavilion, with a collection of porcelain; *see* p.215.

Planétarium National, 10 Avenue de Bouchout (Laeken), ✆ 478 95 26. *Open according to a timetable of audio-visual-style presentations; adm 120 BF.* Primarily an educational institution.

Service de Chalcographie, 1 Place du Musée, ✆ 519 56 31. *Open Mon–Fri 9–12.45 and 2–4.45, closed Sat and Sun; adm free.* Not so much a museum as a sales outlet for an impressive collection of historical prints; *see* p.114.

Tour Japonaise, 44 Avenue van Praet (Laeken), ℂ 268 16 08. *Open 10–4.45, closed Mon; adm 80 BF.* Japanese pagoda constructed in 1900, with an ornate interior containing a collection of *samurai* weapons and armour; *see* p.215.

Monuments and Other Attractions

Atomium, Boulevard du Centenaire (Laeken), ℂ 477 09 77. *Open Sept–Mar 10–6; April–Aug 9–8; adm 140 BF.* Famous Brussels landmark: a giant model of an iron atom composed of nine metal spheres linked by tubes; with a panorama at 100m. The dull Biogenium exhibition in the lower spheres traces the development of medicine; *see* pp.216–17.

Basilique Nationale du Sacré Cœur, 1 Parvis de la Basilique (Koekelberg), ℂ 425 88 22. *Easter–early Nov 8–7, winter 8–5; adm free. Panorama from dome Mar–Oct Mon–Fri 11am and 3pm; adm 70 BF.* The green-copper dome that dominates northwestern Brussels belongs to what is often cited as the city's least loved building. Begun in 1905 (another brainchild of Leopold II) and eventually completed in 1930, it belongs to the 'bring-your-own-spirituality school' of ecclesiastical architecture: if you don't, you'll find it about as inspiring as a public swimming bath.

Bois de la Cambre, southern end of Avenue Louise. *Always open.* The wooded park that until 1842 formed the northern tip of the Forêt de Soignes. A favourite spot for walks and picnics, the park includes a large artificial boating lake, cafés and a roller-skating rink.

Brasserie Belle-Vue, 43 Quai du Hainaut, ℂ 410 19 35. *Open Tues 2–6pm, Wed–Fri 10–6, Sat 10–4; adm free.* Guided tours of Interbrew's *lambic* and *gueuze* brewery, with free sample drinks; telephone appointments advisable.

Bruparck, Boulevard du Centenaire (Laeken), ℂ 477 03 77. *Free admission to village.* A pleasant reconstructed gabled village of restaurants and boutiques, which acts as the hub for a variety of leisure attractions: **Mini Europe** (*see* below), **Océade** (swimming-pool complex), and **Kinepolis** (multi-screen cinema complex); *see* p.217.

Cathédrale Saint-Michel, Parvis Sainte-Gudule, ℂ 217 83 45. *Summer 7–7, winter 7–6; adm free.* The Gothic cathedral of Brussels, commonly referred to as Sainte-Gudule; choir currently under restoration; *see* pp.120–21.

Forêt de Soignes. Vast beech forest bordering southeast Brussels, covering 4000 hectares; a remarkably wild area given its proximity to the city, and ravishingly beautiful in its golden colours of autumn. Plenty of good paths for walkers—take your own picnic. A popular starting point is the Abbaye du Rouge-Cloître, a former 14th-century monastery at Auderghem. The forest includes two major tree collections, the **Arboretum Géographique de Tervuren** (Old and New World. trees), and the **Arboretum de Groenendaal** (400 forest species).

Jardin Botanique National, Domaine de Bouchout (Meise), © 269 39 05. *Park open 9am–sunset; adm free. Palais des Plantes (greenhouses) open Mon–Thurs 1–4pm, Sun and public holidays from Easter to last Sun of Oct 2–5.30pm; adm 120 BF.* Park and national botanical collection in the grounds of a château that belonged to Charlotte, Empress of Mexico (sister of Leopold II).

Kasteel van Beersel, Beersel (8km south of Brussels), © 331 00 24. *Open Mar–mid Nov Tues–Sun 10–12 and 2–6; mid Nov–Dec and Feb Sat and Sun 10.30–5 only, closed Jan; adm 60 BF.* Robust medieval castle on a small lake. It consists of three massive towers joined by a curtain wall; the interiors are stark but atmospheric.

Mini Europe, Bruparck, Boulevard du Centenaire, © 478 05 50. *Open April–June and Sept–Oct 9.30–6, July–Aug 9.30–8, Nov–early Dec 10–6; closing extended by 1 hr on Sun May–Sept; closed early Jan–late Mar; adm 380 BF, children under 12 years old 290 BF.* Some 300 architectural landmarks of Europe reduced to head-height models; *see* p.217.

Palais de Charles de Lorraine, 1 Place du Musée, © 519 53 71. *Guided tours only, by telephone appointment; adm free.* Elegant, if sparsely furnished, 18th-century apartments in palace of fashionable Austrian governor.

Palais de Justice, Place Poelaert, © 508 61 11. *Mon–Fri 9–4; adm free.* The vast law courts that dominate southern Brussels, the supreme example of megalomaniac neoclassical architecture, *see* pp.136–7.

Palais Royal, Place des Palais. *Open for guided tours during August; consult the tourist office.* Grandiose, somewhat soulless staterooms in the royal palace, built 1904–12, *see* p.114.

Porte de Hal, *see* Musée du Folklore.

Serres Royales de Laeken, Domaine Royal (Laeken). *Open for guided tours in April–May only; consult the tourist office and book early.* Superb series of greenhouses in the grounds of the royal palace of Laeken; designed in the 1870s by Alphonse Balat; *see* p.214.

Peripheral Attractions

THE ERASMUS HOUSE

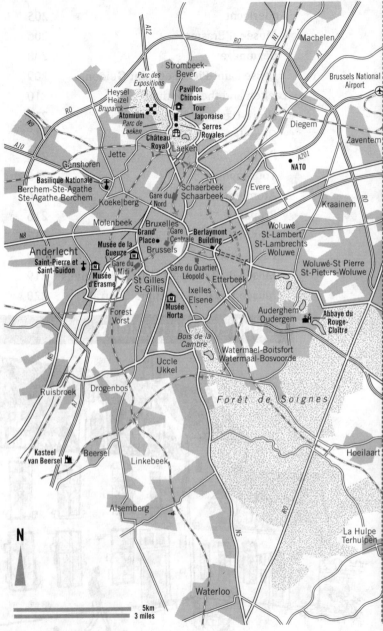

The main sights of Brussels are packed conveniently close to the city centre, but there are a few others that justify a short journey to the outskirts. Some of these are well publicized, such as the Atomium: resembling an outsized model from a school physics lab, it has virtually become a city emblem. Others are lesser-known gems, such as the Béguinage at Anderlecht and the Tour Japonaise at Laeken.

Anderlecht

This excursion could be combined with visits to the Musée des Egouts (see p.198, Wed only) and the Musée de la Gueuze (see p.196); Bus 47 connects Porte d'Anderlecht with the Place de la Vaillance. Also the Basilique de Koekelberg (see p.201); use the Métro link between Saint-Guidon and Simonis.

Start: *Saint-Guidon.*

Walking time: *it takes no more than 15 minutes to walk this circuit, but allow a further 2 hours to see the sights.*

The name Anderlecht will set bells ringing in the mind of any soccer fan: Anderlecht is one of Europe's premier football teams, and its 28,000-seat stadium in the Parc Astrid is situated in the heart of this commune. Anderlecht was once an outlying village of Brussels, clustered around an old and atmospheric church, until the late 19th century when it was radically transformed into an industrialized suburb. However, it still retains the independent atmosphere of a village, and there is a distinct air of prosperity in its many shops and restaurants.

During the 13th century a small *béguinage* was founded in the shadow of the church; this is now a charming small museum. Three hundred years later the great humanist Erasmus came to live nearby for a brief period, and his house is also a museum now. The museums are closed Tuesdays and Fridays.

lunch/cafés

Café-Brasserie Bellevue, corner of Rue de Veeweyde and Place de la Vaillance. Modern brasserie where locals come to eat simply but well. Standards such as *tomate-crevettes grises* (485 BF), washed down with *gueuze*.

In de Stad Brugge, 29a Place de la Vaillance. Cosy old-fashioned brasserie serving steak and chips at 450 BF.

Le Béguinage, 3 Place de la Vaillance, ℭ 523 08 44. Stylish, agreeable tavern-cum-restaurant, open all day every day for *la cuisine française non-stop*, including a *plat du jour* Mon–Fri at 295 BF.

*Walk out of the curious circular Métro station of Saint-Guidon and turn left down the main road, Avenue Paul Janson (note the late Art Nouveau façades at Nos. 28 and 8). Take the first left, which leads into the Place de la Vaillance, a pretty, early 20th-century evocation of a Flemish Renaissance square. The church at the top of the square is the Eglise Saint-Pierre et Saint-Guidon. Take the first right in the square, the Rue du Chapitre. Cross the road and walk through the archway in the brick wall facing you to enter an attractive courtyard leading up to an L-shaped, step-gabled house. The date 1515 is written in wrought iron on one façade. This is the **Musée d'Erasme** (Erasmus Museum). Open 10–12 and 2–5, closed Tues and Fri; adm 50 BF, plus 20 BF for the loan of an invaluable catalogue (in English) of the 663 exhibits.*

Desiderius Erasmus (*c.* 1469–1536) was one of the great scholars of the Renaissance, and did much to release intellectual thought from the shackles of Christian dogma and medieval superstition. Born Geert Geerts in Rotterdam, the illegitimate son of a priest, he did what many a bright boy of his time did and joined a monastery to pursue a life of learning, taking on the name of Desiderius ('beloved') Erasmus (after St Erasmus, *see* p.210). In 1492 he was ordained as a priest. However, he became frustrated with the restricted intellectual life of the monastery and went to a college in Paris, where he earned a reputation as an inspired teacher. He began his life of travelling from one scholarly establishment to another, in the Netherlands, Italy and England (Oxford in 1499 and Cambridge in 1509–14).

During his stay in England he became friends with Thomas More, who encouraged him to write his most famous work *In Praise of Folly* (1509), a satire directed mainly against theologians. In 1516 he became adviser to the young Duke of Brabant, shortly to become the great Emperor, Charles V, and wrote *The Education of a Christian Prince* for him. That same year he also published his ground-breaking Latin translation (from Greek) of the New Testament.

Erasmus taught piety, pacifism, equality for women, and tolerance, illuminating the world with the torch of humanism. Strictly, humanism referred to a new emphasis on secular studies (the humanities)—informed by the rediscovery of classical literature—as opposed to religious studies. Its development coincided with the growth of universities as the leading centres of education, at the expense of the monasteries. (Erasmus helped to found the famous College of Three Languages at Leuven in 1517–21.) But humanism was also a reassertion of the dignity of human life. Previously the Church alone had controlled moral and intellectual issues; ordinary people were generally classed as sinful and could not hope for anything but eternal damnation. The humanists placed people back at the centre of the stage, offering them the choice of leading moral, dutiful and Christian lives in return for the opportunity to reassess and reshape their world.

This intellectual emancipation required enormous courage, diplomacy and determination, with the hugely powerful forces of the Church and vested political interests ranged against it. The prejudices of Erasmus's detractors were soon confirmed: his attacks on the abuses of the Catholic Church (notably in *Colloquia*, 1519) were considered to have a direct influence on the Reformation which had been set in motion by Martin Luther in 1517.

Although Erasmus distanced himself from the Reformation and contested the theology of Martin Luther, he found himself in the midst of religious controversy—a life-threatening game then as now. In the latter years of his life he was based in Basle, but was forced to flee to Germany between 1529 and 1536 when religious fanatics made life too hot for him there. He returned to Basle in 1536 and died the following year, aged 67.

In 1521 Erasmus spent five months at this house, as a guest of Canon Wijkman, enjoying the country air and the relaxing atmosphere. 'I would be dead by now had I not left the stench of the city [Brussels],' he wrote in one of his thousands of charming, witty and erudite letters.

The brevity of his stay here undermines the museum's claim to be the 'House of Erasmus', but don't let that put you off. Restored in the 1930s, after a century of neglect, it consists of a series of rooms containing a rich collection of books, furniture, paintings and engravings from the life and times of Erasmus. Furthermore, it is a rare opportunity to see the interior of a 16th-century gabled house. The centrepiece, the Salle de Renaissance, is decorated with embossed Spanish leather wall-hangings—rare today but a common treatment in their time. In the cabinets here you'll find various editions of *In Praise of Folly* and the *Colloquia*, as well as a chilling collection of books that have been censored. Sections of Erasmus's work have been ripped out, inked over or scored through; in one case even the genitals of cherubs on a title page have been covered over. There is a list of books dated 1537 in which Erasmus's works have been crossed out by the Inquisition and the following inscription inserted: '*Auctor damnatus: opus vero permissum-correctum est*' ('Condemned author: work authorized after correction'). Also in this room is the museum's most remarkable painting: an Epiphany triptych by Hieronymus Bosch (1450–1516), featuring red-nosed peasant numbskulls gathered around a lowly cowshed in a medieval Flemish landscape.

> On leaving the museum, walk towards the east end of the church. To the right of the church you will see a white signpost pointing to the **Béguinage/Begijnhof**. Open 10–12 and 2–5, closed Tues and Fri; adm 20 BF.

This tiny enclave—it's really just two shuttered, red-brick cottages facing each other across a courtyard with a well—is the only surviving béguinage in Brussels.

Béguinages were communities of single women which developed during the 13th century, mainly in response to the imbalance caused by the Crusades: for several centuries there just weren't enough men to go around. Rather than living in isolation or with married relatives, many unmarried women preferred to join a *béguinage* until a suitable partner turned up. Widows (themselves often young) could also stay in a *béguinage*. By and large, the women came from fairly well-off backgrounds, as they had to pay an entry fee and maintenance. These were pious communities, usually closely connected to a church, but the *béguines* were not nuns. They made simple vows of chastity and obedience to their superiors (the elected *maîtresses*), applicable for the duration of their stay. They led modest but comfortable lives, assisted by servants and estate workers, and spent their time in prayer, in making lace, biscuits and sweets, in looking after the sick in their infirmary, and in distributing gifts to the poor. The origin of the word *béguinage/begijnhof* remains obscure. One legend refers to Saint Begga, a 7th-century noblewoman who founded a convent and seven churches near Namur after her son found a hen shielding seven chicks from his hounds. A more plausible derivation recalls a priest from Liège, Lambert le Bègue ('the Stutterer'), who encouraged crusaders' widows to form communities, an idea that quickly spread throughout the Netherlands and Germany. Béguinages remained a widespread feature of society in the Low Countries—the larger ones had over a thousand members—until the 18th century, and a few continue to operate to this day. Even when deserted, they have a unique atmosphere of care, moderation and tranquillity.

This *béguinage*, founded in 1252, had a complement of just eight béguines. The tiny rooms have now been set out as a museum, evoking the atmosphere of the *béguinage* when it was in operation, with its minuscule chapel, a simple bedroom, and a kitchen with rush chairs set around the cast-iron stove. The first room on the left-hand side contains photographs of Anderlecht in the late 19th century when it was still semi-rural. The attic has been set aside as a local folklore museum. In the right-hand side one room has been arranged as the *béguines'* shop, where they would sell *speculoos* biscuits (shaped in wooden moulds) and festive loaves decorated with plaster discs illustrating children's stories and so forth. Look out too for the display cabinet devoted to St Guidon (or St Guido, *c.* 950–1012), a local saint who is celebrated as the protector of stables and cowsheds and the healer of livestock and of human contagious diseases. The cabinet contains *ex voto* offerings, made to accompany some special plea: miniature cast-iron limbs, wax models of cows and pigs, tin noses.

> *As you leave the Béguinage, turn right and walk around to the door in the south side of the church, the* **Eglise Saint-Pierre et Saint-Guidon**. *Open Mon–Tues, Thurs–Sat, 9–12 and 2.30–6, Wed 9–6 (closes at 5 in winter), Sun 9–12.*

This is one of Brussels' few surviving Gothic churches, a robust piece of late medieval architecture with thick stone walls and a roofline bristling with dragon-like gargoyles and crockets. A spire was added in the 19th century—an airy confection of stonework as delicate as Brussels lace. Chapels on this site date back to at least the 10th century, but this church was designed largely by Jan van Ruysbroeck (architect of the old Hôtel de Ville, *see* pp.91–2) and built between 1470 and 1515. Sadly, the fabric of the exterior is in such a sorry state that much of it has had to be fenced off.

Once the streets around this church thronged with horses and cattle, for it was the focus of the cult of St Guidon, whose tomb lies in the 11th-century crypt. Until about 20 years ago, local people still brought their animals—particularly their horses—to the church at Pentecost and on the saint's feast day (the first Sunday after 12 September) in order to have them blessed. The interior is cool and dingy, with cylindrical grey-stone columns and shadowy recesses, redolent of its medieval past. To the left of the entrance door is the Chapelle de Saint-Guidon, tacked on to the church in the first half of the 16th century. It was here that pilgrims would bring their *ex voto* offerings to plead for St Guidon's intercession. Further up on the south side of the church is the Chapelle de Notre-Dame de Grâce, which contains a statuette of the Virgin Mary that has been venerated here since 1449. This chapel was dedicated to St Guidon and is decorated with original 15th-century frescoes depicting his life. The pulpit in the nave also takes up the theme of St Guidon, showing him with a full-sized cow and a horse.

The church was once lavishly decorated with early 16th-century wall-paintings, some of which were discovered beneath a layer of whitewash in 1840. In the north wall of the nave is a graphic depiction of the martyrdom of St Erasmus, whose guts were slowly wound on to what looks like a kind of barbecue spit. St Erasmus (also called St Elmo) was an early Christian who became the patron saint of sailors. His symbol was the windlass, and this somehow got translated in the medieval mind into an instrument of torture.

In the north transept there is a 15th-century relief sculpture, which serves as a memorial to Albert Ditmar (d.1439), doctor to various Dukes of Burgundy, including Philip the Good (*see* p.54). Ditmar is portrayed kneeling before the Virgin and Child, and St Guidon features in one corner surrounded by his animals. A curiously lifelike black-stone effigy of a 14th-century knight in armour (Jean de Walcourt) lies on the left-hand side of the choir. Opposite is the memorial to Arnoul de Hornes (died 1505) and his wife Margaret of Montmorency, who were forebears of the ill-fated Count Hornes (*see* p.57).

Retrace your steps through the Place de la Vaillance to Ⓜ *Saint-Guidon.*

Laeken and the Atomium

This could be combined with a visit to the Basilique de Koekelberg (see p.201) (use the Métro link between Ⓜ *Heysel and* Ⓜ *Simonis).*

Start: Ⓜ *Bockstael. Alternatively you could cut this walk short and see only the highlights by going to* Ⓜ *Bockstael and taking Bus 53 to the stop called Pagodes (Pavillon Chinois and Tour Japonaise).*

Walking time: *about 3 hours, plus a further hour to look around the Tour Japonaise and the Atomium.*

Laeken is a breezy parkland district of northern Brussels, synonymous with the large royal palace and its extensive domain which accounts for much of the surrounding area. The magnificent royal glasshouses, the Serres de Laeken, built during the reign of Leopold II, are open to the public for only a very limited period in spring, but nearby you can see two outstanding monuments to Leopold's more exotic fantasies, the Tour Japonaise and the Pavillon Chinois—vivid flashes of Orientalism in this remote and unlikely corner of the city.

A walk across the Parc de Laeken leads to the Atomium—a hilarious 1950s space-age fantasy which dominates the northern skyline and has the best panoramic view over Brussels. In its shadow lies Bruparck, an ersatz Flemish village of restaurants and boutiques surrounded by a model villag), a multi-screen cinema complex and an indoor swimming-pool and water-fun complex. The promoters of Bruparck call it 'Europe's leisure capital', but it's not nearly as bad as that. Go for broke: bring your swimsuit!

On Mondays the Tour Japonaise is closed; at weekends the Atomium and Bruparck can get very busy.

---

lunch/cafés

On a fine day the shady Parc de Laeken is a good place for a picnic, with views over the city of Brussels to the south.

Restaurant Adrienne, at the top of the Atomium (take the lift to Panorama), ✆ 478 30 00. *Closed Mon evenings and Sun.* Copious buffet lunch (650 BF, or 750 BF with additional hot dish), with unsurpassed views. Reservation advisable.

Atomium Brasserie, in one of the Atomium spheres, access through Biogenium exhibition. For surrealists: the domed ceiling is covered with a naive map of the northern hemisphere showing where the now defunct Ekla beer was sold. Sandwiches, fantasy ice-creams and pricey omelettes and salads (around 300 BF).

Chez Léon, in Le Village at Bruparck. A new branch of the famous Chez Léon (*see* p.83), serving mussels (550 BF) and other Belgian standards; menu at 645 BF.

L'Arbre d'Or, in Le Village at Bruparck. Convincing traditional-style tavern-restaurant serving reasonably priced lunches.

Simplon-Express, in Le Village at Bruparck. Brasserie in a restored 1929 railway carriage and mock station platform. Inventive menu of authentic regional dishes such as *Brusselse kiek à la broche me kompot* (grilled chicken with apple purée) and *gauffres* (waffles). Three courses for around 800 BF.

Fritekot, in Le Village at Bruparck. A place to sample the famous Belgian chips in 60 BF cornets—with mayonnaise, of course.

---

*From Boekstael turn left down Rue Léopold I, which leads to the extraordinary Neo-Gothic church of **Notre-Dame de Laeken**. Open only during services (Sun am) and first Sunday of the month April–Oct 3–5.*

Laeken has been the out-of-town residence of the royal family since the days of the first king of the Belgians, Leopold I, and Notre-Dame de Laeken is effectively the royal chapel. It was designed after 1853 by Joseph Poelaert (architect of the Palais de Justice, *see* **Walk III**) and completed in 1870. It is exceptional for its sheer lumpy quality, now accentuated by grime—a kind of Lego-land church with a bizarre rocket tip emerging from the choir.

*The church is built over the **Royal Crypt**. Open first Sun of the month April–Oct 3–5; on the anniversaries of the deaths of King Albert (17 Feb, 2–6), Queen Astrid (29 Aug, 2–6), Leopold III (25 Sept, 10–12 and 3–5.45), and on All Saints' Day (1 Nov, 10–12 and 3–5).*

This clinical-looking marbled sepulchre contains virtually every past member of the Belgian royal family, from Leopold I to Baudouin I, who was interred here in 1993. The various queens buried here include Astrid (*see* below) and Charlotte (1840–1927), daughter of Leopold I and wife of the ill-fated Maximilian, Emperor of Mexico, who was executed in 1867.

*If you look south from the church, down the Avenue de la Reine, you can see all the way to the Eglise Sainte-Marie (see **Walk IV**). The Avenue de la Reine crosses the Willebroeck Canal, which slices through northwest Brussels. First completed in 1561 to connect Brussels to Antwerp and the North Sea, the canal played a major role in the city's prosperity. Today it is a large, workaday canal, and not particularly lovely.*

*Walk around the west side of the church, past the solemn monumentt to French soldiers killed on Belgian soil in the First World War and its flame to the Unknown Soldier, to the entrance to the **Cimetière de Laeken** (Laeken cemetery). Open 8.30–4.30, closed on Mondays 15 Nov–20 Sept.*

This is one of Brussels' most celebrated necropolises, tightly packed with ornate tombs topped by broken columns, urns, angels and statues of incongruously sensual grieving maidens. The majority of the tombs near the entrance are late 19th century, many belonging to the great and the good of Brussels' public life. The architects Joseph Poelaert (1817–79) and Alphonse Balat (1818–95) are buried here, as is playwright Michel de Ghelderode (1898–1962). Near the east gate, beyond the remnant of a 13th-century church, is a copy of Auguste Rodin's bronze *The Thinker*, contemplating the tomb of an art critic called Jef Dillen. Although French by birth, Rodin lived and worked in Brussels during the 1870s.

> *The main entrance to the cemetery is also the only exit. Walk back around the church, and cross the Avenue du Parc Royal at the pedestrian crossing on its eastern flank. Turn left and walk up the Avenue du Parc Royal. On the right, just after the Rue des Vignes, is a pretty park of plane trees and copper beeches, set around a temple-like* **monument to Queen Astrid***.*

The Swedish Princess Astrid married the future Leopold III in 1926. She was a vivacious beauty who captured the hearts of the Belgians through her natural charm and charitable works, and who was a gift to the burgeoning photographic press. She had three children: Joséphine-Charlotte, who married the Grand-Duke of Luxembourg; Baudouin I, king of the Belgians 1951–93; and Albert II, the present king. In 1935, however, aged just 29, she died in a tragic car accident in Switzerland, a little over a year after Albert I had died in a climbing accident and her husband had become king.

This somewhat spartan monument was erected in 1955 to mark the twentieth anniversary of her death.

> *Continue walking up the Avenue du Parc Royal. This is a noisy road of fast traffic, and the park itself is screened from view by sheets of metal attached to the perimeter railings. At the first park gate, therefore, cross the road (with care) and take a gravel path that leads through a sliver of woodland between the Avenue du Parc Royal and the large red-brick Caserne Sainte-Anne (barracks). Take the left-hand fork in the path, which leads to the tiny, white-painted Chapelle de Sainte-Anne and, close by, a fountain in a sunken pit which was erected in 1625 during the reign of Infanta Isabella. You are now on the edge of the* **Parc de Laeken***.*

This agreeable, undulating park contains two royal palaces, both sealed off from the public and more or less obscured from view: the Stuyvenberg (to the west) and the Belvédère, over the hill to the north.

In dry weather you can walk across the grass; otherwise turn left up the Avenue des Trembles and first right up the Avenue des Narcisses (no street signs here) to reach the distinctive spire that rises up over the **monument to Leopold I,** *standing on the crest of a low hill.*

This is an extravagant and delicate piece of Neo-Gothic erected in 1881 in honour of Leopold I (r.1831–65). Leopold had turned down the throne of Greece in 1830, but agreed to become the first king of Belgium. Having laid solid foundations for the monarchy, he was victim of an unwarranted indignity at his death. Because he was a Protestant, Cardinal Sterckx refused to allow his funeral to take place inside the church at Laeken. His coffin had to be placed in a cardboard mortuary temple outside the church, before being transferred to the cellar which, two years later, was upgraded as the Royal Crypt.

Leopold has a good view down the Avenue de la Dynastie to the **Château Royal de Laeken** *(not open to the public).*

This palace was first built in 1782–4 by the governors who replaced Charles of Lorraine, Maria Christina of Austria and Albert of Saxe-Teck. After coming close to demolition during the French occupation, it was restored as a personal residence by Napoleon after 1804. He was in residence here with his new wife, Marie-Louise, in 1812 when he received intelligence that Csar Alexander I of Russia had decided to reject the Continental System (the blockade of British goods from Europe). At Laeken, therefore, Napoleon drew up the resolution to begin his disastrous invasion of Russia, which was one of the major factors in his downfall. A fire in 1890 destroyed a large proportion of the palace but it was rebuilt along its original Louis XV lines, with neoclassical façades topped by a dome of black tiles. This is now the royal family's preferred residence, and they tend to use their other palace in the centre of town only for formal occasions.

Walk down the Avenue de la Dynastie and around the fencing to the right of the gates. Then walk up the Avenue du Parc Royal. Before long the pagoda-like Tour Japonaise comes into view, and in front of it the tops of some of the **Serres Royales de Laeken** *(glasshouses). Open only for guided tours at end April–early May; apply (from Jan on) to the tourist office in the Grand' Place.*

Frustratingly, this is all you can see of the glasshouses from outside the Domaine Royal—a view that gives only a faint hint of their scale, and not a whisper of their true magnificence. The Serres Royales are a complex of eleven huge barrel-vaulted galleries and glass domes, the largest of which rises to 25m. This extraordinary 'city of glass' was built for Leopold II during the 1870s by Alphonse Balat (Victor Horta's teacher). Inside are extensive collections of tropical and subtropical plants, some dating back to the 19th century. If you are here in spring when the glasshouses are open to the public, it is well worth making a visit.

> *Continue up the Avenue du Parc Royal. Cross the road where it reaches a junction. Facing you is a copy of the 16th-century* **Neptune Fountain** *in Bologna, Italy—a robustly sexual piece, like many public statues in Brussels. Turn right into Avenue Jules van Praet. Now the Tour Japonaise will be in full view on the right-hand side of the road. This is reached by entering the grounds of the glittering building on the other side of the road, the* **Pavillon Chinois**. *Currently closed for restoration, but due to reopen during 1995.*

Following his visit to the Paris Exhibition of 1900, Leopold II hatched a grand plan of lining this street with exotic architecture for the enlightenment of his nation. He commissioned Alexandre Marcel (1860–1928), a specialist in oriental architecture, to devise the plan. The Pavillon Chinois was designed in 1901–2, and its constituent parts were made in Shanghai over the following two years. The final assembly of the pavilion was completed in 1910, after Leopold's death. Restoration is returning this remarkable two-storey building to its original splendour—an intricate jigsaw of gilded wood, polychrome ceramics, carved screens and balustrades, and dainty finials. The equally lavish interior contains a collection of Chinese porcelain and furniture.

> *By walking around to the right of the pavilion, you reach the entrance (via a tunnel under the road) to the newly restored* **Tour Japonaise**. *Open 10–4.45, closed Mon; adm 80 BF.*

This complex consists of a set of Japanese halls leading up to the base of the five-tiered tower. The entrance halls are the work of Japanese architects and builders, and were designed and built in Japan and then shipped over for the 1900 Exhibition. They now contain an admirable collection of Japanese samurai armour and weaponry. The staircase is pure, unashamed 'Japanoiserie'—a stunning marriage of Art Nouveau and Japanese design. It includes luminous stained-glass panels by J. Galland based on Hokusai and other Japanese printmakers, and superb chandelier lamps by Eugène Soleau consisting of entwined foliage and glass lampshades in the form of petalled flowers. The tower itself was designed by Marcel along the lines of a 17th-century Buddhist pagoda; today only the lower level can be visited, an impressive room decorated with Japanese lacquer panels.

> *Retrace your steps to the Neptune Fountain, but instead of turning left down the Avenue du Parc Royal continue straight ahead, along the Avenue de Madrid. Soon the unmistakable orbs of the Atomium heave into view. After 500m or so you come to a strange modern circular*

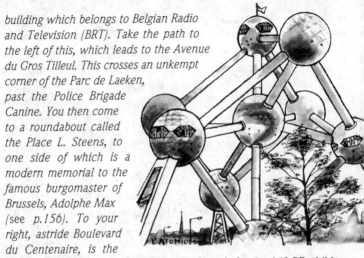

building which belongs to Belgian Radio and Television (BRT). Take the path to the left of this, which leads to the Avenue du Gros Tilleul. This crosses an unkempt corner of the Parc de Laeken, past the Police Brigade Canine. You then come to a roundabout called the Place L. Steens, to one side of which is a modern memorial to the famous burgomaster of Brussels, Adolphe Max (see p.156). To your right, astride Boulevard du Centenaire, is the **Atomium**. Open Sept–Mar 10–6, April–Aug 9–8; adm 140 BF, children 3–12 years old 120 BF. Combined tickets to Atomium and Mini Europe or Océade 470 BF, children 400 BF.

The Atomium was designed as the centrepiece of the Exposition Universelle et Internationale de Bruxelles of 1958—a showpiece of the then-powerful Belgian metal industry. During the 1950s the atomic structure was a popular design theme, first seen on a grand scale at the Festival of Britain Exhibition of 1951 and popularized in the form of 'cocktail-cherry' motifs (coloured plastic beads) found on clocks, coat hangers and record racks of the era. In 1958 a group of Belgian designers went the whole hog, creating this giant-sized version of an iron atom. This is architectural kitsch on a grand scale. Sorely compromised by the practical necessity of grounding the structure to earth with fire escapes, it looks more like a Dan Dare space station than a conceptual image from particle physics. To underline the absurdity of its scale, the Atomium often flies a Belgian tricolour from its top sphere. Yet the Atomium is a remarkable thing: with its nine giant steel balls interconnected by metal tubes (containing escalators) and rising to 120m, it is the Eiffel Tower of Brussels.

Inside, a glass-topped lift whisks you up the central shaft to the Panorama at 100m. From here you can see right across Brussels (assisted by strategically placed maps) to Altitude 100 at Forst, the highest point of the city (100m) way over to the south. You can look down on the Parc de Laeken and over Bruparck. Beside Bruparck, at the top of the Boulevard du Centenaire, is the Parc des Expositions, a huge complex built for another international exhibition in 1935. To its left is the famous Heysel football stadium, where in May 1985 a wall collapsed and 40 people (39 of them Italians) were killed.

Leaving the Atomium, follow signs to **Bruparck**, *which lies 200m to the northeast. Admission to Le Village is free.*

Bruparck was founded in 1987 as a sort of mini theme park. At its heart is Le Village, designed as a traffic-free Flemish town centre, with quaint red-brick, gabled buildings on several levels. These mainly house gift shops and a great variety of pubs and restaurants—Greek, Asian, Belgian, serving everything from burgers and chips to five-course meals. At the centre of Le Village is a children's adventure playground and a small arena where entertainers perform free for much of the year. The atmosphere is peaceful and cheering. The cafés spill out on to the walkways with tables under awnings and umbrellas, filling up with waves of visitors as they drift to and from the three main attractions around Bruparck.

One of these is **Mini Europe**. *Open Apr–June and Sept–Oct 9.30–6, July–August 9.30–8, Nov–early Dec 10–6; opening hours extended by 1hr on Sun May–Sept; closed early Jan–late Mar; adm 370 BF, children under 12 years old 290 BF.*

The Acropolis, the Colosseum, the Leaning Tower of Pisa, the Palace of Westminster, the Eiffel Tower, and much more... Mini Europe contains all the major landmarks of the European Union reduced to one twenty-fifth of their actual size and surrounded by ponds with electronically operated boats and model trains on tracks. However, compared to other model villages (such as the one in The Hague) this is rather sparse and, some might feel, somewhat overpriced.

Bruparck also includes what claims to be the largest cinema complex in the world, **Kinepolis**.

The entrance is either through Bruparck or from the Avenue du Championnat. It includes the Imax theatre (250 BF), which has a vast 600 sq m screen and shows short, specially made films that go for awesome 3D effects (*Fires of Kuwait*, and so on). There are a further 24 screens operating a varying programme.

Lastly, Bruparck offers **Océade**, © *478 49 44. Open 2pm–10pm or 11pm, except during weekends and school holidays when doors open at 10am; closed Mon during school term time; adm for 4 hours 380 BF, children between 1m and 1.3m 320 BF.*

Océade is an inventive complex of indoor swimming pools (at 28°C), saunas, jacuzzis, slides, wave machines and spiralling water shoots, designed for both exhilaration and relaxation in a tropical setting, and suitable for children and adults of all ages.

You can return to the centre of Brussels by taking the Métro from Heysel, which lies just to the north of Bruparck.

Trams and Central Africa

*This excursion could be combined with the museums of the Cinquantenaire (see **Walk V**), and the Forêt de Soignes (see p.202).*

Start: Ⓜ *Montgomery, then Tram 39 or 44 to Dépôt Woluwe. (If you do not wish to stop at the Musée du Transport Urbain, Tram 44 goes all the way to the Tervuren terminus, which is within walking distance of the Musée Royal de l'Afrique Centrale.)*

Walking time: *3½ hours to visit both museums.*

When it came to architecture, King Leopold II did not like to do things by halves. He left his mark in no uncertain terms on various parts of Brussels, notably the centre, and Laeken. At Tervuren, a wooded suburb to the southeast of the city, he built a vast monument to his great colonial endeavour, the Congo (*see **Topics**, pp.34–6*)—a museum to inform the Belgian people about the natural wonders of his vast fiefdom covering much of Central Africa and to tell the story of the brave explorers, soldiers and missionaries who 'liberated' it from slavery and pagan superstition.

Time has virtually stood still in the Musée du Congo, now renamed the Musée Royal de l'Afrique Centrale (or—this being the determinedly Flemish Commune of Tervuren—the Koninklijk Museum voor Middenafrika). The collection of stuffed animals, anthropological spoils and explorers' mementoes is fascinating enough, but the museum itself is also a kind of museum piece. Furthermore, it is set in one of Brussels' most attractive parklands.

At weekends (except in the winter months) you can combine your trip to Tervuren with a visit to the Musée du Transport Urbain Bruxellois—old tramsheds filled with trams of all kinds and ages, run by happy enthusiasts. Add a reclining nude, and you could be in pure Delvaux-land. When the museum is open, historic trams trundle back and forth through the woods to Tervuren.

The Musée du Transport is open only on Saturdays, Sundays and public holidays and closed in winter; the Musée de l'Afrique is closed on Mondays.

Estaminet, at the Musée du Transport. Beer, coffee, light meals (lasagne
etc. for around 200 BF), in a cheery station atmosphere.

La Vignette, 12 Leuvensesteenweg, Tervuren (near the Musée de
l'Afrique Centrale). Straightforward bar-restaurant serving
good Belgian dishes. Set menu at 595 BF.

Le Chalet Vert, 145 Grenstraat, Tervuren (near the Musée de l'Afrique
Centrale), © 767 74 31. French cuisine in a refined yet welcoming
atmosphere, for around 1200 BF. Closed Fri.

---

*To reach these museums by public transport you have to take a tram
along the Avenue de Tervuren from Montgomery. Keep your eyes peeled
near the beginning of this journey: just beyond Square Léopold II, on
the right-hand side, at 275 Avenue de Tervuren, is the **Palais Stoclet**
(not open to the public). For a more leisurely look, you can either walk
the 700m from Montgomery or get off the tram at Père Damien.*

The Palais Stoclet is a classic of modern architecture, designed for a private client
by the Austrian Joseph Hoffman (1870–1956), one of the founder members of the
Vienna Secession. At first glance you would have said it was Art Deco (i.e. post-
First World War): in fact it dates from 1905–9. It is all strident verticals and
receding rectangles, reminiscent of skyscraper architecture. The only element of
decorative whimsy is the four nude male statues, braced to the four winds on the
summit. The interior is also uncompromisingly avant-garde—clear, open rectangular spaces, palatial and luxurious, and a million miles from Art Nouveau which
continued to be the predominantly popular style of this era. Unfortunately you
cannot get nearer than the garden gate.

*The tram continues down the Avenue de Tervuren, past the large, open
Parc Woluwe (on the right), to the stop called Dépôt Woluwe. On the
left side of the road, is the **Musée du Transport Urbain Bruxellois**.
Open 1.30–7 Sat, Sun and public holidays only, from first Sat in April to
first Sun in Oct, adm free, or 125 BF with a historic-tram ride to
Tervuren and back.*

Filling the extensive sheds of this old tram depot are dozens of trams (and some
buses)—essential ingredients in the expansion of Brussels in the 19th century.
The first trams were the horse-drawn *hippomobiles*, introduced in 1835, just
after Belgium's first railway. They went on to dominate urban transport
until 1895, when they were superseded by the electric tram. The museum has

beautifully restored examples of trams of all ages—including the sleek cream and chrome models of the 1950s and 1960s—plus plenty of tram memorabilia, guaranteed to pluck the strings of nostalgia somewhere along the line.

The modern-day Tram 44 runs all the way to Tervuren, passing through woodland at the very northern tip of the Forêt de Soignes; when the Musée du Transport Urbain is open this line is also used by a selection of historic trams, which visitors to the museum can (and should) use. The trams leave from the museum forecourt and run to a published schedule. (The journey takes about 20min each way.)

These historic trams date from the 1920s, but with their panelling and wooden seats they evoke an even earlier era. The ticket collector and the driver dress in period uniforms; you can watch the driver working the primitive controls. At the stops the ticket collector signals to the driver with a duck-like horn.

*At Tervuren, turn left as you leave the terminus and walk 200m down the Leuvensesteenweg (past the petrol station) to the **Musée Royal de l'Afrique Centrale** (or Koninklijk Museum voor Middenafrika). Open 16 Mar–15 Oct, 9–5.30; 16 Oct–15 Mar 10–4.30; adm 50 BF. To reach the entrance, walk through the gates to the back of the building.*

There was once a pleasure palace on this huge domain where Charles of Lorraine liked to hold hunting parties and other festivities, and he died here in 1780. The vast, domed Louis XV-style château that now dominates the park looks as though it might have been built in that era: in fact it was designed expressly as a museum at the end of the reign of Leopold II—at about the same time as the Palais Stoclet. It first opened its doors to the public in 1910, a year after Leopold's death.

The museum contains a large and absorbing collection of historical, anthropological and zoological artefacts: fetishes, jewellery, baskets, weapons, sculpture, masks and headdresses, stuffed wildlife—many of which were collected for the Congo exhibit at the Brussels Universal Exhibition of 1897. Among the most memorable exhibits are an enormous pirogue—a 22.5m long canoe, big enough for 100 men, hewn out of a single tree; a battered trunk used by Dr Livingstone on his last voyage; Stanley's peaked cap; an explorer's tin travelling case that doubled as a hip-bath; slaving manacles; and a pickled coelacanth (the living 'fossil fish', believed to have been extinct for 70 million years until it was discovered off Africa in 1938). Since the 1960s, artefacts from the Americas and Pacific Islands have been added to the collection.

After visiting the museum you can walk down to the lakes at the foot of the park, a place for afternoon strollers, anglers and children feeding the ducks. The thick woods of towering beech trees turn golden brown in autumn—a ravishing spectacle on a bright October day.

Food and Drink

221

> *So prodigiously good was the eating and drinking on*
> *board these sluggish but most comfortable vessels [travel-*
> *ling between Bruges and Ghent], that there are legends*
> *extant of an English traveller, who, coming to Belgium for*
> *a week, and travelling in one of these boats, was so*
> *delighted with the fare there that he went backwards and*
> *forwards from Ghent to Bruges perpetually until the rail-*
> *roads were invented, when he drowned himself on the*
> *last trip of the passage-boat.*

William Makepeace Thackeray, *Vanity Fair* (1847–8)

It is now a well-known secret that Belgium's food ranks among the best in Europe—and that even the French are prepared to admit it. Belgium—and not just Brussels—has an armful of garlanded restaurants over which even the most hardened international gastronomes will bill and coo. You can eat extremely well in Belgium but, more importantly, it is almost impossible to eat badly. Since virtually everyone in the entire nation is an expert on food, restaurants that dare to serve sub-standard fare simply cannot survive. Belgians have a great enthusiasm for eating out. This means that decent restaurants are well patronized and are able to keep their prices competitive. Standards are invariably high—in the humble *friterie* on a street corner as well as at the dizzying pinnacles of *haute cuisine*. The foundations of this impressive tradition are laid by the quality of produce. Everyone in the food production chain takes immense pride in their profession, and they are likewise held in high regard by their clients, provided that the Belgians' fastidious standards are consistently met. Butchers' shops, often family-owned, are run by white-coated staff who will advise customers and discuss their needs—and weather their criticism if ever they should fall below expectations. *Pâtisseries* offer a sumptuous array of glistening *tartes aux fruits*, light and fluffy *tartes aux fromage*, elaborate gâteaux and chocolate extravaganzas.

Good pastries are considered an inalienable part of Belgian living, and *pâtisserie* has been raised to an art form there; even run-down urban districts have a *pâtisserie*, sometimes striking an incongruous note of luxury. The preoccupation with quality extends even to the large supermarket chains, such as Delhaize and GB, where standards are almost as good as in the numerous specialist high-street, family-run concerns. Even so, a fair amount of Belgium's food is grown in the back yard, where small *potagers* are coaxed into producing immense quantities of nutrition from tightly packed rows of carrots, sprouts, beans, endives, artichokes, asparagus, celery and tomatoes.

Some Belgian Specialities

Belgian food is solidly northern European, hearty and copious—with a touch of genius that lifts it above the ordinary. Clearly it is closely allied to French cuisine, but its most famous dishes are still firmly rooted in burgher traditions and by and large the Belgians have little patience with the over-priced preciousness to which *la haute cuisine française* can so easily fall victim.

A famous anecdote about Victor Hugo speaks of these differing traditions. Eating in a Brussels restaurant during his exile in Belgium after 1858, Hugo was addressed by a fellow customer. 'I can see you must be French,' he said, 'from the amount of bread you eat with your meal.' 'I can see you must be Belgian,' retorted Hugo, 'from the amount you eat!' *Asterix and the Belgians* has a similar leitmotif: to Obelix's delight the huge meals provided by his Belgian hosts merge into one continuous feast, lasting most of the day.

Steak and chips is virtually the national dish. The steak will be first-class (perhaps a huge *entrecôte à l'os*, or a melt-in-the-mouth *filet pur*) and the chips, of course, have no rival in Europe (*see* p.224). *Moules et frites* (mussels and chips) comes a close second. No dainty soup bowls scattered with mussels here, but a kilo per person, which comes to the table in a casserole the size of a bucket. *Moules marinière* is the standard preparation: cleaned live mussels are cooked on a bed of sweated celery, onion and parsley until the shells open. Few elaborations improve on this simple formula.

Most restaurants offer French-style cuisine, but in down-to-earth establishments heartier northern dishes will feature on the menu, too. On the lighter side you may find delicately flavoured soups, such as *soupe de cresson* (watercress); excellent fish—in particular, turbot, flounder, plaice, monkfish and bream; tasty, substantial salads, such as *salade Liégeoise* (a warm salad of green beans or *salade frisée* and bacon pieces); and *steak à l'américaine* (or *américain préparé*), raw minced steak with capers, chopped raw onion, Worcestershire sauce and even a raw egg. Typically Belgian dishes often crop up on menus. The most famous is *waterzooi*, a soothing soup-like dish in which chicken is cooked with cream and vegetables. The *waterzooi* formula has recently been applied to fish, such as turbot. *Carbonnades flamandes*, another classic Belgian dish, is a hearty, sweetly flavoured beef stew cooked in beer.

Pork is an important meat, and there is a wide variety of home-produced pork products, such as *andouillettes* (rich sausages made of offal) and the excellent *boudin blanc* and *boudin noir* (soft meat and blood sausages, usually served with apple purée). Game (*gibier*) in season includes pigeon, hare, pheasant and venison, often made succulent with berries, raisins or braised chicory. Look out for unusual seasonal vegetables, such as salsify and *jets de houblon*—hop shoots, served in spring with a peppery cream sauce and poached eggs.

Belgian food is to some extent regional, but the country is too small to make any great issue of this. Nonetheless, the origins of famous regional dishes are respected: if you want the best *waterzooi* you have to go to Ghent. For the best seafood head for the coast. Eels are seldom better than around the lakes of Overmere, east of Ghent, where the great speciality is *paling in 't groen* (called *anguilles au vert* in French). This is a kind of stew, in which substantial chunks of eel are cooked in handfuls of chervil, sorrel and parsley—a delicious dish when done well. The Ardennes region is famous for its game dishes, and also for its cured *jambon d'Ardennes*. Abbeys like Chimay, Orval and Maredsous, produce their own brands of cheese as well as beer (*see* pp.228–9), and there are numerous other provincial cheeses, such as Herve, Limburger and Boulette de Romedenne. Brussels, too, claims its own cuisine, often presented under picturesque *bruxellois* titles. The most famous dishes include *bloedpens* (blood pudding), *carbonnades* cooked with the local *lambic* or *gueuze* beer, and various vegetable and meat purées known as *stoemp*. *Choesels* is a celebrated dish made of seven kinds of offal cooked in *lambic*. The crucial ingredient is beef pancreas and it has to be eaten as fresh as possible—traditionally on the day of slaughter.

Belgian biscuits are almost as famous as their chocolates. These include the crumbly, buttery biscuits of the kind made by Dandoy in the suitably named Rue au Beurre adjacent to the Grand' Place. The southern Belgian town of Dinant is famous for its fancy biscuits called *couques* (the most elaborate are intended to be hung on walls, not eaten), while *speculoos*, a hard, buttery biscuit, is a well-known speciality of Flanders. A box of inexpensive, wafer-thin almond biscuits produced by Jules Destrooper makes a good present. At the other end of the scale, you can sink your teeth into a luscious, freshly cooked *gaufre* (waffle) sprinkled with icing sugar, a familiar fast food at any market or fairground.

Chips

If you want a quick snack in Belgium, you could do worse than stopping at a *friture/frituur* van and ordering a cone of chips (French fries). Belgian chips—*frites*—are quite simply the best: no thicker than your little finger, served piping

hot, golden brown and *croustillantes*, or crispy. The traditional accompaniment is a dollop of mayonnaise. One of the reasons Belgian *frites* are so good is the choice of potato—usually a sweeter one such as Bintje. Belgians bring critical appreciation to their potatoes, just as they do to any other aspect of food: hang the shelf life. Take, for instance, the Saint-Nicholas, a delicious, waxy potato with a yellowish hue and an aromatic, nutty flavour; served boiled with fish or meat, this is not just a lump of carbohydrate filler but a vegetable of distinction.

Belgium, in fact, has a close connection to the history of the potato in Europe. After Sir Walter Raleigh brought the tuber back from the Americas in the 16th century it was virtually forgotten, but a Flemish botanist called Charles de l'Ecluse, working in Emperor Maximilian II's gardens in Vienna, saw its potential and kept it in cultivation. Over 100 years later it still hadn't caught on: it was a food of last resort, fed to farm animals, prisoners and soldiers. It was growing in the province of Hainault by 1715, and came into its own after a wheat-crop failure in 1739–40, whereafter it supplanted cereals as a staple until the growth of grain imports from Canada and the USA in the late 19th century.

So what is the secret of making good Belgian chips? First select an appropriate potato variety; cut the potatoes to the correct size, keeping them fairly thin. Lastly, fry them *twice*: the first time round so that they are cooked but not brown; then, after allowing them to cool, cook them a second time until golden brown and *bien croustillantes*!

Chicory

The French-speaking Belgians call them *chicons*, the French call them *endives*, the Flemish call them *witloof*, the English-speaking world refers to them as chicory in the UK and Belgian endives in the US—a suitably mysterious confusion for this bizarre little vegetable. Chicory consists of a head of firm, bullet-shaped leaves—white, yellow and pale green—with a crunchy texture and a distinctive, bitter flavour. It is often eaten raw, in salads, but with simple cooking, chicory is transformed into one of the most delicious and surprising of Belgium's foods.

Melt some butter in a saucepan, drop in a handful of chicory, put on the lid and cook very slowly until it has collapsed into its own aromatic juices and transmogrified into sweet, succulent delicacy. Chicory wrapped in slices of ham and baked in a cheese sauce (*chicons gratin*) is a classic, warming Belgian dish.

Chicory is essentially a winter crop. The roots of the *chicorée* lettuce are replanted and allowed to shoot, but are kept in the dark to make the shoots white. The process was apparently discovered by accident in about 1840 by the head gardener at the botanical gardens of Brussels, who was simply trying to over-winter some rootstock. He kept the shoots in the dark by gently piling up the earth over them, and this is the method still used by gardeners in the *potagers* today. Commercial growers, however, used darkened sheds and hydroponics to maintain a thriving export industry.

Chocolate

When it comes to chocolate, 'Belgian' is synonymous with quality—so much so that unscrupulous foreign operators will use the term liberally as a sales tool when their product contains only the merest fraction of Belgian chocolate, or is simply prepared in Belgian style. Imitation may be a form of flattery, but do not be misled: only the Belgians produce the chocolates that are responsible for this reputation, and the best place to buy them is in Belgium itself. This is partly because freshness counts: Belgian chocolates are sumptuous, fresh-cream confections with a limited shelf life (three weeks in the fridge, if you are lucky); furthermore, because the Belgians themselves are enthusiastic consumers of hand-made chocolate, turnover is high and the price is remarkably low. A kilogram of Leonidas chocolates costs just 380 BF, and the 250gm box (the perfect small gift from Belgium) costs just 95 BF; they would be at least twice this price abroad.

Three factors have given rise to the unassailable reputation of Belgian chocolate: the cream fillings, white chocolate, and—most important of all—the quality of the plain chocolate. The Belgians may not have been the first to put fresh cream in chocolates, but they pioneered fresh-cream fillings for the mass market. White chocolate is a comparative newcomer; in fact it is barely chocolate at all, but a milk-based confection mixed with cocoa butter and sweetener. The best plain Belgian chocolate contains a very high proportion of cocoa solids—at least 52 per cent, usually more like 70 per cent (90 per cent is the feasible maximum). These cocoa solids are the crushed and ground product of cocoa beans (usually from South America), from which some of the oily cocoa butter has been extracted. This valuable cocoa butter is later reintroduced to make high-quality chocolate (in poor-quality chocolate, vegetable fat is substituted for cocoa butter and there is also a much lower percentage of cocoa solids). Cocoa butter makes a significant difference, as any chocolate addict will tell you: the natural oils in the cocoa butter evaporate in your mouth, provoking a slight cooling, refreshing sensation.

Leonidas, Godiva, Corné de la Toison d'Or, and Neuhaus are the most famous manufacturers in Belgium, but there are many more, some of them tiny individual concerns with just one outlet. Of the big names, Leonidas is probably the cheapest, but this has little bearing on quality: many Belgians actually prefer Leonidas and find the others too rich. Leonidas appears to produce chocolates on an industrial scale, and has numerous outlets. Some have large counters opening directly on to the street, so that the staff can shovel out boxes of chocolates to passing customers with the minimum of delay. Only in Belgium could chocolates be treated as a kind of fast food. Godiva, however, has the greater international reputation: the company now has 1400 shops worldwide, selling 120 different kinds of chocolate at the luxury end of the market, and is noted especially for its chocolate truffles. Why, you may ask, is a Belgian chocolate company named after Lady Godiva, the nobleman's wife who rode naked through the streets of Coventry in the 11th century? The answer is simply that, in 1929, the founders of the business liked the image, which seemed to represent the qualities of their chocolates: elegant, rich, sensual and daring.

You will find chocolates (or *pralines*, as they are generically known) on sale everywhere in Brussels. If you want to buy a handful of boxes in a hurry to take home with you, there's a Godiva shop in the Grand' Place (No. 22) and a large Leonidas shop at 46 Boulevard Anspach, close to the Bourse.

Beer

Belgian beer enjoys an unparalleled reputation. For beer lovers, it is the object of pilgrimage and reverence. For others it can be a revelation. Belgium has some 400 different kinds of beers produced by 121 breweries (in 1900 there were 3223 breweries). Each has its own distinctive style, and all are good quality. Even the ubiquitous Stella Artois and Jupiler, made by the brewing giant Interbrew, are a cut above your average lagers.

A word first of all about how beer is made. The essential ingredient is grain—usually barley, but sometimes wheat. (This explains why beer is the historic beverage of grain-growing northern Europe, just as wine is the drink of warmer climes further south.) The barley is soaked in water to stimulate germination, then dried in a kiln to produce malt. The malted barley is then crushed and boiled before being left to ferment, during which process the natural sugars (maltose) and any added sugars are converted into alcohol. Yeast is the agent of fermentation. Some yeasts rise to the top of the brew, forming a crust that protects the beer from the air; this process creates a richly flavoured 'top-fermented' ale. Other yeasts sink to the bottom to make a lighter, clearer, lager-type 'bottom-fermented' beer. The choice of barley, the preparation of the malt, the quality of the water, and the type of yeast used all influence the final taste of the beer. Hops provide a spicy, bitter tang and may be added at various stages of brewing.

With Belgian beer there is no great concern about whether it is served from the keg or in bottles. Some do come in kegs, but many of the best are bottled. The labels on the bottles give the vital statistics, including the all-important alcohol content. By and large Belgian beer has a higher level of alcohol by volume than equivalent British or American beers. Specialist bottled beers start at about 5 per cent; stronger brews measure 8 or 9 per cent. The maximum alcohol content for beer is about 12 per cent—four times the strength of most lager. Bush beer is one of several brands that claims to be Belgium's strongest beer: one bottle is very pleasant; after two bottles you feel as though your knees have been hinged on backwards. Some breweries (especially the abbeys) classify their beer as *double/ dubbel* (dark and sweet, about 6.6 per cent) or *triple/tripel* (paler and lighter, but stronger, about 8 per cent). Labels also instruct you about the correct temperature at which to serve the beer and the shape of glass to be used. Every brew is assigned its own glass shape, from tumbler to goblet, and this is something that any bartender instinctively understands. Only in the appropriate glass can the merits of a particular beer be fully savoured.

The most famous bottled beers are those produced by the Trappists—the order of Cistercian monks which observe the strict (these days not quite so strict) order of silence. In the 19th century the monasteries produced beer for the consumption of the monks, but then they began to sell it to the outside world in gradually increasing quantities. Trappist beer is now a major income-earner for the monasteries, produced on a semi-industrial basis, nowadays largely by lay workers rather than monks. Nonetheless, the monasteries retain strict control over their product and have resisted offers of expansion into the large-scale export markets, which would rapidly lap up any increased production. These Trappist beers are top-fermented ales, with extra yeast added at bottling to produce a second fermentation in the bottle. As a result a white sediment forms: allow the beer to stand to let it settle, then when you open the bottle pour the entire contents off all at once to avoid disturbing the sediment (it is not harmful, just rather yeasty).

The most famous Trappist beer is probably Chimay, produced by the abbey of Notre-Dame de Scourmont, which in the 1860s became the first to release its beers to the public. Today Chimay is available as 7, 8 and 9 per cent alcohol by volume are indicated by red, white and blue labels respectively. Kept for several years, Chimay Bleu becomes ever richer, its flavour drifting towards port.

The Trappist abbey of Orval, whose brewery is run entirely by lay staff, produces one brand only, sold in distinctive pear-shaped bottles. This is an excellent pale brew, pitched at a fairly modest 5.2 per cent alcohol. Its distinctive spicy flavour derives from the dry hops added at the end of fermentation. Excellent Trappist beers are also produced in the traditional copper kettles of the abbey at Rochefort, including a power-packed version at 11.3 per cent, while the abbey of Westmalle, near Antwerp, produces famous *dubbel* and *tripel* ales.

Only Trappist monasteries are allowed to produce Trappist beer. Other monasteries produce similar 'abbey beers'—sometimes franchising their names to commercial brewers, so the monastery connection may be tenuous. Leffe is an abbey beer now owned by Interbrew, but it is still an excellent brand, with several styles from pale to rich and dark, including the warming Radieuse (8.5 per cent).

For a refreshing change, try the remarkable 'white' beers—*witbier/bière blanche*. The most famous are produced at Hoegaarden, to the east of Brussels. Hoegaarden (also a brand name) is a wheat beer flavoured with a touch of coriander; it has a delicious peppery tang and a modest alcohol content (5 per cent)—excellent for that jaded moment in the late afternoon. Some *blanche* drinkers even add a slice of lemon to their glass. It is often a little cloudy—don't send it back: that is how it should be! Other good white beers are Brugs Tarwebier and Blanche de Namur.

Numerous beers in Belgium belong to no category but their own. Duvel is a famous brand produced at Breendonk in Flanders—strong (8.5 per cent), pale and with a distinctive hoppy bitterness. De Verboden Vrucht (Forbidden Fruit) is a good strong ale (9 per cent) from Hoegaarden, which benefits from secondary fermentation in the bottle; it has a sumptuous label, portraying Adam and Eve in the Garden of Eden clasping glasses of beer. Bruges has its deliciously spicy Brugse Tripel, which weighs in at 9 per cent. Kwak, from east Flanders, is most readily associated with the large one-litre, trumpet-shaped glasses in which it is traditionally served. There is a knack to drinking from these: novices tend to tip it too fast at a critical moment and get a dowsing. A number of breweries produce special Christmas brews with festive labels, such as Blanche de Noël and the power-packed Bush Noël.

Last but by no means least is the family of *lambic* beers, unique to the valley of the River Senne. What makes *lambic* so special is that it is 'spontaneously' fermented by the agency of naturally occurring airborne yeasts—tiny fungi called *Brettanomyces* that are found only in Brussels itself and in the countryside to the west. Fermentation begins within three days, but the beer is allowed to age for a year or more. *Lambic* is a fairly strong (about 5.5 per cent), still beer with a distinctive sour, winey flavour—something of an acquired taste. Cherries (formerly from the Brussels suburb of Schaerbeek) may be macerated in *lambic* to produce the fruity beer called *kriek*; raspberries are added to make *framboise*; and sugar and caramel are added to make *faro*. Blended *lambic* of different ages is allowed to ferment a second time in bottles to become the slightly fizzy sour beer called *gueuze*. These are really essential flavours of Brussels, and worth seeking out in bars where they are available on tap. Or better still, go to the Musée Bruxellois de la Gueuze (*see* p.197), housed in the Cantillon brewery where *gueuze* is still made on cold winter nights in the traditional way.

Eating Out

There are over 3000 restaurants in Brussels, and you can bet that 95 per cent of them are good. Given this *embarras du choix*, how do you decide where to eat? The Bruxellois have the same problem: most of them end up with their own selection of favourite restaurants, usually near where they live—why go further when excellence is on your doorstep? Here are a few tips to avoid disappointment. Look out for busy restaurants, patronized by locals; avoid restaurants that appear to cater mainly for tourists. Don't be afraid to ask for recommendations—all Belgians are experts on food and only too happy to advise. Newspapers and magazines, such as *Le Soir* and *The Bulletin*, have regular restaurant reviews, which are reliable guides to the places that are currently on form.

Restaurant hours are generally 12–2.30 and 6–10.30 or 11, although many of the smaller *bistrots* and brasseries serve *cuisine* non-stop from about 11am to midnight. Many restaurants are closed for Saturday lunch and on Sunday, and some shut down completely in July or August. Always phone first to check opening times. It's advisable to make a reservation for the more upmarket establishments. There are restaurants to suit all palates and appetites; menus at the door will show what's on offer. The fixed-price *menu du jour* or *plat du jour* is often a bargain, and you will find that even luxury restaurants usually feature a cheaper menu at lunchtime. Many cafés serve a limited range of light dishes for lunch and supper, and bars may offer '*petite restauration*'—snacks of sandwiches, *croque monsieur* (grilled cheese and ham on toast), *toast cannibale* (raw minced steak on toast) and so forth. Such food is usually also available in the *estaminets*—a class of rare, old-world taverns celebrated for their antique clutter and relaxed atmosphere.

Some food shops and pâtisseries have tables and chairs where you can sit and eat a snack: *dégustation* (sampling/tasting) at a specialist food shop can often end up as a full-scale meal.

Belgian food has few exotic influences, but if you fancy something a little different there are a fair number of restaurants offering foreign food: North African, Japanese, Thai, Indian, Italian and Spanish. Many of these are extremely good—they have to be, to survive in this competitive world!

Value Added Tax (TVA/BTW) at 19.5 per cent is generally already included in the price of restaurant meals. In principle, if you eat in a restaurant you must insist on a VAT receipt and take this out of the restaurant with you. VAT officials may demand to see your receipt, and failure to produce one can entail a fine, and a penalty for the restaurant owner. However, this recently introduced, uncharacteristically officious regulation appears to have had little impact in Belgium.

Vegetarians

Meat plays a central role in Belgian cuisine, but it would be wrong to assume that vegetarians are completely left out in the cold. Belgian chefs have become increasingly aware of the call for lighter dishes, and that sometimes means vegetarian. Even traditional Belgian cooking includes noted vegetarian dishes, such as *flamiche aux poireaux*, a kind of flan filled with leeks in a cream sauce. Egg dishes are excellent, and although vegetarians often get tired of being fobbed off with yet another omelette, omelettes in Belgium are actually extremely good. Asparagus, chicory and hop shoots often feature in meatless dishes. In restaurants, you may fare better if you pick and choose from the edges of the menu, ordering a starter instead of a main course and filling up on delicious, substantial puddings. Foreign restaurants, particularly Italian, Indian and Thai, usually cater more than adequately for vegetarians. There are also several specialist vegetarian restaurants, including La Tsampa in Rue de Livourne, whose inspired cooking has come to the attention even of carnivore gastronomes.

Restaurants in Brussels

Most of the restaurants listed below are in central Brussels; there is no shortage of good restaurants in the suburbs, however, and the ones included here are just a personal selection. It's very difficult to give a hard and fast guide to prices. You can eat relatively cheaply at expensive restaurants if you stick to special *prix fixe* menus. The price categories used here indicate the cost of a three-course meal (without wine), for one person, from the à la carte menu.

expensive	—	over 1500 BF
moderate	—	700–1500 BF
inexpensive	—	below 700 BF

expensive

Les Brigittines, 5 Place de la Chapelle, ✆ 512 68 91. *Closed Sat lunch, Sun and Aug.* Lobster, truffles and other delights in a *belle époque* setting.

Au Cheval Marin, 25 Rue du Marché aux Porcs, ✆ 513 02 87. *Closed Sun.* A highly respected old-world fish restaurant: a Baroque salon inside a gabled building dating from 1680. *Menu du jour* for 900 BF.

Chez Marius en Provence, 1 Place du Petit-Sablon, ✆ 511 12 08. *Closed Sun.* Stylish, much-loved restaurant specializing in southern French food and famous for its *bouillabaisse*. Prices can escalate to 3000 BF, but there are set menus at around 1000 BF.

Comme Chez Soi, 23 Place Rouppe, ✆ 512 29 21. *Closed Sun and Mon and July.* Owned and run by Pierre Wynants, one of Europe's most fêted chefs, this is Brussels' premier restaurant—but with just 23 places you need to book weeks in advance. Exquisite concoctions of snipe, eel, truffle, lobster, beautifully presented. Expect no change out of 5000 BF.

L'Ecailler du Palais Royal, 18 Rue Bodenbroeck, ✆ 512 87 51. *Closed Sun.* One of Brussels' most celebrated fish restaurants: classy and welcoming, with absolutely *comme il faut* cuisine. The set lunch at 950 BF is a bargain.

La Maison du Cygne, 2 Rue Charles Buls, ✆ 511 82 44. *Closed Sat lunch, Sun and three weeks in Aug.* Sumptuous and justly famous restaurant in one of the Grand' Place guildhouses, serving top-notch French cuisine at matching prices. Lunch menu at 1300–1600 BF; dinner would set you back at least three times as much.

Le Quai, 14 Quai aux Briques, ✆ 512 37 36. Tiny restaurant with a dozen tables or so, but *the* place to eat lobster.

moderate

Aux Armes de Bruxelles, 13 Rue des Bouchers, ✆ 511 21 18. *Open noon– 11, closed Mon.* Sophisticated busy restaurant, with impeccable service.

La Belle Maraîchère, 11 Place Sainte-Catherine. *Closed Wed and Thurs.* With its elegant late-19th-century air, this is one of the great fish restaurants of Place Sainte-Catherine. The changing three-course menu, 900–1100 BF, includes such wonders as *saumon braisé au champagne*.

Le Café de Paris, 12 Rue de la Vierge Noire, ✆ 512 39 30. *Closed Sat lunch and Sun.* Art Nouveau setting for good-quality brasserie-style food, majoring in fish. Three-course menu for 985 BF; lunch menu at 450 BF.

In 't Spinnekopke, 1 Place du Jardin aux Fleurs, ✆ 511 86 95. *Open 11–11, Sat 6–11, closed Sun.* One of Brussels' oldest *estaminets* (its name means 'at the sign of the little spider'), dating back to 1762, now a charming restaurant noted for traditional Belgian cuisine. *Coquilles Saint-Jacques* (scallops) cooked in Trappist beer. Bargain lunch menu at 295 BF.

L'Ogenblik, 1 Galerie des Princes, ✆ 511 61 51. *Closed Sun.* Friendly, stylishly low-key brasserie serving elegant—if pricey—dishes of scallops, *gâteau de homard*, wild duck etc.

Rôtisserie Vincent, 8 Rue des Dominicains, ✆ 511 23 03. *Closed Aug.* Totally *bruxellois* atmosphere in a colourfully tiled restaurant entered through the steaming kitchen and fronted by what looks like a butcher's shop window. Good, solid cooking; *menu du patron* at 940 BF.

Taverne du Passage, 30 Galerie de la Reine, ✆ 512 37 31. *Open noon–midnight, closed Wed and Thurs in June and July.* Classic old-style restaurant, where elderly ladies speak in hushed voices over crisp linen. Specializes in Belgian cuisine, such as *andouillette grillée* and *waterzooi.*

La Villette, 3 Rue du Vieux Marché aux Grains, ✆ 512 75 50. *Closed Sat lunch and Sun.* Named after the old slaughterhouses of Paris—boldly advertising that this is a decidedly meat-oriented restaurant in a fish-dominated district. Charming, intimate and stylish. Light meals of salads, *américaine maison* (steak tartare), plus serious steaks to satisfy all waistlines.

inexpensive

Chez Léon, 18 Rue des Bouchers, ✆ 511 14 15. *Open noon–11.* The jam-packed, multi-storeyed original (founded in 1893) of what has now become a small chain, specializing in *moules-frites* and other Belgian standards. Tourists enthuse, but the Bruxellois remain sniffy.

't Kelderke, 15 Grand' Place, ✆ 512 36 94. *Open noon–2am, closed Sat lunch.* Medieval cellar setting for authentic shoulder-to-shoulder dining. Hearty *bruxellois* food at reasonable prices.

La Marée, 99 Rue de Flandre, ✆ 511 00 40. *Closed Mon.* Charming, family-run fish restaurant with an escalating reputation.

East Brussels   *Restaurants*

expensive

Bernard, 93 Rue de Namur, ✆ 512 88 21. *Closed Mon evening and Sun.* Entered through the marbled hallway of an upper-crust delicatessen, this is a hallowed shrine to fish cookery.

Mon Manège à Toi, 1 Rue Neerveld (Woluwe-Saint-Lambert), ✆ 770 02 38. *Closed Sat, Sun and last three weeks of July.* This rather ordinary-looking suburban house is home to one of Brussels' great restaurants. Inventive French cuisine, beautifully presented; garden terrace in summer.

Moulin de Lindekemale, 6 Avenue J. F. Debecker (Woluwe-Saint-Lambert), ✆ 770 90 57. *Closed Sat, Sun and Aug.* Good French cuisine in a picturesque old watermill. Set menus at 1500 BF upwards.

3Couleurs, 453 Avenue de Tervuren (Woluwe-Saint-Pierre), ✆ 770 3321. Closed Mon, Tues and Sept. Comfortable elegant and justifiably celebrated for its supreme Frence cuisine.

moderate

Colmar, 71 Boulevard de la Woluwe (Woluwe-Saint-Lambert), ✆ 762 98 55. Friendly, well-respected family restaurant (children's menu 199 BF).

Les Jardins de l'Europe, Woluwe Shopping Center, 202/98 Rue Saint-Lambert (Woluwe-Saint-Lambert), ✆ 762 61 82. *Open 11–10, closed Sun lunch.* Busy and comfortable brasserie-style restaurant serving admirable food—far better than you might expect in a shopping centre! *Menus du jour* at 375 BF and 695 BF.

Sukhothai, 135 Avenue d'Auderghem, ✆ 649 43 66. *Closed Sat and Sun lunch.* Friendly rattan-furnished Thai restaurant, with the full range of Thai favourites, such as *tom yam koong* (spicy soup with prawns and lemon grass). Lunch menu at 425 BF.

Taj Mahal, 12 Avenue des Gaulois, ✆ 734 51 55. *Closed Sat lunch and Mon evening.* Tandooris and tikkas served in the Raj-like splendour of a *tous-les-Louis* salon on the first floor of a *maison de maître*. Set lunch 580 BF.

Vimar, 70 Place Jourdan, ✆ 231 09 49. *Closed Sat lunch and Sun.* A stylish setting of crisp linen for serious fish cuisine. Lunch menu at 850 BF.

inexpensive

L'Annexe, Woluwe Shopping Center (Woluwe-Saint-Lambert), ✆ 771 90 24. *Last orders 7pm, closed Sun.* Shop and bistro rolled into one, where you can *déguster* meat specialities such as *rillettes*, with a glass of wine.

Noé, 25 Rue de Trèves, ✆ 512 85 20. *Open 11.30–3, closed Sat and Sun.* Agreeable vegetarian restaurant which specializes in supplying hurried office staff with a wholesome, balanced *plat du jour* for around 300 BF.

Oceanis, Woluwe Shopping Center, next to L'Annexe (Woluwe-Saint-Lambert), ✆ 771 90 24. *Last orders 7pm, closed Sun.* Another shop-cum-bistro. Here you can sample oysters, *bouillabaisse* and *anguilles au vert* (eels).

South Brussels   *Restaurants*

expensive

L'Amandier, 184 Avenue de Fré (Uccle), ✆ 374 03 95. *Closed Sat lunch.* Good French food served amid very elegant décor designed by Ralph Lauren: what the Francophones would call *huppé* (very select).

A'mbriana, 151 Rue Edith Cavell (Uccle), ✆ 375 01 56. *Closed Sat lunch and Tues.* Elegant Italian restaurant, one of the best in Brussels. *Carpaccio* (thinly sliced raw beef) 445 BF, grilled prawns, etc. Good-value set menu for 895 BF, including wine.

En Plein Ciel, 27th Floor, Hilton Hotel, 38 Boulevard de Waterloo, ✆ 504 11 11. Famous for its fabulous champagne brunch (smoked salmon, etc.), with views over Brussels, served on Sundays only, 10–2. Set price of 1190 BF; children pay 100 BF per year of age. Get there early. Other days: buffet lunch 600–1200 BF.

La Maison du Boeuf, Hilton Hotel, 38 Boulevard de Waterloo, ✆ 504 11 11. Its high standards of Belgian and French cuisine have earned this restaurant a seriously good reputation. On the first floor overlooking the Jardin d'Egmont. Set lunch at 1450 BF.

Tagawa, 279 Avenue Louise, © 640 50 95. *Closed Sat lunch and Sun.* First-class Japanese food—*sashimi, tempura* and so on. Up to 4000 BF for a full meal, but lunch menu at 1500 BF.

Taishin, Hôtel Mayfair, 381–3 Avenue Louise, © 649 98 00. *Closed Sun.* Japanese food with French influences, 1500–2000 BF.

La Villa Lorraine, 28 Chaussée de la Hulpe (Uccle), © 374 31 63. *Closed Sun and July.* Luxurious elegance at the edge of the Bois de la Cambre; much admired French cuisine. Up to 5000 BF, but lunch at 1800 BF.

moderate

La Canne en Ville, 22 Rue de la Réforme, © 347 2926. *Closed Sat lunch and Sun.* Charming restaurant in three small rooms decorated with 1900s tilework, paintings and walking sticks. Well-known for its first-rate French cuisine. Bargain lunch at 380 BF.

Les Foudres, 14 Rue Eugène Cattoir, © 647 36 36. *Sat lunch and Sun.* A wine-lover's paradise: a restaurant with wine shop attached (a *foudre* is a large wine cask). Excellent, well-balanced cuisine—primarily fish—and fine wines. Set menus at around 1000 BF.

Leonardo da Vinci, 6 Rue du Postillon (Uccle), © 347 02 92. *Closed Sun.* Pleasant pizzeria and restaurant serving above-average Italian food. Lunch menu at 495 BF.

La Quincaillerie, 45 Rue du Page, © 538 2553. *Closed Sat lunch.* The name means 'hardware store' and that's what it is—a wonderful, invigorating restaurant newly installed between the ranks of wooden drawers in an authentic 1900s shop. Well-prepared French cuisine at around 1000 BF.

Rick's Café, 344 Avenue Louise, © 647 75 30. Open 11–11. Best of the new-wave American-chic cafés, noted for its Sunday brunch.

La Tsampa, 109 Rue de Livourne, © 647 03 67. *Closed Sat evening and Sun.* A cut above the average vegetarian restaurant, beautifully set out at the back of a health-food shop. Japanese, Indian and Vietnamese touches add colour to an inventive menu, with main dishes at 350–430 BF.

inexpensive

La Baie de Tunis, 11 Rue de Moscou, © 539 10 97. *Closed Tues.* One of a cluster of North African restaurants, serving a range of couscous dishes (around 400 BF) as well as other North African specialities, such as *scampi à la Sfaxienne* (in coriander sauce) and *briks*, a kind of omelette wrapped in paper-thin rice-flour pastry.

Chez Mustafa, 79 rue de l'Eglise (under the Beni Znassen sign). *Open evenings only.* Celebrated cheap couscous restaurant (around 200 BF).

El Yasmine, 234 Chaussée d'Ixelles, © 647 51 81. Friendly restaurant serving some of the best Tunisian food in Brussels. Couscous for around 480 BF.

expensive

Bruneau, 73–5 Avenue Broustin, ℗ 427 77 70. *Closed Sat lunch and Sun.* Famously luxurious, much-garlanded restaurant, with three Michelin stars. Impressive *haute cuisine française*, and prices to match (5000 BF or more).

inexpensive

Le Béguinage, 3 Place de la Vaillance, ℗ 535 08 44. Stylish, agreeable tavern, serving food all day. *Plat du jour* at 295 BF.

expensive

De Ultieme Hallucinatie, 316 Rue Royale, ℗ 217 06 14. *Closed Sat lunch and Sun.* Famously authentic Art Nouveau restaurant (*see* p.162), with separate bar; an adventurous menu includes such delicacies as *magret de canard aux figues* and warmed *foie gras* with honey. Lunch menu at 950 BF.

moderate

La Ferme du Wilg, 164 Chaussée de Wemmel, ℗ 427 83 14. *Closed Tues.* Delightful converted 14th-century farmhouse (with garden in summer) known for its buffet meals (650 BF) and Scotch beef.

Restaurant Adrienne, at the top of the Atomium (take the lift to Panorama), ℗ 478 30 00. *Closed Mon evenings and Sun.* Copious buffet lunch (650 BF and 750 BF), with unsurpassed views. Surprisingly good, and good value given that this is a major tourist site. Booking advisable, in which case ask for a table on the south side, overlooking Brussels.

inexpensive

Le Jardin des Palmiers, 166 Boulevard Lambermont (Schaerbeek), ℗ 215 25 63. Relaxed, oriental setting for good-quality Moroccan (and Western) food; *couscous royal*, 590 BF.

Bars and Cafés in Brussels

A la Mort Subite, 7 Rue Montagne aux Herbes Potagères. This famous bar, decked out like a large Rococo boudoir, has had a type of *gueuze* named after it. *Gueuze* from the barrel at around 75 BF and *petite restauration*.

L'Archiduc, 6 Rue Antoine Dansaert. Designed like the interior of a 1930s cruiser, with piano player, this is one of numerous bars near the Place Saint-Géry that positively zings late at night and at weekends.

L'Avant-Nuit, 50 Rue Antoine Dansaert. *Closed Sun.* One of a growing number of gallery-cafés. Imaginative salads and light dishes for around 300 BF, served amid the art.

La Bécasse, 11 Rue de Tabora. Famous drinking hall, at the end of a narrow passageway; founded in 1793 as a coaching inn.

La Belgica, 32 Rue du Marché au Charbon. Famously thrusting rock dive, with standing-room only; lip-readers at an advantage.

Café de l'Opéra, 4 Place de la Monnaie. Welcoming café in 1920s style, with pavement terrace overlooking the Théâtre de la Monnaie; offers *petite restauration*.

La Chaloupe d'Or, 24–25 Grand' Place. Celebrated and stylish Grand' Place bar/restaurant, popular with well-heeled locals. Light meals and cold snacks at marginally inflated prices: *demi-poulet garni* 370 BF; *croque-monsieur* 220 BF.

Falstaff, 19 Rue Henri Maus. Large, classic Art Nouveau café dating from 1903. Light meals of Belgian cuisine; lunch menus at 325 BF.

La Fleur en Papier Doré, 55 Rue des Alexiens. Splendid old *estaminet* (*see* p.98). Good beers from the barrel, plus light snacks and sandwiches from around 120 BF.

H₂O, 27 Rue du Marché au Charbon. A softly candlelit bar playing classical music: the ultimate '*feutré*' (felt-like) environment.

Le Métropole, 31 Place de Brouckère. One of the grandest and most elegant cafés in Brussels. Chandeliered luxury, wicker chairs on the pavement. *Petite restauration* at acceptable prices, given the location.

Le Roy d'Espagne, 1–2 Grand' Place. An institution: a wonderfully atmospheric bar/restaurant, with waiters in starched, medieval aprons. You pay for its magnificent position in the Grand' Place, but not excessively so. Light lunch menu of, for example, *waterzooi de volaille* for around 500 BF.

South Brussels — *Bars and Cafés*

Chez Moeder Lambic, 168 Rue de Savoie. Celebrated bar boasting 1000 different kinds of beer.

Au Père Faro, 442 Chaussée d'Alsemberg (Uccle). Famous old pub; décor devoted to the brewer's art. Within staggering distance of Au Vieux Spijtigen Duvel.

Au Vieux Spijtigen Duvel, 621 Chaussée d'Alsemberg (Uccle). *Closed Sun.* Atmospheric tavern, one of the oldest *estaminets* in Brussels.

Indigo, 160 Rue Blaes. *Open 9–3, closed Mon.* Busy, arty, joyous café decorated from head to toe in miscellaneous *brocante* (junk), which is for sale along with well-crafted salads (avocado, Roquefort and bacon, 220 BF), wine and mouthwatering slabs of cake (95–120 BF). Open terrace to the rear.

North Brussels — *Bars and Cafés*

De Ultieme Hallucinatie, 316 Rue Royale. Famous Art Nouveau bar (*see* p.162). Drinks and light meals (plat du jour 250 BF) from the bar; for the restaurant, *see* above.

Where to Stay in Brussels

As a major centre for business and tourism, Brussels has scores of hotels, ranging from extremely cheap—and very central—youth hostels to venerable old luxury hotels of the highest standard. In the middle range there are some agreeable family hotels and dozens of good establishments of the international, 'I-could-be-anywhere' sort: a little soulless they may be, but by and large they are competitively priced and efficiently run, by staff who manage to welcome their endless turnover of guests with a smile.

Reservations may not always be essential but they are certainly advisable at busy times of the year—such as during the school holidays in the summer, around Easter and Christmas/New Year, and at weekends between May and September. It is so simple to make a reservation—by telephone or fax—that there seems little point not reserving in advance if you can. Almost all reception staff speak good English—or certainly enough English to take a reservation. You may be asked to send a deposit or give a credit-card number to secure the reservation but this is not always the case.

You can also make reservations, free of charge, through the central hotel organization BTR (Belgian Tourist Reservation), Boulevard Anspach 111 BF, 1000 Brussels, ✆ 513 74 84, fax 513 92 77. If you arrive in the city without a hotel reservation, the tourist office in the Grand' Place (see p.27) can offer advice and make reservations for you in return for a small fee.

The hotels in this list have been divided into five categories based primarily on price, although five-star hotels earn their extra star for their exceptional elegance and note of luxury. These star ratings are not the official ones, which are based on facilities rather than character and comfort. The prices indicated below are for a double room for one night; a light 'continental' breakfast is often included in the overnight price—it is worth establishing this when you make your reservation, as breakfast can otherwise add 250–800 BF to the bill. Prices are only marginally cheaper for single travellers, who will probably occupy double rooms anyhow.

Note that many of the larger hotels frequently offer special discounts for weekends and off-season stays: ask about these if telephoning in advance. Also note that some of the smaller hotels (usually in the one-star category) do not accept payment by credit card.

These days almost all hotel rooms in Brussels—except the very cheapest—have their own *en suite* bathroom—sometimes squeezed into a space about the size of a telephone kiosk. Most also have a television and telephone, and perhaps a small fridge with 'mini-bar'.

- ★★★★★ *luxury*; 6000 BF or more—often much more.

- ★★★★ *very expensive*, first-class; 6000 BF or more.

- ★★★ *expensive*; 3500–6000 BF.

- ★★ *moderate*; 2000–3500 BF (sometimes more, on account of location).

- ★ *inexpensive*; up to 2000 BF.

Central Brussels — *Hotels*

- ★★★★★ **Amigo**, 1–3 Rue de l'Amigo, 1000 Brussels, ✆ 547 47 47, fax 513 52 77. Elegant modern hotel on the site of the old prison (*see* p.92), a stone's throw from the Grand' Place.

- ★★★★★ **Métropole**, 31 Place de Brouckère, 1000 Brussels, ✆ 217 23 00, fax 218 02 20. Brussels' grandest old hotel: marbled, gilded halls and palm court—the picture of Belle Epoque elegance otherwise encountered only on film sets; expect to pay up to 10,500 BF for a room.

- ★★★★★ **SAS Royal**, 47 Rue du Fossé aux Loups, 1000 Brussels, ✆ 219 28 28, fax 219 62 62. The most impressive modern hotel in Brussels, with a towering atrium containing trees, waterfalls and fountains. Very polished service—as you come to expect from this chain owned by Scandinavian Airline System—and super-luxurious, with prices to match.

- ★★★★ **Bedford**, 135 Rue du Midi, 1000 Brussels, ✆ 512 78 40, fax 514 17 59. Sleek stylish modern international-mode hotel; a member of the Best Western chain.

- ★★★★ **Carrefour de l'Europe**, 110 Rue du Marché aux Herbes, 1000 Brussels, ✆ 504 94 00, fax 504 95 00. Centrally situated hotel, built in 1992; gabled exterior and international-style comfort inside.

- ★★★★ **Le Dixseptième**, 25 Rue de la Madeleine, 1000 Brussels, ✆ 502 57 44, fax 502 64 24. Elegant and charming hotel of just 21 rooms occupying the 18th-century residence of the Spanish ambassador, sympathetically restored; close to the Grand' Place. Note that breakfast (800 BF) is not included in the room rate.

- ★★★★ **Jolly Atlanta**, 7 Boulevard Adolphe Max, 1000 Brussels, 217 01 20, fax 217 37 58. Good, well appointed and central; part of the smart Italian Jolly chain.

- ★★★★ **Jolly Grand Sablon**, 2–4 Rue Bodenbroek, 1000 Brussels, ✆ 512 88 00, fax 512 67 66. Another member of the Jolly chain, with the distinct advantage of its location off the Place du Grand-Sablon.

- ★★★★ **Royal Windsor**, 5 Rue Duquesnoy, 1000 Brussels, ✆ 511 42 15, fax 511 60 04. Supremely first-class elegance, all highly modernized, but in elegant antique style.

- ★★★ **Arenberg**, 15 Rue d'Assaut, 1000 Brussels, ✆ 511 07 70, fax 514 19 76. Modern, no-nonsense hotel, close to the cathedral; part of the City Hotels chain.

- ★★★ **Novotel Brussels Off Grand' Place**, 120 Rue du Marché aux Herbes, 1000 Brussels, ✆ 514 33 33, fax 511 77 23. Modern hotel dressed in a Flemish-style exterior; efficient, international, and a cut above its neighbour, the Ibis.

★★★ **Orion**, 51 Quai au Bois à Brûler, 1000 Brussels, ✆ 221 14 11, fax 221 15 99. Apartment hotel in the old fishmarket district close to Place Sainte-Catherine; small but adequate accommodation, with special rates for the week or month.

★★ **Arlequin**, 17–19 Rue de la Fourche, 1000 Brussels, ✆ 514 16 15, fax 514 22 02. Small, friendly, modern hotel in the thick of touristic central Brussels: some rooms have a view of the Grand' Place.

★★ **Auberge Saint-Michel**, 15 Grand' Place, 1000 Brussels, ✆ 511 09 56, fax 511 46 00. This cheap(ish), family-run hotel could not be more central. Every room is different, furnished with character, and some (more expensive) overlook the Grand' Place itself. Breakfast, delivered to your room, costs an additional 200BF.

★★ **Ibis**, 100 Rue du Marché aux Herbes, 1000 Brussels, ✆ 514 40 40, fax 514 50 67. Very central, efficient, smart-but-no-frills hotel—and competitively priced.

★★ **Ibis Sainte-Catherine**, 2 Rue J. Platteau, 1000 Brussels, ✆ 513 76 20, fax 514 22 14. Comfortable, modern, if somewhat characterless hotel, in a good location close to the city centre.

★★ **La Madeleine**, 22 Rue de la Montagne, 1000 Brussels, ✆ 513 29 73, fax 502 13 50. Agreeable small hotel, close to the Grand' Place.

★ **Elysée**, 4 Rue de la Montagne, 1000 Brussels, 511 96 82, fax 733 74 75. Very basic, family-run hotel with shamelessly shoddy 1950s décor, but clean and very central. The cheaper rooms have shared bathrooms. Breakfast in bed is included—there's no restaurant.

★ **Noga**, 38 Rue du Béguinage, 1000 Brussels, ✆ and fax 218 67 63. Welcoming modern hotel in a quiet street.

★ **Pacific**, 57 Rue Dansaert, 1000 Brussels, ✆ 511 84 59. 'Clean and cheap' declares the 3rd-generation owner of this utterly charming, very central hotel—but it is much more than this. More like a private home, every room has bags of old-world character, down to the original 1910 plumbing. A full breakfast (included) is served in an authentic Art-Nouveau-style restaurant.

★ **Sleep Well**, 23 Rue du Damier, 1000 Brussels, ✆ 218 50 50, fax 218 13 13. Remarkably stylish, brand-new 'youth hotel', friendly, very central and very cheap. Monastically simple accommodation in rooms with one, two, three, four or six beds; shared bathrooms. Some youth hostel rules apply, such as no access to rooms during the day; no linen (sheets can be rented for 100 BF). Reservation advised.

★ **Windsor**, 13 Place Rouppe, 1000 Brussels, ✆ 511 20 14, fax 514 09 42. Quiet, clean and comfortable—a small hotel of just 24 rooms, but with a warm welcome that sets its apart.

Upper Town: Congrès and Porte Louise   *Hotels*

★★★★★ **Astoria**, 103 Rue Royale, 1000 Brussels, ✆ 217 62 90, fax 217 11 50. Ranked alongside the Métropole as a grand old hotel of Brussels—timeless elegance, originally opened in 1908 and superbly renovated.

★★★★★ **Brussels Hilton**, 38 Boulevard de Waterloo, 1000 Brussels, ✆ 504 11 11, fax 504 21 11. Ugly modern monolith, but comfortable and with splendid views; noted not only for its service but also for the high standards of its restaurants.

★★★★★ **Conrad Hilton**, 71 Avenue de Louise, 1050 Brussels, ✆ 542 42 42, fax 542 43 42. Super-luxurious modern hotel in a cocktail of architectural styles designed to impress.

★★★★★ **Royal Crown Hotel**, 250 Rue Royale, 1210 Brussels, ✆ 220 66 11, fax 217 84 44. Superlative luxury hotel.

★★★★ **Copthorne Stéphanie**, 91–3 Avenue Louise, 1050 Brussels, ✆ 539 02 40, fax 538 03 07. One of the Copthorne chain, a name associated with comfortable, well-run luxury; indoor swimming pool.

★★★ **Argus**, 6 Rue Capitaine Crespel, 1050 Brussels, ✆ 514 07 70, fax 514 12 22. Pleasant small hotel offering good-value accommodation close to upmarket Porte Louise area.

★★★ **Delta**, 17 Chaussée de Charleroi, 1060 Brussels, ✆ 539 01 60, fax 537 90 11. Functional, with all mod-cons, if short on character; one of the City Hotel chain.

★ **Congrès**, 42 Rue du Congrès, 1000 Brussels, ✆ 217 18 90, fax 217 18 97. A friendly welcome in a fine converted *maison de maître*, with *fin-de-siècle* touches.

★ **Duke of Windsor**, 4 Rue Capouillet, 1060 Brussels, ✆ 539 1819. A tiny hotel with just five rooms, close to the Porte Louise.

★ **Résidence Osborne**, 67 Rue Bosquet, 1060 Brussels, ✆ 537 92 51. A 19th-century *maison de maître* with just 10 rooms, and a garden.

East Brussels: Around the EU *Hotels*

★★★★★ **Montgomery**, 134 Avenue de Tervuren, 1150 Brussels, ✆ 741 85 11, fax 741 85 00. Brand new, very splendid hotel with 62 richly upholstered rooms, furnished in antique style of various inspirations; fax machine and video in every room; to the east of the Parc du Cinquantenaire.

★★★★★ **Stanhope**, 9 Rue du Commerce, 1040 Brussels, ✆ 506 91 11, fax 512 17 08. Sumptuously elegant, extremely expensive hotel with just 50 rooms, decorated in the refined style called *à l'anglaise*; strategically placed between the main EU buildings and the city centre.

★★★★ **Brussels Europa**, 107 Rue de la Loi, 1040 Brussels, ✆ 230 12 33, fax 230 36 82. Conveniently located modern hotel, near the EU and close to Maelbeek métro station, run with aplomb by staff who know what the business community needs.

★★★★ **Park Hotel**, 21–2 Avenue d'Yser, 1040 Brussels, ✆ 735 74 00, fax 735 19 67. Business hotel in a renovated townhouse on the other side of the Parc du Cinquantenaire from the main EU buildings.

★★★ **Archimède**, 22 Rue Archimède, 1040 Brussels, ✆ 231 09 09, fax 230 33 71. Popular hotel with a keynote in post-modern design flair, currently undergoing major expansion from 56 to 245 rooms; close to the Euro-centre.

★★★ **City Garden**, 59 Rue Joseph II, 1040 Brussels, ✆ 230 09 45, fax 230 64 37. Well-appointed, business-orientated apartment hotel, with special rates for the week or month.

★★★ **Euro-flat**, 50 Boulevard Charlemagne, 1040 Brussels, ✆ 230 00 10, fax 230 36 83. Hotel also offering apartments, with special rates for the week or month.

★★ **Armorial**, 101 Boulevard Brand Whitlock, 1200 Brussels, ✆ 734 56 36, fax 734 50 05. For something a little different, at surprisingly low prices: an atmospheric *maison de maître* with just 15 individually furnished rooms; to the east of the Parc du Cinquantenaire.

★★ **Lambeau**, 150 Avenue Lambeau, 1200 Brussels, ✆ 732 51 70, fax 732 54 90. Agreeable family and business hotel to the east of the EU.

★ **Derby**, 24 Avenue de Tervuren, 1040 Brussels, ✆ 733 08 19, fax 733 74 75. Popular, straightforward business and tourist hotel to the east of the Parc du Cinquantenaire; sister to the Hotel Elysée. Breakfast (130 BF) not included.

South Brussels — *Hotels*

★★★ **Mayfair**, 381–3 Avenue Louise, 1050 Brussels, ✆ 649 98 00, fax 640 17 64. East meets West: classy hotel in the Japanese Chisan chain, with Laura Ashley interior.

★★★ **Cadett Mövenpick**, 15 Rue P. Spaak, 1050 Brussels, ✆ 645 61 11, fax 646 63 44. Spotless scion of the Swiss-owned international Mövenpick chain, offering spacious and comfortable accommodation.

★★ **Capital**, 19 Chaussée de Vleurgat, 1050 Brussels, ✆ 646 64 20, fax 646 33 14. Pleasant, modest and friendly new hotel; no extras, but comfortable rooms and efficient, helpful staff.

North-central and North Brussels — *Hotels*

★★★★ **Sheraton Brussels**, 3 Place Rogier, 1210 Brussels, ✆ 224 31 11, fax 224 34 56. Huge, top-quality international hotel, as the name would suggest, with swimming pool on the 30th floor—but on the margins of the decidedly iffy Gard du Nord district.

★★★ **Albert Premier**, 20 Place Rogier, 1210 Brussels, ✆ 217 21 25, fax 217 93 31. Smart, friendly hotel converted in functional modern style, behind an Art Deco façade of the 1930s.

★★ **Père Boudart**, 592 Romeinsesteenweg, 1853 Stombeek, ✆ 460 74 96, fax 460 78 16. Pleasant guesthouse within walking distance of Heysel and the Atomium.

Apartment Hotels

There are several of these in Brussels: by providing bedrooms with small kitchens attached they combine the advantages of self-catering with hotel service, and are particularly useful for families. They are available for stays of just one night, but prices become increasingly competitive the longer the stay. There are over twenty apartment hotels in the city: three are listed above: the Orion in the city centre and City Garden and Euro-flat in east Brussels.

Bed and Breakfast

It is possible to find accommodation in family homes in Brussels, staying on a bed-and-breakfast basis. The conditions vary from household to household, of course, but it can be a remarkably cheap alternative to hotels (around 1200–1500 BF per night for two) and can, if successful, provide a rewarding insight into Belgian life. Some of the addresses in Brussels are extremely well located. Details change from year to year, so cannot reliably be published here. There is a useful booklet called *Bed and Breakfast: Benelux Guide*, which is given away free by some of the Belgian tourist offices abroad (*see* p.27). Alternatively, apply directly to the publishers: Taxistop, 28 Rue Fossé aux Loups, 1000 Brussels, © 223 23 10.

Youth Hostels

There are four main youth hostels *(auberge de jeunesse/jeugdherberg)* in the city. Prices per head per night range from about 300–620 BF, depending on the number of beds in the room. Auberge de Jeunesse Jacques Brel and the Vlaamse Jeugdherberg Bruegel are both located close to the centre and represent outstanding value for money. You don't really have to be a youth, by the way; young at heart will do.

Vlaamse Jeugdherberg Bruegel, 2 Rue du Saint-Esprit, © 511 04 36; fax 512 07 11. In a prime position at the foot of the Sablon district. Here you have to be a member of the International Youth Hostel Association.

Auberge de Jeunesse Jacques Brel, 30 rue de la Sablonnière, 1000 Brussels, © 218 01 87, fax 410 39 05. In the Congrès area.

CHAB (Centre d'Hébergement de l'Agglomération de Bruxelles), 8 Rue Traversière, 1030 Brussels, © 217 01 58, fax 219 79 95. Close to the Jardin Botanique.

Auberge de Jeunesse Jean Nihon, La Fonderie, 4 Rue de l'Eléphant, 1080 Brussels, © 410 38 58, fax 410 39 05. In Molenbeek, west Brussels.

Entertainment and Nightlife

The best entertainment and nightlife in Brussels is in the restaurants and bars—they are great places to while away the evening and in many of the bars you can drink well into the small hours. Brussels has all the mainstream cultural attractions of a large European city—a wide choice of international films, imported rock concerts, jazz venues and discos. It also has an armful of theatres (fine, if you speak the language), some seriously good classical music and the opera of the Théâtre de la Monnaie, which commands considerable international respect. Unique to Brussels are the famous Toone puppets, which are to theatre what the Manneken-Pis is to sculpture. That makes it a truly *bruxellois* institution—there's something in the nature of the Belgians that prevents them getting too prissy about their culture.

Listings

The best listings magazine for the English-speaking visitor is the pull-out supplement called *What's On* (in Brussels and other towns and cities) which comes with the weekly publication *The Bulletin* (out on Thursdays, 80 BF). The magazine itself also contains reviews of what's currently on offer. The most widely available French listings magazine for Brussels is the monthly *Kiosque* (60 BF). The tourist office also publishes a free guide to the main cultural events in the city.

Ticket Agencies

Tickets to mainstream events can be booked (for a small charge) through the TIB tourist office in the Grand' Place, ℰ 513 89 40 (*see* p.27). Other agencies include:

Auditorium 44, 44 Boulevard du Jardin Botanique, ℰ 218 27 35.

La Clé des Loisirs, ℰ 763 07 28.

FNAC, City 2, 123 Rue Neuve, ℰ 209 22 11.

Info Ticket, ℰ 512 85 54 or 504 03 99.

Cultural Centres

There are a number of these in central Brussels as well in the suburbs. They put on a broad range of events, such as theatre, performances by foreign dance troupes, and concerts (classical, folk, blues, etc.). The most important are:

Le Botanique, 236 Rue Royale, ℰ 218 37 32. The cultural centre for the French community of Brussels, housed in the elegant domed glasshouses of the old botanical garden, *see* p.161.

Palais des Beaux-Arts, 23 Rue Ravenstein, ℰ 507 82 00. The cultural centre designed by Victor Horta between the wars; *see* pp.115–6.

Beurschouwburg, 22 Rue Auguste Orts, ℗ 513 82 90.

Centre Culturel d'Auderghem, 185 Boulevard du Souverain, ℗ 660 03 03.

Centre Culturel d'Uccle, 47 Rue Rouge, ℗ 374 64 84.

Centre Culturel de Woluwe-Saint-Pierre, 93 Avenue Charles Thielemans;
℗ 773 05 88.

Centre Culturel d'Anderlecht, Avenue de Scheut, ℗ 387 30 92.

Centre Culturel Jacques Franck, 94 Chaussée de Waterloo, ℗ 538 90 20.

Opera and Classical Music

Belgium must be the only country in the world that was born out of an opera. A performance at the Théâtre de la Monnaie led directly to the revolution of 1830 (*see* p.62). La Monnaie/De Munt is still the jewel in the crown of Brussels' cultural life. Its company is renowned for the high quality of its productions, its inventive staging, and as a nursery for talent (while the big stars, and their big fees, are shunned). Opera tickets may be hard to come by, but there is no shortage of classical music concerts. There are a number of well-established concert halls, but look out also for one-off performances held at other venues, such as the churches (Cathédrale Saint-Michel, Eglise Notre-Dame du Sablon, Eglise Sainte-Catherine, Eglise des Minimes, and so forth).

Le Cercle, 20–22 Rue Sainte-Anne, ℗ 514 03 53. Venue for small-scale classical music and jazz concerts.

Cirque Royal, 81 Rue de l'Enseignement, ℗ 218 20 15. Venue for visiting opera companies and dance troupes—as well as rock groups.

Conservatoire Royal de Musique, 30 Rue de la Régence, ℗ 511 04 27. Brussels' venerable Conservatory, which runs a busy programme, mainly of chamber music.

Forest National, *see* 'Jazz, Rock, World Music', below.

Maison de la Radio, Place Eugène Flagey, ℗ 507 82 00. Classical and contemporary music concerts in this outlandish 1930s landmark (*see* p.194).

Théâtre Royal de la Monnaie, Place de la Monnaie, ℗ 217 22 11. Brussels' most celebrated theatre, devoted to opera, ballet and classical music concerts since 1850; many of the tickets are taken by season-ticket holders, and the rest are snapped up fast—so book early; *see also* pp.147–8.

Palais des Beaux-Arts, 23 Rue Ravenstein, ℗ 507 82 00. This is the home the Philharmonique and the Orchestre National de Belgique/Het Nationaal Orkest van België, and is also one of the key venues for visiting orchestras.

Dance

The name Maurice Béjart is still uttered in hushed and reverent tones in Brussels. He created his 'Ballet du XXᵉ Siècle' during his long residence at the Théâtre

Royal de la Monnaie, producing his own kind of modern-dance grand spectacle. Like it or loathe it, Béjart's work laid the foundations for an enthusiastic appreciation of modern dance in the city. The Monnaie's resident ballet is now directed by Anne Teresa De Keersmaeker, to considerable acclaim.

Cirque Royal, *see* 'Opera and Classical Music', above.

Théâtre Royal de la Monnaie, *see* 'Opera and Classical Music', above.

Théâtre du Résidence Palace, *see* 'Theatre', below.

Theatre

Brussels has its fair share of theatres and theatre companies putting on a spread of plays ranging from French classics by Molière, Corneille and Racine, to Feydeau farces, to modern classics by Ionesco, Michel de Ghelderode and the like, and works by contemporary Belgian playwrights. For better or worse, however, there is no equivalent of Broadway or London's West End, dominated by musicals that any visitor might appreciate. Theatre-goers in Brussels will need a good grip of French or Flemish—or of *bruxellois* if they are going to enjoy that most famous of Brussels plays, the knockabout comedy *Le Mariage de Mademoiselle Beulemans* (1910) by Frans Fonson and Fernand Wicheler.

Espace Delvaux/La Vénerie, Place Keym (Auderghem), ✆ 672 14 39. Specializes in humorous café-theatre performances.

Koninklijke Vlaamse Schouwburg, 146 Rue de Laeken, ✆ 217 69 37. The main Dutch-language theatre of Brussels, built in grand Edwardian style.

Magic Land Theatre, no fixed address. Unpredictable and inventive street theatre troupe, worth looking out for.

Plan K, Rue de Manchester, ✆ 523 18 34. Home of the hard-hitting avant-garde, in a converted sugar refinery.

Rideau de Bruxelles, Palais des Beaux-Arts, 23 Rue Ravenstein ✆ 507 83 60. Intimate theatre with a respected and long-established company, performing classic modern Belgian work by authors such as Michel de Ghelderode and Maurice Maeterlinck, as well as contemporary work.

La Samaritaine, 16 Rue de la Samaritaine, ✆ 511 33 95. Warm-hearted café-theatre currently considered on form.

Théâtre 140, 140 Avenue Plasky, ✆ 733 97 08. For over 30 decades one of Brussels' leading venues for contemporary theatre and other performances.

Théâtre de Poche, 1a Chemin du Gymnase (Bois de la Cambre), ✆ 649 17 27. Widely respected small theatre presenting contemporary, often experimental work in pleasant woodland surrounds.

Théâtre de Quat'Sous, 34 Rue de la Violette, ✆ 512 10 22. Tiny, friendly theatre of 50 seats, performing mainly modern French plays.

Théâtre National de Belgique, Place Rogier, 217 03 03. Modern francophone plays, often by Belgian authors, located in an ugly tower-block.

Théâtre du Résidence Palace, 155 Rue de la Loi, ✆ 231 03 05. A 1920s Art Deco-style theatre, with resident company; and also a dance venue.

Le Théâtre Royal des Galeries, Galeries Saint-Hubert, ✆ 512 04 07. A theatre founded in 1847, with a well-worn tradition of comedies and melodramas, these days supplemented by some more challenging productions.

Théâtre Royal du Parc, 3 Rue de la Loi, ✆ 512 23 39. Splendid 18th-century theatre mounting respected seasons of plays in French, both classical and modern (Pagnol, Pirandello, Ionesco, Ibsen and so forth).

Théâtre Varia, 78 Rue du Sceptre, ✆ 640 35 50. Progressive theatre at the cutting edge of Brussels' avant-garde—often inspired.

Puppets

The Théâtre Toone is a famous Brussels institution, with a history that goes back over 150 years. On a small stage in a loft off an ancient alleyway, the great works of Aristophanes, Shakespeare and Corneille, as well as more jolly entertainments, are played out with characteristic relish and verve by troupes of large puppets made of wood and *papier mâché*, manipulated by a few rather crude strings. No subject is too elevated for these characters: at Easter they take on The Passion. The first Toone theatre was established in 1830 by Antoine Genty (Toone is a shortened form of Antoine), and the tradition has been handed down from generation to generation (though not always within the family). It started off in the Marolles, but has been in its present home since 1966.

The Toone puppets are famous for their performances in a French-based *bruxellois* dialect, and José Géal, who now leads the 20 or so puppeteers in the 7th generation of this theatre (Toone VII), is not just a famous face in Brussels but also a noted expert on the language. If you want to hear *bruxellois*, this is the place to come—although you should note that for some of the classical plays only certain performances are in dialect. Some plays are also performed in English.

It may seem folksy, something to take the kids along to, but it is not. These plays are staged in the evening for good reason: they are serious productions, hard to follow and—so say those who can follow them—often outrageously bawdy. However much you can take in, an evening with Toone VII is an unmistakably *bruxellois* experience.

For children, there is the Théâtre Peruchet in Ixelles, a delightful puppet theatre which stages a varied programme based on fairy-tales, in a converted farmhouse; it also has a puppet museum, open during performances. The Théâtre Ratinet also puts on puppet shows for children, mainly new workings of fairy-tales.

Théâtre Toone, Impasse Schuddeveld, 21 Petite Rue des Bouchers, ✆ 513 54 86 or 511 71 37. *Performances at 8.30pm, not every day.* Reservations by telephone or at the theatre bar (*estaminet*) after 12 noon. The Toone puppet museum is open during the intervals.

Théâtre Peruchet, 50 Avenue de la Forêt, ✆ 673 87 30. *Performances on Wed, Sat and Sun, closed July and Aug.*

Théâtre Ratinet, 44 Avenue de Fré (Uccle), ✆ 375 15 63. *Afternoon performances.*

Jazz, Rock, World Music

Although Belgium does have its own rock culture and some energetic bands, the world still awaits a Belgian band of truly international distinction. Meanwhile, Brussels attracts many of the major international stars, who seem to respond well to their enthusiastic reception, and to the comparatively modest scale of most of the venues.

Jazz has a loyal and devoted following, and blossoms during the annual three-day Brussels Jazz Rallye *(end April, early May)*, when mainly European artists invade dozens of bars and small venues in and around the city centre in a happy festival of drinking and foot-tapping.

Le Botanique, *see* 'Cultural Centres', above.

Le Cercle, *see* 'Opera and Classical Music', above.

Cirque Royal, *see* 'Opera and Classical Music', above.

Chez Lagaffe, 4 Rue de l'Epée, ✆ 511 76 39. *Closed Sat lunch and Sun.* Restaurant with piano bar, which on Tuesday and Saturday evenings becomes a noted jazz venue, primarily Dixieland.

Forest National, 36 Avenue du Globe, ✆ 347 03 55. This is the largest and somewhat soulless rock venue in Brussels—an arena for 6000 adoring fans; also plays host to opera and classical music events.

Les Halles de Schaerbeek, 22a Rue Royale Sainte-Marie, ✆ 218 00 31. Formerly the main rock venue, now emerging from massive renovation.

La Luna, 20 Square Sainctelette, ✆ 218 59 59. The big new rock venue of Brussels.

Maison de la Radio, *see* 'Opera and Classical Music', above.

Le Paradoxe, 329 Chaussée d'Ixelles, ✆ 649 89 81. *Closed Sun.* Vegetarian restaurant which on Fridays and Saturdays doubles up as a popular venue for jazz, blues, folk and World music.

Sounds, 28 Rue de la Tulipe, ✆ 512 92 50. Jazz, folk, funk and South American.

La Soupape, 26 Rue A. de Witte, ✆ 649 58 88. A café-theatre which specializes in Belgian singer-songwriters.

Travers, 11 Rue Traversière, ✆ 218 40 86. One of the key jazz and World music venues, which also hosts occasional theatre.

UGC–De Brouckère, *see* 'Film', below.

Nightclubs and Discos

On Fridays and Saturdays the young-at-heart head for the trendy bars, then those with energy still to burn dance until sunrise. This is a lively and, by and large, amicable scene, but it's the people rather than the venues that make it work. Ask around in the livelier bars for tips about which places are currently on form.

Do Brasil, 88 Rue de la Caserne, ✆ 513 50 28. *Closed Sun and Mon.* Thumping Brazilian fun: tropical food with flair, and samba music to dance to.

L'Equipe, 40 Rue de Livourne, ✆ 538 31 84. *Open every night.* Standard-fare, fun disco for all-comers.

Le Garage, 16 Rue Duquesnoy, ✆ 512 66 22. *Every day after 11pm; Sun gay night.* Spacious disco with energetic light show—throbs when the crowds swell at weekends.

Jeux d'Hiver, Chemin du Gymnase (Bois de la Cambre). *Thurs and Sat; adm free (priority to members).* Disco at the edge of the woods, next to the Théâtre de Poche, frequented by the youthful smart set—*BCBG (bon chic, bon genre).*

Mirano Continental, 38 Chaussée de Louvain, ✆ 218 57 72. *Sat only, after 11pm.* A converted cinema, now one of the city's best and most popular dance spots.

La Rose, 21 Rue des Poissonniers, ✆ 513 43 25. *Wed–Sun 5pm onwards.* A *café/bardansant* close to the Bourse, with live band, spangled reflector-globes and toyboys in flares: weird but pure Jacques Brel.

Vaudeville, 14 Rue de la Montagne, ✆ 514 12 60. *Fri and Sun.* Wild dancing in a former music-hall.

Cabaret and Revues

Cabaret is always a mixed bag, and no more so than in Brussels. It ranges from small-scale comedy pieces, accompanied by singers and illusionists, to glam shows just this side of sleaze. If it is true sleaze that you want, follow your nose around the Gare du Nord.

Le Black Bottom, 1 Rue Lombard, ✆ 511 06 08. *Mon–Thurs 10.30 and 11.30pm; Fri and Sat 12 and 1am.* Cabaret and varieties, magicians and comics.

Chez Flo, 25 Rue au Beurre, ✆ 512 94 96. *Wed–Sat only, 8pm.* A ritzy transvestite show with dinner, the classiest of its kind in town. All good, clean fun—after a fashion. Dinner and show 1470 BF.

Domino, 54 Rue du Pont Neuf, ✆ 219 51 00. Cabaret, with a strong emphasis on its female artistes.

Garden's Club, 203 Avenue d'Auderghem, ✆ 647 13 66. Upmarket strip club around the EU—but looks innocent enough on a credit-card statement.

Moustache, 61 Quai au Bois à Brûler, ✆ 217 01 67. Fish restaurant with famous comedy cabaret on Saturdays; menu with show 1350 BF.

Le Pré Salé, 20 Rue de Flandres, ✆ 513 43 23. Restaurant serving Belgian cuisine, famous for its jocular 'playback' (mimed) show on Fridays; dinner with show 1250 BF.

Film

The eyes of the film world may not usually be trained on Belgium, but the joint directors Rémy Belvaux, André Bonzel and Benoit Poelvoorde bucked the trend in 1992 with their acclaimed arthouse movie *Man Bites Dog*. The touching semi-surrealist films of André Delvaux such as *L'Homme au crâne rasé* (1965) and *Un Soir, un train* (1968) are also worth looking out for. By and large, however, films in Belgium are imported, and the most successful tend to be mainstream Hollywood ones. The new releases are usually shown in their original language *(VO, version originale)* with subtitles in French or Flemish (or both), but older and widely popular films often have the soundtrack dubbed *(doublé)*. *The Bulletin* gives listings of performances in English.

For a comprehensive programme of classic international films, look out for the programme of the Musée du Cinéma; films shown there usually have the original soundtrack with French subtitles.

Remember that in Belgium (as in France) it is customary to tip the cinema attendant who shows you to your seat (about 20 BF).

Musée du Cinéma, Palais des Beaux-Arts, 9 Rue Baron Horta, ✆ 507 83 70. Daily menu of classic films, and two performances of silent movies with live piano accompaniment; a ticket of 80 BF to the museum entitles you to see a film as well. The museum publishes a monthly schedule of films, usually organized around a central theme; *see* pp.121–2 for further details and how to book.

Other Major Cinemas

Actor's Studio, 16 Petite Rue des Bouchers, ✆ 512 16 96.

Arenberg-Galeries, 26 Galerie de la Reine, ✆ 512 80 63.

Aventure, Galerie du Centre, ✆ 219 17 48.

Kinepolis, Bruparck (Heysel), ✆ 478 04 50. A mega-cinema with 24 auditoriums showing primarily mainstream films, plus the Imax theatre (vast screen with 3D effect); *see* p.217.

Movy Club, 21 Rue des Moines, ✆ 537 69 54.

Styx, 72 Rue de l'Arbre Bénit, ✆ 512 21 02.

UGC–Acropole, 8 Avenue de la Toison d'Or/17 Galerie de la Toison d'Or, ✆ 511 43 28.

UGC–City 2, 235 Rue Neuve (City 2), ✆ 219 42 46.

UGC–De Brouckère, 38 Place de Brouckère, ✆ 218 06 07. Also a venue for jazz concerts.

Vendôme-Roy, 18 Chaussée de Wavre, ✆ 512 65 53.

Shopping

What will you take home from your trip to Brussels? Fresh-cream chocolates for the neighbours, a few bottles of Belgian beer? A tablecloth of the finest hand-made Brussels lace? A set of Tintin classics to help improve your French? How about a 19th-century engraving of Brussels, an Art Nouveau lamp, or a party mask of Gilles de Binche?

Remember, the very character of Belgium was forged by the strong traditions of its artisans and traders. Shops and stores are in the mainstream of Belgian life, and the Belgians love to shop. To enhance the feel-good factor for those parting with their money, there are numerous elegantly styled *galeries*—covered arcades filled with shops, as well as restaurants and cafés for those who need refuelling between bouts of spending. You could pass most of the day in one: many Belgians do.

If you are in search of a bargain and local colour, there are several regular markets, although these are not quite the cultural feast that they are in, say, France and Italy. Towards the end of the year the traditional Christmas markets—selling crafts, decorations and seasonal fare—strike an authentic festive note, summoning up childhood memories of Christmas as it used to be.

Many of the supermarkets are vast emporia, selling food, wine and beer (including all the best Trappist beers), plus a huge range of goods such as toys, books, stationery, garden furniture, cheap clothes, anything. They are excellent places to stock up on basics and to gauge the range of goods generally available in Belgium. However, to find the best and largest of them, you will have to travel to the suburbs.

Value Added Tax

All shop prices include Value Added Tax (TVA/BWT) where applicable. At the time of writing this stands at 19.5 per cent. Non European Union visitors may claim back the VAT on purchases in excess of 7000 BF made in any one shop. This is a fairly complex procedure, most effectively dealt with if you are departing from Brussels international airport (Zaventem)—allow extra time.

When making your purchase, ask the shop for a form called a 'Tax-free Shopping Chèque'. Staple the receipt to it and fill out your personal details. When you reach the airport, have the Shopping Chèque stamped by customs (who may wish to inspect the goods), then take it to the refund office in the departure hall, which will refund to you the VAT paid.

Refunds are also available at the Interchange offices in central Brussels (88 Rue du Marché aux Herbes) and in Antwerp (36 Suikerrui). If you prefer, you can apply for a refund by post through Interchange. For further information ask at any major shop, the tourist office, or the specialist agency Europe Tax-free Shopping, 13/1 Jan Sobieskilaan, 1020 Brussels, ✆ 479 94 61.

The Main Shopping Districts and the *Galeries*

The centre of Brussels is packed with shops. The best-known shopping street is the Rue Neuve, a thronging pedestrianized thoroughfare within short walking distance of the Grand' Place. It contains many of the large chain stores such as Sarma and C&A, plus hundreds of clothing boutiques, record shops, camera suppliers and so forth. Despite its reputation, the Rue Neuve has become a little tawdry. This is not a criticism that could be levelled at the other main shopping area of Brussels, the area around Place Louise and the adjoining Boulevard de Waterloo/Avenue de la Toison d'Or. It is noted in particular for its chic clothes shops, and all the best names in *haute couture* are here, lining a broad avenue busy with traffic. Close at hand are two of the most famous modern *galeries*, the Galerie Louise and the Galerie de la Toison d'Or.

The *galeries* are the Belgian equivalents of shopping malls, and since the Belgians have been building them since the 1840s they have had plenty of time to perfect the formula. The best have quality written all over them: they entice then flatter the shopper with their style and elegance. Larger modern versions tend to be labelled 'Shopping Centers', and have a more down-to-earth range of shops, but here again architects have wisely developed the theory that the pleasure of the shopper is conducive to good trade.

Anspach Center, off Boulevard Anspach and Rue de l'Evêque. Busy, glitzy shopping centre, mainly clothes and accessories—smart, but not exclusive. It is connected to the Centre Monnaie and close to the Grand' Place.

Centre Monnaie, Place de la Monnaie and Boulevard Anspach. Another central shopping centre, along similar lines to the Anspach Center.

City 2, top of Rue Neuve, off Place Rogier. A warren of shops, restaurants and cinemas. Its wide range of quality shops includes the mega-book-and-record store FNAC, and the department store Inno.

Galerie Agora, off Rue des Eperonniers, Rue de la Colline and Rue du Marché aux Herbes. A surprisingly upmarket setting for this bazaar of subculture T-shirts, leather, jewellery, baseball caps, body-piercing, and other forms of alternative exotica, all within a stone's throw of the Grand' Place.

Galerie Bortier, between Rue Saint-Jean and Rue de la Madeleine. A 19th-century *galerie*, now a centre for second-hand books; *see* pp.93–4.

Galerie de la Toison d'Or, between the Avenue de la Toison d'Or and the Chaussée d'Ixelles. Often paired with its neighbour, the Galerie Louise, and of matching high standards. Clothes, accessories and much more.

Galerie Louise, off Avenue de la Toison d'Or and Avenue Louise. Sleek and tasteful, at the upper end of the shopping spectrum—mainly high-class clothing stores and shoe shops. Expensive, but the throngs of customers include many an average Bruxellois(e) out to buy that little number for the coming season. *See* p.138.

Galeries Royales de Saint-Hubert, off Rue du Marché aux Herbes. The oldest and most elegant of them all; marbled halls and a relaxed café ambience in which to window-gaze at exquisite shoes and clothes in luxurious boutiques, as well as browse around some excellent bookshops. *See* pp.94–5.

Woluwe Shopping Center, Rue Saint-Lambert (Woluwe-Saint-Lambert). A huge shopping emporium, an excellent example of its kind. Good restaurants and plenty of parking. You could easily spend a day here.

Antiques and Fine Art

Like everywhere else in Europe these days, antique dealers in Brussels know the value of everything, down to the last bit of junk that deserves no living space at all. There are few bargains here, but at least prices are not always exorbitant. The dealers range from traders in old carpets and bits of typewriter at the Place du Jeu de Balle to the owners of chichi antiques galleries of the Place du Grand-Sablon (the headquarters of the antiques trade), selling genuine pointillist paintings and beautifully veneered Biedermeier cabinets. Brussels, naturally enough, offers a particularly strong line in Art Nouveau objects, from door furniture to much sought-after lamps.

The Place du Grand-Sablon is also one of the two main centres for the fine art trade, and home to a number of small art galleries. The other is at the upper end of the Avenue Louise.

Argus, 45 Place du Grand-Sablon. Specializes in Art Nouveau and Art Deco: lamps, sculpture, furniture and so on.

Au Vieux Magasin, 39–41 Rue Godecharle (Quartier Léopold). An Aladdin's cave of appealing junk: ancient biscuit tins, *objets d'art*, furniture, Art Nouveau lamps. Must be a bargain somewhere in all this.

Isy Brachot, 62a Avenue Louise. Respected gallery dealing in surrealists and contemporary art.

Librairie van de Plas, 10 Rue des Eperonniers. Appropriately dingy and antique setting for a large selection of old prints and engravings: old views of Brussels, fashion plates, Art Deco posters, erotic engravings by Félicien Rops, and stacks more.

Sablon Shopping Gardens, 36 Place du Grand-Sablon. A cluster of some 40 sophisticated antique and art shops.

W. Sand, 28c Rue du Lombard. A long-established dealer in antique sculptures, musical instruments, jewellery and so forth from Africa and the Orient—an anthropological treasure trove.

Yannick David, 26 Boulevard de Waterloo. A respected purveyor of antique *objets d'art*, one of a cluster of antique and fine-art shops at this address.

Antiques Fairs and Flea Markets

Place du Grand-Sablon. A small, well-established, and rather upmarket antiques fair: old prints, books, 18th-century furniture, porcelain, Art Deco figurines, bakelite. *Sat 9–6, Sun 9–2.*

Place du Jeu de Balle. The premier flea market in Brussels: hunt for bargains; be astounded at what some people attempt to sell. *Every day, but even more stalls on Sun, 7–2.*

Stamps

Brussels is a leading European centre for philatelists. There are numerous stamp shops of all kinds and levels all the way down the Rue du Midi, from the Bourse to the Place Rouppe. Here is just a selection:

Belgasafe, 24 Rue du Midi. One of a cluster at the upper end of the street: mainly modern stamps from all over the world, for the general collector.

Maurice Baeton, 7 Rue du Midi. August antique stamp dealer and auctioneer, for the expert whose passion means spending serious money.

Philatelie Corneille Soeteman, 131 Rue du Midi. A major auction house, but also exhibits the *crème de la crème* for purchase in its showroom.

Books and Music

There are hundreds of bookshops in Brussels, selling primarily works in French and Flemish, of course. However, the large English-speaking community has given rise to a handful of excellent English-language bookshops. Belgium also has a strong music culture and the wide availability of recordings reflects this.

Centre Belge de la Bande Dessinée, 20 Rue des Sables. Thousands of comic-strip titles—in French and Dutch.

English Shop, 134 Chaussée de Waterloo and 186 Rue Stevin. Both branches sell a range of English books (mainly paperbacks), as well as English food .

FNAC, City 2, 123 Rue Neuve. French megastore selling a huge selection of books (in French, English and other languages), CDs and cassettes, and computers. Also has a ticket agency for concerts, etc.

Free Record Shop, Gaité Theatre, 18 Rue du Fossé aux Loups. Impressive recently converted record/CD and videocassette megastore in a venerable old music hall.

House of Paperbacks, 813 Chaussée de Waterloo (Uccle). English paperbacks and some hardbacks, with a good selection of children's books.

Musées Royaux des Beaux-Arts, 3 Boulevard de la Régence. Good selection of art books, particularly on Belgian painters.

W. H. Smith, 71–75 Boulevard Adolphe Max. Unlike most of the British chain of the same name, this is much more than just a stationer with a stock of popular books: this is a serious English-language bookshop, with a huge range of titles.

Strathmore Bookshop, 110 Rue Saint-Lambert (Woluwe). Small but impressive English-language bookshop.

Tropismes, Galerie des Princes, Galeries Saint-Hubert. Famously elegant bookstore, a joy to browse in. Has some English titles.

Chocolates

For the background to Belgian chocolates, *see* pp.228–30. The manufacturers listed below are the best-known and have numerous outlets throughout Brussels; these are all branches close to the city centre.

Corné, 24–6 Galerie de Roi, Galeries Saint-Hubert. One of the big names in luxury chocolates.

Godiva, 22 Grand' Place. Celebrated and expensive.

Leonidas, 46 Boulevard Anspach. Good value, and, in many people's opinion, the best.

Neuhaus, 27 Galerie de la Reine, Galeries Saint-Hubert. Refined, restrained, perhaps *the* place for the chocolate addict.

Clothes and Accessories

You can buy good-quality clothing of any kind in any price range in Belgium—from American-style children's clothing in the supermarket to Parisian *haute couture* and hot-off-the-press fashions by the Antwerp Six (*see* p.340). If you are in search of a touch of Euro-chic, have a stroll around Place Louise and Boulevard de Waterloo, where you'll find the likes of Chanel, Hermès, Giorgio Armani and Gianni Versace, and take a look at the adjoining Galerie Louise and Galerie de la Toison d'Or for lesser-known names and high-quality shoe shops. Rue Antoine Dansaert, close to the Bourse in the city centre, has a growing reputation for shops at the sharp end of fashion; for slightly less elevated boutiques, try the Anspach Center and the Rue Neuve.

Bouvy, 52 Boulevard de Waterloo. Famous, elegant sportswear shop that was established over half a century ago: who cares if you can't play tennis if you look this good?

C&A, 27 Rue Neuve. The Dutch chain stocking surprisingly good off-the-peg clothes at competitive prices.

Delvaux, 22 Boulevard Adolphe Max, 31 Galerie de la Reine in Galeries Saint-Hubert, and 27 Boulevard de Waterloo. The ultimate sophistication in leather goods.

Dujardin, 82–4 Avenue Louise. This famous shop sells chic children's clothes, all designed and made in Belgium. Recently rescued from oblivion by Delvaux, it is now housed in a vampishly renovated *maison de maître*.

Elvis Pompilio, 60 Rue du Midi. Hats wild and wonderful, stylish and fanciful—just how far can Elvis go? His most extravagant creations are virtually sculptures fashioned in felt. But don't expect any change out of 6000 BF.

Kat, 32 Rue Antoine Dansaert. Stylish off-the-peg children's clothes. Knitwear, smocks and winning woolly hats, for 0–14 years.

Marks & Spencer, 17–21 Rue Neuve. A well-stocked representative of the British chain: clothes, toiletries and some food.

Naf Naf, 42 Passage du Nord. A representative of the upbeat French chain stocking fashionable clothes for men and women. One of a cluster of clothing multiples in and around the Rue Neuve. Others include Etam (67–9 Rue Neuve), H&M (37 Rue Neuve) and La Redoute (9 Rue Neuve).

Peau d'zèbre, 40 Rue du Midi. Remarkable clothes for younger children, designed and made on the premises. Charming, stylish yet practical, in inspired autumnal colours—russets, greys and blacks. Most remarkable of all, they are incredibly good value: dungarees for 700 BF; nothing costs more than 1600 BF.

Stijl, 74 Rue Antoine Dansaert. Well-established avant-garde fashion boutique—a good place to hunt for your new outfit by Cries van Noten or Ann Demeulemeester.

Virgin, 10 Rue Antoine Dansaert and 13 Rue des Eperonniers. Gritty, modish boots and shoes, where black rules. For those who want street cred with style, and are prepared to pay for it.

Food Specialities

There are hundreds of first-class *traiteurs*, *pâtissiers* and other specialist food producers in Brussels. Below is a list of just a few shops of outstanding quality. Many standard specialities—including Trappist beers, *jambon d'Ardennes*, *saucisses de campagne*, cheeses and so forth—are available from the larger supermarkets, but specialist shops earn their keep by being a cut above the rest in a highly competitive market. For chocolates, *see* p.258.

Bernard, 93 Rue de Namur. Marbled delicatessen on the ground floor of a celebrated fish restaurant, specializing in mouthwatering fish and seafood preparations.

Dandoy, 31 Rue au Beurre and 14 Rue Charles Buls. Famous for its buttery, crumbly biscuits: *speculoos* and many other specialities.

Dragées Maréchal, 40 Rue des Chapeliers. Fine old store founded in 1848, specializing in the sugared almonds and fancy porcelain containers that are traditionally offered to guests at christenings.

Langhendries, 41 Rue de la Fourche. Supreme selection of beautifully conditioned French, Italian, Dutch and Belgian cheeses from 'dare you to' strong *crottes* to slabs the size of truck tyres, all presented with the true passion of a *maître-fromager*.

Pandin, 47 Rue de la Fourche. When you have bought your cheese from Langhendries, choose some patés, *charcuterie* or delicious ready-made dishes from this ravishing display of the *traiteur*'s art.

Wittamer, 12–13 Place du Grand-Sablon. The most celebrated *pâtisserie* in Brussels. Eat one of their chocolate cakes and you'll see why: angels will dance on your tongue.

Lace

For a summary of Belgian lace, *see* pp.36–8. There are numerous outlets selling lace around the Grand' Place—anything from glass-mats and handkerchiefs to tablecloths. The price varies according to provenance and quality, and there is a fair bit of imported lace, made in the Far East. Good lace shops, such as the ones listed below, should tell you where the lace is made. You only have to watch it being made to understand why there is no such thing as cheap Belgian lace.

Maison Rubbrecht, 23 Grand' Place. Central outlet for good-quality lace, much of it hand-made.

La Manufacture Belge de la Dentelle, 68 Galerie de la Reine, Galeries Saint-Hubert. Expensive, but good.

Louise Verschueren, 16 Rue Watteeu. Part exhibition, part shop, and a reliable source for real hand-made Belgian lace, *see* p.139.

Toys

You can buy good-quality toys in the department stores and a wide range of cheaper ones in supermarkets. The best specialist toy shops are a model mixture of alluring interior design and childhood magic. They include:

Christiaensen, 123 Rue Neuve, 22a Avenue de la Toison d'Or, and other branches. Comprehensive selections of international toy brands, anything from Barbie to radio-controlled speed-boats.

La Courte Echelle, 12 Rue des Eperonniers. Everything for the doll's house—plus the house itself. A magical world of miniaturization where craftsmanship is the guiding principle.

Picard, 71 Rue du Lombard. If you are going to a fancy-dress party, look no further—children and grown-ups alike. Fantasy outfits, masks, jokes, tricks, splendidly frivolous accessories, in a carnival of colour.

Serneels, 516 Galerie de la Toison d'Or. Tasteful toys and clothes based on comic-strip heroes such as Babar.

Supermarkets and Department Stores

The leading supermarket chains in Belgium are Delhaize, GB and Sarma. Smaller branches are found around the city, while in out-of-town sites they can take on gigantic proportions. They not only stock all the basics but also have respectable delicatessen counters as well as books, stationery, cheap clothes and toys.

Cora, Avenue Ariane, off the E40 (Woluwe Saint-Lambert). A vast megastore selling everything. Fill up your car with beer, wine and chocolate. Good also for cheap clothes, shoes, toys and toiletries.

GB, City 2, top of Rue Neuve. One of a vast chain of standard supermarkets, specializing in food and drink—good-quality, competively priced.

Inno, 111 Rue Neuve. The best-known department store in Brussels: clothes, sports goods, furnishings and domestic appliances, perfumes, textiles—the great department-store mix.

Sarma, 15 Rue Neuve. Large inner city superstore which stocks a good range of food and clothes.

Unusual and Miscellaneous

Art and High-class Decoration, 81 Rue de Laeken. Personalized marionettes made to order (or off-the-peg). Choose the face, specify the clothes: the marionette of your choice can be created to any degree of sumptuousness, for from 1500 BF to 15,000 BF or more.

Atelier de Moulages, Parc du Cinquantenaire (Rue Nerviens). Go home with an authentic plastercast of Leopold II; *see* pp.177–8.

Boutique de Tintin, 13 Rue de la Colline. Models, T-shirts, stationery, plus the books themselves, featuring Tintin, Captain Haddock, Snowy *et al.*

Cartes, 25 Rue Neuve. Postcards and greetings cards of all kinds and descriptions, featuring everything from work by classic photographers to filmstars, joyous kitsch and the outrageously lewd.

Euroline, 52 Rue du Marché aux Herbes. One of several Euro-shops, selling postcards, stickers, nailbrushes, flags—and just about anything with a flat surface that can be emblazoned with the bespangled Euro-flag.

Jean-Pierre Forton, 7 Rue des Carmes. Hand-crafted pipes and exotic tobaccos; *see* p.97.

La Boule Rouge, 52 Rue des Pierres. Artist's materials of every description in neatly ordered stacks and shelves, the very sight of which is inspiration to pick up a brush and have a go.

Lauffier, 26 Rue des Bouchers. Equipment for the chef, professional and amateur alike. Ranks of superb knives, glistening steel saucepans, precison-made spatulas, wooden moulds for *speculoos* biscuits—you can even buy yourself a full chef's outfit and crown yourself with a genuine *bonnet de chef.*

Le Jardin d'Apollon, City 2, Local 232, Rue Neuve. Tired of saying it withflowers? How about a bonsai tree instead? Prices start at just 300 BF.

New Second Light, 29–31 Rue Léopold. An inspired collection of the latest in domestic lighting. The shop also stocks 4500 kinds of electric bulb.

Service de Chalcographie, 1 Place du Musée. Over 5000 historical and contemporary prints from the royal library collection of plates; *see* p.114.

The Box Store, City 2, 126 Rue Neuve. Everything to do with boxes and domestic storage, including some ingenious solutions.

Markets

For **Antique and Flea Markets** see p.257.

Gare du Midi. *Sun am*. The biggest market in Brussels, filling the Boulevard de l'Europe and selling everything from couscous to cars. The bicycle market at the upper end of the Boulevard du Midi is a famous place to pick up a second-hand bike.

Grand' Place. *Sun 8am–12.30pm*. Bird market: half the square fills with traders selling parrots, love birds, budgies and fancy chickens. A delightful tradition enhanced by a relaxed Sunday mood. (The daily flower market in the Grand' Place consists of little more than a couple of stalls—barely a market at all.)

Parvis Saint-Gilles. *Tues–Sun 6am–12.30pm*. A busy food market a short walk from the Porte de Hal. Mainly fruit, vegetables and other necessities, displayed in vivid Technicolor—and also some speciality hams and cheeses.

Place de la Duchesse de Brabant (Molenbeek). Horse market (*Fri 6am–12 noon*), should you wish to buy a horse. Rural Belgium in an urban setting.

Place du Châtelain (Ixelles). *Wed 2–7 (and sometimes later)*. A charming evening food market (often referred to by the appealing expression *marché nocturne*), where basic groceries and vegetables are sold, along with interesting breads, ready-made pasta dishes and other specialities.

Rue Ropsy Chaudron (Anderlecht). *Sat 7am–1pm and Sun 8am–1pm*. A lively market for pets, poultry and North African food, held in and around the impressive ironwork shelter of a late 19th-century abattoir. The modern slaughterhouse next to this old abattoir is still active: hundreds of cattle and sheep are brought here to be sold for slaughter on Tuesdays (cattle, from 6am) and Wednesdays (calves and sheep, from 6pm, summer only)—not for the faint-hearted. Committed carnivores come to eat at the restaurants that are clustered around the abattoir gates.

Christmas Fairs

These take place in the run-up to the Fête de Saint-Nicolas (6 December) and Christmas itself (contact the tourist office for dates and times). The best-known are held in the **Place du Grand-Sablon**, and the **Place Cardinal Mercier** (Jette). The stalls sell decorations, candles, foods associated with the festive seasons, hand-crafted gifts, and so on, but their particular appeal is the joyous mood and vivid colour which bring light and warmth to those chill and gloomy December days.

People from all over the world want to come and live in Belgium, and Belgian bureaucracy seems to do as much as it can to put them off. Getting permission to stay is one thing; finding a job and somewhere to live that is halfway decent and reasonably priced is another. If you come from a country in the European Union, the hurdles are lower and further apart, but there are hurdles nonetheless. Don't be put off: provided you have the right qualifications to compete in the job market, and the stamina to go through the turmoil of relocation, you should be able to find your feet—and, with luck, join the many members of the international community who find living and working in Brussels both rewarding and a pleasure.

Living and Working in Brussels

The Paperwork

EU passport holders have the right to stay in Belgium and take up work without a work permit. However, your passport allows you to stay for 90 days only; and after this you have to register with the police to acquire a three-month residence card *(certificat d'immatriculation)*, renewable for a further three months. You can do this at the local town hall *(maison communale/gemeente-huis)*. The application procedure is straightforward; all you will need is three passport-style photos. You will have to pay a small charge and may be asked also to give your fingerprints. After your first or second three-month visa you can apply for a five-year identity card *(certificat d'inscription au registre des étrangers,* CIRE*)*. Note that if you come to Brussels with the intention of finding work you should not wait the 90 days to register at your local *maison communale*; strictly speaking, you should register within eight days of your arrival, since you need to have done so before applying to a recruitment agency (see 'Finding a Job').

If you are from **outside the EU** your passport entitles you to a visit of 90 days or whatever visa restriction applies. A non-EU national coming to work in Belgium must obtain a work permit before entering the country, as well as entry permits for any accompanying family. The standard work permit is a B permit (valid for one year, not transferable to any other job besides that specified); an A permit (transferable to other employment, valid for five years) may be granted after residence of five years. There are various other pieces of documentation and complications to wrestle with, so it is best to apply to your nearest Belgian consulate as early as possible before you leave; the process can take several months.

Once you achieve your work permit you can apply for an identity card which is valid for one year, for yourself and your family—although this again requires a handful of documents to prove family connection and a certificate as evidence of good conduct and general desirability (the *Certificat de bonne vie et moeurs/Bewijs van Goed Gedrag en Zeden*, signed by your local police). You are permitted to bring all your possessions with you into Belgium—although it's best if all items are over six months old, to avoid the suspicious scrutiny of Customs. Once in Belgium, for further information or clarification about legal formalities (such as permit renewal), you can apply to the **Service des Etrangers/ Vreemdelingendienst**, Square de Meeüs, 1040 Brussels, ℰ 514 22 70.

Finding Somewhere to Live

There are no short cuts to finding accommodation in Brussels. Property values across the board have shot up, trailing rented accommodation in their wake.

Rents begin at about 10,000 BF per month (rock-bottom), average 20–50,000 BF and stretch into the millions. The city also has its share of good and bad landlords. It may be worth staying in an apartment hotel (see p.243) to begin with, while you find your way around. All the usual rules of house-hunting apply. Certain areas of the city—such as Ixelles, Uccle, Saint-Gilles, Woluwe and Watermael-Boitsfort—seem to be more popular with Western foreigners than others. (Note, however, that the following municipalities do not grant residence permits to non-EU nationals: Anderlecht, Forest, Molenbeek, Saint-Gilles, Saint-Josse and Schaerbeek). Properties for rent are advertised in the national newspapers such as *Le Soir* and *De Standaard*, and there are also useful listings in *The Bulletin*, where owners will be expecting to deal with English-language clients. By far the best, however, are to be found in the weekly journal *Vlan*. This reaches newspaper shops first thing on Monday morning, and the best properties are snaffled within hours, if not minutes. After Thursday *Vlan* is distributed free of charge to letter-boxes throughout Brussels. Look out also for the orange and black 'to let' signs *(A Louer/Te Huur)* posted in windows. Alternatively, you can apply to any of the estate agencies *(agence immobilière)* which deal with rented property. They receive their cut from the landlord, so you don't have to pay for their services—but remember that their loyalties ultimately lie with the landlord. There are also some property agencies that offer a scouting service in return for a fee.

Examine the terms of the lease very carefully. Leases for unfurnished properties are usually for a period of three, six or nine years, although shorter leases are available. Furnished properties can be rented for any length of time but a year is usual. You will be asked to put down a deposit *(garantie)*—usually the equivalent of three months' rent. These days it is standard practice to set up a *garantie bancaire* by opening a *compte bloqué* in your own bank, with two signatures, yours and your landlord's; without both signatures the money cannot be withdrawn.

Leases are normally accompanied by a document called the *état des lieux*—a survey of the precise condition of the property, and the benchmark against which the condition of the property at the end of the lease will be measured. This is drawn up by an independent assessor and costs about 7000 BF, split two ways between between landlord and tenant. It is for the protection of both parties: if there is no *état des lieux*, this is always to the advantage of the tenant. An alternative is for the tenant and landlord to do this survey together—a less formal arrangement, and free of charge. If you do this it is important above all to list anything in the property that is new, and anything that is broken or worn out. You should allow a few weeks at the beginning of your tenancy to see if any survey covers all faults—if not, include any further observations before signing it. When visiting the property, check its state of repair carefully. See whether the heating system works and how much hot water it generates—Brussels can be very cold and damp in winter. You will be expected to take responsibility for paying the bills; these are usually due every two months and must be paid within 10 days of receipt. If you go away a lot this can be a hazard: to avoid this, pay your bills by standing order *(domiciliation des paiements)*. Tenants also have to pay fire insurance, but note that the landlord is legally obliged to pay property tax. When you enter the property you may well have to get all the services reconnected. This means that you will have to pay deposits. For gas and electricity, however, it may be possible to arrange a joint meter-reading with the tenant who is leaving, and to complete a document which is supplied by the local office and signed by both parties. This avoids all the inconvenience of reconnection.

In apartment blocks, a regular bone of contention is the 'common parts': the staircase, landings and lifts. Find out who looks after these. It seems virtually impossible to live in any flat in Brussels without having some kind of running dispute with a neighbour—about dustbins, noise, car parking or dogs. If you enter into a dispute with your landlord you do have some recourse to the law. If you encounter problems that are not put right in reasonable time you should send a letter by registered mail to the landlord, formally requesting that repairs are carried out. If this doesn't work, you may have to engage the services of an *avocat*, a professional lawyer.

Lastly, three months before vacating the property you should write to your landlord to announce that you intend to leave. Failure to do so can be interpreted as a wish to renew the lease, and can incur penalties. Also before you leave, you'll have to scrub the property from top to bottom, and make sure it is up to the standards stipulated by the *état des lieux*. Since the Belgians generally have very high standards of cleanliness, it may be wise to seek professional help for this task.

Finding a Job

With over a quarter of the Brussels population of foreign extraction, and half of these from EU countries, it goes without saying that foreigners can get jobs in Brussels. The majority of these are executive and governmental posts, which are by and large arranged from abroad. For people from non-EU countries it is really only at this level that any work opportunities exist at all, and it is virtually impossible for them find legal casual or temporary work. For people from the EU, in contrast, the situation is rather different. In principle, they can apply for jobs at any level. In practice, however, the main vacancies fall into two categories: executive posts, and temporary work for experienced personnel. There are extremely few temporary menial jobs available to the outsider; these are mostly spoken for by the local labour force. Note that the construction industry is unable by law to employ temporary staff. Executive posts are advertised in the leading national newspapers, such as *Le Soir, La Libre Belgique, De Standaard,* and also in *The European* and *The New York Herald Tribune. The Bulletin* also lists vacancies, but these tend to be primarily for secretaries, PAs and other office staff.

All EU citizens are entitled to use the services of a Belgian government job agency, which advertises general vacancies. In Brussels, this is the **Office Régional Bruxellois de l'Emploi** (look in your telephone directory to find your local office). The chances of finding employment through one of these offices, against local competition, are slim, but they can offer useful advice about employment generally, and about the comparability of qualifications.

A major employer is the **European Union**, and many of its staff—at all levels—are recruited locally. You can contact it directly by applying to **The Commission of the European Communities**, Recruitment Unit—COM/A/724, 200 Rue de la Loi, 1049 Bruxelles, ✆ 235 11 11. There is also a London office: European Commission, 8 Storeys Gate, London SW1P 8AT, ✆ (0171) 973 1992.

Because Belgium's employment laws guarantee substantial benefits after a year's service (paid holidays, pension schemes, sickness benefit, maternity benefits and so on), many employers prefer to keep their overheads down by taking on temporary staff. As a result, there are opportunities in the multinationals and in the EU for temporary office work, and in computer-based service industries, and nursing. Experience, training and qualifications come into play: competition is tight. It also helps to be able to speak French and/or Flemish competently, although this is not always essential: there are some job environments (such as in some departments of the EU) where the language may be almost exclusively English. The temporary work sector is serviced and more or less controlled by the **employment and recruitment agencies** called *agences intérimaires.* Here are some of the best known—but there are dozens more, listed in the Yellow Pages *(les Pages d'Or)* of the telephone directory under *Intérimaires.*

ADIA Interim, office work: 52 Boulevard Adolphe Max, ✆ 219 30 85; European affairs: 28 Rue Montoyer, ✆ 230 50 26.

Creyf's Interim, 21–3 Rue de l'Ecuyer, ✆ 218 83 70; and 226a Avenue Louise, ✆ 646 27 02.

Randstad Interim, 8–10 Rue des Princes (Place de la Monnaie), ✆ 209 12 11.

The best advice to anyone seeking work in Brussels is to register with one or more of these agencies—though you must first of all register as a resident at the *maison communale (see* above). An *agence intérimaire* does not charge you for placing you in work: it receives a commission from the enterprise which takes you on. However, when you get work the *agence intérimaire* will be your employer, will issue you with a contract (often of five or six weeks' duration, renewable), and will be responsible for paying you. You may be lucky and find that an agency already has something on its books that suits you. More likely, however, you will have to wait—but telephone the agency regularly to let it know that you are keen. Such is the grip of the *agences intérimaires* that most major employers will be under some sort of obligation to recruit through them. Hence you may find that, even if you have a personal contact within a company, you will still have to be employed through an *agence intérimaire*. However, your contact (known in the trade as a *piston*) can legitimately root for you and make fairly sure that you are the person recruited. One group of people who will not be served by the *agences*, however, is **students under the age of 25**. This is because of a legally enforced supplement (14.8 per cent of the salary) called the *pécule de vacances* which employers are obliged to give to their employees to cover holiday pay. To protect young people from exploitation, and to prevent a flood of temporary labour during the summer holidays, employers are obliged to pay a full year's *pécule de vacances* if they take on any student before he or she has left education for a full four months. This means that ex-students cannot take up temporary work until 1 November, since the school year is deemed to end on 30 June. It also means the *agences intérimaires* are not keen to take on students, and that if you are under 25 and seeking work for the first time after full-time education you should come with documents showing that you have left education at least four months previously.

One further agency is worth singling out. **Focus Career Services** (23 Rue Lesbroussart, ✆ 646 65 30) offers not just the services of a recruitment agency, but also training programmes to help newcomers to find jobs, whether paid employment or voluntary work. It is particularly valued by families who have relocated but where one spouse, for whatever reason, cannot pursue his or her normal career. The agency also publishes a document called *Getting Started Legally*, which offers advice about setting up a business in Belgium.

Survival Guides

If living and working in Belgium seems an uphill struggle, remember that you are not alone. There are several publications produced that anticipate the concerns of the expatriate community, including the bi-annual *Newcomer*, which is produced as a supplement to *The Bulletin* in March and September. It is an excellent review of the problems of moving to Belgium, and their solutions; as well as a guide to life in Brussels, and contains numerous addresses and advertisements for schools, clubs, removal companies, employment agencies, services and so on. It is offered free of charge, and distributed by the publishers to Belgian embassies abroad, which then send it out to applicants who are intending to live in Belgium. It is also available from several of the major relocation agencies (*see* below). If you have difficulty getting hold of a copy, you could contact the publishers (Ackroyd Publications SA, 329 Avenue Molière, 160 Brussels, ✆ 343 99 09, fax 343 98 22), but they may be unwilling to mail individual copies unless you send an international postal order to cover the cost of postage for a package weighing 500g. Another similar publication, produced annually, is called *Living in Belgium* (about 500 BF), which is available in English-language bookshops such as W. H. Smith (*see* pp.257–8).

It is also worth contacting the **Belgian embassies** abroad for any advice about living and working in Belgium. The embassy in London supplies a document called *Working in Belgium*, which gives useful general advice, as well as addresses of recruitment agencies in Belgium and in the UK, plus details about sickness and unemployment benefit, state pension schemes and so on.

The **British Department of Social Security** publishes a document (SA 29) called *Your Social Security Insurance, Benefits and Health Care Rights in the EC*, available at your local DSS office, or from the Department of Social Security Overseas Branch, Newcastle-upon-Tyne, NE98 1YX, ✆ (0191) 213 5000. For information about benefits in Belgium, contact the **Office National de la Securité Sociale**, 76 Boulevard de Waterloo, 1000 Bruxelles, ✆ 509 31 11.

EU nationals are entitled to use, the Belgian **state school system** free of charge—which on the whole is very good. There are also numerous private schools of all kinds in Brussels, which are specifically set up to cater for the international community. The publications for newcomers listed above offer general surveys of these, and carry numerous advertisements submitted by the schools. Belgian embassies abroad are also able to help with this.

The quickest way to find your feet, however, is to ask people who have done it before. There are numerous clubs and associations that bring together nationals with common interests, be it sport, culture, religion—or just nationality. Alternatively, for a price, you can make use of one of the handful of specialist **relocation services agencies** which advertise in publications such as *Newcomer* and *Living in Belgium*. For a fee, or for payment by the hour, they will undertake to advise you on entry requirements, housing, schooling, and generally hold your hand while you become accustomed to your new life in Belgium.

Newcomers and resident expatriates alike should look out for the annual **Brussels Welcome Fair**—a dynamic event at which numerous agencies and services in Brussels set out their wares. This includes property agencies, tax consultants, insurance brokers, schools, clubs and associations, even restaurants. In 1994 it took place in the *Palais des Congrès* during the last weekend of September, but the date and location may alter in future (for information ℂ 675 82 67).

Addresses and Contacts

American Chamber of Commerce: 5 Avenue des Arts, 1040 Brussels, ℂ 513 67 70, fax 513 79 28.

American Library: 1c Square du Bastion, ℂ 512 21 29.

British and Commonwealth Women's Club: 509 Rue du Bois, 1150 Brussels, ℂ 772 53 13.

British Chamber of Commerce: 30 Rue Joseph II, 1040 Brussels, ℂ 219 07 88, fax 217 84 58.

British Council and Library: 5 Avenue Galilée, 1030 Brussels, ℂ 219 36 00.

Childcare: Apply to the Office National de l'Enfance (ONE), ℂ 739 39 79 for a list of crèches and child-care facilities in your area. Nannies Incorporated (international nanny agency), ℂ 374 31 81.

Crisis helpline: Community Help Service, 102 Rue Saint-Georges, Box 20, 1050 Brussels, ℂ 647 67 80; 24-hr crisis helpline, ℂ 648 40 14. An English-speaking organization to help and advise on family problems, educational difficulties, depression, drug addiction.

Electricity: See your bills or meters for the contact number of the company that serves your property; central office and emergencies ℂ 511 19 70.

Gas: See your bills or meters for the contact number of the company that serves your property; central office and emergencies ℂ 511 41 11.

Help and Information: Bruxelles-Accueil, 6 Rue de Tabora, ℂ 511 27 15, 511 81 78. Organization funded by the Catholic Church offering help and advice to all comers of any denomination (students, refugees, anyone) about the law, accommodation, acclimatization, courses, etc.

Language Schools: There are dozens of these, teaching both French and Flemish. The largest are Berlitz, 306 Avenue Louise, ℂ 649 61 74; and Linguarama, 19 Avenue des Arts, ℂ 217 90 55. See publications such as *Living in Belgium* for further details or ask around. The style of language learning that suits you depends very much on personal preferences.

Telephone: Belgacom (central office), 17 Boulevard de l'Impératrice, ℂ 513 89 81, but it is better to deal with your local office.

Water: Compagnie Intercommunale Bruxelloise des Eaux, 70 Rue aux Laines, ℂ 518 81 11; emergencies ℂ 739 52 11.

Belgium is a small country, and Belgians think nothing of travelling from Brussels to the coast, or to the valley of the River Semois in the far south, for lunch. The truth is that a guide book to the whole of Belgium could be entitled 'Day Trips from Brussels'. Places like Bruges, Ghent, Liège, Antwerp, and Ostende are all within easy reach. These day trips, however, are all to places lying within 30km of Brussels.

Day Trips from Brussels

Of all the Flemish cities, Mechelen is the most charming. It is an unpretentious working town, a cluster of crooked streets centred upon a sprawling market-place—as much its commercial heart today as in its flamboyant medieval past. Dotted about the city are Renaissance palaces, wizened old abbeys, solid churches—all dominated by the stupendous bell tower soaring like a vast medieval rocket from St Rombout's Cathedral. Its startling proportions are eclipsed only by the extraordinarily ambitious nature of the original plans. Despite its quiet charms, Mechelen tends to be left off the usual tourist trail, perhaps because, the cathedral apart, it cannot boast any high-profile attraction. With its lively atmosphere, prosperous streets and evocative medieval backwaters, it is remarkably unspoilt.

History

Mechelen grew up as a fortified trading centre on the River Dijle (Dyle) in the early medieval period, and became prosperous through its textiles and weaving. It developed into an important administrative centre under the Dukes of Burgundy, and in 1473 Charles the Bold set up the Grand Council here. This was the supreme court of the land, and it remained in Mechelen until the end of the eighteenth century. When Charles the Bold died in 1477, his widow Margaret of York came to live in Mechelen, and when Margaret of Austria, acting as regent for the infant Charles V, became governor of the Netherlands in 1507 she made Mechelen her capital. This was the city's heyday as a European centre of power, culture and learning. However, following Margaret of Austria's death in 1530, the court moved to Brussels and Mechelen retired from the limelight. In 1559, in the gathering storm of religious troubles, it became an archbishopric. The diocese was combined with Brussels in 1962, but the archbishop of Mechelen-Brussels holds the title of Primate of Belgium, the leading figure in the Catholic Church. Mechelen returned to prosperity in the 17th and 18th centuries, during which it became famous for its lace, tapestry, embossed leather wall-hangings and with Baroque woodcarving.

Getting There

Mechelen (Malines in French) lies halfway between Brussels and Antwerp, just off the A1/E10 autoroute. The railway station (direct connections with Brussels Nord/Central/Midi) lies to the south of the town, a 25-minute walk from the centre. There is a fair amount of public parking, which is controlled by pay-and-display tickets available from machines. The **tourist information** office (open Mon–Fri 8–5, Sat and Sun 10–12, 2–4.30) is in the Stadhuis in the Grote Markt.

Grote Markt and Stadhuis

The **Grote Markt** is the largest of the market squares at the centre of the city: no petite Renaissance gem this, but a business-like open space, bordered by picturesque buildings containing restaurants and tea rooms and, on its eastern side, the **Stadhuis** (town hall). The Stadhuis is made up of two contrasting but adjoining buildings: the plainer 14th-century Lakenhalle (clothmakers' hall) to the right as you face it, with its squat, unfinished belfry; and the north wing, in 16th-century flamboyant Gothic, flanked by an arcaded walkway. This was originally intended to be the seat of the Grand Council, and building was commenced following designs by the celebrated architect Rombout Keldermans in 1530; however, the project was abandoned in 1543 after the court moved to Brussels, and it was only finally completed to Keldermans' plans in 1911. The statue in the middle of the Grote Markt is an unflattering 19th-century impression of Margaret of Austria. Nearby, immediately in front of the tourist office, is a modern statue of Op Signoorke being tossed in a sheet (*see* p.275).

Leading into the Grote Markt from the south is the **Ijzerenleen**, which also serves as a marketplace. It is fronted by the **Oud Schepenhuis** ('old sheriff's office'), a squat gabled and turreted tower built in 1374, which served as the seat of the Grand Council from 1474 to 1618.

St-Romboutskathedraal

The real centrepiece of Mechelen is **St-Romboutskathedraal** *(open about 9.30–dusk)*. It is named after the Irish missionary St Rombout (St Rombold), who brought Christianity to this region in the 8th century. A restoration programme is bringing its 14th- and 15th-century stonework back to pristine condition. Enter by the south door, from the marketplace. The immensity of the interior and its sombre, timeless poise immediately impress themselves upon you. The mighty columns, decked with sympathetic 17th-century statues of the apostles, recede into the soft gloom. The choir has been radically altered by black and white marble Baroque installation around the altar, which was designed by the Mechelen-based sculptor Luc Fayd'Herbe (1617–97). A bronze plaque in front of the altar marks the entrance to the crypt, where all the archbishops of Mechelen have been laid to rest, bar one (*see* below).

A treasured collection of paintings lines the ambulatory. Immediately to the right of the south door is a *Crucifixion* (1627) by Antoon van Dyck, full of passion and verve. Continuing to the right of the choir, there is a triptych of the *Martyrdom of*

St Sebastian by Michiel Coxie (1499–1592), who was born in Mechelen. Another triptych featuring St Luke painting the Virgin is by Abraham Janssens (1575–1632), an Antwerp painter who might have risen to greater stardom had he not been overshadowed by his famous contemporary, Rubens. On the left-hand side of the choir is a triptych of the *Martyrdom of St George* (c. 1588), again by Michiel Coxie, showing the strong influence of his Italian training.

The chapel immediately to the west of the north door contains the tomb of Desiré Joseph Mercier, cardinal-archbishop of Mechelen from 1906 until his death in 1926. During the First World War he bravely stood up against the occupying German authorities, and in the 1920s he attempted to bring about a reconciliation between the various Churches of Europe, particularly the Church of England and the Roman Catholic Church, by conducting a series of conferences called the 'Malines Conversations'. It is a sign of the esteem in which Mercier was held by the people of Mechelen that he was buried separately from his predecessors.

The oak pulpit in the nave is a classic piece of 18th-century Baroque woodcarving by the Antwerp sculptor Michiel Vervoort the Elder, and represents the Conversion of Saint Norbert (occasioned by a scrape with death when he fell from his horse). Vervoort was noted for his animal sculptures, and if you look closely you can find various small beasts among the foliage, such as a lizard, a snail, a frog and a squirrel. The pulpit was originally intended for another location where it was to be set against the wall. To fit this site, it has been ingeniously cut and altered to wrap around the pillar.

Near the west door is a model of the cathedral following original plans discovered in Mons. The massive tower was going to be almost twice its present size, rising to 167m—the tallest in Europe. Work began in 1452 but, for unknown reasons, stopped in the 1520s. In its present form the tower is remarkable enough: for 87 of its full 97m it rises as a hollow tube, bridged only by six wooden floors, before reaching its lowest stone vault. Depending on the season and the availability of staff, visitors can join a guided tour and climb the staircase of 514 steps to the upper gallery. The tower contains two celebrated bronze carillons, one dating back in part to the 17th century—a total of 98 bells, weighing 80 tons. The bells are operated by an ingenious system connected to a keyboard, and concerts are given on Monday evenings during the summer months (*8.30–9.30pm*).

From the Cathedral to the Speelgoedmuseum

Leaving the cathedral by the north door, turn left into the Wollemarkt and follow it around to the right. The bishop's palace can be seen on the left, a surprisingly secular-looking neoclassical building (1717) in need of a lick of paint.

The road leads past a quaint cluster of houses, including the beautiful 16th-century red-brick **Refugie van de Abdij van St-Truiden** (Refuge of the Abbey of St Truiden), a charming stack of stepped gables and steeply pitched roofs. Beyond it, down Schoutetstraat is the **Refugie Abdij van Tongerlo**, which is now the home of the Gaspard de Wit workshops, royal tapestry manufacturers *(open Sat only, guided tour 10.30)*.

Virtually opposite is **St-Janskerk** (St John's Church), a massive stone edifice in 15th- and 16th-century Gothic with a contrastingly delicate belfry over the crossing. It contains a remarkable triptych of the *Adoration of the Magi* (1619) by Rubens, a fascinating encounter between maternal tenderness and male swagger and power. Isabella Brant, Rubens' first wife, posed as the model for the Virgin.

On the corner of Frederik de Merodestraat, east of St-Janskerk, is the home of a famous carillon school, where people come from all over the world to learn to play these unusual Flemish bells. A short way down the same street on the left is the **Museum Hof van Busleyden** *(open 10–12 and 2–5, closed Tues; adm 75 BF)*. This pretty little palace was built in 1503–17 for Hieronymus van Busleyden, a friend of Erasmus and a councillor to Charles V. It now houses the Beiaardmuseum (carillon museum) and the municipal museum, which contains an interesting mixed bag of paintings and sculpture by Rubens, Gaspard de Crayer, Michiel Coxie and others, plus various artefacts such as the old wooden Op Signoorke doll, beloved mascot of Mechelen, which used to be tossed in a sheet at festivals. Its name dates back to 1775 when a man from Antwerp—Mechelen's great rival—was accused of trying to steal the doll. Op Signoorke comes from '*señor*', a reference to Antwerp's Spanish connections and once a nickname for the people of Antwerp, used in Mechelen as an expression of contempt.

Retrace your steps to the crossroads, then continue east to the **Sint Pieter en Sint Pauluskerk** (Church of SS Peter and Paul), which has a Baroque façade topped by an impressive Jesuit sunburst. A little beyond this, in Keizerstraat on the left-hand side, is the **Paleis van Margaretha van Oostenrijk** (palace of Margaret of Austria), a fine Renaissance building of the early 16th century, set around a formal garden of clipped box hedges *(garden open to the public)*. It was the seat of the Grand Council from 1618 to 1794 and still serves as law courts.

The best museum in Mechelen lies at the end of a 10-minute walk further east along Keizerstraat, beyond the noisy bypass road. It is the **Speelgoedmuseum** (toy museum), at 21 Nekkerspoel *(open 10–5, closed Mon; adm 100 BF, children 3–12 80 BF)*. This major collection of toys takes as its starting point a painting by Bruegel called *Children's Games* (1560) to demonstrate the timeless fascination of toys. Set out on several floors, there are trains, boats, board games, early Meccano, Dinky toys, Fisher-Price, Lego, Barbie and Ken—you name it. The thousands of exhibits are attractively presented in historical order to underline the theme of continuity with the present. It is very much a museum designed for children, and they are welcome to romp around and encouraged to play with exhibits where appropriate. Look out for the exhibit devoted to the Brussels-born illustrator Peyo (Pierre Culliford, 1928–92), who in 1957 invented the Smurfs (called Schtroumpfs locally) and went on to make a fortune for himself. The museum also has its own café (*see* below). All in all, it's a joy.

Other Attractions

Clock Museum: Horlogeriemuseum, 13 Schipstraat *(open 10–12 and 2–6, closed Sun; adm 120 BF)*. Small museum devoted to historic clocks and watches, many of them charming and unusual.

Tours in a Horsedrawn Carriage: from the tourist office in the Grote Markt; 2–5, Easter–end Nov, Sat and Sun only, July and Aug every day. 400 BF for up to 5 people.

Festival: Hanswijkprocessie, Sunday before Ascension Day (May). A statue of the Virgin Mary from the Hanswijk Basilica is paraded around the streets in an annual pageant, celebrating deliverance from the plague in 1272.

Eating Out

D'Hoogh, 19 Grote Markt, ℰ (015) 21 75 53. *Closed Sun evening and Mon.* Serious, high-quality restaurant, offering dishes such as Canadian braised lobster with *witloof* (chicory). Fresh, seasonal produce from the market is used to produce the 'market lunch' for 1650 BF.

In den Beer, 32–3 Grote Markt. Brasserie, serving anything from hamburgers (345 BF) to braised pheasant (545 BF). Two-course set lunch for 695 BF.

In den Witten Bijbel, 7/1 Niewwerk (at eastern end of cathedral). *Closed Thurs.* Cheap, family-run tavern, with terrace dining in summer. Homemade soups (75 BF), robust stews (450 BF), and daily menus.

Club Bizare, 35 Ijzerenleen. Not quite as bizarre as it likes to think, but a fun, post-modern interior, where light meals of pasta, *Spinaziestoemp* and the like are served for around 230 BF.

Speelgoedmuseum (toy museum), 21 Nekkerspoel, ℰ (015) 20 03 86. A fun place to take the children, this café attached to the toy museum *(access with museum ticket only)* is very reasonably priced. Dishes include lasagne (195 BF), waffles and fruit tarts—and you are also welcome to bring your own picnic.

Leuven is famous above all for two things. It is the seat of one of the great, historic universities of Europe—the oldest in Belgium and still the largest, with 23,000 students. It also has the most beautiful Stadhuis (town hall) in the country: like a bejewelled reliquary casket writ large, it is the ultimate example of Flamboyant Gothic style. It rather puts everything else in the shade in this compact and user-friendly town, but other highlights include the art museum inside the Sint Pieterskerk, which has a notable collection of medieval and Renaissance painting, and the Stedelijk Museum Vander Kelen-Mertens, which presents a rewarding mixture of furnished rooms, paintings and ceramics. A stroll to the south of the town leads to the picturesque and extensive *béguinage*, the Groot Begijnhof.

History

There may have been a Roman settlement on this site at the highest navigable point of the River Dijle (Dyle), and the Vikings appear to have made a base here from which to launch their raids. After they were ousted at the end of the 9th century a fortress was built, and the town began to develop at its feet. It became the capital of the Duchy of Brabant after 1190 and blossomed with the growth of the Flemish textile industry, swelling to fill two successive rings of town walls. However, the strife between the weavers and the nobles, which affected all of Flanders during the 14th century, was particularly acute in Leuven, and ended up with a defenestration: in 1379 rioters pitched 17 nobles from the windows of the old Stadhuis on to the pikes of the guildsmen below, incurring the wrath and vengeance of the then ruler of Brabant, Wenceslas of Luxembourg. At this point weavers left Leuven in droves, emigrating mainly to England. The town went into a decline and under the Dukes of Burgundy the capital of Brabant was moved to Brussels. However, in 1425 a university was founded at Leuven, and a century later, in 1517, the great humanist Desiderius Erasmus (*see* pp.206–208) and others founded the Collegium Trelingue (College of Three Languages), which encouraged a ground-breaking synthesis of religious and classical studies. Mercator the geographer and Vesalius the physican were among the alumni. However, the rise of Protestantism in northern Europe caused the authorities to retrench and Leuven became a bastion of Roman Catholic orthodoxy. Erasmus's doctrine was condemned, and his dreams of liberalized education were demolished.

The university had a rocky career through the religious disputes of the 16th and 17th centuries. **Cornelius Jansen** (1585–1638) taught here and Leuven became a focus of the subsequent Jansenist movement, which promoted an ascetic way of life and a firm belief in predetermination; it was later declared heretical. In 1835 a new Catholic University established in Mechelen was transferred to Leuven. Despite a constant power struggle between liberal and conservative Catholics, the university built up noted faculties in science, engineering and the humanities.

Language has been a bone of contention throughout most of this century, resulting in what many look back upon as a regrettable series of events for a great university. During the 19th century all lectures were in French (except those on theology, which were delivered in Latin). After a series of riots in the 1920s the university adopted a dual language approach. In the 1960s the dispute was revived when Flemish agitators demanded that French be abandoned completely. Amid growing protests and acrimony it was decided in 1968 that the university should be split in two. In 1980 the Université Catholique de Louvain was transferred to a brand new university city called Louvain-la-Neuve to the south of Brussels, while the K.U. Leuven (Katholieke Universiteit Leuven) became the exclusive preserve of Flemish speakers.

Getting There

Leuven (Louvain in French) lies 20km to the east of Brussels, just off the A3/E5 autoroute to Liège. Trains from Brussels' Nord/Central/Midi take you to the station to the east of the city, about 15 minutes' walk from the centre. Parking in the centre is limited, especially in the busy summer season, and you may need to leave your car on the outskirts—which is still within walking distance of the centre. The **tourist office** (open Mon–Fri 9–5, Sat 10–5; March–Oct 10–5) is in Namsestraat, behind the Stadhuis. Note that a **combinatieticket** (50 BF) allows you to see all four of the *stedelijk* (municipal) museums.

Stadhuis

The pride of Leuven is the magnificent **Stadhuis** *(guided tours only, 11am and 3pm weekdays; Sat and Sun 3pm only; March–Oct Sun only, 3pm; on Sat and Sun tickets must be purchased at the tourist office around the corner in Namsestraat)*. The Stadhuis is a spectacular agglomeration of crockets and finials, lace-like balustrades, pinnacles, niches, dormer windows and pepper-pot spires, all smothered in carving. There is not a flat surface in sight. The foundation stone was laid in 1439, during the reign of Philip the Good, Duke of Burgundy and, not surprisingly the building took 30 years to complete. The aim was to outdo Brussels' new town hall—and it succeeded triumphantly. Hundreds of small carvings, mainly of biblical scenes on the theme of sin and punishment, were included as part of the original plan, while some 300 niches remained empty until the larger statues of historical figures and saints were created for them during much-needed restoration that took place in phases between 1828 and 1907.

Changing tastes in municipal grandeur have taken their toll on the interior. Its gilded 18th- and 19th-century décor is lavish but soulless, as public function rooms so often are. The collection of painting and sculpture includes work by Gaspard de Crayer, Constantin Meunier and Jef Lambeaux.

The cellars of the Stadhuis (separate entrance on the left of the building) now contain the **Stedelijk Brouwerijmuseum** (municipal brewery museum) *(open Tues–Sat 10–12 and 2–5; adm 50 BF)*. Its collection of brewing artefacts and photographs serves as a reminder that brewing was a mainstay of Leuven's economy from the 18th century onwards. A brewery called Den Horen ('The Horn') is known to have existed as early as 1366, and this was taken over by the master brewer Sebastien Artois in 1717. When his brewery produced a Pilsner-style beer in 1926 it was named Stella Artois (Artois Star), but the emblem on the label is still the horn.

Sint Pieterskerk

The Stadhuis sits on the edge of the rather cramped Grote Markt, the middle of which is occupied by the grimy hulk of the **Sint Pieterskerk** *(hours as for the museum,* see *below)*, built in Gothic style during the 15th century. Damaged by fire at the start of the First World War, this is no longer one of the land's great churches, and now the choir has been turned into the **Stedelijk Museum voor Religieuze Kunst** (museum of religious art) *(open Mon–Sat 10–12 and 2–5, Sun 2–5 only; 16 Oct–14 March; closed Mon; adm 50 BF)*. The paintings are displayed against the old stone walls of the side-chapels, among the tombs and fonts.

The star of the show is **Dirk Bouts** (1415–75), who was born in Haarlem, studied in Brussels under Rogier van der Weyden, then in 1457 moved to Leuven, where he remained for the rest of his career. His triptych of the *Last Supper* (1464–7) is one of the great paintings of the period. The scene is set in a contemporary Gothic hall, and the view glimpsed through the window to the left is probably the marketplace of Leuven. The side panels show a series of biblical scenes set in Flemish landscapes. These have had a wayward history: they were sold off several times, finally ending up in Germany, then returned to Leuven in 1918 as part of the war reparations package, only to be carried off again during the Second World War, which they spent in a salt mine. A second famous painting by Dirk Bouts is the *Martyrdom of St Erasmus*, in which his intestines are being wound on to a windlass. No one in the scene, not even the saint himself, seems particularly bothered about this; the picture is imbued with a wonderful beatific calm which was considered appropriate for scenes of martyrdom at the time. The collection also includes a reduced copy (1440) by **Rogier** van der Weyden (*c.* 1400–64) of his own *Descent from the Cross* (now in the Prado, Madrid), filled with the realistic anguish that Bouts' work lacks.

One of the eastern side-chapels of the Sint Pieterskerk contains the reliquary shrine to **Fiere Margriet** (Proud Margaret), a local saint. Margaret was servant to an innkeeper, and a witness to his murder, in 1225. The miscreants seized her and carried her off, and then one of them attempted to impose his favours upon her ('marry' is the term used in some versions). When she resisted she too was murdered, and her body was cast into the river. The story is told in pictures on the reliquary shrine, and also in the neighbouring chapel through a series of paintings by **Pieter Josef Verhaegen** (1728–1811), who lived in Leuven for most of his life and was court painter to Charles of Lorraine.

The crypt was filled in during the 15th century, but revealed by bombing in 1944. Re-excavated, it now contains a set of magnificent embroidered bishop's robes, which incorporate panels depicting religious scenes, such as the Agony in the Garden. They are in perfect condition—quite remarkable since some of them are nearly 500 years old.

In the main body of the church, there is a lavish oak pulpit by Jacques Bergé of Ninove; like the Mechelen pulpit, its central theme is the conversion of St Norbert. The choir is separated from the nave by an impressive rood loft over three arches, erected in 1488, on top of which there is a life-size calvary scene carved in stone in 1500. There is also a model of the ambitious Gothic towers designed in 1507 by Joos Metsys, with a spire that would have risen to 168m; however, the ground proved unstable, work was abandoned, and the towers were levelled to the roofline in the early 17th century.

Stedelijk Museum Vander Kelen-Mertens

Open Tues–Sat 10–5, Sun 2–5, closed Mon; adm 50 BF.

Set in a 17th- and 18th-century private mansion donated to the municipality by the Vander Kelen-Mertens family in 1918, the museum in Savoyestraat presents a series of furnished interiors decorated during the 19th century in retrospective historical styles: hence a Baroque sitting room, with high-backed William-and-Mary-style chairs and *famille-rose* Chinese vases, a Renaissance salon, and a rococo dining room. The modernized galleries upstairs contain the municipal collection of treasures, acquired mainly through the confiscation of private property by the occupying French Revolutionary Army in the 1790s, and through subsequent donations. The paintings are primarily by early Renaissance Flemish artists, including **Quentin Metsys** (1466–1530), who is credited with bringing Italian verve to the rather stilted compositions of northern European medieval art. Metsys was born in Leuven, but he spent most of his working life in Antwerp. His

Mourning over Christ has an almost expressionist intensity. The collection includes a splendidly bizarre, Bosch-like *Temptations of St Anthony* (anon), as well as a fine *Crucifixion* triptych by Michiel Coxie, dated 1571, which shows the kind of flowing Italianate composition that influenced Rubens. Elaborately embroidered vestments from the 16th and 17th century are displayed in the galleries, as well as gold- and silverware, stained glass and an extensive collection of porcelain, delftware and other ceramics from Japan, China and Belgium itself.

Groot Begijnhof

At the southern end of the town at the other end of Namsestraat, where many of the university colleges are located, is what was once one of the largest *béguinages* in the land (for an explanation of *béguinages, see* pp.208–209), and is now a tidy collection of 72 modest red-brick homes and grassy courtyards, set out along crooked cobbled streets and pathways that crisscross branches of the River Dijle and lead up to an early 14th-century church. The *béguinage* was founded in the 13th century, and most of the buildings date from the 14th to 18th centuries. The nearby river played an important part in one of the *béguines'* principal activities: making sheets. However, flooding and the language of the passing bargees were regular sources of complaint. The *béguinage* reached its apogee in the 17th century, when there were 300 *béguines*; after this the falling numbers meant that the properties had increasingly to be rented out. By the turn of this century, the *béguinage* was in a very decrepit state, and eventually, in 1962, it was bought by the university for use as college residences. Since then it has been spruced up and restored, but—alas—some of its character has been thrown out with the bathwater. The last *béguine* soldiered on throughout these changes and died in 1988.

Other Attractions

Sint Antonius Kapel: This modern church on Pater Damiaanplein to the north of the Groot Begijnhof is where the body of Father Damien (1840–89) was eventually laid to rest. He was a missionary who ran a leprosy colony on the island of Molokai in Hawaii, where, having himself succumbed to the disease, he died. As part of the long process of becoming a saint he was beatified during the Pope's visit to Brussels in 1994.

Norbertine Abbey of Park-Heverlee: An ancient abbey in a rural setting, situated to the south of Parkpoort in the southwest of the town. The 17th-century library has an elaborate stuccowork ceiling. *(Library and refectory are open on Sundays at 4pm; adm 80 BF.)*

There are numerous restaurants in and around the city centre, including various brasseries and cafés in the Grote Markt itself, and in Muntstraat behind the Stadhuis.

Sire Pynnock, 10 Hogeschoolplein, ✆ (016) 20 25 32. *Closed Sun evening and Mon, and Sat lunch 15–31 Jan and 15 Aug–6 Sept.* Serious and inventive *haute cuisine* by a garlanded young chef, with inspired Japanese touches. Three-course lunch for 1250 BF.

Tijl, 8 Hogeschoolplein, ✆ (016) 21 04 78. Relaxed brasserie atmosphere for French-style cooking. Lunch menus start at 600 BF.

Japans Restaurant, 25 Oude Markt. Japanese food, priced within reach of the students: *miso* soup for 140 BF, *tempura* for 300 BF, and a four-course set meal for 1050 BF.

Kampuchea, 3 S'Meiersstraat, ✆ (016) 23 11 21. Mouthwatering Cambodian and Vietnamese cuisine, including chicken with ginger, frogs' legs with lemon grass, duck with bananas. Set menus from 495 to 1310 BF.

Waterloo

The Battle of Waterloo represents one of the great turning points of European history, when Napoleon's Empire was finally demolished after two decades of tumult and radical change across the continent. For all that, Napoleon remained a great European hero (even today, most Belgians regard the battle as the defeat of Napoleon rather than the victory of Wellington and the Allies). In the more settled years that followed, industrialization gathered pace and the modern shape of Europe began to emerge, yet many people still yearned for the élan and the sense of new horizons which had died when the Napoleonic era ended.

The significance of the battle of Waterloo, the romantic tales of bravery and tragedy that emerged from it and Napoleon's enduring fascination, made the battlefield a scene of touristic pilgrimage almost before the bodies had been carted off for burial. The site, therefore, can claim over 150 years of tourism. This heritage accounts to some degree for the strangely amateur and tacky nature of many of the museums connected with the battlefield, but their musty, antique air is part of the unique flavour of the place. The exception is the brand new Visitors' Centre at the battlefield site—but even that is barely able to cope with the hordes of tourists who swarm through it. As a result, this can be a disappointing visit unless you know what you are looking at: you have to do a little homework and then let your imagination flow. If you can get away from the crowds it is not difficult to people the landscape with soldiers in your mind's eye. A short walk from the

Butte du Lion to the Château de Hougoumont, for instance, will help you to get a feel for the lie of the land, and allow you to contemplate in peace the momentous events that took place in this unlikely rural landscape one Sunday in the middle of June 1815.

History

Napoleon, self-proclaimed Emperor of France, had been the master of continental Europe for nearly two decades when he took the fatal decision (in Brussels) to invade Russia. His armies were thwarted as much by the freezing Russian winter of 1812–13 as by the harrying bands of cossacks, and were forced back to Leipzig, where they were decisively defeated by a combined army of Russians, Prussians and Austrians. When Paris fell, Napoleon was forced to abdicate, but as a concession he was allowed to rule over a tiny dominion on the Italian island of Elba, to which he withdrew in May 1814 accompanied by 400 loyal campaigners of the Old Guard. Meanwhile, the Allies met at the Congress of Vienna, where they redrew the map of Europe once more and Belgium was placed under the control of William of Orange, King of the Netherlands.

It was an absurd hope that a man of Napoleon's ambition would allow himself to be confined to Elba. After just ten months he broke out at the head of an army of 1000 men and made a daring advance on Paris. The rotund and unpopular new king of France, Louis XVIII, despatched an army to see Napoleon off, led by Marshal Ney who promised to bring his old master back to Paris 'in an iron cage'. Instead, he and his troops once again fell prey to Napoleon's charisma and joined him on his march to Paris. Louis XVIII fled to Ghent in terror.

The Allies—Russia, the Netherlands, Austria, Britain, Prussia and the other German states—looked on with horror. They declared war on Napoleon, and in April 1815 they began to assemble in Brussels, which was considered a suitable base from which to march on Paris. In May Arthur Wellesley, the Duke of Wellington, took up command. The British army was in a ragged state after the war of 1812 in the USA (fought over a shipping dispute arising from the Napoleonic Wars), which had resulted in defeat at New Orleans in January 1815. Nonetheless, in Brussels a holiday atmosphere reigned: as the political confrontation intensified, the '100 Days' of Napoleon's revival passed in a ceaseless round of dinners and balls. Napoleon's immediate strategic task was to remove this hostile force from his doorstep. By aiming for Brussels, he could drive a wedge between the British and the large Prussian force stationed in western Belgium. Wellington planned to take the initiative, but Napoleon beat him to it: on 15 June his army of 125,000 men crossed the border, took Charleroi and came within 25km of the Belgian capital. On the evening of 15 June the Duchess of Richmond held her famous ball (at the Rue des Cendres) in Brussels, which was attended by all the leading British military figures. At 8pm Wellington gave orders for his troops to march at daybreak before going off to the ball. At 11pm he brought forward his army's departure by two hours, putting Brussels in turmoil (*see* p.117–18), then he retired to bed. Many of his officers, however, danced on through the night and rode into battle in their ballroom shoes.

The following day, in torrid weather, two preliminary confrontations took place: the Prussians, led by the 72-year-old Marshal Blücher, were put to flight at Ligny, to the northeast of Charleroi, while Wellington's forces were pushed back from Quatre Bras, a crossroads to the south of the village of Genappe on the road between Charleroi and Brussels. Sensing his advantage, Napoleon sent Marshal Grouchy at the head of 33,000 men in pursuit of Blücher to prevent the Prussians joining up with Wellington. Meanwhile, he concentrated his main forces on his old adversary Wellington, whom he had never before confronted directly in battle. Wellington knew that he now had to hold the line before Brussels, and he chose a site on a ridge overlooking a shallow valley to the south of Waterloo, a place he had surveyed a year before and recognized as defensible. To reach it the French would have to fight uphill.

Throughout the night of 16 June and all the following day Wellington effected a carefully disguised retreat under the cover of teeming rain and the general confusion resulting from the battle the previous day. As the foul weather turned the undulating fields into a quagmire, Marshal Ney was unable to cut off the Allied retreat. Napoleon, seeing his advantage wane, greeted Ney with insults: 'You have ruined France!' he declared. But it was Grouchy who was making the more significant error. He allowed Blücher to retreat north towards Brussels, to a position from which he could rejoin Wellington.

As a hazy dawn broke on Sunday 18 June, the bedraggled ranks of cavalry, artillery and infantry in their brilliant regimental colours, huge embroidered ensigns held aloft, faced each other across the muddy valley. The French numbered 72,000. Wellington had 67,000 men under his command of which only a third were British; the rest were from the Netherlands (under the Prince of Orange), Belgium, and the German states of Brunswick, Nassau and Hanover. Somewhere in the hinterland were the 52,000 Prussians commanded by Blücher.

Napoleon was anxious to begin battle as soon as possible but was persuaded to hold off until the sodden ground could dry out a little. His plan was simple: he would begin by attacking the Château de Hougoumont, a large farmhouse on the Allies' right. This was a diversionary tactic intended to provoke Wellington into weakening his centre, and Napoleon entrusted this task to his famously inept brother, Prince Jérôme. Battle commenced at 11.35am. Although heavily out-numbered, the British defenders at Hougoumont refused to be budged, and Wellington kept his centre intact. Jérôme became obsessed with his task and what began as a diversion ended up as a full-scale attack that lasted all day.

At 1.30pm Napoleon launched a massive infantry attack on Wellington's left and on the farm in the middle of the field, La Haie-Sainte. It was presaged by a thunderous artillery barrage, which failed to strike the farm, leaving the French infantry under Quiot to fight hand-to-hand. Another barrage followed and then Ney, leading a cavalry force of 15,000, launched an attack on Sir Thomas Picton's forces in the centre. Meanwhile the French commander Durutte took the Papelotte farm on the Allied left from troops from Nassau. Picton—like Wellington, dressed in civilian clothes, but with a top hat and carrying an umbrella—then mounted a devastating counter-attack, during which he was killed. It was clear that everything depended on the prompt intervention of Blücher's forces, who were by now within 6km and fighting off a French force sent out to meet them. Wellington ordered his troops to march back 100 paces beyond the crest of the ridge. There they formed up into defensive squares and were submitted to countless attacks from the French cavalry, interspersed with repeated bombardments by artillery. They became badly depleted but held firm. 'Will the English never show their backs?' demanded Napoleon.

The battle raged all day, the result held finely in the balance: 'A damned near thing,' as Wellington later put it, 'the nearest run thing you ever saw in your life.' The roar of cannon fire was deafening: even before news of the battle reached England. The *Kentish Gazette* reported from Ramsgate, over 200km away on the other side of the Channel, that 'a heavy and incessant firing was heard from this coast on Sunday evening in the direction of Dunkirk'. At 5.30pm the first of the Prussians reached the field on the French right, and Napoleon threw his remaining cavalry into the fray. Again Wellington's defensive squares held their ground, under immense pressure, while the Allied cavalry counterattacked under Lieutenant-General Uxbridge, taking great losses. Wellington's centre had been decimated and was strewn with the bodies of the dead and wounded.

The French now had to commit some 14,000 troops to their right to hold off the Prussians but Napoleon was determined to launch another attack on the centre. Major Baring and 350 troops of the King's German Legion had held La Haie-Sainte all afternoon, causing considerable damage from their crossfire. The battle now raged around the farm, which the French were determined to win at all costs, and it finally fell at 6.30pm, when Baring retreated with just 42 survivors. However, it was too late for the French: Blücher had begun to break through their right. At 7.30pm Napoleon was forced to throw in his élite Imperial Guard, who strode forth courageously, ignoring heavy losses, and pushed through the Allied lines almost as far as the Ferme de Mont-Saint-Jean. For a moment Napoleon thought victory was at hand, but then the Guard came under heavy counterattack by the Belgians led by General Chassé, followed by fierce onslaughts from other infantry divisions. When the Imperial Guard was eventually forced to retreat—for the first time in its history— panic spread among the French. Wellington ordered the counterattack, riding down the ranks on his chestnut horse Copenhagen and shouting: 'Go on! Go on! They will not stand!' The British and Prussians surged forward in pursuit. Napoleon, staring defeat in the face, had to be bundled into a carriage and whisked back to Paris. He left behind him a field of carnage, where 13,000 soldiers had died and 35,000 had been wounded. Many of the wounded, their limbs shattered by the low-velocity missiles, were cared for by local people; others were transported to field hospitals, where the standard treatment was amputation. It took days to clear the bodies from the battlefield. Wellington had seen a number of his closest associates killed or fatally wounded, including his aide-de-camp Sir Alexander Gordon and his young Quartermaster-General, William de Lancey, who was blown off his horse by a ricocheting cannonball at Wellington's side. Wellington is said to have broken down and wept as the casualty list was read out to him: 'Next to a battle lost,' he later wrote, 'the greatest misery is a battle gained.'

On 22 June Napoleon abdicated for a second time. The British government decided to hold him captive in perpetuity, exiled to St Helena, a lonely island in the middle of the South Atlantic, where he died in 1821. Marshal Ney had a more abrupt fate. Castigated for his military failure, and reviled by the Royalists as a turncoat, he was court-marshalled and executed by firing squad in December 1815.

Getting There

The Battle of Waterloo didn't take place at Waterloo at all. Wellington sent a dispatch announcing his victory over Napoleon from the small town of Waterloo, some 15km south of Brussels and as was the custom, the battle took this name. In fact the fighting was closer to Braine-l'Alleud, about 4km south of the centre of Waterloo. The battlefield covers a considerable area, so it is best to visit Waterloo with a car. There are two principal sites: the old inn in the centre of Waterloo where Wellington had his headquarters, now signposted the **Wellington Museum**, and the battlefield itself, clearly identifiable from a distance by the **Butte du Lion**, the mound with a statue of a lion on top (follow signs marked QG Napoléon then Butte de Lion to the south of Waterloo on the

Charleroi road, the N5). The **Waterloo Visitors' Centre**, the main exhibition site, is clustered around the Butte du Lion. There is a regular bus service from Brussels to Waterloo and the Butte du Lion which departs from Place Rouppe about once every hour. For organized coach trips, ask at the Brussels Tourist Office. Trains leave for Waterloo from Bruxelles Nord, Central and Midi; the station is about 1km from the centre at Waterloo. It is possible to rent bicycles at the next station down the track, Braine l'Alleud, under the 'Train et Vélo' scheme.

Tourist Information

149 Chaussée de Bruxelles, Waterloo, ✆ 345 99 10. Open 1 April–15 Nov 9.30–6.30, 16 Nov–31 March 10.30–5.

Re-enactment

A full-scale re-enactment of the Battle of Waterloo, carried out by enthusiasts dressed in replica uniforms, takes place once every five years on the Sunday nearest to 18 June. The next re-enactment is due in 1995.

The Wellington Museum

Open 1 April–15 Nov 9.30–6.30, 16 Nov–31 March 10.30–5; adm 70 BF.

The old Bodenghien Inn at the centre of Waterloo was chosen by Wellington as his headquarters. He stayed here on the night of 17 June before the battle, making meticulous plans with remarkable composure and sending out dispatches and correspondence. It's an evocative old building, now converted into a small museum of the history of the town of Waterloo and the battle. Displays include weapons, pieces of uniform, engravings, and the bed in which Sir Alexander Gordon died. To the rear is a modern exhibition with panels giving blow-by-blow plans of various stages of the battle. In fact this information is also available in a booklet called *Waterloo 1815* that can be bought at the museum shop—a good investment as it provides an excellent source of information when visiting the battlefield itself.

La Chapelle Royale

This pretty and unusual neoclassical church faces the Wellington Museum and was built in 1690 by the Governor-General of the Spanish Netherlands, the Marquis of Castanaga, as an expression of his wish that Charles II of Spain would produce an heir (he didn't). It was deconsecrated by the French revolutionaries and sold in 1799, bought back by the parishioners in 1806 and enlarged in 1823. After 1815 it became a kind of shrine to various British and Dutch officers killed at Waterloo. The domed, circular entrance contains a bust of Wellington and inside the nave are various memorial plaques which make remarkable reading.

One, for instance, commemorates William Livingstone-Robe of the Royal Horse Artillery, who fell at Waterloo—his 33rd battle, of which many were fought in the Peninsular War. He was 24 years old.

The Visitors' Centre and the Butte du Lion

Open April–Oct 9.30–6.30, Nov–March 10.30–4; adm Lion 40 BF, Lion plus film 250 BF, Lion plus film plus Panorama 280 BF.

This is at the heart of the battlefield, 4km south of the centre of Waterloo itself and part of a cluster of attractions that also includes the Panorama and the Wax-work Museum (*see* below). The Visitors' Centre is a modern complex fronted by a brash and shameless souvenir shop. Tickets come in the form of *jetons*, which you push into ticket barriers to gain entry to each section. The film is in fact a two-part show. First there is a kind of miniature *son-et-lumière* based on a model of the battlefield—far from perfect but at least it gives an insight into how the battle developed. Next there is a 15-minute film in which children are seen wandering the battlefield, imagining the battle. The battle scenes used in this come from Sergei Bondarchuk's film *Waterloo* (1970), which starred Rod Steiger as Napoleon and Christopher Plummer as Wellington. Neither is exactly a classic work of cinema, but the Bondarchuk film contains powerful footage of the battle, graphically portraying the sheer weight of numbers and the violence of the conflict, which is otherwise hard to picture.

The Butte du Lion is the most prominent monument of the battlefield. Rising 143m and with 226 steps leading up to the top, it was built in 1824–26 and dedicated to the Prince of Orange, who was wounded at the battle. The large bronze lion on the summit was cast in the Liège workshops of the British entrepreneur John Cockerill, and it was female workers from his factory who piled up the earth into the mound—all 300,000 cubic metres of it—in wicker baskets. The lion stands at about the mid-point of the Allied lines and the view from the summit offers a magnificent panorama of the battlefield. There is very little documentation at the summit so if you want to study the view in detail, bring your own map.

Panorama de la Bataille

Open Mon–Sat 9.30–6, Sun 9.30–6.30; adm 60 BF.

In the latter part of the 19th century there was a vogue for painting large-scale panoramas in circular buildings—a kind of early form of 3D cinema. The Waterloo Panorama belongs to this tradition: erected in 1912 and painted by a French artist called Louis Dumoulin (1860–1924) and a team of assistants, it measures 110m long by 12m high and consists of a well-executed portrayal of

Marshal Ney's attack on the centre of Wellington's army at 3pm. The Panorama is a historical piece in its own right—even if it isn't exactly virtual reality.

Musée de Cires (Waxwork Museum)

Open April–Oct 9–6.30, Nov–Mar weekends only 10–4.45; adm 60 BF.

Major E. Cotton, a former British hussar and a veteran of the battle, set up a museum of mementoes on this site as early as 1825 to satisfy the curiosity of the numerous visitors to the battlefield. This oddball, scruffy little museum is heir to his tradition, with a few cabinets of military junk, handwritten labels, and astonishingly wooden waxworks (the uniforms, however, are good). It is barely worth the entrance fee, unless you can draw some pleasure from its idiosyncrasy. The main focus, of course, is on Napoleon.

Château de Hougoumont

Private property; visitors may walk in the yards but are expected to behave discreetly.

A narrow road, the Chemin des Vertes Bornes, leads along the ridge to the southwest of the Butte du Lion. From here it is a 20-minute walk to the Château de Hougoumont, past the points at which the Allied squares were drawn up. Hougoumont is not really a château at all but a large and attractive fortified farmhouse—a modest prize considering that 6000 soldiers died here. It was defended by the British against Prince Jérôme's persistent attacks from the very start of the battle, and their valiant resistance was a major contribution to the Allied victory. Inside the farmyard is a tiny chapel where many of the defenders expired.

La Ferme du Caillou

Open April–Oct 10–6.30, Nov–March 1.30–5, closed Mon; adm 70 BF.

This farm was Napoleon's base, where he worked out his battle plans with Marshals Ney and Soult on the night of 17 June and morning of 18 June. The house (much altered since 1815) now serves as a Napoleonic Museum, filled with uniforms, furniture, plans and various battle mementoes.

Other Monuments and Sites

Napoleon directed the battle from a farm called **La Belle Alliance** (named after a marriage between a farmer and his servant in the preceding century), which lies a little to the north of La Ferme du Caillou. The **Ferme de la Haie-Sainte**, which stood at the centre of the battlefield, lies on the main Waterloo–Namur road to the south of the Butte du Lion. Just to the north of this is **Gordon Monument**, a single broken pillar in memory of Wellington's loyal aide-de-camp, who was fatally wounded on this spot. Further north, also on the Waterloo–Charleroi road is the **Ferme de Mont-Saint-Jean**, where British military doctors working behind the lines in the most crude conditions did what they could to save the wounded—without, of course, the aid of anaesthetic. On either side of the Ohain road (once a deep ditch that formed a part of Wellington's defensive strategy), to the east of the Butte du Lion, are two monuments to the fallen. To the south is the sober Hanoverian Monument, erected in 1818. Hanover came under British control after 1814; the German Legion, consisting of troops from Hanover, Nassau and Brunswick, fielded a contingent of 20,000 men at Waterloo and played a significant role in the centre of the battle, around La Haie-Sainte.

To the north of the road is the **Monument to the Belgians**. The Belgians played a somewhat equivocal role in the events leading up to the Battle of Waterloo. By and large the nation welcomed the defeat of Napoleon and the French forces that had occupied their territory between 1794 and 1814. Yet there were also many Belgians who had come of age in this period, who had gained much from it and remained committed Bonapartists. The nation was divided in its reaction to Napoleon's comeback in 1815. Some Belgians joined the French army while others joined the Allies and in some cases brother fought brother. Wellington was unsure about the commitment of the Belgians in his army. Nonetheless about 6000 took part in the battle, and some played a decisive role in the defence of La Haie-Sainte and the defeat of the Imperial Guard.

Eating Out

It's all beer and *frites* and tourist menus around the Butte du Lion, in a group of tired old inns that have been trampled by countless tourists for generations. In Waterloo itself there is a cluster of more attractive small restaurants in the Passage Wellington, opposite the Wellington Museum—a pizzeria, a sandwich shop, chic bars serving *plats du jours*, and **La Coupole**, a more upmarket establishment serving mussels and other standard Belgian fare. There is a large, well-run **McDonald's** at the Sarma Shopping Centre on the Chaussée de Charleroi just south of Waterloo, complete with playground and London bus—a reward for patient children perhaps. For a more memorable meal you will have to travel further afield. You could combine your trip to Waterloo with a visit to Louvain-la-Neuve, for example (*see* p.278), which has an astonishing range of restaurants—traditional brasseries, plus Vietnamese, Cambodian and Chinese restaurants. You probably won't go wrong wherever you choose to eat, but **Le 1900** (26 Rue Rabelais, © (010) 45 12 38) is worth singling out for its exceptional atmosphere. It serves coffee, beer and snacks from 8am onwards and also boasts an impressive list of excellent lunch and dinner dishes: oysters, *bisque de homard*, venison steaks in bordelaise sauce, for around 250–500 BF.

Here are a few other recommendations:

La Fontanell', 27 Avenue Theodore Roosevelt, Genval, ✆ 652 03 81, *closed Wed*. Good Italian restaurant and pizzeria next to the tranquil Lac de Genval. *Carpaccio*, veal, fish, wild boar. Main dishes for around 650 BF.

Le Shangri-La du Lac, 96 Avenue du Lac, Genval, ✆ 654 12 44. Overlooking the Lac de Genval, an above-average Chinese restaurant serving *dim-sum*, duck pancakes and other tasty and well-chosen dishes. 500–1000 BF.

Restaurant Victoria, 17 Marcel Félicéstraat, Hoeilaart, ✆ 657 07 38, *closed Tues and Wed*. Run by the same family for nearly 40 years, this popular and typically Belgian restaurant serves excellently prepared dishes such as *anguilles au vert* and *entrecôte à l'os*. Set menus at 995–1350 BF.

Walibi

Getting There

The Walibi amusement park (✆ 41 44 66) lies just to the south of the town of Wavre, 16km southeast of Brussels. If you are going by car, take the Brussels–Namur motorway (E411) to Wavre, then follow signs to Walibi from Exit 7. This is the circuitous official route, devised to discourage the thousands of visitors from taking the much shorter route through the centre of Wavre. The park is open for two weeks over Easter and from mid-April to late September, 10am–6pm; on Sun, public holidays and in July and Aug the park remains open until 7pm; adm 590 BF for the day, children aged 3–6 540 BF. The entrance ticket includes the cost of all rides, plus admission to the Aqualibi swimming complex, which is also open in the evenings and during the winter (*see* below). The vast car park costs an additional 60 BF: make a mental note of where you leave your car—the spaces are not numbered. Walibi is also accessible by train. It lies on the line linking Ottignies and Leuven, and the nearest station is Bierges, which is just 300m from the park. Take your swimming things and even a change of clothes: many of the rides are water-based and can result in a soaking, which may not be so welcome on a chilly day.

Walibi, founded in 1975, is Belgium's premier amusement park. It offers dozens of rides suitable for all ages—from a gentle, old-fashioned roundabout and track-guided jalopies for the very young, to thrills and spills on high-powered modern rollercoasters. These are laid out in a series of thematic 'villages' joined by a network of tree-shaded walkways, set around a cluster of lakes. Countless souvenir shops, snack bars and restaurants jostle for position beside the walkways, along with the various stages, marquees and covered halls where animal and circus acts are performed to a posted schedule. The atmosphere is friendly and fun-loving, and Walibi can make an enjoyable family day out—provided that you observe some important ground rules. The name Walibi, by the way, is simply a contraction of the names of the three local communities: Wavre, Limal and Bierges.

The park attracts as many as 15,000 people a day. This can result in exasperating queues to the best attractions. Avoid weekends in the summer season. Go early: aim to be at the gates for opening time at 10am—there is easily enough in Walibi to occupy you for a whole day. Note also that although many of the rides and shows are in covered areas, if it rains you are likely to get cold and wet.

The entrance ticket allows you to spend 1¼ hours in the adventure swimming centre called Aqualibi located at the park gates—although you can extend your visit at the extra cost of 60 BF per half hour. *(Aqualibi is also open in winter, weekdays 2–10pm, weekends 10–10; in summer 6–10pm; adm 420 BF for 4 hours.)* This complex contains a range of pools of various shapes and forms, including ones with wave machines, and a huge hot-bath and jacuzzi , plus enormous tubular water chutesand gushing water slides. Walibi's own advice should be taken: go to Aqualibi as soon as you reach the park in the morning, as it may become very crowded later on. The sheer weight of numbers can be alarming in the more popular chutes and slides. Some of these are for confident swimmers only, and this is not always as clear as it should be from the notices. Once in the shoots it is virtually impossible to beat a retreat, except by being hoicked out ignominiously by one of the pool attendants.

Other key attractions in the Walibi park include: a big wheel, the runaway train, a train that loops the loop at 80 km/hr, 'river rafting' (be prepared to get wet), a magical water journey through animated scenes from Ali Baba, and a similar ride on the theme of Tintin's *The Secret of the Unicorn*, adventure playgrounds, waterskiing from a drag-line around the lake, a 3D cinema, and performing parrots, sea lions *(otaries)* and magicians.

Eating Out

The park contains numerous restaurants and theme-based snack bars, selling sandwiches, hamburgers, grilled sausages, Chinese food and, of course, *frites*. Prices are high and the quality is not brilliant, so you may prefer to bring a picnic with you.

Bruges

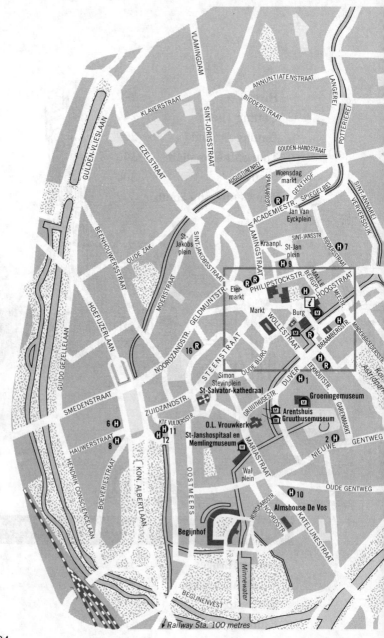

VLAMINGDAM

ANNUNTIATENSTRAAT

LANGEREI

KLAVERSTRAAT

SINT-JORISSTRAAT

BIDDERSTRAAT

EZELSTRAAT

GOUDEN-HANDSTRAAT

POTTERIEREI

AUGUSTIJNENREI

SPANJAARDSTR.

GENTHOF

Woensdag markt

SINT-ANNAREI

R 17

ACADEMIESTR.

SPIEGELREI

St-Jakobs plein

SINT-JAKOBSSTRAAT

VLAMINGSTRAAT

Jan Van Eyckplein

VERVERSDIJK

OUDE ZAK

MOERSTRAAT

Kraanpl.

St-Jan plein

SINT-JANSSTR.

RIDDERSTRAAT

H 7

BEENHOUWERSTRAAT

H 9

R

R

PHILIPSTOCKSTR.

WALLE

BERGPL.

HOOGSTRAAT

VESTE

Eier-markt

GELDMUNTSTR.

H

Markt

Burg

M

HOEFIJZERLAAN

WOLLESTRAAT

M

R

BRAAMBERGSTR.

MINDERBROEDERSTR.

R 16

NOORDZANDSTR.

STEENSTRAAT

OUDE BURG

R

H

Kon. Astridpark

GUIDO GEZELLELAAN

SMEDENSTRAAT

ZUIDZANDSTR.

Simon Stevinplein

St-Salvator-kathedraal

DIJVER

GRUUTHUSESTR.

EEKHOUTSTR.

H 1

GARENMARKT

M Groeningemuseum

M Arentshuis

M Gruuthusemuseum

H 6

H 11

KTE VULDERSSTR.

O.L. Vrouwkerk

MARIASTRAAT

H 2

NIEUWE

GENTWEG

HAUWERSTRAAT

H 8

H 12

St-Janshospitaal en Memlingmuseum

M

BOEVERIESTRAAT

HENDRIK CONSCIENCELAAN

KON. ALBERTLAAN

OOSTMEERS

Wal plein

OUDE GENTWEG

H 10

WINGAARDSTR.

Almshouse De Vos

KATELIJNESTRAAT

NOORDSTR.

Begijnhof

BEGIJNENVEST

Minnewater

↓ Railway Sta. 100 metres

Bruges

400 metres
400 yards

Bruges is a Cinderella city. When most of the other major Flemish cities set off for the ball of industrialization during the 19th century, Bruges was left behind in its medieval rags. In 1908 George W.T. Omond was able to write (in his travelogue-cum-history *Belgium*): 'Bruges is a city of the dead, of still life, of stagnant waters, of mouldering walls and melancholy streets, long since fallen from its high estate into utter decay.' In the 20th century, however, Bruges found her prince: he is called Tourism. As it turned out, Bruges's centuries of decline proved to be its saving grace. Gradually travellers, artists, writers, then tour-operators became aware of a city preserved in a time-warp, an unpolished gem barely touched by modernization, with crooked streets and crumbling guildhouses and palaces, stone bridges over mirror-still canals reflecting the gables, spires and towers of a medieval skyline.

Bruges has since prospered by its famous charm, and it is now the most visited city in Belgium after Brussels. But there has been a price to pay. The coachloads of tourists, the trample of thousands of feet, the gaze of countless eyes have gradually smoothed away the authentic texture of the city's character, and hardened the souls of many of its citizens, who have simply seen too many daytrippers pass through their gates. The deadening combination of restoration and tourism is bringing Bruges perilously close to sanitization, to making it into a sterile museum city. As a result of this—and of unhealthy over-promotion of the city's virtues with misleading epithets such as 'the Venice of the North'—not a few visitors to Bruges come away sadly disappointed.

That is a shame, for Bruges's charms are real enough. The intimate, pocket-sized city is indisputably one of the most remarkable urban heirlooms of Europe, while its two triumphant collections of medieval art would alone justify the visit. And if the crowds get too much, steal away from the main thoroughfares and find a quiet sunny corner, where the old soul of the city still speaks. The more tranquil streets north of the Markt—Vlamingstraat, Grauwwerkersstraat, Academiestraat, Jan van Eyckplein, Spiegelrei—are off the main museum trail, but are dotted with historic buildings redolent of Bruges's properous past. Or catch the city in its slumber at either end of the day, as the dawn mists rise off the canals, or the setting sun throws the layered architecture into startling relief.

Better still, stay a few days in one of the handful of superb small hotels that cluster around the centre of the city; enjoy some of the best cooking in Belgium in some of the land's most attractive and fêted restaurants. Be fair to Bruges: allow it the opportunity to reveal its famous charms in its own time.

History

Once upon a time Bruges was linked to the sea by a river, the Reie, which led to a deep coastal inlet called the Zwin. It was here that Baldwin Iron-Arm, the first Count of Flanders, decided to build a castle to protect the coast from Viking raids, and gradually a town developed around it, thriving on the trade that came to it on the Reie and to Damme on the Zwin. As with the other Flemish cities, textiles were the key to Bruges's early prosperity, closely linked to the wool trade with Britain. In 1093 Robert the Frisian made it the capital of the Duchy of Flanders, and by the 13th century Bruges was one of the wealthiest cities of northern Europe and a major player in the Hanseatic League, the powerful association of north European (mainly German) trading cities.

During 1297 to 1300 the city surrounded itself with a mighty oval ring of defensive walls and ramparts, reinforced by a moat, and channelled the River Reie into a system of interconnecting canals. The Minnewater, the lake just to the south of the city, was receiving some 150 ships a day, exchanging Flemish cloth for wool, lead, tin, coal and cheese from England, pigs from Denmark, wood and fish from Scandinavia, wine from Spain and Germany, furs from Russia and Bulgaria, and silks and oriental spices from Venice and Genoa.

Bruges claims to have had the first stock exchange in Europe: merchants would buy and sell shares and credit notes outside the house (at No. 35 Grauwwerkersstraat) of a leading family of merchants called Van ter Beurse, hence the origin of the term *beurs* or *bourse* by which many European stock exchanges are known. And when Philip the Fair, King of France, came to the city on a state visit in 1301, his wife Joanna of Navarre was so impressed by the wealth and luxurious clothes of the inhabitants that she made her famous remark: 'I thought I alone was Queen, but I see that I have 600 rivals here.'

But, as elsewhere in Flanders, this prosperity was achieved against a backdrop of political strife. Flanders was a duchy of France, a status supported by the the French-speaking patricians, who were called the *leliaerts* (after the *fleur de lis* or lily, the French royal emblem). The Flemish masses, as well as many leading merchants, however, were proudly Flemish and had acquired a considerable amount of autonomy over the years. Called the *clauwaerts* (from the claws of the Flemish lion), they lived in constant tension with their French overlords.

Philip the Fair came to Bruges in 1301 to reassert French authority and to reduce the city's autonomy. To add insult to injury, the citizens of Bruges were asked to foot the bill for his ostentatious reception. In 1302 Pieter de Coninck, Dean of the Guild of Weavers, and Jan Breydel (or Breidel), Dean of the Guild of Butchers, led a *clauwaert* revolt in response to the arrival of a new French garrison of 2000 men, which the citizens of Bruges believed had been sent to suppress them. Early in the morning, during the so-called 'Bruges Matins', the French troops were massacred—as indeed was anyone who was unable to pronounce in convincing Flemish the shibboleth '*Schild en Vriend*'. This revolt stirred up a widespread rebellion and led to the famous Flemish victory over the French six weeks later at the Battle of the Golden Spurs near Kortrijk (*see* pp.52–3). But after this brief spell of independence the French regained control. Their policy of crushing suppression led to a period of instability and confusion throughout Flanders, which coincided with the outbreak of the Hundred Years' War, and the emigration to England of a large number of weavers.

In 1381–2 Philip van Artevelde (*see* **Ghent**, p.318) led a briefly successful revolt against Louis de Male, count of Flanders, and took Bruges, before himself being defeated by the French. The situation was only resolved in 1384 when Philip the Bold, Duke of Burgundy, inherited Flanders through his marriage to Margaret, daughter of Louis de Male. Under the Dukes of Burgundy Bruges entered its second great period of prosperity, particularly during the reign (1419–67) of Philip the Good. He came to Bruges in 1419 to marry his wife, Isabella of Portugal, an occasion celebrated by one of the most stupendous bean-feasts of the medieval era. It was also later marked by the foundation of the prestigious Order of the Knights of the Golden Fleece. Bruges was by now a truly international city. By 1500 the population had reached 200,000; the population of London at this time was 75,000. This was also a dazzling period for Flemish art. Jan van Eyck (1390–1441) worked and died in Bruges, and painted the *Adoration of the Mystic Lamb* here (now in Ghent cathedral). Hugo van der Goes (?1435–82) spent his last years in Bruges, whilst Hans Memling (1430/5–94) spent most of his working life in the city.

Two factors brought about Bruges's decline after the 15th century: the silting-up of the Zwin, which was virtually complete by 1550, cutting off the city's access to the sea; and the general collapse of the Flemish textile trade. Antwerp's star was rising, and many of Bruges's old merchant families relocated. During the next century Bruges became the focus of revolt, both of the iconoclasts, and of the '*Gueux*', the rebels fighting against Spain. Bruges slid quietly into a forlorn state of decay, earning itself the title 'Bruges-la-Morte'. It remained virtually unchanged, girdled by its moat and old city walls until the end of the 19th century.

In the early 20th century, however, the Boudewijn Canal was built to link Bruges with a new port at Zeebrugge. Completed in 1907, it encouraged some industrial development; this, however, was curtailed by the two World Wars, during which much of the canal was destroyed. The link to the sea was restored during the 1950s, and now Bruges has a thriving industrial sector (set well away from the historic city) producing glass, electrical goods and chemicals. It is also the seat of Europa College, a respected postgraduate centre for European studies—but it is tourism that is the mainstay of its modern prosperity.

Getting There

Bruges (Brugge in Flemish) is about 100km northwest of Brussels, connected by the E5 autoroute. It is a small city, and highly conscious of its limited capacity for traffic. The authorities have therefore set up several well-organized **car parks** in the south and west of the city. Since these are not expensive (around 215 BF per day), and not a huge distance from the centre, the best advice is to go straight for one of these. Illuminated signs indicate *vrij* if there are spaces free. The largest are the underground car park at 't Zand, and the coach/car park near Katelijnepoort. If you are staying overnight, ask your hotel about parking when making your reservation. There is very limited street parking, mainly around the shopping area in the west of the city (maximum 2 hours, 80 BF, tickets from machines). The **railway station** is to the south of the city, about 20 minutes' walk from the centre. There is a direct train link from Brussels (Gare du Nord, Gare Centrale, Gare du Midi) via Ghent.

Getting Around

Bruges also has its own **bus service**, which links the centre with outlying districts, such as 't Zand. **Taxis** are available from stands at the railway station and at the Markt.

Because of Bruges's restrictive traffic policies, it is a pleasant place to cycle. Bruges station offers **bicycles for hire** under the 'Trein + Fiets' scheme, and there are other bike-hire shops in the centre, such as 't Koffieboontje, 4 Hallestraat; and Eric Popelier, 14 Hallestraat. Note that bicycles are permitted to travel in both directions in one-way streets.

Taking a **boat-trip** on the canals offers a picturesque introduction to the city—but is madly popular and attracts long queues in summer. All the starting points are along the canal connecting the Minnewater to the Burg, mainly close to Blinde Ezelstraat and the Vismarkt. Trips last approximately 30 minutes. *Available daily 10–6 March–Nov, Dec–Feb weekends only; adults 150 BF, children 4–12 65 BF.* You can also see the city from the back of a **horse-drawn carriage**, departing from the Burg: *March–Nov 10–6, 800 BF per carriage for 35 minutes.*

Tourist Information

The **tourist office** is in the centre of the town, 11 Burg, © (050) 4486 86, open April–Sept Mon–Fri 9.30–6.30, Sat and Sun 10–12 and 2–6.30; Oct–March Mon–Fri 9.30–5, Sat 9.30–12.45 and 2–5. There is also a new tourist office at the railway station (similar hours, closed Sun). They offer a guide service (1000 BF for 2 hours), or you can join the daily guided tour in the summer, starting at 3pm at the Burg tourist office *(100 BF per person)*. If you are travelling as a family, note that many of Bruges's museums have 'family tickets' which offer discounts for parents and children under 18. The tourist offices can also arrange hotel bookings.

Festivals

The principal festival of Bruges is the **Heilig-Bloedprocessie** (Procession of the Holy Blood), which takes place annually on Ascension Day (40 days after Easter). Following an 800-year-old tradition, the holy relic is paraded through the streets surrounded by participants wearing medieval and biblical costumes in a mixture of pageant, fun and serious religion. Tickets (about 400 BF) for the grandstand are available from the tourist office from 1 March onwards.

The Centre and South

Markt

The old marketplace is at the very heart of the city—once the scene of great trade fairs, medieval jousts and public executions. This is a good place to start, although architecturally it is somewhat disappointing. Lacking the gilded brilliance of the Grote Markt of other Flemish towns, it is flanked by 17th-century gabled houses, much altered and now housing banks, souvenir shops, and the kind of restaurants that offer menus in four languages. On the eastern (lower) side is the **Provinciaal Hof**, the imposing provincial government building (Bruges is the capital of the province of West Flanders). It was built in Neo-Gothic style betwen 1881 and 1921, on the site of the old Waterhalle, a covered hall over the River Reie where cargoes of market goods were unloaded. In the centre of the square is a statue (1887) by Paul de Vigne of Pieter de Coninck and Jan Breydel, leaders of the 1302 rebellion against the French. The most arresting feature of the Markt, however, is the **Belfort** *(open April–Sept 9.30–5, Oct–March 9.30–12.30 and 1.30–5; adm 100 BF)*. Bruges's belfry is one of its great landmarks, which for centuries served as a watchtower, clocktower and symbol of Bruges's independent spirit. It is a remarkable hybrid building, with three main tiers rising to 83m through a series of architectural styles. The lower part of the tower dates from 1282–96, the four corner towers from 1396, and the octagonal belltower from 1482–87. There used to be an additional spire, but this was destroyed by lightning in 1741.

You have to be fit to climb the 366 steep steps to the top; they take you past the 47-bell carillon *(played on summer evenings, Mon, Wed and Sat; and on winter afternoons, Sun, Wed and Sat)* and the mechanism of the clock installed in 1748. From the summit there are unrivalled views over the waterways and rooftops of the city.

The Belfort rises up from a low building set around an austere courtyard. This is the Halle, an old covered market originally built in 1239, but added to over the next three centuries.

Burg

If the Markt is the centre of Bruges, the Burg is its historical heart, the site of the castle around which Bruges grew. This small square boasts a handful of the city's most impressive civic buildings, and its most interesting church. From the Breidelstraat entrance (from the Markt), to your left is the **Proostdij** (Provost's House), a grey-stone Flemish-Baroque building dating from 1662, with an elaborate entrance crowned by blind Justice. It used to belong to the provost of the church, later cathedral, of Saint Donatian (or Donatus), which stood on the neighbouring open space until 1799, when it was destroyed by the French. The church was a major landmark: Jan van Eyck was buried here; and here too was Charles the Good, Count of Flanders, murdered by a nephew of the provost in 1127, the victim of bitter clan warfare. This was the trigger for a bout of vicious slaughter, after which the streets of the Burg are said to have run with blood.

On the right-hand flank, in the centre, is the **Stadhuis** (*see* below), with its tall Gothic windows and pepperpot onamental towers. To its right (occupying the corner site) is the **Heilig Bloedbaseliek** (*see* below), built of grey stone with golden figures and ornate ogive arches. To the left of the Stadhuis is the Oude Griffie (Old Recorder's House), pierced by the arched entrance to an alleyway, and also surmounted by a statue of blind Justice. A Gothic and Renaissance building dating from 1534–7, it acted as an annexe to the lawcourts next door between 1883 and 1984. Beside it is the entrance to the Museum van het Brugse Vrije (*see* below).

The far flank is occupied by the mainly 18th-century, neoclassical **Gerechtshof** (lawcourts), where justice was dispensed until 1984, but which now contains city administrative offices, as well as the tourist information office. The building covers much of the site of the old Landshuis van het Brugse Vrije (the palace and lawcourts of the 'Bruges Liberty'), built in 1525, although the façade overlooking the canal was retained. The Bruges Liberty was an area of legal jurisdiction that stretched over a large area around from Bruges and as far west as Dunkirk.

Heilig Bloedbaseliek

There are two separate parts to the small 'Basilica of the Holy Blood'. The lower church is known as St Basil's Chapel after the relic (four vertebrae) of St Basil the Great that was brought back from Caesarea in the Holy Land in 1099. The chapel is effectively a kind of undercroft, a robust piece of 12th-century architecture with massive pillars of raw, rough-hewn stone rising to Romanesque arches. The tone is bleak and thoroughly medieval: you could imagine crusaders clanking around here, haunted by distant memories of Jerusalem. To the right of the choir is a wooden polychrome statue of the Virgin and Child dating to 1300, and there is a primitive stone sculpture over the arch leading back from the side aisle to the nave, possibly of the baptism of St Basil. Upstairs, reached by a splendid, broad spiral staircase, built in 1523, is the Chapel of the Holy Blood, a 15–16th century addition, destroyed by the French in the 1790s but rebuilt, and richly decorated, in the 19th-century. The relic of the Holy Blood—apparently blood washed from the body of Christ by Joseph of Arimathea—was, according to tradition, given to Derick of Alsace, Count of Flanders, in 1148, during the Second Crusade. When it arrived in Bruges in 1150, the blood in its rock-crystal phial appeared to be dry, but it miraculously suddenly became liquid again, and would repeat this phenomenon every Friday. It became the focus of fervent devotion and miraculous healings took place among the worshippers who assembled before it on Fridays. This tradition is still maintained: the relic is displayed for veneration in the chapel on Fridays *(8.30–11.45 and 3–4)*—but it hasn't turned liquid since 1325.

The chapel is appealing in its bespangled, multicoloured way, enhanced by the ingenious pulpit in the form of a complete globe, designed by Hendrick Pulincx and carved from a single piece of oak in around 1728.

Next to the church entrance upstairs is a tiny museum *(open April–Sept 9.30–12 and 2–6, Oct–March 10–12 and 2–4; adm 40 BF)*, the focus of which is an elaborate gold reliquary made by Jan Crabbe in 1617. This is used in the Heilig-Bloedprocessie, when the relic is paraded around the city on Ascension Day. Among the precious stones decorating it is a large diamond said to have belonged to Mary Stuart. There are also two fine paintings (actually the wings of a triptych), dated 1556, portraying the very sanctimonious-looking Members of the Brother-hood of the Precious Blood. These were painted by Pieter Pourbus (1524–84), who lived and worked in Bruges, married the daughter of the painter and archi-tect Lancelot Blondeel and founded a dynasty of distinguished painters.

Stadhuis

Open April–Sept 9.30–5, Oct–March 9.30–12.30 and 2–5; adm 60 BF.

The town hall dates originally from 1376–1420, making it the oldest in Belgium; it is also one of the finest. The building has been heavily restored over the cen-turies, with the result that it is part medieval, part 19th-century medieval fantasy, part modern renovation. The statues of the Counts and Countess of Flanders in the niches between the windows were originally medieval, but were pulled down by French Revolutionaries in 1792, and replaced in modern times.

The Gothic Hall, on the upper floor still has its original vaulted wooden ceiling, dating from 1385. It has been beautifully restored, so that the decorated vault keys (illustrating scenes from the New Testament) and consoles next to the walls (illustrating the twelve months of the year and the four elements) can be seen in their full splendour. The walls have been decorated with rich and well executed murals depicting scenes from Bruges's history, painted in 1895 by Albert and Julien Devriendt—a monument to medievalism and visually stunning. A neigh-bouring room contains a selection of prints relating to Bruges's canal system.

Museum van het Brugse Vrije

Open April–Sept 10–12, Oct–March 10–12.30 and 1.30–5; adm 20 BF.

This small museum is housed in part of the 14th-century Schepenzaal, where magistrates of the Brugse Vrije used to meet. Its unique exhibit is the huge oak and black marble chimneypiece (1529–33), a robust and sensuous installation in pristine condition, designed by Lancelot Blondeel (1496–?1561). It is a monu-ment to the ruler of the day, Charles V, whose oak statue appears in the centre, flanked by his two pairs of grandparents, Maximilian of Austria and Mary of Bur-gundy (left), and Ferdinand of Aragon and Isabella of Castile (right).

Vismarkt, Groenerei and Rosenhoedkaai

The archway and vaulted passage beneath the Oude Griffie in Burg leads to Blinde Ezelstraat (Blind Ass Street—probably a reference to a tavern, since disappeared), and immediately you cross the main canal on one of the Bruges's many bridges. The number of bridges in Bruges is said to have earned the city its name (*brug* means bridge in Flemish). But another theory suggests that the name is derived from the Norse word *bryggia*, meaning a landing place.

You are now in one of the most picturesque parts of Bruges. On the other side of the bridge is the old **Vismarkt** or fishmarket, where fish is still sold every morning except Sundays and Mondays on the stone slabs set out beneath covered colonnades, erected in 1826. The street that follows the canal to the left leads to the Groenerei, which offers some of the most famous views of the Burg, the Belfort, and the fetchingly crooked houses that overlook the canal. On the right-hand side of the **Groenerei** (Nos. 8–12) is an old almshouse, De Pelikaan, dated 1714. The date is significant as an indicator of the distress of Bruges during the 18th century, when there were some 300 almshouses (*Godshuisen*) in the city, set up by wealthy families and the guilds to shelter the aged and indigent.

To the west of the Vismarkt is the picturesque **Huidenvettersplein** (Tanners' Square), in the middle of which stands a statue of two lions (1925), emblems of the tanners' guild. This square leads to the **Rosenhoedkaai**, which offers views of the Belfort in one direction and Onze Lieve Vrouwekerk in the other. On the next bridge is a statue to St John Nepomuk (1767, erected 1811). This St John was confessor to the queen of Bohemia, but when in 1393 he refused to pass on the contents of her confessions, King Wenceslas IV had him thrown into the River Moldau from a bridge in Prague. Hence he is patron saint of bridges.

Groeningemuseum

Open April–Sept 9.30–5, Oct–March 9.30–12.30 and 2–5, closed Tues; adm 130 BF.

Entered through an archway and a series of courtyards from the canal-side street called Dijver, the low-rise modern building housing this municipal museum comes as something of a surprise. Even greater is the surprise of the treasures within—one of Europe's most dazzling collections of medieval art. The museum is actually too small to exhibit its entire collection, so paintings are shown in rotation. Almost everything in it is of outstanding quality. It's a delight—provided that you can stomach the subject matter of so many of the exhibits: gruesome martyrdom painted with loving attention to every horrific detail.

The great star of the collection is **Jan van Eyck**'s *Madonna with Canon van der Paele* (1436), a large work filled with stunning detail. The Madonna sits enthroned with Christ on her knee, while Canon van der Paele (who commissioned the work) kneels to her left, spectacles in hand. Behind him is St George, his patron saint, kitted out in a full set of ceremonial armour, and opposite him is St Donatian dressed in sumptuous vestments. (St Donatian was a Roman who in 390 became Bishop of Reims; his relics were brought to Bruges during the 9th century.) This is not simply a religious work, but a portrait of living people, surrounded by the kind of luxurious setting that existed in Burgundian Bruges. Note the oriental carpet, and the African parrot held by Christ—evidence of the scope of Bruges's trade. In terms of technique, and of the sophistication of detail, this painting outstrips anything that was produced in Italy by at least three decades.

St Luke Drawing a Portrait of Our Lady, by van Eyck's pupil **Roger van der Weyden**, is in its way another snapshot of contemporary life: the Virgin gives her breast to a rather starved-looking baby Jesus, surrounded by Renaissance textiles and architecture. **Dirk Bouts** is represented by a triptych of featuring the Martyrdom of St Hippolytus, in which the saint is being pulled asunder by four horses, with ropes attached to each limb. This is upstaged only by *The Judgement of Cambyses* (1498) by **Gerard David** (?1460–1523), who lived and died in Bruges and was the last great artist of the Bruges school. It depicts the corrupt judge Sisamnes being flayed alive with surgical precision by knaves in boots and cloaks; Cambyses, king of Persia in the 6th century BC, and other surrounding figures, including a mangy dog, are painted in great detail and look entirely unconcerned. The painting was commissioned for the Stadhuis by the contrite magistrates of Bruges following a famous incident in 1488. Reacting to the erosion of their privileges and an increase in taxation, the Bruges authorities ill-advisedly held captive for three months Maximilian, the governor of the Low Countries and future Holy Roman Emperor. Pieter Lanchals, treasurer to Maximilian, attempted to intervene and was summarily executed in the Markt. Maximilian was freed, but the damage was done: thereafter he took a dim view of Bruges, and favoured Antwerp, hastening Bruges's decline.

A series of panels depicting the legends of St Ursula, by the Master of the Legends of St Ursula and dated to before 1482, tells the story of the saint and the fate of her 11,000 virgins. According to the legend, St Ursula, daughter of a king of Britain, escaped to Rome to avoid being married against her will, accompanied by a retinue of virgins. They then went to Cologne in Germany, where they were murdered simply because they were Christian. All this is based on a small inscription in Cologne, but it clearly caught the imagination of the medieval mind and snowballed into a legend in which an original contigent of 11 virgins became 11,000, plus a few bishops for good measure.

This is a subject taken up more famously by **Hans Memling** in the Memling museum. Here he is represented by the large and impressive Moreel triptych (1484), named after the donor Willem Moreel, burgomaster of Bruges. Willem Moreel is depicted in the left-hand panel, his wife in the right-hand panel. The saints in the central panel are Saints Christopher, Maurus and Giles. The painting shows the greater confidence in figure work, and in the use of perspective and scale, that Memling brought to Bruges painting.

Other highlights include a nightmarish *Last Judgement* by Hieronymus Bosch; the *Allegory of the Peace of the Netherlands* (1577) by **Pieter Claessens the**

Younger, one of a distinguished family of Bruges painters; and the startling portraits of Archduke Albert and Isabella the Infanta by **Frans Pourbus the Younger** (1569–1622). The collection peters out in the period between the 17th century and late 19th century, when it picks up again with work by **Emile Claus**, **Fernand Khnopff**, **Léon Frédéric**, **Jean Delville**, **Gustave de Smet**, **Constant Permeke**, **Edgar Tytgat**, **Rik Wouters**, **Magritte** and others.

Arentshuis/Brangwynmuseum

Open April–Sept 9.30–5, Oct–March 9.30–12.30 and 2–5, closed Tues; adm 100 BF.

This rewarding little museum, housed in an 18th-century neoclassical mansion at Dijver 16, contains a set of paintings, prints and drawings donated to Bruges by Frank Brangwyn (1867–1956), an Anglo-Belgian artist. Brangwyn was associated with the Pre-Raphaelites and for a time joined the workshop of William Morris, but always held an affection for Bruges, the city of his birth. The collection also includes lace, porcelain and other ceramics, numerous pewter objects, and (outside, opposite the entrance) a group of historic carriages and sleighs.

Onze Lieve Vrouwekerk

This is Bruges's most imposing and endearing church. Built over some 200 years from 1220, it has a stark, medieval feel to it. Its soaring, pinnacle-like tower rises to 122m, and is one of the highest in Belgium. The cream-painted interior has a bold simplicity, with hefty columns and black and white flagstones. This austerity is offset by outbursts of massive baroque ornament in the side chapels, and in the exuberant pulpit (1743) by **Jan Garemijn**, decked with cherubs and a depiction of Wisdom sitting on a globe.

At the head of the southern aisle, protected by a glass screen, is one of Bruges's great treasures: the Madonna and Child (1504–5) by **Michelangelo**, one of the very few Michelangelo sculptures outside Italy. Originally intended for the cathedral of Siena, it was acquired by Jan van Moscroen, a wealthy merchant, and donated to this church. In this deeply and delicately sculpted work, Michelangelo has succeeded in turning stone into an image of great tenderness: it puts to shame virtually any other sculpture in Belgium.

The main altar sits oddly in the middle of the church; the choir behind it is fenced off as a museum *(open April–Sept 10–11.30 and 2.30–5, Oct–March 10–11.30 and 2.30–4.30; adm 60 BF)*. The main exhibits are the elaborate tombs of Charles the Bold and his daughter, Mary of Burgundy. Mary married Maximilian of Austria but died after a fall from a horse in 1482 at the age of 25. Her fine tomb was constructed in 1495–1502, surmounted by a gilt-brass effigy of her in contemporary costume; her feet are resting on a pair of dogs, the symbol of fidelity. Her father, Charles the Bold, was the son of Philip the Good, whom he succeeded in 1467. He reigned for ten years before waging a disastrous war against France. He was killed at the Battle of Nancy in 1477, where his body was buried after, apparently, being half-eaten by wolves. It was Charles V who ordered that the body should be brought to Bruges in 1550, a move fiercely resisted by the people of Nancy, who may have substituted the body of a knight instead. It eventually reached Bruges and was placed in a tomb similar to that of his daughter, made in 1559–62. His feet rest on a lion, the symbol of strength.

In the crypt, visible through glass panels, you can see simple mural paintings of crucifixions dating from the 13th and 14th centuries, as well as the coffins of three canons. Crouch down, and beyond these you can see the coffin of Mary of Burgundy (it's not in her tomb), and on top of it an urn containing the heart of her son, Philip the Handsome (father of Charles V), who died in 1506.

Also in the choir is a fine altarpiece by **Bernard van Orley** (1499–1541), and there are several paintings by Pieter Pourbus; these include a *Last Supper* (1562), and the wings of a triptych (1573). Pieter Lanchals, the treasurer executed in 1488, is commemorated in a chapel off the south ambulatory, which also contains medieval coffins excavated from the crypt.

In the wall of the north ambulatory of the choir is a wooden gallery, which overlooks the altar. Built in 1472, it belonged to the Lords of Gruuthuse, whose mansion was next door (*see* below).

Memlingmuseum

Open April–Sept 9.30–5, Oct–March 9.30–12.30 and 2–5, closed Wed; adm 130 BF. Closed for restoration during 1995.

There are just six works by Hans Memling (1435–94) in this museum, which occupies a chapel in the old Sint-Janshospitaal—a city hospital dating back to the 12th century and still in operation until 1976. Born in Germany, Memling was probably a pupil of Roger van der Weyden before he settled in Bruges and became a citizen in 1465. Celebrated particularly in the 19th century as one of the masters of Flemish art, his prodigious output is now scattered around many of the world's great galleries.

The most celebrated work in the collection is the Ursula Reliquary. Just one metre long, made of gilt wood, it is contains a dozen or so small painted panels that tell in vivid and beautifully rendered detail the story of St Ursula and her 11,000 virgins (*see* above). The *Mystic Marriage of Saint Catherine* (1479) also demonstrates Memling's sparkling attention to detail. The painting shows baby

Jesus sliding a ring onto the finger of St Catherine (with the broken wheel on which the Romans attempted to martyr her), while St Barbara reads a book beside her. St Catherine is believed to symbolize Mary of Burgundy, and St Barbara her mother, Margaret of York. This polyptych was commissioned for this chapel, and the wings show the two St Johns (patrons of the hospital), with John the Baptist spurting blood after decapitation, and St John the Divine (the Evangelist) on the island of Patmos, to which he was exiled. St John the Divine can also be seen being boiled in a vat in Rome, which he is supposed to have survived—but the story is apocryphal. Other works include the *Adoration of the Magi* (1479), a *Pietà* (1480) and a striking portrait of a patron, Maarten van Nieuwenhove (1487).

As you leave the Sint-Janshospitaal, go in the door to the left of the exit, which leads to a 15th-century pharmacy (same ticket), complete with glass jars, ceramic pots and box-drawers. It remained in use until 1971.

Gruuthusemuseum

Open April–Sept 9.30–5, Oct–March 9.30–12.30 and 2–5, closed Tues; adm 130 BF.

This 15th-century mansion next to the Brangwynmuseum owes its name to the building that originally stood on the site—where grain (groats) was prepared for brewing. A tax on beer was later the perk of an honorific title, 'Lord of Gruuthuse'. The old Gruuthuse mansion, much restored, now contains a splendid collection of all the kinds of things that enriched the lives of the merchant classes of Bruges. Most of the objects are solid and utilitarian, but beautifully crafted and often charmingly decorated. Follow the room numbers to pursue a serpentine course through the museum, past weapons, kitchen implements, Delftware, linenfold cupboards, leather trunks, clocks, scales, spinets and hurdy-gurdies, textiles and lace—and criminals' shackles and a guillotine. Look out for the little wooden gallery that leads across a bridge to the balcony-like oratory overlooking the choir of the Onze Lieve Vrouwekerk.

In Guido Gezelleplein, between the Onze Lieve Vrouwekerk and the Gruuthusemuseum, is a statue to Guido Gezelle (1830–99), one of Flanders' most celebrated poets. Born and bred in Bruges, he joined the priesthood in 1854 and is noted in particular for his nature poems which demonstrate his conviction of the presence of God in all things.

Sint-Salvator-kathedraal

Squat and built of yellow brick, this gloomy church is not the dominant building that its title would suggest, but then it only inherited the role in 1834 after the destruction of the cathedral of Saint Donatian in 1799. It contains an elaborate pulpit (1778–85) by Hendrick Pulincx, as well as some large religious paintings by the Antwerp painter Erasmus Quellinus (1607–78), a pupil of and assistant to Rubens, who had considerable success after his master's death. There is also, unusually, a series of Brussels tapestries, dating to around 1731, depicting religious scenes such as the Nativity and Adoration. The oldest part of the cathedral is the choir, which contains the original choir stalls commissioned when the Order of the Golden Fleece was founded in 1430; these are not accessible, however. The cathedral has its own museum just off the north transept *(open April–Sept 10–12 and 2–5, closed Wed; Oct–March 2–5; adm 40 BF)*, containing numerous ecclesiastical treasures , including works by Dirk Bous and Hugo van der Goes. The most arresting feature of the church, however, is the remarkable baroque organ (1682) at the base of the nave, a mighty confection topped by angels and cherubs playing celestial music. The central statue, of the Creator, is by Artus Quellinus (1625–1700), brother of Erasmus Quellinus.

In Simon Stevinplein, a little way along Steenstraat towards the Markt, is a statue to Simon Stevinus (1548–1620), a Bruges-born mathematician and physicist who demonstrated the impossibility of perpetual motion and is credited by some as the inventor of the decimal point.

South Bruges—Begijnhof and Minnewater

The south of Bruges relaxes into a pretty network of tree-shaded canals. The Begijnhof (*béguinage*) has occupied its site since 1235: this was once, presumably, a vineyard, hence the full title, the Prinselijk Begijnhof ten Wijngaarde. Today it appears more like an island, accessed by a bridge and a gatehouse (dated 1776). (For a history of *béguinages see* pp.208–9.) Tranquil, white-painted gabled houses are set around a spacious patch of grass and cobbled walkways shaded by tall trees, which is awash with daffodils in spring. The church was built in 1602 to replace and earlier one that was burnt down; it has a simple wood-panelled interior and a contrasting baroque altarpiece. There is also a small museum *(open April–June 11–12 and 1.45–5.30; July and Aug 10–12 and 1.45–6; Sept–March 10.30–12 and 1.45–5; adm 50 BF)*, containing mementoes of the Begijnhof, and an evocation of how the interiors looked. The nuns seen in the Begijnhof are not *béguines*, by the way, but Benedictine sisters, who moved here in the 1930s; they have, however, adopted the habits once worn by the *béguines*.

Just south of the Begijnhof, the Minnewater— a broad stretch of water connected to the canals, and eventually the sea—was once a hive of activity as dozens of ships from all over the world jockeyed for position along the quays. Today it is a quiet backwater, enjoyed by strollers and the swans, perhaps now more atune to its peculiar name which means 'Lake of Love'. The old Poedertoren (Powder Tower), built in 1398, was once an arsenal, part of the defensive ramparts protecting the port. There is a good view of the spires of Bruges across the water from the bridge at the base of the Minnewater.

Eastern Bruges

Brugse Brouwerij-Mouterijmuseum ('De Gonden Boom')

Open June–Sept Thurs–Sun 2–5; adm 100 BF (includes one free drink.

This brewery museum, at 10 Verbrand Nieuwland, is housed in a malthouse built in 1902 and used until 1976. It contains artefacts and documents relating to the 31 breweries operating in the city before the First World War.

Beer has been brewed in Bruges for centuries, and there are still several well-known breweries here. De Gouden Boom (next to the museum) was founded in 1584 and produces the excellent Brugse Tripel as well as the spicy wheat beer *(blanche)* called Brugs Tarwebier. The Straffe Hendrik brewery in Walplein was founded in 1546, and produces a beer of that name ('Strong Henry') which is sold only locally *(guided tours only, 10–5; adm 150 BF)*.

Museum voor Volkskunde

Open April–Sept 9.30–5, Oct–March 9.30–12.30 and 2–5, closed Tues; adm 80 BF.

This folk museum in Balstraat is situated in one of the prettiest quarters of old Bruges, among rows of tiny cottages and almshouses. It consists of several cottages knocked together—formerly cobblers' almshouses—and contains all kinds of furniture, tools, domestic implements, toys, lace, paintings and clothes, as well as replicas of a cobbler's workshop, an old grocery and pharmacy, and so on. It also has its own pub, De Zwarte Kat.

Jeruzalemkerk and Kantcentrum

The Jeruzalemkerk is an unusual church for several reasons—not least its polygonal tower surmounted by two tiers of wooden polygonal lanterns and crowned by a tin orb. It could be mistaken for a water tower. The first chapel on this site was built by the Adornes family, Genoese merchants who settled in Bruges in the 13th century. This was replaced in 1427 by the present church, the design of which is based on the Church of the Holy Sepulchre in Jerusalem. It contains the fine tomb of the founder, Anselm Adornes, and his wife, and a replica of the Holy Sepulchre itself. The church is still privately owned by the descendants of the

Adornes family. Adjacent to it is the Kantcentrum (lace centre) *(open April–Sept Mon–Fri 10–12 and 2–6, Sat 10–12 and 2–5, closed Sun; adm 40 BF)*. Its small museum, housed in former almshouses, contains examples of Belgian lace—tablemats, handkerchiefs, collars, cuffs and borders—and underlines the important role that lace has played in fashion over time. In the demonstration room a crowd of practitioners sit chatting and laughing as their operate with lightning speed the numerous bobbins and pins on the cushions on their knees.

Schuttersgilde Sint-Sebastian, Schuttersgilde Sint-Joris

The archers' guilds were celebrated clubs that far outlived the age of bows and arrows as military weapons. Archery remained a social sport, and its traditional form is still practised today: the target is an artificial bird attached to a high pole. When Charles II, future king of England, settled in Bruges between 1656 and 1658 (the year of Cromwell's death), he was made 'King of the Archers' Guild of Saint Sebastian'. He was joined in Bruges by his brother James (the future James II) and a gang of cronies who were well noted for their dissolute ways and their perpetual inability to pay their bills—all of which was carefully noted with relish by Commonwealth agents sent to spy on them. The royal connection has been maintained by the guild: all British sovereigns have been members of the guild since the days of Charles II. Today the old and atmospheric guildhouses both contain small museums. The Schuttersgilde Sint-Sebastian, the longbow archers' guild, is housed in a pretty red-brick house (dated 1565) in Carmerstraat *(open Mon, Wed, Fri and Sat 10–12 and 2–5; adm 40 BF)*; it contains paintings, goldwork and various mementoes of royalty. Its rocket-shaped tower is one of the few survivors of an architectural peculiarity which was once so prevalent that Bruges was often compared to an oriental city.

Schuttersgilde Sint-Joris (Saint George), the crossbow archers' guild, is in Stijn Streuvelstraat *(open 2–6, closed Wed and Sun; adm 50 BF)* and contains paintings, archives and a collection of crossbows.

The Windmills and Kruispoort

There use to be 20 windmills lining the earth ramparts around Bruges, and today three still stand overlooking the canal on the eastern edge of the old city. From north to south they are: De Nieuwe Papegai (an old oil-mill, brought here in 1970), Sint-Janshuysmolen (a grain mill, built here in 1770 and, after restoration, still in use) and Bonne Chiere (brought here in 1911). It is possible to visit the Sint-Janshuysmolen during the summer *(May–Sept 9.30–12 and 12.45–5; adm 40 BF)*. To their south is the Kruispoort, a massive hulk of a bastion dating from 1402, one of the four surviving city gates.

Other Attractions

Just to the south of Bruges, off the A17, is **Boudewijn Park** (© (050) 38 38 38), a large amusement park with numerous rides including a big wheel and water shoots, crazy golf and a large dolphinarium. *Open May–Aug 10–6, and Easter and weekends in Sept; all-in tickets 420 BF for adults, 380 BF for children aged 6–12, 340 BF for children under 6, children under 1m tall are free.*

Shopping

The main **shopping district** is in the west of the city, in and around Steenstraat and Zuidzandstraat. The shops these days are upmarket and all very tasteful—even the chain stores have wrought-iron shop signs. Lace is a famous Bruges product, and much of it is still hand-made locally. There are good lace shops in Breidelstraat, between the Markt and Burg, and a lively fish market (Vismarkt, *see* pp.303–4).

Bruges © (050–)

Where to Stay

Some of the small hotels in central Bruges are historic mansions and town-houses, beautifully restored and converted, and looking like photographs from glossy interior-design magazines—the stuff of dreams. The cheaper hotels are more run-of-the-mill, but it may be worth sacrificing comfort for a more central location.

★★★★★ **De Tuilerieën**, 7 Dijver, 8000 Brugge, © 34 36 91, fax 34 04 00. Pampered luxury in a 15th-century town house, on the Dijver, a pretty stretch of canal near the centre. Has swimming pool. 6000–10,000 BF.

★★★★ **De Snippe**, 53 Niewe Gentweg, 8000 Brugge, © 33 70 70; fax 33 76 62. A hotel-restaurant with celebrated cuisine (*see* below). The 18th-century house has been sympathetically restored to comfortable elegance. 4500–6000 BF.

★★★★ **De Swaene**, Steenhouwersdijk (Groenerei), 8000 Brugge, © 34 27 98, fax 33 66 74. A 15th-century mansion overlooking the canal close to the Vismarkt, restored in 1981 in Louis XV-cum-Laura Ashley style. 4850–5850 BF.

★★★★ **Duc de Bourgogne**, 12 Huidenvettersplein, 8000 Brugge, © 332038, fax 344 037. Hotel-restaurant in a very central historic house with good restaurant (*see* below). Nine rooms only; 3500–5000 BF.

★★★★ **Holiday Inn Crowne Plaza**, 10 Burg, 8000 Brugge, © 34 58 34. Sleek modern hotel bang in the centre, with pool and parking. 6000–6700 BF; children free if sharing with parents.

★★★ **Pandhotel**, 16 Pandreitje, 8000 Brugge, ✆ 34 06 66, fax 34 05 56. A fine 18th-century burgher's house converted into a cosy, elegant hotel, part of the Romantic Hotels chain. Close to the centre. 4500 BF.

★★★ **Park Hotel**, 5 Vrijdagmarkt ('t Zand), 8000 Brugge, ✆) 33 33 64; fax 33 47 63. Comfortable modern hotel on 't Zand, about 15 minutes' walk from the centre. 3600–5400 BF.

★★★ **Patritius**, 11 Riddersstraat, 8000 Brugge, ✆ 33 84 54, fax 33 96 34. A big old mansion, converted into a medium-priced hotel, spacious and central but with few frills. 2900–4000 BF.

★★★ **Pullman**, 2 Boeveriestraat, 8000 Brugge, ✆ 34 09 71; fax 34 40 53. Modern hotel behind the façade of a 17th-century monastery on 't Zand, about 15 minutes' walk from the centre. Has a swimming pool. 4000–5000 BF, without breakfast.

★★ **Campanile**, 20 Jagerstraat, 8200 St Michiels, ✆ 38 13 60; fax 38 45 42. A family-run hotel in Sint-Michiels to the south of the station. 2600 BF.

★★ **Cordoeanier**, 16–18 Cordoenierstraat, 8000 Brugge, ✆ 33 90 51, fax 34 61 11. A small hotel, good value for its central position. 2000 BF.

★★ **Ibis Brugge Centrum**, 65A Katelijnestraat, 8000 Brugge, ✆ 33 75 75; fax 33 64 19. Large modern hotel with all mod-cons, close to the Begijnhof in the south of the city. 2300 BF.

★★ **Groeninghe**, 29 Korte Vuldersstraat, ✆ 34 32 55. Small guesthouse with the atmosphere of a private home, in the west of the city not far from Sint-Salvator-kathedraal. 2300 BF.

★★ **'t Putje**, 31 't Zand, 8000 Brugge, ✆ 33 28 47, fax 34 14 23. Well-run, clean and friendly modernized hotel backing on the 't Zand, about 15 minutes' walk from the centre. 2600–3400 BF.

youth hostels

There are several *jeuglogies* in Bruges, where you can find cheap and cheerful accommodation—fine if you don't mind sleeping in a dormitory.

Bauhaus International Youth Hotel, 135–137 Langestraat, 8000 Brugge, ✆ 34 10 93, fax 33 41 80. Room for 32 people, about 20 minutes' walk from the centre. 320 BF per person.

Passage, 26 Dweerstraat 8000 Brugge, ✆ 34 02 32, fax 34 01 40. Capacity for 42, a stone's throw from Sint-Salvator-kathedraal. 310–375 BF.

International Youth Hostel, 143 Baron Ruzettelaan, 8310 Assebroek, ✆ 35 26 79, fax 35 37 32. The modern youth hostel, located in Assebroek, a suburb to the east of the city. 335 BF.

The fame of Bruges's best restaurants has spread far beyond the borders of Belgium. It has some outstanding chefs working in beautifully decorated restaurants. Treat yourself. Besides, finding good, inexpensive food in Bruges is more of a problem: tourism has taken its toll, and in some of the more prominent tourist restaurants the fare can be decidedly mediocre.

expensive

Den Braamberg, 11 Pandreitje, ✆ 33 73 70. *Closed Sun eve and Thurs*. Elegant restaurant in an 18th-century house, with award-winning cuisine. Menu at 2000 BF.

De Karmeliet, 19 Langestraat, ✆ 33 82 59. *Closed Sun eve and Mon*. Chic restaurant with an excellent reputation. Lunch menu at 2300 BF.

De Snippe, 53 Nieuwe Gentweg, ✆ 33 70 70. *Closed Sun and Mon lunch*. Hotel-restaurant in a tastefully renovated *maison de maître*, with an orangerie overlooking the garden, serving superb *haute cuisine française*—dishes such as *queues de langoustines à la ciboulette*. Lunch menu at 1650 BF; four-course evening menu for 3400 BF (with wine).

De Swaene, Steenhouwersdijk (Groenerei), ✆ 34 27 98. *Closed Sun and Mon lunch*. Elegant hotel-restaurant which prides itself on its French-style cooking. Lunch menu at 1050 BF.

Duc de Bourgogne, 12 Huidenvettersplein, ✆ 33 20 38. *Closed Mon and Tues lunch*. Classy hotel-restaurant in a former palace gatehouse, overlooking the canal at the heart of the city, with canal views from the restaurant. Gastronomic menu at 2050 BF.

Patrick Devos, 41 Zilverstraat 33 55 66. *Closed Sun and Mon*. Much fêted restaurant in an elegant turn-of-the-century house with garden. Patrick Devos is noted for his French cuisine prepared with an ingeniously light touch. Lunch menu at a bargain 750 BF, gourmet menu at 3000 BF.

De Witte Poorte, 6 Jan van Eyckplein, ✆ 33 08 83. Specialist in Belgian cooking, of exceptional quality. Lunch menu at 1100 BF.

moderate

De Beiaardier, 34 Markt, ✆ 33 41 37. Pleasant, down-to-earth restaurant, specializing in traditional Bruges fare, such as country sausages with sorrel-flavoured potatoes; around 800 BF.

inexpensive

Café des Arts, 32 Markt. Agreeable if touristy, with local dishes for 575 BF.

Of all the great Flemish cities, Ghent wears the robes of its prosperous and noble past with the most dignity: 'majestic' might not be too strong a word. Stately step-gabled façades line the tranquil canals, while the pinnacled and gilded spires of its great monuments shape the skyline, constantly reappearing from all angles across the city.

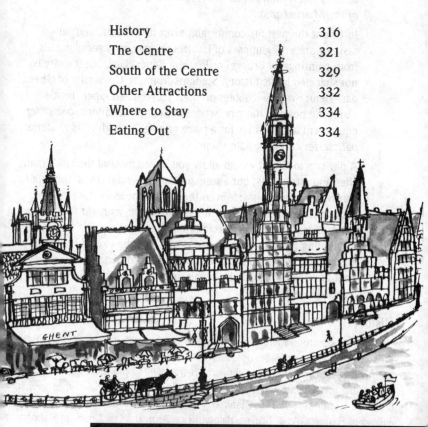

Ghent

A number of Ghent's museums surpass expectations—notably the Museum voor Sierkunst (decorative arts), the Museum voor Volkskunde (folk museum) and the Bijlokemuseum (a rich historical ragbag). Its *begijnhof* (*béguinage*) is one of the most charming and evocative in Belgium. And there is a remarkable and dazzling jewel in this crown: in a kind of sanctuary within its fine cathedral is one of the great masterpieces of European art, Jan van Eyck's *Adoration of the Mystic Lamb*.

In Ghent the past fits comfortably with its dynamic and self-assured present: glimpses of its street scenes may recall details from paintings by Bruegel or Joachim Beuckelaer, but the city is not shackled by its history. Students from the University of Ghent dart about over the cobbles on their bicycles. Shoppers bustle about the heart of the city, where daring new fashions, computer equipment and CDs vie for a place among the high-class groceries, *pâtisseries* and chocolate shops.

A day trip to Ghent would allow you to see most of the city's main sites and attractions, but a weekend break would reveal more of its warm and friendly heart. Even though Ghent lacks the range of sumptuous hotels of Bruges or even Antwerp, as night falls the atmosphere relaxes in expectation of pleasure, and the soft and welcoming lights of the numerous bars and the excellent restaurants—many of them housed in centuries-old historic buildings—glow across the canals and in the recesses of the crooked streets.

History

Ghent grew up around two 7th-century abbeys, those of St Baaf and Sint Pieter, built among a group of 30 or so islands scattered across the marshy ground where the Rivers Lys (Leie) and Lieve converge before joining the River Scheldt just to the south. (The name Ghent may well derive from the Celtic word *ganda*, meaning 'confluence'.) These later developed into two of the most powerful abbeys in Flanders. As at Bruges, Baldwin Iron-Arm, the first Count of Flanders, built a castle here in the 9th century to protect the abbeys from raids by the Vikings, who could penetrate far inland in their shallow-draft ships.

Ghent became rich from the cloth trade and in the 13th century forged a canal link with Bruges. At the start of the Hundred Years' War, however, the Count of Flanders, Louis de Nevers, sided with France; the effect was to throttle trade with

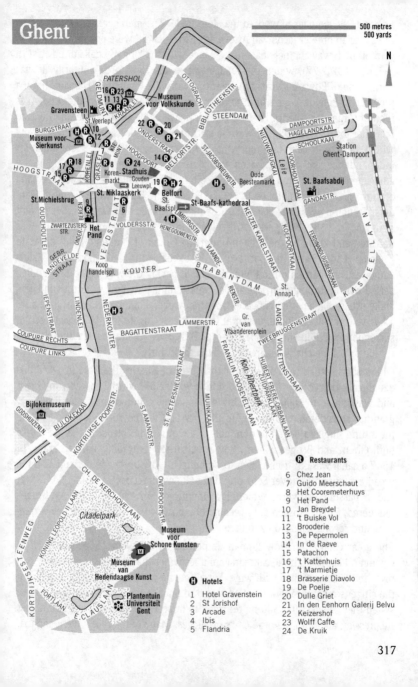

Ghent

500 metres
500 yards

N

PATERSHOL

Museum voor Volkskunde

Gravensteen

St. Veerlepl.

BURGSTRAAT

Museum voor Sierkunst

GELDMUNT

KRAANLEI

OTTOGRACHT

STEENDAM

BIBLIOTHEEKSTR.

DAMPOORTSTR.
HAGELANDKAAI

SCHOOLKAAI

Station Ghent-Dampoort

ONDERSTRAAT

HOOGPOORT

BELFORTSTR.

ST-JACOBSNIEUWSTR.

NIEUWBRUGKAI

VOORHOUTKAAI

Lele

St. Baafsabdij

GANDASTR.

HOOGSTRAAT

GRASLEI

KORENLEI

MINT

Korenmarkt

Stadhuis
Gouden Leeuwpl.

St. Niklaaskerk

Belfort
St. Baafspl.

St-Baafs-kathedraal

LIMBURGSTR.

Oude Beestenmarkt

KEIZER KARELSTRAAT

KOEPOORTKAAI

FERDINAND LOUSBERGSKAAI

KASTEELLAAN

St. Michielsbrug

OUDEHOUTLEI

ZWARTEZUSTERS STR.

Het Pand

BERGEN

ONDER

VELDSTRAAT

VOLDERSSTR.

HENEGOUWENSTR.

VLAAND.

VLAANDERENPLEIN

BRABANTDAM

St. Annapl.

GEBR. VANDEVELDE STRAAT

LINDENLEI

IEPENSTRAAT

COUPURE RECHTS
COUPURE LINKS

NEDERKOUTER

Koophandelspl.

KOUTER

BAGATTENSTRAAT

LAMMERSTR.

Gr. van Vlaanderenplein

REINSTR.

LANGE VIOLETTENSTRAAT

TWEEBRUGGENSTRAAT

HUBERT FRÈRE-ORBANLAAN

ZUIDPARKLAAN

Bijlokemuseum

GODSHUIZENLN.

BIJLOKEKAAI

Lele

KORTRIJKSE POORTSTR.

ST. PIETERSNIEUWSTRAAT

ST-AMANDSTR.

MUINKKAAI

FRANKLIN ROOSEVELTLAAN

Kon. Albertpark

CH. DE KERCHOVELAAN

OVERPOORTSTR.

Citadelpark

Museum voor Schone Kunsten

KORTRIJKSESTEENWEG

KONING LEOPOLD II LAAN

FORTLAAN

E. CLAUSLAAN

Museum van Hedendaagse Kunst

Plantentuin Universiteit Gent

R Restaurants

6 Chez Jean
7 Guido Meerschaut
8 Het Cooremeterhuys
9 Het Pand
10 Jan Breydel
11 't Buiske Vol
12 Brooderie
13 De Pepermolen
14 In de Raeve
15 Patachon
16 't Kattenhuis
17 't Marmietje
18 Brasserie Diavolo
19 De Poelje
20 Dulle Griet
21 In den Eenhorn Galerij Belvu
22 Keizershof
23 Wolff Caffe
24 De Kruik

H Hotels

1 Hotel Gravenstein
2 St Jorishof
3 Arcade
4 Ibis
5 Flandria

317

England, the supplier of wool to the cloth trade. The merchants of Ghent, led by the patrician brewer Jacob van Artevelde (1287–1345), were powerful enough to go their own way and negotiated an alliance with the king of England, Edward III (reigned 1327–77), which the English were able to enforce militarily. It was during one of Edward's visits to Ghent that his wife, Philippa of Hainault (now a province of Belgium), gave birth to their third son, who was thereafter known as John of Gaunt (or Ghent). He later ruled in place of his ageing father, and was to be father to the Tudor line. It was the start of a troubled history for Ghent, a city which, despite its calm face today, has always had something of a reputation for independence and revolt. Jacob van Artevelde was murdered in 1345 by guildsmen who had tired of the near-dictatorial powers that he had acquired and did not agree with his proposal to make Edward the Black Prince Count of Flanders. French power over Flanders subsequently waxed and waned in a constant struggle. In 1381 Philip van Artevelde (son of Jacob) led a revolt, but was defeated and killed by the French under the Count of Flanders, Louis de Male (reigned 1346–84)at the Battle of Westrozebeke in 1382. Louis de Male's daughter was married off to Philip the Good, paving the way to the Burgundian period which, through marriage and conquest, united the Low Countries and generally ushered in a period of peace. Ghent, however, continued to resist, and after a five-year revolt ending in defeat at the Battle of Gavere in 1453 was forced to surrender as Philip the Good, Duke of Burgundy, made the leading citizens parade out of the city gates dressed only in their shirts.

Ghent soon settled the score. After the death of Charles the Bold in 1477, his daughter and successor Mary of Burgundy was held in virtual captivity in Ghent and was forced to sign (in the Sint-Jorishof, now a hotel) the Great Privilege, granting considerable autonomy to the city and the power to legislate. In the meantime England began to dominate the cloth trade, bleeding the life out of both Ghent and Bruges. Ghent, however, turned its trading skills to grain. In 1547 a canal was cut from Ghent to Terneuzen (now in the Netherlands) on the broad estuary of the River Scheldt, giving Ghent direct access to the North Sea, and bypassing Antwerp, which lay downriver on the Scheldt. As Bruges foundered, Ghent prospered, to become the most powerful city of the Low Countries, and second in size only to Paris.

The great Charles V, Holy Roman Emperor from 1519 to 1556, was born in Ghent and baptized in the cathedral amid festivities that included a three-day carnival and fountains filled with wine. For a time he was Ghent's favourite son, but the citizens grew weary of taxation raised to finance his extravagant campaigns. When they rebelled in 1540 he returned to impose his authority with a ruthless suppression and withdrew the city's privileges. Many of the rebels were hanged, earning the citizens of Ghent the nickname *stroppendragers* ('noose bearers'), an event still recalled in folk processions, such as the Gentse Feesten. This tragedy helped to shape Ghent's outlook through the turmoil of the Counter-Reformation, during which Ghent had a sizeable minority of Protestants and suffered at the hands of the Inquisition. There was a Calvinist revolt in 1566, eventually brought under control by the Duke of Alva, but not before the iconoclasts had caused widespread damage to the churches and monasteries. In 1576 William of Orange, Stadholder of the Protestant Netherlands, pushed his army southwards and took Ghent, forcing the treaty known as the Pacification of Ghent by which Philip II of Spain undertook to withdraw his troops from the 17 United Provinces of the Netherlands and to grant them religious freedom. For just under ten years Ghent remained under Dutch rule and for a time Protestants dominated the city council. Sint-Baafskathedraal became a Protestant church. But in 1585 Alexander Farnese, Duke of Parma, retook Ghent on behalf of Philip II and pushed the border back to more or less the current frontier with the Netherlands. After 1648 the Netherlands sealed off the Scheldt estuary, cutting off Antwerp's access to the sea and one of Ghent's two canal links to the coast, and crippling their trade. The fortunes of the two trading cities were only released from this stranglehold when the French Revolutionary Army overran both Flanders and the Netherlands in 1794.

Ghent's subsequent revival is largely attributed to a merchant called Lieven Bauwens (1762–1822), who in 1800 managed to smuggle a Spinning Jenny out of England piece by piece, along with a group of skilled operators. He set up a cotton-spinning business of his own, and by 1810 cotton had boomed into an industry employing some 10,000 workers. By the late 19th century Ghent had developed into a major industrial centre, with cotton and linen as the mainstays of its fortunes. (The River Leie became known as the 'Golden River', because the quantities of flax treated on its banks stained it yellow.)

Ghent's industry has continued to thrive; textiles still play an important role, now supplemented by chemicals and steel. The old canal to Terneuzen was massively enlarged in the 1820s, when Belgium was ruled by the Dutch prior to independence, and in the 1960s the width was doubled in size to 200m. Today ships of up to 60,000 tonnes can dock in the midst of the sprawling industrial complex to the north of the city, and Ghent's port constitutes the second largest port in Belgium after Antwerp. Ghent is also the capital of the province of East Flanders.

Getting There

Ghent (Gent in Flemish and Gand in French) is just 50km northwest of Brussels, connected by the E40 autoroute. By **train** Ghent is a 40-minute journey from Brussels. The main station (Gand-Sint-Pieters) is 2.5km to the south of the city centre. There are tram links (trams 1, 11 and 12) to the centre, and also taxis.

Getting Around

Ghent has a good **bus and tram** network covering the city. Maps are available from the ticket and information office on the Korenmarkt, at the western end of Sint-Niklaaskerk. Driving in the city is complicated by a system of one-way streets around the centre, and the presence of trams. Once in the centre, **parking** can be a real problem. There are numerous parking spaces in Gouden Leeuwplein, in the shadow of the Belfort, but these are fiercely contested and you have to be lucky to come across upon a car vacating a space. There are other car parks in and around the Kouter to the south of the centre, and in the Vrijdagmarkt to the north, and a small one on Sint-Veerleplein close to the Gravensteen.

Boat trips on the canals depart from the Graslei and Korenlei. The trip around the city centre lasts about 35 minutes *(April–Oct 10–7; about 130 BF per person)*.

Horse-drawn carriages make half-hour trips around the main sites of the city centre, starting at Sint-Baafsplein *(Easter–Sept/Oct 10–7; about 700 BF per carriage)*.

Tourist Information

The tourist information office is in the crypt of the Stadhuis, open daily April–Oct 9.30–6.30, Nov–March 9.30–4.30, © (09) 224 15 55. This is not a great source of literature, but staff are on hand to answer questions. Most practical information is available in a single pamphlet on the city, called simply 'Ghent', published annually by the tourist authority.

Festivals

The **city illuminations** regularly create a spectacular sight. Many of the city's monuments are lit up every night from May to October, and on Friday and Saturday for the remainder of the year.

Ghent's most spectacular festival is its flower show, the **Gentse Floraliën**, which takes place at the Flanders Expo (a huge international trade fair centre to the southwest of the city) over ten days in late April every five years (on the decade and half-decade: for example, 22 April–1 May 1995). Ghent—or rather the land to its east, known as the Bloemenstreek (Region of Flowers)—is an important centre for the horticulture industry, famous above all for its begonias, azaleas, rhododendrons and roses.

The Flanders-wide **Festival van Vlaanderen** is a major European festival of classical music that takes place annually in the last two weeks of September and the first week of October; some concerts are staged in Ghent's historical buildings. This is not to be confused with the annual **Gentse Feesten** (Ghent Festivities), which is held over ten days in early July and consists of a variety of folk processions, street theatre and musical events.

The Centre

Sint-Baafskathedraal

Open April–Sept Mon–Sat 9.30–12 and 2–6, Sun 1–6; Oct–March Mon–Sat 10–12 and 2.30–4, Sun 2–5.

Ghent's cathedral, one of the finest in Belgium, was named after the city's most cherished early-Christian saint. St Bavo (or Bavon) lived in the 7th century. In the early part of his career he was a wealthy man, with a wife and daughter and extensive properties in his native Brabant. He was also a thorough degenerate. However, after his wife died he was inspired to reform: he gave his fortune to the poor and devoted himself to good works. As a follower of St Amand, he undertook several missionary expeditions to France and Flanders before retiring to live as a hermit in woods near Ghent. When he died in about AD 653 he was buried in one of the monasteries, which later became known as Sint-Baafsabdij (*see* below). The present cathedral was founded originally in the 10th century as a church dedicated to St John the Baptist, but it was rebuilt in Gothic style over nearly three centuries, from 1290 to 1569. It was renamed after St Bavo in 1540, when Charles V had the old Sint-Baafsabdij pulled down in order to build a castle on the site. The exterior has an impressive simplicity, crowned by its 85m-tall belltower (1462–1534) adorned by crocketed spires.

The great treasure of the cathedral is the *Adoration of the Mystic Lamb*, displayed in a rather cramped room to the left of the west (main) door to the cathedral (*adm 50 BF; ticket includes admission to crypt*). It is a large polyptych of twelve panels, painted by Jan van Eyck between 1426 and 1432; a Latin inscription on the reverse claims that it was begun by Jan's brother Hubert (of whom no other works are known) and continued by Jan after Hubert's death, but there is little other information to corroborate this story. Given that this is one of the earliest known oil paintings, the proficiency with which the new medium was used is astonishing. There are some 280 figures, painted with almost translucent clarity and pinpoint detail. In the upper tier Christ enthroned is flanked by the Virgin Mary and John the Baptist, musicians and singers, and Adam and Eve of such raw and sensual nakedness that they were replaced in the late 18th century, during the reforming era of Joseph II, by clothed versions (now on view by the west door). The lower tier shows a Flemish landscape with the Fountain of Life and an altar in the mid-distance on which stands the Lamb of God (symbol of Christ sacrificed to redeem the world), surrounded angels, patriarchs, prophets and apostles. Processing towards the altar from the rear left are martyrs and confessors; from the right, virgins. To the left and right in the foreground are further crowds of judges, knights, monks, clerics, and hermits. The right-hand panel shows St Christopher and a crowd of pilgrims. The left-hand panel of the just judges was stolen in 1934 and was never recovered, so has been replaced by a copy made in 1941. The reverse side of the panels have also been painted, in statuesque monochrome. Here we can see the Annuncation, St John, a view of Ghent (top right), and in the centre, portraits of the donors who commissioned the painting, the cloth merchant Joos Vijd and his wife Isabella Borluut.

In the nave is a fine pulpit (1741–5) by Laurent Delvaux (1696–1778) made of an unusual mixture of oak and marble—Baroque, but with a Rococo lightness of touch. On the crest, a serpent wriggles around the Tree of Knowledge adorned with golden apples. The 13th- and 14th-century choir, built of grey-blue Tournai stone, has been compromised by 18th-century neoclassical screen to draw focus to the altar; this altar was designed by Hendrik Verbruggen (creator of the extraordinary pulpit in the cathedral of Brussels) and shows the *Apotheosis of St Bavo*. The ambulatory has been divided into a series of dimly-lit chapels, one of which (to the left of the altar) contains *The Vocation of St Bavo* (1623/4) by Rubens. It is Rubens at his best, with a dramatic, sweeping composition, full of animation and with a real sense of the physical presence of the figures depicted. The face of St Bavo is said to be a self-portrait of Rubens.

The crypt was part of the original Romanesque church (black tiles on the floor indicate the limit of the original church foundations), and it has the faded but beautiful remnants of murals, dating from between 1480 and 1540, on the columns and vaults. Today the crypt serves as a kind of museum of extravagant church ornaments and reliquaries, but also includes a few exceptional altar pieces, notably a Crucifixion by Justus van Gent (?1435–80), in which the artist struggles to portray distress amid all the medieval finery. Painted in about 1464–8, it appears to precede the painter's voyage to the court of Urbino, during which he may well have provided a crucial link between Flemish and Italian art.

Belfort

Open 10–12.30 and 2–5.30 daily; adm 80 BF.

The belfry of Ghent is one of the city's great landmarks. It rises majestically to the gilded copper dragon at 91m, and has a weathervane that can trace its history back to 1377, set above a crescendo of black-tiled pinnacles and roof-tops, dappled with gilded crockets. Built originally between 1381 and 1380, it was heavily restored in the 19th century. It used to contain an alarm bell called Roeland (it was said to have the tongue of the chivalric hero Roland), which was removed on the instruction of Charles V because the bell had been used to call the citizens of Ghent to revolt in 1540. It was replaced by the 'Triomfante' in 1660. This in turn cracked in 1914, and now sits in the square below, towards the western end of the Sint-Niklaaskerk. Today the tower contains not only its clock, but also a 52-bell carillon, 37 of which date back to 1660. *(Carillon concerts: Fri and Sat 11.30am–12.30; also at 9–10pm on Sat in July and Aug.)* Visitors can reach the parapet at 65m by lift from which there are good views of the city.

At the foot of the belfry is Lakenhalle (cloth hall) *(guided tours only, same hours as the Belfort; adm 100 BF)*, a classic Flemish Gothic building dating to about 1425, with a roofline studded with gabled and shuttered dormer windows. Attached to both the Belfort and the Lakenhalle, on the Stadhuis side, is the former prison (1741) called the Mammelokker ('Suckler') because of the relief carving on the façade which shows a man being suckled by a young woman. This relates to a Roman legend about an aged prisoner who was condemned to death by starvation and was saved in this way by his daughter.

The square between the Belfort and the cathedral (Sint-Baafsplein) was occupied by buildings until 1913. In front of the Schouwburg theatre (1891), is a monument to Jan-Frans Willems (1793–1846), set on a angled slab of marble over which water satisfyingly flows. Willems was a writer and historian who specialized in Flemish history and literature, and was an early champion of Flemish culture and the Flemish national identity.

Stadhuis

Guided tours in Flemish, March–Sept at 2pm, on certain days only; contact the tourist office in the crypt below.

This imposing town hall has three faces: you can see two of them by standing at the corner of the Botermarkt and Hoogstraat. Overlooking Hoogstraat is the Flamboyant Gothic façade (1518–60), a cornucopia of stonework ornamentation. Overlooking the Botermarkt is the more restrained Renaissance façade of 1581, reflecting the cooler outlook of the then Protestant administration. The third is a complex of antique wonky rooflines which lies virtually hidden, glimpsed only from the Gouden Leeuwplein, housing the working parts of the building.

Still serving as a centre for city administration—and still the focus of the occasional demonstration—the interior contains a mixture of grand halls, function rooms and offices of various eras, but mainly dating from the restoration that took place after 1870. However, included among them is the 16th-century Pacificatiezaal where the Pacification of Ghent was signed.

Sint-Niklaaskerk

Open 9–12 and 2–5.

This fine church, built mainly in the 13th century in what is known as Scheldt Gothic, is currently emerging from two decades of renovation, and the entrance for the time being is on the southern side. It has a atmospheric interior, with plain walls of knibbled stone set against concertinaed ranks of dressed-stone buttresses and side-chapels and the elegant curvature of the Gothic arches. This was once the church of the guilds, where each guild had a chapel, but it was badly damaged by the iconoclasts in 1566 and was used as a stable by the French Revolutionary Army in the 1790s. Outside, on the northern side of the church you can still see the remnants of the houses and shops that were once built against the church walls, most of which were removed during the 19th century. There is a remarkable building overlooking the street on the south side of the Sint-Niklaaskerk. An ancient gabled house is topped by exuberant dancing, prancing medieval characters, teetering on the pinnacles in their long pointy shoes and playing tambourines and bagpipes. These modern statues are 'Moresken' (dancers in Moorish style; the same derivation as Morris dancers) by the Ghent sculptor Walter de Buck; somehow, through their scale and pure exuberance perhaps, they escape triumphantly the usual crassness of medievalism. The building itself, much restored, is the old Metselaarshuis, a guildhouse of the masons.

In Burgemeester Braunplein, between the eastern end of Sint-Niklaaskerk and the Belfort, there are two monuments. The first is the old cracked bell called 'Triomfante' (*see* under 'Belfort' above). The second is a bronze version of the *Fontein der Geknieden* (Fountain of Kneeling Youths) by George Minne (*see* 'Museum voor Schone Kunsten' below).

Sint-Michielsbrug

This bridge is Ghent's most famous viewpoint, and justly so. To the east is the spectacular line-up of the towers of Sint-Niklaaskerk, the Belfort and Sint-Baafskathedraal. To the north is the city's most beautiful stretch of canal, with the Graslei to the right and the Korenlei to the left. Behind you is the imposing cruciform hulk Sint-Michielskerk *(not open to the public)*, a church begun in 1440 and built over two centuries, although the tower was never completed.

Graslei and Korenlei

The waterway (the canalized River Leie) leading between these two quays was at the heart of the old port of Ghent. The Graslei on the eastern side has the most striking frontages, a fetching jumble of step-gables, stone carving and ranks of elegant windows. The buildings go as far back as the 12th century, added to over the next 500 years, but are mainly Flemish Renaissance in style. From north to south, they are as follows.

The building with high pinnacles topped by gilded gryphons is the Gildehuis van de Metsers (Guildhouse of the Masons), built in 1521. Next comes the 15th-century Korenmeterhuis (also spelled Cooremeterhuys; the Guildhouse of the Grainmeasurers). Grainmeasuring was an important function because Ghent was a major shipping centre for grain after the 15th century, and customs duties could be paid in kind with grain. This grain was stored in the building next door, the broad-fronted Korenstapelhuis, built originally in 1130 and still retaining its romanesque arches. Beside this is the minuscule gabled Tolhuisje (1682), which is the customs house. Then follows the broad Gildehuis der Graanmeters (Grain-measurers—their second house on this frontage), built in 1698 and decorated with escutcheons. The last of the set, and the finest, is a beautifully designed Renaissance house (1531), with a elaborately sculpted gable and a façade filled with windows; over the doorway is a relief sculpture of a ship. This is the Gilde-huis der Vrije Schippers (Free Boatmen), a symbol of the power of the boatmen who had the monopoly for shipping grain and other goods in and out of the city.

To the north of the Graslei and the Grasbrug is the confluence of the Rivers Lieve and Leie. Lining the towpath on the right-hand side of the River Leie is the old meat market, the Groot Vleeshuis, built 1406–10—a long and elegant building with a row of gabled dormer windows poking up through the base of its steep-pitched roof.

Het Pand

This old Dominican monastery stands next to the river beside the Sint-Michielskerk. It is now the property of Ghent University and is used as a cultural centre, with two restaurants and halls for civic receptions. You are free to wander around it, and by following the stone staircases can reach the corridors lined with the former cells of the monks (now used as offices).

A staircase on the left-hand side of the building leads up to the Bibliotheca Dominicana *(open Tues 9–12, Wed 2–4)*, a library originally founded by Margaret of York, wife of Charles the Bold. The collection was destroyed by the iconoclasts in the 1570s, who burnt the monastery and threw the books into the river; some of these were salvaged, however. The monastery was again sacked by the French Revolutionary Armies, but in the 1830s the library was rehabilitated in its original site, and now contains 10,000 volumes, some of the oldest and most precious of which are displayed in a glass cabinet.

The Museum Glasramen *(open April–Sept Thurs–Sat 11–12.30 and 2–5.30, Sun 2.30–5.50; Oct–March Thurs–Sat 11.30–12.30 and 2–4, Sun 2–4; closed*

Mon–Wed; adm) contains a collection of early stained glass which was salvaged from the monastery and rediscovered during restoration in 1982.

Museum voor Sierkunst

Open 9.30–5, closed Mon; adm 80 BF.

This museum of the decorative arts is one of the most rewarding and delightful in Belgium. It is set out in a series of rooms in a grand 18th-century townhouse built for a wealthy family of cloth merchants called De Coninck. The house was purchased on behalf of the public for its historical interest in 1921 and became a museum of the decorative arts in 1958, and it has an excellent collection of antique furniture, arranged according to function and date. At the rear of the museum is a modern annexe, completed in 1992, which has moving floors to enable it to house temporary exhibitions at different heights. This annexe contains a superb collection of modern design, from Art Nouveau to Post-Modernism.

The suggested route through the museum takes you past rooms of 17th–19th furniture first—with such items as bombé commodes veneered with delicate marquetry, glass chandeliers and Delftware. It then leads to the lower floor of the modern section, and here the real feast begins, tracking the development of modern design through dozens of pioneer pieces, many of them classics, starting with a Thonet bentwood chair of 1860. There is Art Nouveau glassware by **Emile Gallé** and the **Daum** brothers from the Nancy workshops; carpets, furniture and lighting by **Gustave Serrurier-Bovy**; chairs by **Victor Horta**; a table by **Louis Majorelle**; wrought-iron lamps by **Paul Hankar**; textiles and cutlery by **Henri van de Velde**; perfume bottles by **René Lalique**. Look out for the work of the British designer **Christopher Dresser**, a leading campaigner for industrial design against the tide of the Arts and Crafts movement. His letter-rack, decanter and sugar bowl here look like pieces of Art Deco: in fact they date back to the 1880s. There are two classic Modernist chairs of the same era: a 1925 version of the Wassily Chair, the first to be made of tubular steel, by **Marcel Breuer**, and a 1929 version of the X-frame Barcelona Chair by **Ludwig Mies van der Rohe**.

The collection has been kept fresh by some skilful buying over the last decade or so, which demonstrates vividly how Post-Modernism has the same kind of appeal, élan and shock that Art Nouveau and Art Deco both had in their day. There are some splendidly wild and garish pieces from the Milan School, rewriting the very concept of furniture, such as the glass constructions by Ettore Sottsass, multimedia items from the Memphis Studio, and post-Rococo pieces by Alchimia. Some of the highly original cutlery and tea and coffee sets by Aldo Rossi and Richard Meier (for Alessi) have already become design classics. The 'Banana

Chair' by Muriel Adam is composed entirely of a heap of textile bananas and beckons you to throw yourself onto it—but, alas, you are not allowed to.

Visitors are now led back through the old building past rooms furnished with an excellent collection of Directoire and Empire furniture and accessories, which show how these too brought with them the shock of the new during the French Revolutionary and Napoloeonic periods. Finally you reach the original dining room of the house, a beautiful wood-pannelled room with a painted ceiling, and display cabinets containing *famille-rose* ware. In the centre is a magnificent wooden chandelier (1770) by the Ghent sculptor J. F. Allaert, richly decorated with carved animals, and cherubs wearing turbans, Indian headdresses and elephant masks and riding camels and crocodiles and so forth. Each represents one of the 'four corners of the world' (Europe, America, Africa, Asia)—a monument to the European trading prowess that helped to make Ghent rich.

Gravensteen

Open April–Sept 9–6; Oct–March 9–5; last admission 45 mins before closing; adm 80 BF.

This grim and muscular fortress comes as something of a shock after the more dainty Gothic architecture of Ghent's other prominent monuments. Its name means 'Castle of the Counts', and it was built in 1180 by Philip of Alsace, Count of Flanders, on the site of the original 9th-century castle of Baldwin Iron-Arm. Philip of Alsace had fought in the Crusades, and the influence of Crusader architecture is clear to see. After the 14th century the castle was no longer needed as a military stronghold, and thereafter it had a more mundane career as a jail (until the 18th century) and a cotton mill. It was restored between 1894 and 1913 with a decidedly heavy hand, which makes it rather disappointing to visit; it is at its best when seen from a distance over the water of the River Lieve that lines its dramatic outer walls on two sides.

Inside, the lower parts of the castle are the most impressive: the huge piers and arches give a tangible sense of the massive nature of this bastion. To bring alive the empty banqueting hall higher up, you have to picture the medieval scene—for instance, the occasion when Edward III and Queen Philippa feasted with Jacob van Artevelde in 1339: the stone walls would have been decorated with tapestry, and the floors peopled with figures clothed in luxurious medieval textiles. Winding staircases lead up to the parapet, from which there is a good view across the rooftops of Ghent.

The adjoining Count's House contains the small but finely vaulted room where the Council of Flanders once met. In the very next room is an 'oubliette', a deep shaft down which miscreants would be hurled and left to expire—a grim reminder of the realities of the medieval world, and no doubt a sobering influence on council members. As if to reinforce this, the upper rooms serve as a museum of instruments of torture and execution, a sickening collection of shackles, thumb-screws, brands and guillotine blades.

This will put you in a suitable mood to reflect that the small square in front of the castle gates, called Sint-Veerleplein, formerly served as a place of execution. Victims of Inquisition were burned here between 1550 and 1576.

Museum voor Volkskunde

Open April–Oct 9–12.30 and 1.30–5.30; Nov–March 10–12 and 1.30–5; closed Mon; adm 50 BF.

There are numerous folk museums in Belgium, but they don't come much better than this. It is housed in a dainty little cluster of whitewashed almshouses dating originally from 1363. Not all almshouses (also referred to as hospices) were created as acts of pure charity: the Rijm family was forced to fund this one as a form of punishment in settlement of a bitter dispute between rival families, the Rijms and the Alijns, during which Henry and Seger Alijn were murdered at Mass in the church that is now Sint-Baafskathedraal. Substantially rebuilt in the 16th century, the hospice housed 18 indigent elderly women until the mid-19th century. It became a museum of folklore in 1940 and now contains an impressive collection of furniture, toys, dolls, tools, clothes, utensils, funerary mementoes, and so on. Much of the museum is laid out as furnished rooms, shops and workshops representing daily life in Ghent in about 1900. There is also a puppet theatre where marionette shows are performed *(Wed 2.30pm, Sat 3pm; no performances in Aug; tickets 50 BF)*.

The museum is in the picturesque Patershol district, a web of atmospheric little streets lined with old gabled houses, which provides a glimpse of how the residential quarters of Ghent looked a hundred years ago.

Dulle Griet and the Vrijdagmarkt

A huge cannon sits beside the River Leie in Kanonenplein at the top of the street called Lange Munt. Some 4m long and weighing 16 tonnes, it was cast in iron in about 1430 and was capable of firing ammunition the size of a beachball. It has earned the name Dulle Griet ('Mad Meg'), the name of a legendary medieval character who symbolized violent madness and disorder.

To the east is the large, open expanse of the Vrijdagmarkt, surrounded by shops and restaurants in gabled buildings. True to its name, a big general market is held here on Fridays *(7–1pm)* and Saturdays *(1–5pm)*. In the centre of the square is a statue (1863) of Jacob van Artevelde by the ubiquitous sculptor of public monuments, Paul de Vigne. It is an appropriate site, for it was here that a pitched battle took place between rival factions after the murder of Jacob van Artevelde in 1345. The gabled, turreted building by the southeastern entrance to the square is the Toreken (1480), which belonged to the Guild of Tanners. It now serves as a branch of the KB Bank.

Duivelsteen

This grim, turreted fortress to the east of the cathedral is named after its original owner, a knight called Geraard de Duivel (Gerard the Devil), who built it as his residence in 1245. After latter-day service as a mental hospital, arsenal and fire station, it now houses the state archives and is currently undergoing a massive programme of renovation.

Sint-Baafsabdij

Open 9.30–5, closed Mon; adm 80 BF.

This abbey was one of the two original 7th-century monasteries of Ghent, and the focus of a string of key events in Ghent's history. However, little now remains of it besides the refectory, decorated with fragments of 12th-century frescoes, and some medieval tombs. In the cloisters is the Museum voor Stenen Voorwerpen (lapidary museum), a collection of religious stone sculpture. Unless this is your special subject, the abbey—despite its history—barely justifies the 1km trek from the city centre.

South of the Centre

Bijlokemuseum

Open 9.30–5, closed Mon; adm 150 BF.

This rich and pleasantly unfocused historical museum is housed in the Abdij (abbey) van de Bijloke, which can be reached from the city centre by walking along the picturesque canals on the Recollettenlei and Lindenlei. The abbey itself is a beguiling set of red-brick buildings in traditional Flemish style. It was formerly a nunnery, founded originally in about 1204. It was sacked by Calvinists in the 1570s, and closed down in 1797 by the French, although the hospital continued to function until the 1980s. Fortunately the fabric of the building has remained largely intact, including the refectory—a large hall with a wooden vaulted roof like the hull of an upturned ship, and with walls painted with murals lit by the slanting rays of the sun penetrating the church-like windows.

The museum is casually set out in the cloisters and former dormitories of the abbey. It contains an vast array of historical objects of all kinds, much of it of high quality: furniture, paintings, measuring instruments, carnival masks, donated collections of Chinese ceramics and jade, a sedan chair, crossbows and other weapons, costumes and accessories, 14th-century religious sculptures.

Museum voor Schone Kunsten

Open 9.30–5, closed Mon; adm 80 BF.

The grand neoclassical entrance, built in 1902, and Ghent's long artistic tradition promise much, but this municipal gallery of fine art is, alas, faintly disappointing. The collection, however, is punctuated by a few treasures which will make the journey from the centre of the city worthwhile. The collection could be divided into two segments: from the Flemish primitives to Rubens, and then the 19th and early 20th centuries. Of the two the latter is the more rewarding.

The early section is composed largely of second-rate works by top-drawer painters of the Flemish School. However, one outstanding piece is the *Bearing of the Cross* by **Jeroen (Hieronymus) Bosch** (1450–1516), who worked in 's-Hertogenbosch in the Netherlands and whose imagery was immensely influential even in his own day. Christ, painted with a sublime expression of suffering and inner peace, is surrounded by a dense throng of grotesque degenerates, many of whom exhibit the kind of piercings that would be the envy of any modern punk. Other notable works include *The Virgin with a Carnation* by **Rogier van der Weyden** (*c.* 1400–64); a *Pietà* by **Hugo van der Goes** (*c.* 1435–82), who was in the service of the Dukes of Burgundy in both Bruges and Ghent; and two pieces by **Pieter Bruegel the Younger** (1564–1638), after originals by his father.

The collection contains four market scenes by the Antwerp painter **Joachim Beuckelaer** (1530–74). These are a curious mixture of still-life, landscape and figure painting, but their sense of movement, the complexity of their composition and their technical ease speak more of the era of Rubens than the 16th century. The works by **Rubens** here, *The Scourging of Christ* and *St Francis receiving the Stigmata*, both caught him on an off-day, but there is a splendidly sensual *Jupiter and Antiope* by **Antoon van Dyck** (1599–1641), in which a crusty old supreme god is about to furnish the sleeping object of his passion with twins.

Among the 19th-century works there is a good collection of paintings by French artists, including a intense *Portrait of a Kleptomaniac* by **Théodore Géricault** (1791–1824), and landscapes by **Daubigny**, **Rousseau**, **Corbet** and **Daumier**.

There are a few wooden-looking neoclassical works which show admirably how Belgian art went adrift in this period; see, for example, *Anthea returning to the Temple of Diana at Ephesus* by **Joseph Paelinck** (1781–1839).

The collection, however, picks up in the late 19th-century, which has some excellent examples of work by leading painters of the period. There is the *Reading by Emile Verhaeren* by the Ghent-born painter **Théo van Rysselberghe**

(1862–1926). A founder member of Les XX in Brussels, he adopted the pointillist style of Seurat and Signac in the 1880s and 1890s and developed it as a technique for landscape, interiors and portraits. The post-Impressionist **Henri Evenepoel** (1872–99) is represented by his striking *L'Espagnol à Paris*. There is a winter scene by the 'Luminist' **Emile Claus**, and a large social-realism work entitled *The Funeral Dinner* by **Léon Frédéric**. The painting of a raddled old woman surrounded by masks, *La Vieille Dame aux Masques* (1899), is a typically bizarre contribution by **James Ensor**. The early 20th-century includes a silhouette self-portrait (1907) by **Léon Spilliaert**, *Seated Wife* (1915) by **Rik Wouters** and works by the idiosyncratic Flemish Expressionists **Jean Brusselmans** (1884–1953) and **Edgar Tytgat** (1879–1957).

Not unnaturally, a special emphasis is given to the artists associated with the **Sint-Martens-Latem School**. Sint-Martens-Latem is a small village on a strikingly pretty stretch of the River Leie, to the west of Ghent. The sculptor and painter George Minne (1866–1941) came to the village in 1898, where he was deeply impressed by the work of a naïve painter Albijn van den Abeele (1835–1918). Minne went on to produced some of the most powerful and expressive sculpture of the period, often of emaciated figures hewn tenderly out of unpolished marble. He was joined in 1899 by the Symbolist poet Karel van de Woestyne and his brother, a painter called Gustave (1881–1947), who developed a style of mystical, poetic painting, similar in mood to Symbolist work, but more daring and challenging in its naïveté, and often technically brilliant. The painter Valerius de Saedeleer (1867–1941)—noted for his mysterious, fairytale-world landscapes, often inspired by Bruegel—joined the group in 1904. Albert Servaes (1883–1966) arrived in 1905. His highly charged religious paintings caused a considerable stir, and anticipated Expressionism. Other painters at Sint-Martens-Latem at this time included Gustave de Smet (1877–1943), who had settled in Sint-Martens-Latem after 1901 and later went on to become a founding figure in Flemish Expressionism; his brother Leon (1881–1966); and Frits van den Berghe (1883–1939). But the most influential newcomer was the remarkable painter Constant Permeke (1886–1952), who lived in the village from 1909 to 1912. He later developed a highly distinctive style to paint disturbing, anguished portraits of rural life with crude layers of dark, earthy colours.

After the First World War these same artists, particularly the more Expressionist group around Permeke, returned to the banks of the River Leie at various intervals, staying in Sint-Martens-Latem, Afsnee, Deurle and Astene. Successful group exhibitions in 1924 and 1925 established their identity as a school, but each of the artists ploughed his own furrow and responded in individual and often highly original ways to the developments in post-war 20th-century art.

The collection includes work by **Gustave van de Woestyne**, **Valerius de Saedeleer**, **Gustave** and **Leon de Smet** and **Constant Permeke**. It also has the marble version of **George Minne**'s *Fontein der Geknieden*—sculptures of six contemplative, naked boys kneeling around a fountain.

Museum van Hedendaagse Kunst

Open 9.30–5, closed Mon; adm 80 BF.

The museum of contemporary art contains the largest collection of modern paintings and sculpture in Belgium, founded in the 1950s. However, the museum currently occupies a building adjoining the Museum voor Schone Kunsten that is simply too small to accommodate both the permanent collection and its programme of temporary exhibitions. As a result the temporary exhibitions take precedence, and the permanent collection is usually only on view in the summer. The museum directors are anxiously awaiting the opportunity to transfer to larger premises nearby, a move which may begin in 1995. The permanent collection includes not only work by post-1945 Belgian artists—such as the participants of La Jeune Peinture Belge and Cobra (*see* p.76)—but numerous pieces by leading figures of the international art scene, such as Francis Bacon, Andy Warhol, Joseph Beuys, and Gilbert and George.

Klein Begijnhof

Open daily; gates close at 9pm; entrance on Lange Violettenstraat.

Of the many *béguinages* in Belgium, this is one of the most charming, with its neat and peaceful lines of little red-brick houses set around an open area of grass and trees and a Flemish Baroque chapel. (For a general background to *béguinages* *see* pp.208–9). Founded in 1234 by Joanna of Constantinople, patroness to numerous early *béguinages*, it has changed little since the 17th century. The houses have are given an added air of seclusion and privacy by the high white-washed walls that cloister their small yards. There have been no *béguines* at the Klein Begijnhof for some years, however, and the houses are slowly being converted for secular use—although several remain in a state of sad but evocative decay, inhabited only by feral cats which prowl around the weed-filled gardens.

Other Attractions

Slot van Laarne and Donkmeer

Lying 15km east of Ghent on the N345, the Slot (castle) of Laarne *(open Feb–Dec 10–12 and 2–6, closed Mon; adm 120 BF)* is a 17th-century Renaissance mansion built onto a set of robust 14th-century castle towers that once formed part of a defensive ring around Ghent. One of Flanders' best-preserved châteaux, it contains tapestries and furniture, and also a major collection of 15th–18th century silver and gold ware.

A further 10km east on the N345 is a set of lakes near Overmere, notably Donkmeer and the new reservoir Nieuwdonk. This is a popular place to come for walks, boating, swimming, but above all eating, for this is *the* place in Belgium to eat eels—baked or *in 't groen*—in a green herb sauce (*see* De Nieuwe Pluim under 'Eating Out'). After lunch you can walk down Brielstraat and then along footpaths between the lakes to the Eendenkooi Natuurpark *(early April–early Oct, Mon–Sat 1-8, Sun 10.30–8; adm 50 BF)*, an agreeable woodland animal sanctuary where there are deer, goats, wild boar, ducks, geese and exotic pheasants.

Sint-Martens-Latem and Kasteel van Ooidonk

Sint-Martens-Latem is a village famous for the school of artists which assembled here at the turn of the century (*see* p.331). At Sint-Martens-Latem itself you can see the Museum Gevaert-Minne *(open Thurs–Sun 3–6; adm)*, the house of the artist Edgard Gevaert, son-in-law of George Minne, which displays work by both. At nearby Deurle there are three museums. The Museum Dhondt-Dhaenens *(open April–Sept, Wed–Fri 2–6, Sat and Sun 10–12 and 2–6; March, Oct and Nov Wed–Fri 2–5, Sat and Sun 10–12 and 2–5; closed Dec–Feb; adm)* contains a private collection of work by various members of the school. The Museum Gustave de Smet *(open 15 March–Sept Wed–Sun 10–12 and 2–6; Nov and 1–15 March Wed–Sun 10–12 and 2–5; adm)* shows this artist's work in the house in which he lived from 1935 until his death in 1945. The Museum Leon de Smet *(open 2–6 daily, Sat and Sun 10–12 and 2–6; adm)* contains work by this artist, brother of Gustave.

At little further west, near Deinze, is the 16th-century Hispano-Flemish Kasteel (château) of Ooidonk *(open Easter–Sept Sun 2–5, July–Aug Sat and Sun 2–5; adm 120 BF)*, a romantic confection of stepped gables and turrets surmounted by belvederes, spires and orbs. This was formerly the home of the Montmorency family: Philippe de Montmorency was also the Count of Hornes, executed by the Spanish with Count Egmont in 1568 (*see* p57). Extensively renovated in the 1870s, the château contains a collection of furniture, tapestries and porcelain.

It is possible to travel by boat on the River Leie from Ghent to Deurle, Sint-Martens-Latem and Ooidonk. Regular excursions depart from Recollettenlei (Justitiepaleis) at 1pm in July and August; the return journey takes about 5 hours. (Contact the Ghent tourist office for more information).

The main **shopping districts** are to the south of the Belfort, down Mageleleinstraat and Volderstraat, along Koestraat and around the Kalandenberg square, and also along the Lange Munt to the north of the Groentenmarkt. A market is also held in the Vrijdagmarkt (*see*.p.328).

Ghent ℂ (09–) **Where to Stay**

★★★   **Hotel Gravenstein**, 35 Jan Breydelstraat, B 9000 Gent, ℂ 225 11 50, fax 225 18 50. A grand and elegant 19th-century 'Second Empire' townhouse-mansion, modernized but in keeping with its date. Close to the Gravensteen castle and the city centre. 4000–4500 BF.

★★★   **St Jorishof, 2 Botermarkt**, B-9000 Gent, ℂ 224 24 24, fax 224 26 40. Dating originally to 1228, this claims to be one of the oldest hostelries in Europe. Napoleon slept here in 1805. In fact it is mainly neo-baronial in style, and most of its rather unspectacular rooms are in a more modern annexe across the street. Good restaurant, and welcoming and efficient staff, however. 3300 BF.

★★   **Arcade**, 24 Nederkouter, B-9000 Gent, ℂ 225 07 07, fax 223 59 07. Modern, functional hotel—comfortable, efficient, but with no frills. Just to the south of the centre, close to the Justitiepaleis. 3400 BF.

★★   **Ibis**, 2 Limburgstraat, B-9000, ℂ 33 00 00, fax 33 10 00. Very central, well-run but straightforward international-style hotel. Opposite Sint-Baafskathedraal. Limited parking on site; most guests have to make use of the Vrijdagmarkt car park. 3400 BF.

★   **Flandria**, 3 Barrestraat, ℂ 223 06 26, fax 223 77 89. Modest, agreeable family-run hotel with 22 rooms, near the centre. 1300–1600 BF.

     Youth Hostel: De Draecke, 11 Sint-Widostraat (Gravensteen), ℂ 233 70 50, fax 233 80 01.

Ghent ℂ (09–) **Eating Out**

expensive

Chez Jean, 3 Catalioniëstraat, ℂ 223 30 40. *Closed Sun and Mon.* Stylish restaurant—in a gabled house dated 1634—serving carefully prepared seasonal food, such as pheasant in millefeuille pastry with endives. Five-course menu for 1800 BF.

Guido Meerschaut, 3 Kleine Vismarkt, ℂ 223 53 49. *Closed Sun and Mon.* A modern restaurant run by a master-fishmonger, whose family has been in the business since 1846. Delicious, very fresh fish, but at sensible prices. Main courses for 420–1000 BF, lunch menu at 880 BF.

Het Cooremeterhuys, 12 Graslei, ✆ 223 49 71. *Closed Wed and Sun.* An elegant restaurant in this fine old guildhouse overlooking the Graslei. Sophisticated French cuisine, with main courses for 750 BF. Business lunch at 980 BF.

Het Pand, 1 Onderbergen, ✆ 225 01 80. *Closed Sun.* A stylish and upmarket restaurant on the upper floor of this former monastery. Expect gastronomic excursions based on such ingredients as lobster and goose liver. Menu at 1750 BF.

Jan Breydel, 10 Jan Breydelstraat, ✆ 225 62 87. *Closed Mon lunch and Sun.* Genteel, partitioned *fin-de-siècle* setting for *haute cuisine française* of fish and game. Two-course menu for 1250 BF.

St Jorishof, 2 Botermarkt, ✆ 224 24 24. *Closed Sun evening.* The baronial décor of this famed hotel-restaurant provides a suitable backdrop for a mixture of adventurous French cuisine and good-quality, robust Belgian cooking, with dishes such as *Gentse waterzooi* and *paling in 't groen.* Four-course menu at 1450 BF.

't Buiske Vol, 17 Kraanlei, ✆ 225 18 80. *Closed Sun, Wed evening and Sat lunch.* Inventive *haute cuisine française*, such as *petite soupe en croûte aux poireaux et curry*, in the small and beautifully decorated ground floor of a canal-house. Menu at 1750 BF.

moderate

De Kruik, 5 Donkersteeg, ✆ 225 71 01. *Closed Sun.* Follow the menu of the day for excellent French-style cuisine (notably fish), served with the chef's choice of wine for about 1250 BF all in. At this price it astounds even the French.

De Pepermolen/Moulin à Poivre, 25 Kraanlei, ✆ 224 28 94. *Closed Wed.* Relaxed and sociable canal-house restaurant on two floors, the sort of place where you can eat according to you appetite—anything from a salad and *magret de canard, sauce aigre-douce* to a slab of Scotch beef.

In de Raeve, 2 Schepenhuisstraat (off Onderstraat), ✆ 223 31 03. *Closed Sun and Mon.* Elegant meat and fish dishes with a touch of panache cooked on an open grill in what feels like a private house. Main courses at about 500 BF, menus from 1050 BF.

Patachon, 24 Korenlei, ✆ 225 89 02. *Closed Wed.* Evocative restaurant and grill in a medieval undercroft close to Sint-Michielsbrug. Mussels, squid, salmon, mussels at reasonable prices.

't Kattenhuis, 7 Hertogstraat, 224 31 88. *Closed Tues.* The place to eat if you are a cat-lover: cat carvings, cat pictures, even a live cat in a basket on the counter. Warm and welcoming ambience for French cuisine, where meats and brochettes (650 BF) are grilled over an open fire.

't Marmietje, 14 Korenlei, © 224 30 13. *Closed Sun evening and Mon evening*. Ghent and Flemish specialities served in a welcoming and unassuming atmosphere on the Korenlei. Try *waterzooi*, a speciality of Ghent, or *Gentse stoverij*, described as 'steak and kidney pie without the kidney and without the pie—cooked in beer with mustard'. Main courses for about 400 BF.

De Nieuwe Pluim, 9 Brielstraat, Overmere-Donk (overlooking the Donkmeer lake), © 367 80 70, serves eel dishes for about 550 BF.

inexpensive

Brasserie Diavolo, 17 Drabstraat, © 233 10 05. *Closed Mon*. Young and adventurous atmosphere of loud jazz, stripped pine, weird and wild décor drooling with colour. Salads, pastas, stews and bakes served for lunch and supper for 280–360 BF.

Brooderie, 8 Jan Breydelstraat, © 225 06 23. *7.30–6, Sun 9–6, closed Mon*. Tasteful olde-worlde bakery selling delicious cakes and crusty loaves, and serving health-food-style lunches of soup, sandwiches and salads for around 300 BF.

De Poelje, 7 Botermarkt, © 223 83 26. *Closed Wed*. A fresh-faced bistrot and café, open all day, with rattan chairs and a relaxed mood (provides toys for children, and magazines). Salads and light meals, such as *witloof gegratineerd* (230 BF).

Dulle Griet, 250 Vrijdagmarkt. An atmospheric candlelit bar, dripping with beer-drinkers' fetishes and mementoes, and selling 250 different sorts of beer to justify its claim to be a *bieracademie*.

In den Eenhoorn Galerij Belvu, 2 Kammerstraat, © 224 23 14. *Closed Sun lunch and Wed*. Friendly, admirably priced café-restaurant serving a daily rota of lunch dishes, plus pastas and omelettes for around 200 BF.

Keizershof, 47 Vrijdagmarkt. *Closed Sun*. Agreeable and popular tavern serving Palm and other beers from the barrel and good platefuls of home-cooked food, such as *Gentse hutspot*. Lunch dish of the day for around 260 BF.

Wolff Caffe, 27 Kraanlei. *Food at lunchtime only*. Coolly elegant, spacious café in a gabled canal house, with an open fire in winter to warm the conversation of the literary crowd who assemble here. Light lunches for 200–300 BF.

Antwerp

Antwerp

ST LAUREISKAAI
Bonaparte Dok
Willemdok
6 H
GODEFRIDUSKAAI
BROUWERSVLIET
OUDE LEEUWENRUI
Falconplein
FALCONRUI
KLAPDORP
MUTSAERTSTR.
ORTELIUS
MINDERBROEDERS RUI
VENUSSTRAAT
NOSESTRAAT
PAULUSSTRAAT
DOORNIK STRAAT
Vee Markt
St-Pauluskerk
5 H
JORDAENS
Nat. Scheepvaartmuseum
Rockoxhuis
KEIZERSTRAAT
1
Museum Vleeshuis
14
OUDE BEURS
15
St-Carolus Borromeuskerk
KIPDORP
Volkskundemuseum
10 R
Stadhuis
R
LANGE NIEUWSTRAAT
ERNEST VAN DIJCK KAAI
SUIKERRUI
Grote Markt
O. L. Vrouwe-Kathedraal
ST KATELIJNE VEST
13 R
11 R
16 R H 3
R
12
Vlaeykensgang
OUDE KOORNMARKT
MELKMARKT
EIERMARKT
VLASMARKT
17
19
Groen-Plaats
18 R
REYNDERSSTR.
SCHOENMARKT
MEIR
OEVER HOOGSTR.
Museum Plantin-Moretus
WAPPER
STEENHOUWERS VEST
HUIDEVETTERSSTR.
MUNT-STR.
9
AUGUSTIJNEN STR.
Augustijnen
H
NATIONALE STRAAT
KAMMEN STRAAT
St-Andrieskerk
OUDAAN
Museum Mayer v. d. Bergh
ARENBERGSTR.
LANGE GASTHUISSTRAAT
Maagdenhuis
4 H
MAAR GERARDSTRAAT
LEOPOLDSTRAAT
OUDE VAARTPLAATS
Leopold Plaats
BEGIJNENSTR.
ST. ROCHUSSTRAAT
KRONENBURGSTRAAT
KLOOSTERSTRAAT
SCHELDESTRAAT
VOLKSTRAAT
Marnix Plaats
KASTEELPLEINSTR.
BRITSE LEI
COCKERILLKAAI
Museum voor Hedendaagse Kunst
WAALSE KAAI
De Wael Plaats
Kon. Museum Schone Kunsten
VLAAMSE KAAI
Prov. Museum voor Fotografie
AMERIKALEI

Schelde

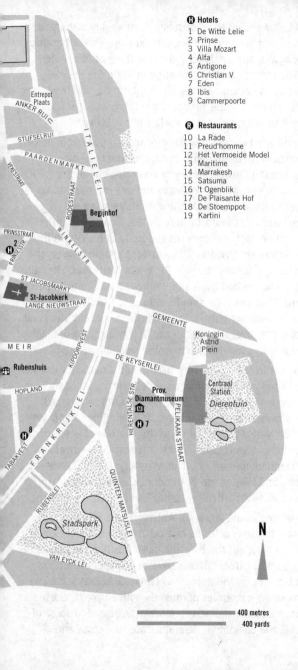

⊕ Hotels

1 De Witte Lelie
2 Prinse
3 Villa Mozart
4 Alfa
5 Antigone
6 Christian V
7 Eden
8 Ibis
9 Cammerpoorte

ℝ Restaurants

10 La Rade
11 Preud'homme
12 Het Vermoeide Model
13 Maritime
14 Marrakesh
15 Satsuma
16 't Ogenblik
17 De Plaisante Hof
18 De Stoemppot
19 Kartini

Entrepot
Plaats
ANKER RUIE
STIJFSELRUI
PAARDENMARKT
VEKESTRAAT
ROPESTRAAT
ITALIELEI
WINKELSTR

Begijnhof

PRINSSTRAAT
PRINSESTR
⊕ 2

ST JACOBSMARKT
St-Jacobkerk
LANGE NIEUWSTRAAT

GEMEENTE

MEIR

Koningin
Astrid
Plein

DE KEYSERLEI

Rubenshuis

HOPLAND

KIPDORPVEST

Prov.
Diamantmuseum

Centraal
Station

Dierentuin

⊕ 8

HERENTALSE STR.
⊕ 7

PELIKAAN STRAAT

FRANKRIJKLEI

TABAKVEST

RUBENSLEI

QUINTEN MATSIJSLEI

Stadspark

N

VAN EYCK LEI

400 metres
400 yards

A bitter wind, straight off the North Sea, hurries down the wide estuary of the River Scheldt, rattling the old store-sheds that line the riverside quays, and briskening the heartbeat of this invigorating city. The old city centre, crowding in upon the delicate, lace-like spire of its cathedral and a Grote Markt to rival the Grand' Place of Brussels, lies a stone's throw from the quays, yet has turned its back to the river as if to shelter from this wind.

Upon this same wind came Antwerp's fortunes: goods from around the world which were traded with products from the whole of northern and central Europe. Antwerp was once one of the great cities of the continent: proud, powerful and adventurous. It has all those qualities today, rekindled by new industries and its sprawling docklands to the north. It feels like a city awakening from a period of neglect, its concerns suddenly in tune with the new Europe. It was apt that in 1993 Antwerp should take on the mantle of Cultural Capital of Europe for a year. This was, after all, the city where Rubens had lived and worked, the brightest star in a galaxy of artistic talent. The manifestations of the city's artistic tradition can be seen not only in the city gallery—one of the great collections of art in Belgium—but in the rich collections of many of the churches and in a handful of charming small museums.

And the tradition lives on. Antwerp has earned a name for itself as a city where things are happening. Its recent successes in the fashion world are a symbol of its new mood: clothes designers from Antwerp have shot to prominence, following the accolades in London in 1986 when a group of them (for reasons of economy) showed together and were labelled the Antwerp Six—Dries van Noten, Ann Demeulemeester, Martin Margiela, Dirk Bikkembergs, Dirk van Saene and Walter van Beirendonck. Several have continued to make waves, particularly Dries van Noten.

There is something in the air: go to Antwerp on a Friday or Saturday night and the streets in the city centre are positively zinging. Youthful crowds pack out the bars and cafés hosting live music; the literary cafés hum to earnest debate over newspapers, beer and chasers; and families fill the numerous restaurants that serve anything from steaming casseroles of mussels with chips, Japanese *sashimi*, Moroccan couscous and Indonesian *rijsttafel* to some of the most recherché cooking in Belgium. Later the clubs and discothèques heat up to a pitch that has made Antwerp's nightlife famous across Europe.

You could not possibly expect to get a feel for all of this in a day. Spend a weekend or more in Antwerp if you can. If a day is all you have, the list below should help you to judge which of the many and varied attractions on offer are the most rewarding—and they are not all what the tourist guides would have you believe.

History

The key to Antwerp's history and fortunes is access to the North Sea, which lies 88km to the north along the broad and deep River Scheldt (Schelde in Flemish, Escaut in French). Over the centuries this access, however, has been at the mercy of political events.

It appears that Frisian seafarers were the first to make a base here, as early as the 2nd and 3rd centuries AD, and over the following centuries it became a settlement of the Franks, who were Roman mercenaries before they acquired power of their own after the Fall of the Roman Empire. A fort ('castellum') was built during the era of Charlemagne (AD 768–814), and enough of a community gathered around it to justify visits from several noted early Christian missionaries such as St Amand and St Bavon. The Vikings destroyed the castle in AD 836, and under pressure of Viking raids the Frankish Empire was carved up along the divide of the River Scheldt by the Treaty of Verdun in AD 843. Antwerp, on the eastern bank of the river, became part of Lotharingia (Lorraine) while the rest of Flanders formed part of the French-dominated West Francia. This accounts for a different and less traumatic medieval history than that of Bruges and Ghent.

Antwerp was a Margravate (a border county ruled by a Margrave) during the 10th century under what became the Holy Roman Empire , and in 1106 became part of the Duchy of Brabant, which also included Brussels. It developed as a thriving trading city, the main port of Brabant, with wool and textiles as its staple commodities. A series of ramparts called *vesten* was built around the port, the positions of which are still remembered in street names such as Steenhouwersvest, Lombardenvest and Sint-Katelijnevest. In 1357 Louis de Male, the acquisitive Count of Flanders, seized Antwerp. Through the marriage of Louis' daughter Margaret to Philip the Bold, Duke of Burgundy, in the next generation both Flanders and Brabant were united as they became part of the powerful Duchy of Burgundy.

Bruges and Ghent were initially key ports in the Burgundian era, but Antwerp's star was rising. As Bruges declined, foreign merchants moved to Antwerp, and by the end of the reign of Charles V (Holy Roman Emperor 1519–56) the population of the city had reached 100,000. It was now the trading capital of Europe, and an intellectual and cultural centre. In 1454 Philip the Good had founded the Guild of St Luke for painters, which became a key force in Flemish art.

Antwerp had achieved remarkable wealth by 1550, but with it came an opening chasm between rich and poor and rapidly deteriorating political stability. The prosperous, cosmopolitan and liberal atmosphere in the city had proved fertile ground for the rise of Protestantism, which led to increasing strife as the Spanish authorities attempted to impose the Catholic faith. This flared up in angry bouts of iconoclasm, notably in 1566, when the cathedral was wrecked.

After 1568 Spain was at war with the Protestant United Provinces of the Netherlands, led by William of Orange. Antwerp wavered. In early November 1576 a disgruntled garrison of Spanish soldiers—sent in by the Duke of Alva to occupy the fortress and intimidate the city—mutinied and then ran amok. At the end of the Spanish Fury, as it was called, much of the city had been torched and 8000 people lay dead. After this, many of Antwerp's leading citizens fled, and Amsterdam soon took over as the leading trading city of the north.

That same year, 1576, the United Provinces under William of Orange (William the Silent) pushed west and took Ghent, forcing the Pacification of Ghent; the following year they took Antwerp, and William set up his headquarters in the city. Religious strife continued; in 1585 the Spanish under Alexander Farnese, Duke of Parma, recaptured Ghent and pushed north to lay siege to Antwerp.

The siege lasted for a year. For a time the blockade was broken by ships running down the Scheldt from Flushing, but the supply dwindled as the prices became unacceptable to the beleaguered citizenry; then the Spanish succeeded in building a bridge to close off the Scheldt from the sea. At last Antwerp capitulated. The terms of peace were not harsh, except that Philip II insisted that Antwerp was to be a Catholic city. Again, thousands of Protestants left to settle in the United Provinces. In 1582 the population of Antwerp had been 84,000 people; by 1589 it was 42,000. The city was brought to its knees, not just from this emigration, but also from a blockade of the Scheldt mounted by the Dutch and also by the English under Sir Philip Sidney, who wanted to starve this Spanish city of trade. This blockade lasted for 24 years.

In 1609 the Twelve Years' Truce, signed by the United Provinces and representatives of the Archduke Albert and Infanta Isabella, offered some relief. Antwerp's faltering economy began to recover as it reasserted its role as a regional (if not international) trading centre. Meanwhile the more stable political situation gave rise to an unprecedented cultural flourish, focusing particularly on Pieter Paul Rubens, who achieved international celebrity. Antoon van Dyck, Jacob Jordaens and Frans Snyders worked with him in his studio at various times, and the city was also home to David Teniers the Elder and the Younger, Pieter Bruegel the

Younger and Jan Bruegel, and the sculptor Artus Quellinus the Elder. But in 1648 Antwerp's Golden Age came to a sticky halt. Spain was now in conflict with France, which was an ally of the United Provinces. To concentrate his fire on France, Philip IV of Spain signed the Peace of Münster, which granted formal recognition to the United Provinces. The United Provinces—which held the territory on both sides of the Scheldt to the north of Antwerp—also demanded the right to close off the Scheldt estuary to shipping, and Spain, with other fish to fry, acquiesced.

It was a disaster for Antwerp, which was effectively throttled by the agreement. The port slid into disuse and despair. It was 150 years before the stranglehold was lifted, after the French Revolutionary Armies overran the Austrian Netherlands in 1794 and the United Provinces in 1795. The French opened up the Scheldt to Antwerp shipping—but Europe was at war.

In 1803 Napoleon described the state of Antwerp: 'It is little better than a heap of ruins. It is scarcely like a European city. I could almost have believed myself this morning in some African township. Everything needs to be made—harbours, quays, docks; and everything shall be made, for Antwerp must avail itself of the immense advantages of its central position between the North and the South, and of its magnificent and deep river.' He also recognized Antwerp's strategic potential as 'a pistol pointing at the heart of England' ('*un pistolet braqué sur le cœur de l'Angleterre*'). He made a start, by building new naval dockyards to the north of the city centre. After Napoleon's fall in 1815, Belgium was handed over to the Dutch and Antwerp suddenly found itself at the heart of the new United Kingdom of the Netherlands. When the Dutch had to abandon Belgium following the Revolution of 1830, it was particularly reluctant to give up Antwerp. It was only in 1832 that the Dutch garrison laid down its arms, when French troops came to the assistance of the Belgians in a punishing struggle.

After the armistice, the Netherlands was once again in control of traffic through the Scheldt, and after 1839 demanded heavy tolls. This situation was only resolved by lengthy negotiation, and in 1863 the tolls were lifted. By this time the city's trade had already reawakened. A railway link, the 'Iron Rhine', between Antwerp and the great Rhine port of Cologne had been opened in 1843. By the latter half of the 19th century, Antwerp rated as the third largest port in the world, after London and New York. In the 1880s the river bank was straightened to provide new quays, a development that also necessitated the destruction of some of the oldest parts of the city around the Steen. Antwerp held a World Fair in 1885, and again in 1894. It hosted the Olympic Games in 1920, and a further World Fair in 1930 included pavilions in the daring new Bauhaus and Modernist styles. In 1928 work began on the 27-storey Torengebouw, known locally as the

Boerentoren, at the western end of the Meir—Europe's first ever skyscraper (now identifiable by its large KB (Kredietbank) signs at the top). During the 1930s the west bank of the Scheldt was developed, connected to the city centre by a road and pedestrian tunnels. The Depression of the early 1930s heralded another period of painful decline, but a new revival gathered pace in the 1980s and 1990s, and now Antwerp's modern port (to the north of the city, well away from the centre) is the second biggest in Europe after Rotterdam, with over 120km of docks and a workforce numbering 75,000. With a population of over half a million, Antwerp is also Belgium's second largest city. It basked in the attention received in 1993 as European Cultural Capital, and has grand plans for the future.

Getting There and Around

Antwerp (Antwerpen in Flemish, Anvers in French) is about 45 km north of Brussels and connected by the E10 autoroute. **Trains** from Brussels arrive at the spectacular Antwerpen Centraal station. Antwerp also has its own **airport** at Deurne, in the southwestern outskirts of the city, with direct flights from London, Amsterdam and so forth.

Unlike most of the Flemish cities, **parking** is not a great headache in Antwerp. There are paying car parks around the old quayside sheds along the River Scheldt, close to the city centre, and a number of underground car parks in convenient places. They cost around 400–500 BF per day. Antwerp is served by an efficient **public transport** system (called De Lijn) consisting of trams, buses and the underground Premétro tram line. A 'Netplan' (map) of the system is available from the tourist office (*see* below) and main stations. **Taxis** are available from designated taxi ranks, or by calling © (03) 238 38 38. **Horse-drawn carriages** make tours of the city centre, starting from the Grote Markt *(July and Aug daily 11–7; Easter–June and Sept–Oct weekends only 12–6)*. You can also take **boat trips** on the River Scheldt. The Flandria line offers 50-minute excursions down the river from its quay beside the Steen *(Easter period and May–Sept, every hour on the hour 11–4pm; adults 240 BF, children under 12 120 BF.)* You can also take a 2½-hour boat excursion to the **port of Antwerp** *(Easter period at 2.30; May–Aug daily 10 and 2.30; Sept weekends only Sat 2.30, Sun 10 and 2.30; adults 380 BF, children under 12 200 BF)*. Alternatively, you can visit the port by car following the Havenroute *(see* p.362)*.

Tourist Information

The **tourist office** is at 15 Grote Markt (corner of Wisselstraat), © (03) 232 01 03 (open Mon–Sat 9–6, Sun 9–5). It offers a good selection of pamphlets and brochures, plus maps of the city, advice about what's on, and runs a hotel reservation service.

The Centre

Grote Markt and Stadhuis

The central square of Antwerp is one of the most attractive in Belgium, flanked by ornate guildhouses and the famous **Stadhuis** (town hall). Built in 1564, the Stadhuis was designed by the architect and sculptor Cornelis Floris, or Floris de Vriendt (1514–75). His training in Italy is apparent in this building, in the mathematical distribution of windows as well as in the Renaissance flair of the centrepiece. The flags mounted along the façade give the building an added touch of brio. The figure at the focal point is the Virgin, while below are Justice and Wisdom, with the crests (from left to right) of Brabant, Philip II and the Margravate of Antwerp. Completed in 1565, it was burnt out during the Spanish Fury of 1576 (*see* p.343), but restored after 1579. The interior *(open Mon–Wed and Fri 9–3, Sat 12–4, closed Thurs and Sun; adm 15 BF)* was totally renovated in the 19th century, largely in retrospective historical styles.

The northern side of the square, and the southeastern side facing the Stadhuis, are flanked by lines of old **guildhouses**, crowned by gilded symbols. To single out some of these: No. 5, 'De Mouwe', was the guildhouse of the coopers (1579); No. 7, the 'Pand van Spanje' (1582), was the house of a guild of crossbowmen and is surmounted by a statue of St George and the Dragon (by Jef Lambeaux, *see* below); No. 38 (on the southeast side) is 'De Balans' (1615), guildhouse of the drapers; No. 40, 'Rodenborch', was the guildhouse of the carpenters.

The **fountain** in front of the Stadhuis depicts **Brabo** casting the hand of the giant Antigon into the river. This relates to the old legend that tells how the giant, Druon Antigon, used to enforce a heavy toll on any ship that passed on the River Scheldt. If a ship's captain failed to pay the toll, Antigon would chop off his hand and throw it into the river. One day, however, a brave Roman soldier called Silvius Brabo killed Antigon, chopped off the giant's hand and likewise threw it into the river. Hence the name of the city—so the legend goes—is a corruption of Handwerpen (*werpen* means to throw). A more prosaic derivation is the old Flemish word *aanwerp*, meaning a promontory, hence a landing stage at the river's edge.

The sculpture (1887) is the most celebrated work of the Antwerp sculptor Jef Lambeaux (1852–1908). The overall effect is a strangely effective evocation of a seaweedy marine world.

Onze Lieve Vrouwe Kathedraal

Open Mon–Fri 10–5, Sat 10–3, Sun 1–4; adm 30 BF.

The largest Gothic cathedral in Belgium it may be, but the approach to it through a web of medieval streets gives it a charming human scale. This is not just some historic survivor, held at bay by the godless anarchy of a modern urban life, but a much cherished sanctuary at the very heart of the city.

It strikes a remarkable pose. The spire or tower (it is neither one nor the other) rises to 123m, up and up through a series of sugar-light tiers, each one of which would be a marvel on its own. In the middle of the main roof is an onion-shaped dome. The tower contains a carillon of 47 bells: the largest, named Carolus after Charles V, dates from 1507. Once there were to be two towers, but the second was never built and has been capped off. The earliest parts of the building date from 1352, but the cathedral took nearly three centuries to build, and was not completed until 1521. The first phase was designed by Jan Appelmans; in the last phase the main designers were the influential late Gothic architects Herman de Waghemakere (1430–1503) and his son Domien (1460–1542) and Rombouts Keldermans (1487–1531). When completed, the cathedral was the richest of the Low Countries. The interior was a dazzling treasure trove, glittering with the dozens of shrines and retables set up by the city's guilds. Many of these, however, were destroyed in a fire in 1553, then the building was sacked by iconoclasts in 1566. The cathedral was stripped of its surviving treasures during the French occupation after 1784. Only a part of its original collection of works of art were recovered from France after 1815. The cathedral has recently undergone three decades of restoration, and work continues on the transept and choir.

Despite this history, the cathedral still contains a remarkably rich collection of paintings and sculpture, set against the elegant simplicity of the Gothic architecture, which has an untypically wide and spacious groundplan with seven aisles. These works of art are dotted around the nave and aisles, and their positions are liable to change while restoration continues.

The cathedral is famous above all for its paintings by Rubens, the great triptychs of *The Raising of the Cross* (1610), *The Descent from the Cross* (1612) and the *Resurrection* (1612). These were painted shortly after Rubens' return from Italy in 1608, where he had spent eight years absorbing the lessons of Raphael, Michelangelo and above all Titian and Caravaggio. It was in these years that he developed his distinctive voice as an artist, and these paintings were major landmarks in this process. His fourth work in the cathedral, *The Assumption of the Virgin Mary*, dates from 1626, by which time he had established his influential studio. Other works of note include 15th-century polychrome wooden statues, and paintings by Antwerp painters Maerten de Vos (1532–1603) and Cornelis de Vos (1584–1651).

In the square in front of the west door of the cathedral is a fountain decorated with a delicate metal sculpture of branches and vineleaves, crowned by a sculpture of Silvius Brabo. It is said to have been forged by the great Renaissance painter Quentin Metsys (1466–1530), who began his career as a metalsmith, following in the footsteps of his father.

Volkskundemuseum

Open Tues–Sun 10–5; adm 30 BF.

The folk museum behind the Stadhuis (at 2–6 Gildekamersstraat) contains a small but intriguing collection of artefacts relating to Flemish traditions and ways of life. It includes toys, dolls, playing cards, fairground attractions and organs, and a reconstructed pharmacy.

Etnografisch Museum

Open Tues–Sun 10–5; adm 30 BF.

African masks, drums for New Guinea, a Maori war-canoe, an Inuit child's kayak, Indonesian jewellery, pre-Colombian American pottery, Japanese paintings, Tibetan Buddhas—these are just some of the hundreds of varied objects representing over a century of collecting, housed since 1988 in a new museum on three floors at 19 Suikerrui. The Central Africa collection is particularly strong.

Steen and the Nationaal Scheepvaartmuseum

Open Tues–Sun 10–5; adm 30 BF.

The Steen, the powerful old fortress at the river's edge, was built between the 10th and 16th centuries, originally as the residence of the Margrave of Antwerp—although legend said it was home of the giant Antigon. It was used as a prison until 1823, then rescued from that role and heavily restored in the late 19th century. It is now home to the National Maritime Museum. This contains an interesting and well-presented collection of ship-orientated artefacts, including numerous superb models of ships. Outside, in one of the large, weatherbeaten quayside sheds is a collection of a dozen barges and 30 or so smaller vessels; the interiors of some of these are open during the summer.

The gangly statue (1963) at the entrance to the Steen depicts Lange Wapper, a supernatural character from Antwerp legend who was famous for playing tricks on drinkers—such as growing immensely tall to look through their windows— hence the diminutive figures depicted at his feet.

Vleeshuis

Open Tues–Sun 10–4.45; adm 30 BF.

In a forgotten corner of central Antwerp, cheek-by-jowl with the small red-light district of Burchtgracht, is one of the city's most impressive buildings. This is the Butchers' Hall, the guildhouse and meatmarket of the Guild of Butchers, designed in Gothic style in 1503 by Herman de Waghemakere (one of the architects of the cathedral). Its walls, step-gables and the five hexagonal turrets running up the sides are built in alternating layers of stone and brick—reminiscent of streaky bacon. An atmospheric vaulted passageway leads beneath the western wall into Burchgracht, which follows the line of the old castle moat.

The Butchers' Guild was a powerful institution. The large and robust meat hall inside was for decades the only place in Antwerp where meat could be sold. (The steps up to the entrance were called the Bloedberg ('Blood Hill') because of this trade.) Butchers' families intermarried, and kept the trade from generation to generation until 1794, when the French Revolutionaries abolished the guilds.

The butcher's hall, and other rooms accessed from it, now contain a rewarding collection of historical odds and ends: medieval sculpture, musical instruments (including 17th-century harpsichords made in the famous Ruckers workshop of Antwerp), paintings, crossbows, the mummy of a 10th-century BC Egyptian singer, and strongboxes with elaborate locking devices. One of the prize exhibits is the Averbode Retable by Jacob van Cothem, dated 1514, with the Entombment of Christ sculpted in relief and wings depicting the Crucifixion and the Ascent to Heaven. Retables were a famous Antwerp product from about 1420 to 1550, and the best of them show astonishingly skilled craftsmanship. Retables produced in Antwerp were shipped to other parts of the country, but many of them fell victim to the assaults of the iconoclasts in the late 16th century.

Sint-Pauluskerk

Open May–Sept 2–5.

This strange, hybrid church, with a Flamboyant Gothic body dating from 1517 and a Baroque spire dating from 1679, rises out of a cluster of buildings (some of which are attached to it) in an attractive quarter of alleyways, small shops and atmospheric bars. The Baroque interior, with its elaborately carved wooden stalls, is an expression of a bold architectural style that sang of the triumph of the Counter-Reformation over iconoclasm. It contains a remarkable collection of paintings, including the series of 15 on 'The Mysteries of the Rosary' (1617–19), by various artists such as Cornelis de Vos (*Nativity, Presentation at the Temple*), David Teniers the Elder (*Gethsemane*), Rubens (*Flagellation*), Van Dyck (*Bearing of the Cross*), and Jordaens (*Crucifixion*).

Sint-Carolus Borromeuskerk

Open Mon 10–12 and 2–5, Tues and Thurs 9–12, Wed 9–12 and 2–6, Fri 9–12 and 2–6.30, Sat 9–12 and 3–6.30, Sun 9–12.30; adm 50 BF.

The façade of this church, overlooking Hendrik Conscienceplein, represents one of the great monuments of Jesuit Baroque architecture—a birthday cake of sculpture, gilded urns, pepperpot domes, pineapples and flaming torches, disposed with an elegant pace and rhythm. Tradition holds that it was designed by Rubens. The church was built in 1615–21 and dedicated to **St Charles Borromeo** (1538–84), a church reformer who, having been appointed Cardinal at the age of just 22, set about applying the accords of the Council of Trent, which attempted to address the abuses of the Catholic Church in the face of the rising tide of Protestantism. As Archbishop of Milan he set an unusual example by his modest and virtuous lifestyle, founded Sunday schools for children and tended personally to the sick during the plague.

In 1620 the Jesuits asked Rubens to create three altarpieces and 39 ceiling paintings for the church. The ceiling paintings were the first in northern Europe to employ Venetian-style foreshortening and optical illusion, and were widely fêted. But in 1718 a fire caused by lightning destroyed the lot; all that has survived of them is a large series of preliminary drawings. Given this history, it is barely surprising that the interior is disappointing, although it contains fine late-Baroque woodwork installed after 1718, and a Lady Chapel which survived the fire.

The square in front of the church is named after **Hendrik Conscience** (1812–83), an Antwerp novelist, whose statue stands before the L-shaped public library. His best-known work is *De Leeuw van Vlaanderen* ('The Lion of Flanders'), a colourful evocation of the events leading up to the Battle of the Golden Spurs in 1302; the book did much to popularize a sense of pride in Flemish heritage.

Rockoxhuis

Open Tues–Sun 10–5, closed Mon; adm free.

Nicolaas Rockox (1560–1640) was mayor of Antwerp during many of its years of revival in the early 17th century; he was also a noted humanist, philanthropist and art collector, and a friend and patron of Rubens. The ground floor of his large house, set around a courtyard garden, was converted during the 1970s into a gallery to house a handsome collection of paintings, tapestries and antique furniture from the era. There are sketches and paintings by all the Golden Age Antwerp artists—Rubens, Van Dyck, Jordaens and Frans Snyders, who lived next door at No. 8 (a fine fishmarket scene, typical of his animated still-lifes)—plus work by the preceding generation, including Joachim Beuckelaer and Pieter Bruegel the Younger.

Sint-Jacobskerk

Open April–Oct, Mon–Sat, 2–5, closed Sun; adm 30 BF.

Rubens lies buried in a family chapel in this large, yellow-sandstone church, designed in late-Gothic style during the 15th and 16th centuries by Herman de Waghemakere and his son Domien, and subsequently by Rombout Keldermans. It stands on the site of a chapel built for pilgrims on their way to Santiago de Compostela (hence the connection with St James), but developed as the church of the patricians of the city. The interior is one of the richest in Antwerp and contains the tombs of wealthy Antwerp families and numerous works of art. There are sculptures by Hendrik Verbruggen, Artus Quellinus and Luc Fayd'Herbe; and paintings by Bernard van Orley, Otto Venius (Rubens' master), Rubens himself, Jordaens and Van Dyck.

Begijnhof

Open to the public during daylight hours; the entrance is a big double door at No. 39 Rodestraat.

A gentle and agreeable atmosphere pervades this small *béguinage*, with its typical modest houses fronted by little courtyards set around a shaded garden. (For the background to *béguinages*, *see* pp.208–209). The Begijnhof was built in 1546 to replace an earlier settlement founded in the 13th century elsewhere. It was expropriated by the French in the 1790s and the original church was destroyed, but it was reoccupied by *béguines* after 1815.

Museum Plantin-Moretus

Open Tues–Sun 10–5; adm 30 BF.

This is one of the most celebrated museums of Antwerp. In principle it has the ingredients for a fascinating visit—a 16th-century patrician house, set around a courtyard straight out of a painting by a Dutch master, original furnishings, and the workshop and book collection of one of the great masters of early printing, Christopher Plantin. Somehow, however, it contrives to be somewhat dull and cheerless. A little background information helps to bring it alive.

European printing was launched with a bang in 1455 when the workshop of Johann Gutenberg in Mainz, Germany, produced the 42-line Bible, a printing masterpiece at virtually the first attempt. This was a ground-breaking event, since prior to this every book had to be written out by hand, a desperately slow and expensive process which could not hope to match the accelerating demand of the new universities and growing private libraries.

Gutenberg did not invent the printing press, and he did not invent printing. He is, however, credited with putting together the elements that made book printing in

Europe not simply possible, but economically attractive. The most important of these elements was movable type: individual letters were cast in metal, then assembled into words. Gutenberg, using technology developed by metalworkers, first carved a master-set of individual letters on the ends of hard-metal rods. These were used as punches; each was hammered into a block of softer metal called a strike to make a matrix. The matrix then formed the base of an adjustable mould into which a molten alloy was poured to produce a cast of the letter on the end of a solid block. This was the movable type.

Pages of text composed of movable type were laid out on a flat bed and secured in a frame to make a 'forme'. Ink was applied with leather pads called inkballs, then paper was laid over the forme. This was pushed under the platen of a printing press; the handle of the screw-spindle was pulled to lower the platen and apply pressure, and the type image was transferred to the paper.

Gutenberg's method of printing soon caught on across Europe, and by 1500 some 40,000 editions of books had been printed. His technique remained the standard process of printing for some four centuries. However, whereas Gutenberg deliberately imitated the traditions of manuscript copying, successive printers developed printing as an art in its own right. One of the most influential figures in this process was Christopher Plantin (c. 1520–89)—and indeed his name lives on in the elegant typeface which he designed, called Plantin.

Plantin was French by birth, from Tours, but in 1546, after training as a bookbinder, he moved to Antwerp, which—after its first book had been printed in 1481—had become one of the Low Countries' great centres of printing. One night, so the story goes, he was wounded by some carnival revellers, who had mistaken him for someone else. Paid a substantial sum as compensation or hush-money, he bought his first press, and thereby began a career as a printer. He gradually acquired more presses, and other printing enterprises, until in 1576 (when he moved into this house) he was in control of 22 presses, three times as many as any of his rivals. At that time printers were also publishers, and some of the greatest and most influential works of the day were produced by Plantin.

The breadth of Plantin's publishing programme is astonishing: medical books, accounts of exploration, histories and biography, religious works, classical literature and contemporary French writing—all appeared on his list of publications. His greatest achievement was the eight-volume Polyglot Bible (1568–72), a bible printed in five parallel languages (Latin, Greek, Hebrew, Syriac and Chaldean), with extensive notes and glossaries. This was supposed to have been sponsored by King Philip II of Spain and so was named the *Biblia Regia*; Philip failed to advance any of the promised money, but in 1570 he appointed Plantin as printer to the court and gave him the monopoly for publishing liturgical books for Spain and the

Spanish colonies. This may well have had a ironic twist, for Plantin was probably a Protestant. Plantin left Antwerp after the sack of Antwerp by the Spanish in 1576, and became printer to the University of Leiden in the Netherlands from 1583 to 1585, when he returned to Antwerp. While he was away the Antwerp press was run by his sons-in-law, Francis van Ravelingen and Jan Moerentorff (1543–1610), known as Moretus. After Plantin died in 1589 Moretus took over the press, and the business was passed down through eight generations until 1875, when Hyacinth Moretus allowed the house and workshops to become the Museum Plantin-Moretus that we see today. The house has seen several stages of transformation, first under Plantin himself, then under subsequent generations, in 1620–22, 1637–9 and 1761–3.

The ground floor in the museum consists of two distinct elements: living rooms and working rooms. To the right of the entrance is a pair of grand 16th- and 17th-century reception rooms, hung with tapestries and paintings, including some portraits and *The Lion Hunt* by Rubens. Rubens was a friend and contemporary of Jan Moretus's son Baltasar, who commissioned him to do a number of copper-plate engravings for various books.

A door leads out into the pretty Renaissance courtyard, off which is a series of small rooms, including one that in the 17th century served as a bookshop, the outlet for the products of the printing presses. A passageway leads through a chain of further furnished rooms, including the study used by the humanist scholar Justus Lipsius (1547–1606), a friend of Plantin. The suite of rooms leads to the printing workshop, a large room crammed with old printing presses (the earliest of which may date from Plantin's day), compositors' trays and all the paraphernalia from the days of letterpress printing.

Upstairs a series of rooms leads through various displays which demonstrate the scope of the Plantin family's printing achievements. These include the Polyglot Bible; engravings by Rubens; maps by Gerard Mercator (1512–94) and other early maps showing the Americas gradually being filled in as explorers and traders reported back their discoveries; and a priceless copy of Gutenberg's 36-line Bible which may have been prepared prior to the 42-line Bible, but was published later by his creditors. The upper floors are the most atmospheric. They include a suitably dingy library lined with august leatherbound tomes, and a printers' workroom where the type was cast; on display are the punches, strikes/matrices and moulds. They include a set of punches made by the famous contemporary of Plantin, the French type-designer Claude Garamond (1480–1561).

The square outside is the Vrijdagmarkt, the old Friday market place, where an antiques and jumble market takes place on Wednesday and Friday mornings.

Sint-Andrieskerk

Open Tues–Fri 9–12.

This squat church was built originally in 1514–29, in a district once known for its abject poverty. Its building was interrupted in 1523 because its Augustinian sponsors were accused of sympathy with Martin Luther (who was himself an Augustinian monk). Work was later completed in late-Gothic style, and the church was dedicated to St Andrew, patron saint of Burgundy. The tower was reworked in late-Baroque style in 1769. The result is a peculiar and agreeable hybrid, solid, almost secular in feel, and very Flemish. It contains a number of paintings and a remarkable monument, with a portrait in painted copper, to Mary Stuart (Mary Queen of Scots, 1542–67).

Rubenshuis

Open Tues–Sun 10–5, closed Mon; adm 30 BF.

Pieter Paul Rubens (1577–1640) was the outstanding painter of Antwerp during a Golden Age of exceptional artistic endeavour (*see* pp.71–3 for a brief account of his life and achievements). This was the house that he bought in 1610, when he was already a wealthy man, and in the service of the Archduke Albert and the Infanta Isabella as court painter. But for them, Rubens' name might not have been so closely attached to Antwerp.

Rubens was in fact born in Siegen in Germany. His father and mother, however, were from Antwerp. His father, a prominent lawyer, was probably a Calvinist, and was implicated in the iconoclastic riot of 1566. He escaped to Germany, where he had an affair with Anna, the second wife of William of Orange. When this was discovered, he was banished to Siegen, where he was later joined by his wife. In 1577 they had a son, Pieter Paul. When Pieter Paul was ten his father died; he and his mother then went to live in Antwerp and several years later he began training as an artist, first with Tobias Verhaecht, then Adam van Noort, then with the 'Romanist' Otto Venius. The young Rubens spent eight years in Italy (1600–1608), but returned in haste when he received news that his mother was ill. He arrived too late to see her alive, and was about to return to Italy when he was persuaded to stay by Albert and Isabella. He accepted on condition that he could remain in Antwerp. In 1609 he married Isabella Brant, and the following year bought this house, which over the next 17 years he transformed into a kind of Italian villa. Unfortunately, the Rubenshuis is considered a premier tourist sight of Antwerp, and is inundated with visitors who are despatched by exasperated attendants along the series of rooms which are virtually bare of any furnishings that might make this recognizably a home.

This, to some extent, is an accident of history. The house indeed had an illustrious past. Rubens was the centre of an elevated artistic circle that included his associates Antoon van Dyck (1599–1641) and Jacob Jordaens (1593–1678). His noble patrons—Archduke Albert and the Infanta Isabella, Marie de Médicis (Queen of France) and George Villiers, Duke of Buckingham—visited Rubens in this house. It later fell into sad neglect, and was only saved after 1937, when it was bought by the city and underwent massive renovation. The paintings and furnishings are designed to evoke Rubens's epoch, but are not his own.

There are a few highlights, including Ruben's large and high-ceilinged studio, now used as a concert hall. The court outside is separated from the small garden by magnificent Baroque portico, with elaborate stonework designed by Rubens (though the statues of Mercury and Minerva on the parapet are modern replicas).

The dining room contains a self-portrait (1625–8) by Rubens, and an example of the still-lifes which made the name of Frans Snyders (1579–1657). The Kunstkammer was where Rubens would have displayed the pride of his large personal collection of paintings. Among the paintings here now is the intriguing *Gallery of Cornelis van de Geest* by Willem van Haecht, a contemporary of Rubens. It depicts Isabella and Albert admiring the art collection of a wealthy Antwerp merchant and shows who were considered the most collectable artists of the day: Jan van Eyck, Albrecht Dürer, Pieter Bruegel the Elder, Quentin Metsys, Rubens and Frans Snyder all feature.

At the age of 62, after suffering from gout for several years, Rubens died in the large bedroom upstairs. His soul, one feels, has moved elsewhere.

Museum Mayer van den Bergh

Open Tues–Sun 10–5, closed Mon; adm 75 BF.

This is the most charming and rewarding of Antwerp's small museums—an Aladdin's cave of paintings, antique furniture and much else. These were all the private possessions of Fritz Mayer van den Bergh (1858–91), who turned his back on the trading empire owned by his parents' families to devote himself to collecting, a career cut short by his early death following an accident at the age of 33. After his death, his mother decided to preserve the collection intact and commissioned an architect to design a purpose-built museum in the style of a 16th-century house. It was officially opened in 1904.

The museum consists of a series of furnished rooms, hung with tapestries and paintings, and dotted with display cabinets containing a variety of treasures— some 3000 in all, not including the 2000 coins. An important part of the legacy is the Micheli collection of late-Gothic and early Renaissance sculpture which Fritz

Mayer van den Burgh purchased *en bloc* in 1898, a daring venture which pushed his financial resources to the limit. There are some exceptional works among the paintings, including a fine Calvary triptych by Quentin Metsys (1466–1530), a touching 15th-century *Adoration of the Magi* by an anonymous Master of Hoogstraten, fine portraits by the Antwerp artist Cornelis de Vos (1584–1651), and various paintings, including a *Nativity*, by Jan 'Velvet' Bruegel (1568–1625), son of Pieter Bruegel the Elder.

The most famous painting of the collection, however, is by Pieter Bruegel the Elder (c.1525–69): *Dulle Griet* ('Mad Meg') portrays this medieval allegory of disorder as an armed woman running from a burning town on which she has vented her rage. She is surrounded by a world turned upside down and inhabited by hybrid monsters and visual puns—such as an upturned head with legs in which the mouth becomes the anus, and fish with legs. Bruegel was based in Antwerp from about 1551 to 1563, when he moved with his new wife to Brussels. The painting dates to about the time of this move and may be a comment on the political and religious troubles that had begun to engulf the Low Countries, and Antwerp in particular. Another painting by Bruegel in the collection is the unusual *Twelve Proverbs on Trenchers*, twelve sayings depicted on a series of wooden trenchers, the common equivalent of plates in his time (hence the expression 'a good trencherman').

Maagdenhuis

Open Mon, Wed–Fri 10–5, Sat and Sun 1–5, closed Tues, adm 35 BF.

This small, rather touching museum is housed in an old 16–17th-century girls' orphanage (the 'Maidens' House'), and thereby hang some tragic tales. Foundlings' homes and orphanages were a necessity during the troughs of Antwerp's history. Rather than simply abandoning their children, mothers were encouraged to bring them to orphanages, where they could leave them anonymously in a niche in the wall of the building designed for that purpose. Often they hoped to claim the child back when things improved, and so tied about the child's neck a label in the form of half a playing card or religious image, cut through with a jagged line. They would keep the other half, in order to be able to identify the child later by matching the two halves.

The Maagdenhuis was one of the earliest orphanages in Antwerp, founded in 1552, and the buildings date from two phases of construction, 1564–68 and 1634–36. It remained in operation until 1882. The museum contains mementoes of the orphanage (including some of the labels), as well as antique furniture, stained glass, historical archives, and also a collection of 16th-century Antwerp pottery and porridge bowls.

The Diamond District

It is claimed that 85 per cent of the world's uncut diamonds are traded through Antwerp, and the majority of these are cut and polished in this city where, the story goes, Lodewijk van Bercken developed the art of diamond polishing in 1476. Diamonds are big business, worth an estimated 500 billion Belgian Francs per annum, or 7 per cent of Belgium's total export earnings. The bulk of the business is carried out by four diamond exchanges and some 1500 firms, many of them run by Orthodox Jewish families, employing 30,000 people, all crammed into a square mile just to the southwest of the Centraal Station. The diamond district is now a network of quiet streets that look nothing out of the ordinary besides repeated reference to diamonds in signboards, the large number of kosher restaurants and delicatessens, and the sight of black-coated and behatted Hasidic Jews hurrying about their business. But behind the rather down-at-heel, scruffy façades are workshops where raw diamonds are shaped into gems, and dealing rooms where the products are sold in bulk to jewellery manufacturers and wholesalers and where astronomical sums of money change hands.

For a good introduction to diamonds generally, visit the **Provinciaal Diamantmuseum** at 31–33 Lange Herentalsestraat *(open 10–5 daily; adm free)*. This museum takes seriously its educational mission to inform the public about diamonds and the diamond trade. On several floors, through photographic panels, models and exhibits, it shows how diamonds are found, explains their natural structure, and how they are cut and shaped into facets to produce maximum sparkle. To get an idea of the scale of the diamond trade, go to Pelikaanstraat, where there are dozens of jewellery and gold shops beneath the railway arches. There is nothing fancy about the diamond business here: these outlets are looking for a brisk trade—they stack 'em high and sell 'em cheap. Notices in the windows boast 'Diamond-setting in 15 minutes!'

For a more sedate and reassuring view of diamond commerce, you can visit Antwerp's largest diamond showroom: **Diamondland**, 33a Appelmansstraat *(open Mon–Sat 9–6; adm free)*. Here you can see craftsmen working on the diamonds, and view the huge range of diamonds offered for sale (the principal purpose of this enterprise). Diamonds bought here are fully authenticated and accompanied by certificates. Take you passport if you wish to benefit from tax breaks offered to foreign purchasers. The trade, incidentally, is regulated by the Hoog Raad voor Diamant (HDR, High Diamond Council), 22 Hovenierstraat, © (03) 222 05 11.

Centraal Station

Antwerp's Centraal Station (once called the Middenstatie) is one of the great monuments to the Golden Age of the railways. This is neoclassicism at its most extravagant: the interior—all gilt and marble, columns and stairs—is like a Renaissance painter's fantasy of what classical building should have looked like. It was designed by Louis Delacenserie (1838–1909), a Bruges architect who created similarly extravagant stations at Dresden and Lucerne. The station took seven years to build, 1898–1905, and was recently superbly restored in time for Antwerp's year as European Cultural Capital.

Antwerp Zoo

Open daily Nov–Feb 9–5, March–May and Sept–Oct 9–6, June–Aug 9–6.30; adm 370 BF, children 3–11 years old 225 BF.

Zoos have temporarily slipped out of fashion, and all the great city zoos are feeling the pinch, under two-pronged attack from declining attendance and pressure to find the money to upgrade facilities and provide better environments for their animals. Antwerp's famous zoo, now over 150 years old, has had its share of criticism. This is, nonetheless, a comprehensive collection of over 4000 animals housed in a sizeable city park, with aquariums, reptile house, nocturama and dolphinarium, besides the usual range of lions, monkeys and giraffes.

South of the Centre

Koninklijk Museum voor Schone Kunsten

Open Tues–Sun 10–5, closed Mon; adm 80 BF.

Antwerp's Royal Museum of Fine Art is housed in a pompously overgrand neoclassical temple, built in 1878–90, topped by women charioteers (by the Antwerp-trained sculptor Thomas Vinçotte), and standing in somewhat forlorn grounds. Don't let this put you off, for what lies within is an outstanding collection of north European painting containing numerous treasures—so many, indeed, that many great works spend most of their days in the 'reserve collection' and receive only the occasional airing.

The collection is divided into two parts: the Old Masters of 14th–17th centuries are in the grand old marbled galleries on the upper floor; the 19th–20th century collection is on the ground floor.

To see the two collections in chronological order, head first for the upper floor. Outstanding works from the early collection include **Jan van Eyck**'s unfinished portrait of *Saint Barbara* (1437), sitting with a book on her lap in front of a Gothic cathedral under construction. The crystal-sharp triptych, the *Altar of the Seven Sacraments* by **Rogier van der Weyden** (*c.* 1400–1464), illustrates the seven key sacraments of the Christian Church (Baptism, Confirmation, the Eucharist, Penance, Orders (being ordained), Matrimony and the Extreme Unction), all being played out around a crucifixion set in a Gothic cathedral. A delightful triptych by **Hans Memling** (1430/5–94) portrays Christ surrounded by singing angels and angelic musicians.

The 15th-century collection is particularly strong. This was a period when Italian painting was beginning to influence Flemish art, through artists such as **Bernard van Orley** (1492–1542), whose *Last Judgement and Seven Acts of Mercy* contains figures in a neoclassical setting. Compare this, however, with *The Entombment of Christ*, a magnificent triptych which shows the greater asssurance of the Antwerp painter **Quentin Metsys** (1460–1530). In the left-hand panel Herod is portrayed as an self-centred epicure, while Salome toys idly with St John the Baptist's head; in the right-hand panel St John the Evangelist looks beatific as he is being boiled in a cauldron while eager peasants stoke the fire—grim subjects, but rich in detail and full of vigour.

One of the great figures of 16th-century Antwerp was **Frans Floris** (1519/20–70), brother of Cornelis Floris, the architect of the Stadhuis. Both travelled to Rome in 1540–5, where Frans was deeply impressed by the work of Raphael and by Michelangelo's *Last Judgement* (which he witnessed being unveiled). On his return he met with huge success, and this made him a wealthy man and enabled him to establish a studio where sometimes over 100 students would gather. However, his paintings (such as the *Fall of the Rebel Angels* and *Banquet of the Gods*), sensual and powerfully imagined though they are, never quite match his ambitions to rival the Italians.

There are a number of artists called de Vos. There were two families by that name active in Antwerp. **Maerten de Vos** (1532–1603) was the son of an Antwerp painter, **Pieter de Vos the Elder**; he trained with his father and Frans Floris, then went to Venice, where he worked in the studio of Tintoretto. Another de Vos family came from nearby Hulst. **Cornelis de Vos** (1584–1651) concentrated mainly on religious and allegorical subjects, painted with cool observation that contrasts with the more heated tones of Rubens. He was also a skilled portraitist. His brother **Paul de Vos** (1596–1678) specialized in animal paintings.

The centrepiece of the 17th-century collection are the rooms devoted to **Pieter Paul Rubens** (1577–1640); this being his city, they promise much, but are disappointing. (The collection of the Musées Royaux des Beaux Arts in Brussels (*see* p.110) is far more impressive.) However, there are two classic Rubens here: the

Enthroned Madonna and Child surrounded by Saints has a typically dynamic composition, which leads the eye from the base of the painting up into the heavens; and the *Adoration of the Magi* is a masterpiece of composition, with at least four main centres of focus, in which swaggering kings, camelriders and helmeted soldiers are stopped in their tracks by the sight of the Holy Child.

In a period of numerous stars illuminated by Rubens' talents, probably his most celebrated contemporary was **Antoon van Dyck** (1599–1641), who for a while worked with him as an assistant. He was famous as a portraitist, particularly at the court of Charles I in London, where he spent much of his later career after 1632 and where he died. But he was a painter of considerably wider skills, as his intense *Lamentation of Christ* demonstrates. After the deaths of Rubens and Van Dyck in 1640 and 1641 respectively, **Jacob Jordaens** (1593–1678)—who had worked alongside Rubens for 20 years—was considered the greatest painter of Antwerp. In a Rubens-like composition, his *Martyrdom of Saint Apollonia* shows the saint having her teeth extracted with a pair of pliers. According to tradition this early Christian saint from Alexandria had her teeth removed by her tormentors before walking voluntarily into a fire on which they had threatened to burn her if she did not renounce Christianity. Jordaens became a Calvinist in his later years, and turned increasingly to religious painting; he is, however, rather better known for his voluptuous paintings of fertility and fun, of which *As the Old Sang, the Young Play Pipes* (1638) is a famous example—a cosy middle-class family concert around a table of snacks, which are being eyed by the dog. Other highlights of this section include genre paintings of peasant jollities by **Adriaen Brouwer** (1605–1638) and **David Teniers the Younger** (1610–90); landscapes by **Jacob van Ruisdael** (1628–82); and portraits by **Frans Hals** (*c.* 1580–1666), who was born in Antwerp, but worked in Haarlem in the Netherlands. The fine *Portrait of Eleazer Swalmius* attributed to **Rembrandt** rests under the cloud of dubious authenticity.

The museum virtually dismisses the 18th century and early 19th century to launch into a excellent late 19th- and 20th-century collection. Just about every major figure in Belgian art since 1850 is represented: **Emile Claus, Théo van Rysselberghe, Léon Spilliaert, Henri Evenepoel, Henry van de Velde** (painter turned Art Nouveau designer), artists of the **Sint-Martens-Latem School** (Valerius de Saedeleer, Gustave van de Woestyne, Albert Servaes, Gustave de Smet, Frits van de Berghe, Constant Permeke), Flemish Expressionists **Jean Brusselmans** and **Edgard Tytgat, René Magritte, Paul Delvaux**, the artists of **Cobra** including **Pierre Alechinsky**. It is worth looking out in particular for the collection of work by **James Ensor** (1860–1949), including the *Oyster Eater* of 1882, a watershed date when he began to pursue his idiosyncratic course. Never has oyster-eating been portrayed with such a pungent subtext of sensual pleasure.

The museum also has a major collection of work by **Rik Wouters** (1882–1916), the best known of a group called the Brabant Fauvists (after the short-lived informal grouping of artists dubbed *fauves* (wild beasts), centring on Matisse, that lasted from 1905 to 1908. The Fauvists essentially took the Impressionists' colour to its logical limits, sometimes with garish abandon. This is not a criticism that can be levelled at Wouters, whose paintings are certainly colourful, but judiciously balanced and full of light and joyousness. *Woman Ironing* (1912) is one of his best-known works, a wonderfully spontaneous domestic portrait of his wife Nel, whom he married in 1905 and who was virtually the only model for his paintings and many sculptures (for which he is equally celebrated. *Rik with a Black Eye Patch* (1915) tells another story. He had suffered blinding headaches after 1911; during the war he was called up and then interned in the Netherlands. His headaches grew worse, and in 1915 he was operated on. He went to live in Amsterdam, where he had a second operation in 1916, but died two months later.

Other especially notable works include the socio-realist landscapes and interiors by the Antwerp artist **Jan Stobbaerts** (1838–1914) and his associate **Henri de Braekeleer** (1840–88), and the powerful industrial scenes by **Constantin Meunier**, including and the famous *Le Retour de la Mine*. **Léon Frédéric** (1856–1940) was an enigmatic painter who succeeded in spanning the chasm between socio-realism and Symbolism with paintings of great power and a technical polish. *Les Enfants Wallons, ou Les Boëchelles*, an affectionate portrait of two peasant girls, is a fine example of this. The Belgian artist **Alfred Stevens** (1823–1906), by contrast, was famous for his portraits of women of both high society and the *demi-monde* of the Second Empire in Paris, where he settled and became an associate of Manet. One of his most famous works is *Parisienne Sphinx*, a brilliantly executed portrait, full of spontaneity and sensual mystery.

The collection also includes some interesting pieces by foreign artists, including **James Tissot**, and the *Potato Digger* by **Van Gogh**, painted in 1885 when he was living in the depressing mining district of the Borinage in southern Belgium.

Museum voor Hedendaagse Kunst (MUHKA)

Open Tues–Sun 10–5; adm 150 BF.

The interior of a huge fawn-coloured grain warehouse, built in the 1920s, has been broken up into a series of dazzling white spaces for this avant-garde museum, which presents a permanent collection of post-1970 works and temporary exhibits—sometimes exhilarating, sometimes bemusing, sometimes infuriating. The café on the third floor is a gathering point for artists and writers at the cutting edge.

Provinciaal Museum voor Fotografie

Open Tues–Sun 10–5, closed Mon; adm free.

This modern museum on the Waalse Kaai tracks the history of photography on two floors in a series of well-explained exhibits. (A thorough catalogue to the exhibits, in English, is available free of charge from the reception desk.)

The exhibition begins with the very first experiments in photography and explains the breakthroughs achieved by the pioneers in the 1820s and 1830s such as Joseph Niépce, Louis Daguerre, and William Henry Fox Talbot. It includes beguiling landscapes and portraits by Julia Margaret Cameron, who saw the artistic potential of photography in the 1860s; meanwhile its commercial potential was being exploited by studio photography, which produced portraits in the *carte de visite* format in such quantities that the fad became known as 'cartomania'. The museum contains equipment from such a studio, complete with cameras able to take the huge glass photographic plates, background scenery and the head-clamps used to prevent children moving during the long exposure times. Hobby box cameras, introduced in the 1890s, opened up photography to amateurs, while it began to be taken seriously as an art form through the work of the great American photographers such as Edward Steichen, Alfred Stieglitz, Edward Weston and Ansel Adams, all of whom are represented here by a collection of their work. There are also numerous classic photographs by other greats: Henri Cartier-Bresson, Brassaï, Robert Capa, Irving Penn *et al.* A large collection of cameras traces the technical development of photography, and includes some interesting oddities, such as miniature spy cameras built into cigarette lighters and watches. The Belgian chemist Lieven Gevaert (1868–1935) made an important contribution to photography through the film produced by his company—now a part of the Agfa-Gevaert multinational.

The second floor is devoted to photography that has attempted to portray the world in more than two dimensions—as in the stereoscopes that became all the rage in the late 19th century. It includes the extraordinary Keizers Panorama, a round wooden construction that permitted 26 people simultaneously to see stereoscopic views of places in the world. It was built for the 1905 World Fair, but was trumped by cinematography, which had been developed a decade earlier by the Lumière brothers. The exhibition also has some of the earliest colour photographs, dating to 1907, and follows the evolution of the moving image from flick cards and zootropes to compact discs.

The street outside, the Waalse Kaai, used to be a quay serving the South Dock, with the Vlaamse Kaai on the other side. However, the dock was filled in in 1968.

Other Attractions

Berchem

This southern suburb of Antwerp is famous for its wealth of Art Nouveau/Jugend-stil buildings. They are found mainly in the Zurenborg quarter, in Cogels-Osylei and surrounding streets. Bus No. 9 travels between the city centre and Berchem, and passes down Cogels-Osylei.

The Port of Antwerp

The massive port of Antwerp lies to the north of the city. It is not so much attractive as impressive, and you can tour the harbour by boat (*see* p.341), or by car by following signs marked Havenroute, a 65km round trip (brochures giving details are available from the tourist office of Antwerp). Ranks of cranes line the dock-sides, hunched over rows of cargo ships; seagulls wheel against a sky pricked by the flares of petrochemical installations; goods wagons trundle across acres of bare industrial landscape, connecting the shipyards, chemical and engineering works with the outside world. The port, consisting of over 120km of docks in all, is in fact built inland from the river, and connected to it by seven sea locks. At night the entire scene goes through a magical transformation, as the millions of lights on the ships and industrial plants create their own night sky, converting a grim and sterile world into an unearthly fairytale landscape. Clouds of vapour pour out of the distillation plants, the flares become giant torches, while in corners of the docks seagulls and ducks paddle about incongruously, apparently undisturbed by this unearthly setting.

Shopping

There are good and interesting shops dotted around the city centre, but the main **shopping** street is the Meir—a broad, pedestrianized avenue lined with the major chain stores and smart boutiques, and one of the most impressive shopping streets in Belgium. The eastern end, leading ito Leysstraat and Teniersplein, includes some very grand 19th-century neo-Baroque buildings, now occupied by clothing boutiques and department stores. This procession of good shops continues further eastwards along De Keyserlei up to Antwerpen Centraal Station. Pelikaanstraat, to the south of the station is at the heart of the **diamond district**. There is also a varied market on Theaterplein (*see* p.363).

★★★★★ **De Witte Lelie**, 16–18 Keizerstraat, B-2000 Antwerp, ✆ 226 19 66, fax 234 00 19. Opened in 1993 in a set of three gabled 17th-century town houses, this is the most delightful city hotel of its kind in Belgium. The décor of the individually styled suites and spacious rooms is coolly elegant, with exposed beams, antique furniture and numerous discreet touches of luxury, yet the atmosphere is that of a private home—enveloping guests with its charm and grace. 7500–19,500 BF.

★★★★ **Prinse**, 63 Keizerstraat, B-2000 Antwerp, ✆ 226 40 50, fax 225 11 48. Somehow the renovators have succeeded in removing any sense of history from the interior of this converted 16th-century mansion; nonetheless a comfortable, tranquil hotel, not far from the city centre. 4000–4300 BF.

★★★★ **Villa Mozart**, 3–7 Handschoenmarkt, B-2000 Antwerp, ✆ 231 30 31, fax 231 56 85. A small, tasteful hotel of just 25 Laura-Ashley-decorated rooms, and very central—opposite the west door of the cathedral. The nearest parking is on the other side of the Stadhuis, however. 4500 BF.

★★★ **Alfa**, 30 Arenbergstraat, B-2000 Antwerp, ✆ 231 1720, fax 233 88 58. A stylish modern hotel, part of the well-known Alfa chain. About 20 minutes' walk to the southeast of the city centre, but once inside you could be just about anywhere in the world. 6100 BF (weekends 3700 BF).

★★★ **Antigone**, 11–12 Jordaenskaai, B-2000 Antwerp, ✆ 231 66 77, fax 231 37 74. A good, well-appointed hotel (IKEA meets Art Deco) with rooms overlooking the River Scheldt (and road), close to the centre. 3500 BF.

★★★ **Christian V**, Bonapartedok, St Laureiskaai, 2000 Antwerp 1, ✆ 226 8317, fax 226 03 28. A pleasant alternative: a 'flothotel'—a hotel (and restaurant) on an elegantly converted Norwegian passenger ship built in 1952. The dock, about 1km from the city centre, was built by Napoleon to serve his fleet, but is in fact somewhat forlorn. Note that breakfast (400 BF) is not included in the cabin price. 3600–4500 BF.

★★★ **Eden**, 25–27 Lange Herentalsestraat, 2018 Antwerp, ✆ 233 06 08, fax 233 12 28. A modern, efficient hotel of 66 rooms, with minimalist décor, in the diamond district to the east of the city centre. 3500 BF.

★★★ **Ibis**, 39 Meistraat (Vogelenmarkt), B-2000 Antwerp, ✆ 231 88 30, fax 234 29 21. Safe if somewhat characterless, invigorated by its keen and efficient young staff, about 20 minutes' walk from the city centre. It overlooks the Theaterplein which hosts a large food and clothes market on Saturday, and flea market, food and pet market on Sunday. 3450 BF.

★★ **Cammerpoorte**, 38–40 Nationalestraat, B-2000 Antwerp, ✆ 231 97 36, fax 226 29 68. A fresh-faced, modern hotel, with plain but adequate rooms and a rooftop garage attached. Well-priced for its central location. 3150 BF. There is also a cheaper 9-room sister *pension* around the corner in Steenhouwersvest. 2450 BF.

Youth Hostel: Jeugdherberg op Sinjoorke, 2 Eric Sasselaan, 2020 Antwerp, ✆ 238 02 73; fax 248 19 32. About 2km south of the city centre. Rooms for 4, 6 or 8 people; 320 BF per person; sheets at extra charge of 120 BF.

Antwerp ✆ (03–)   **Eating Out**

There are countless and varied places to eat (and drink) in central Antwerp. If none of the list below strikes a chord, take a wander around the area south of the Grote Markt, such as Grote Pieter-potstraat and Oude Koornmarkt, and see what's on offer. The so-called Quartier Latin, the district around Theater-plein to the southeast of the centre (Schutterhofstraat, Kelderstraat, Leopoldsplaats) is also a good hunting ground for cheaper bars and restaurants with a lively atmosphere.

expensive

La Rade, 8 Ernest van Dijckkaai, ✆ 233 37 37. *Closed Sat lunch and Sun.* Superior restaurant, founded in 1949, in the splendid first-floor rooms of an old mansion decorated in neo-Renaissance style in the late 19th century, overlooking the Scheldt and the Steen. Good *haute cuisine française* elegantly served.

P. Preud'Homme, 28 Suikerrui, ✆ 233 42 00. With its large picture-window overlooking the street, this is elegant restaurant provides a glittering stage upon which exquisitely dressed clients can dine on lobster salad and *haute cuisine* dishes of game and fish costing 1500 BF.

moderate

Het Vermoeide Model, 2 Lijnwaadmarkt, ✆ 233 52 61. *Closed Mon.* A tavern (the name means 'The Sleepy (Artist's) Model') built into the side of the cathedral, with a pleasantly antique, cosy atmosphere, and reasonable prices. Grilled fish or crab for 320 BF, main-course salads for 380 BF.

Maritime, 4 Suikerrui, ✆ 233 07 58. You can smell the sea air on Suikerrui, and this is one of several restaurants offering fresh, straightforward seafood at competitive prices. Mussels for around 650 BF.

Marrakesh, 1 Wisselstraat. A richly exotic atmosphere, like the inside of a nomad tent, where hearty plates of couscous are served for 420–600 BF.

Satsuma, 5 Wisselstraat, ✆ 226 24 43. *Closed Tues.* A Japanese restaurant with approachable prices, serving the usual range of *sashimi, tempanyaki* and the like. A seven-course set dinner for 1100 BF, and lunch for 680 BF.

't Ogenblick, 10–12 Grote Markt, ✆ 233 62 22. *Closed Tues, and Mon and Tues in winter.* Very stylish and lively bar overlooking the Grote Markt, serving inventive light lunches made of the freshest ingedients.

inexpensive

De Plaisante Hof, 25–27 Vlasmarkt, ✆ 231 57 91. Small, low-key and agreeable restaurant serving sandwiches and snacks, as well as substantial and well-cooked dishes of the day (about 600 BF).

De Stoemppot, 12 Vlasmarkt, ✆ 231 36 86. *Closed Mon, Tues and Sat lunch.* This is the place to try out some *stoemp*—the traditional Flemish dish of puréed meat and vegetables. *Stoemp* of all flavours and other rustic dishes for around 350 BF.

Kartini, 61 Oude Koornmarkt, ✆ 226 44 63. *Evenings only, closed Mon.* Tiny Indonesian restaurant serving tasty, authentic dishes at competitive prices, including a monumental 12-course *Rijsttafel Kraton* for 1400 BF.

Entertainment and Nightlife

Antwerp is famous for its vigorous nightlife and club scene. Fashions change with mercurial speed, but here are a few names to start you off. The cost of entry is usually about 250 BF. They start opening around 10, get going around midnight and tend to stay open until 4 or 5am.

Café d'Anvers, 15 Verversrui, ✆ 226 38 70. Old warehouse, very big, very dark, and a popular venue for house music.

Le Chapeau, 5 Maalderijstraat, ✆ 231 40 77. Discothèque.

Le Palais, 12 van Ertbornstraat, ✆ 233 35 15. Large disco, formerly Jimmy's.

Ossepoot, 7–9 Vrijdagmarkt, ✆ 231 15 30. Discothèque, known for 60s music on Sunday afternoons, but in the evening draws a younger crowd.

Paradox, 25 Waalse Kaai, ✆ 237 64 58. Club-discothèque which is famous for its regular parties.

Red and Blue, 13 Lange Schipperskapelstraat. House and soul music in a large converted warehouse. Entry before midnight free, thereafter 250 BF.

Belgium has three official languages: French and Flemish, and German, which is spoken on the eastern border. (For an introduction to the implications of Belgium's language divide, *see* pp.21–2.)

English is not as widely spoken in Brussels—and in Belgium generally—as it is, for example, in the Netherlands. The chances are, however, that in most tourist contexts (hotels, restaurants, museums) the staff will be able to speak English—at least well enough to communicate. Nonetheless, some knowlege of both French and Flemish will inevitably be helpful.

The French spoken in Belgium is very similar to standard French, although the Belgian accent is distinctive—more throaty and rounded, less nasal than Parisian French. There are certain distinctive features—such as the use of *septante* (seventy) and *nonante* (ninety) instead of the standard French *soixante-dix* and *quatre-vingt dix*. The francophone Belgians are also far more casual than the French about the use of *tu* and *vous* (the informal and formal words for 'you').

A Guide to Flemish Pronunciation

Flemish (*Vlaams*) is a variant form of Dutch (*Nederlands*). Two main problems confront anyone trying to learn even just the rudiments. One is the grammatical structure—although if you know German you will be familiar with the broad pattern of the back-to-front word order. The other is pronunciation. It is phonetic language, but you have to begin by shedding any preconceived notion about how written vowels should be pronounced. *A, e, i, o* and *u* are pronounced in a broadly similar way to English—although the *a* is much throatier and ends up more like the *o* in the English 'odd'. When it comes to combination vowels, however, any attempt to interpret them in an English or, worse, a French manner, will end in failure. Wipe the slate clean and relearn! Names of places, or familiar words, will often provide useful aids to memory. For instance *huis* sounds similar to the English word 'house', which is what it means (although the 'ow' sound is more complex, making it more like 'ah-oohss').

Combination Vowels

aa   like aa in the English 'aardvaark'; e.g. *waar* (= where; pron. 'wahr')
ae   like ar in the English 'part'; e.g. Verhaeren (Belgian poet; pron. 'Verharen')

au	like ow in the English 'cow'; e.g. *kabeljauw* (= cod; pron. 'cabbelyow')	
ee	like ai in the English 'hail'; e.g. *een* (= one; pron. 'ayn')	
ei	like ij (see below); e.g *trein* (= train; pron. 'trayne')	
eie	like ay in the English 'say'; e.g. Leie (name of a river; pron. 'Lay')	
eu	like the English 'err'; e.g. Leuven (place name; pron. 'Lerven')	
eeu	ay-ooh; e.g. *leeuw* (= lion; pron. 'lay-oohv')	
ie	ee in the English 'three'; e.g. *drie* (= three, pron. 'dree')	
ieu	ee-oo; e.g. *nieuw* (= new; pron. 'nee-oo')	
ij	like ay in John Wayne; e.g. *wijn* (= wine; pron. 'wayne')	
oe	like oo in the English 'pool'; e.g. Poelaert (Brussels architect; pron. 'Poolart')	
oo	like oa in the English 'boat'; e.g. Te *koop* (= For sale; pron. 'Te cope' or 'Te cohp')	
ou	like ou in the English 'out'; e.g. *zout* (= salt; pron 'zout')	
ui	like ow in the English 'house'; e.g. *huis* (= house; pron. 'ouse' or 'ah-oohss')	
uu	like oo in the English 'hoot'; e.g. Te *huur* (= For rent; pron. 'Te ooer': but round your lips, or you risk enquiring about a *hoer*, a prostitute)	

Consonants

Most consonants sound the same as they do in English, although some combinations present their own difficulties. Here are some of the more troublesome ones:

ch	pronounced like the *ch* in the Scottish 'loch'.
g	pronounced like a gutteral *h*—something similar to the *h* in 'hotel' or (again) like the *ch* in the Scottish 'loch'.
j	pronounced like the English *y*.
v	closer to the English *f*.
w	in Flemish is like a soft English *w*.
sch	at the end of a word is pronounced *s*. At the start of the word it sounds more like *sr*, with a bit of gutteral throat-clearing.

Greetings, Responses and Getting By

English	*French*	*Flemish*
yes	oui	ja
no	non	nee
please	s'il vous plaît	alstublieft (abbrev. a. u. b.)
thank you (very much)	merci (bien)	dank u (wel)/bedankt
hello, good day	bonjour	goedendag, *or simply* dag
good morning	bonjour	goedemorgen
good evening	bon soir	goedenavond
good night (at bedtime)	bonne nuit	goede nacht
goodbye	au revoir	tot ziens

Language

367

How are you?	Comment allez-vous?	Hoe maakt u het?
How are things?	Ça va?	Hoe gaat het?
Very well, thank you.	Très bien, merci.	Goed, dank u.
My name is ...	Je m'appelle ...	Mijn naam is ...
mister/sir	monsieur	mijnheer
mrs/madam	madame	mevrouw
how much?	combien?	hoeveel?
I can't speak French/Dutch	Je ne parle pas français.	Ik spreek geen Nederlands.
Do you speak English?	Parlez-vous anglais?	Spreekt u engels?
a little	un peu	een beetje
I do not understand.	Je ne comprends pas.	Ik begrijp het niet.
I don't know	Je ne sais pas.	Ik weet het niet.
Go away!	Allez-vous en!	Ga weg!
Where is the toilet?	Où est la toilette?	Waar is het toilet?
ladies	dames	damestoilet
gents	messieurs	herentoilet
Watch out!	Attention!	Pas op!
Sorry!	Pardon!	Sorry!/Het spijt me.
Cheers!	Santé!	Gezondheid!/Proost!

Numbers

0	zéro	nul	22	vingt-deux	twee en twintig
1	un/une	een	30	trente	dertig
2	deux	twee	31	trent et un	een en dertig
3	trois	drie	40	quarante	veertig
4	quatre	vier	50	cinquante	vijftig
5	cinq	vijf	60	soixante	zestig
6	six	zes	70	septante (Belgian)	zeventig
7	sept	zeven		soixante-dix (French)	
8	huit	acht	80	quatre-vingt	tachtig
9	neuf	negen	90	nonante (Belgian)	negentig
10	dix	tien		quatre-vingt dix (French)	
11	onze	elf	100	cent	honderd
12	douze	twaalf	101	cent un	honderdeen
13	treize	dertien	200	deux cents	twee honderd
14	quatorze	veertien	thousand	mille	duizend
15	quinze	vijftien	million	million	miljoen
16	seize	zestien	first	premier/première	eerste
17	dix-sept	zeventien	second	deuxième	tweede
18	dix-huit	achttien	third	troisième	derde
19	dix-neuf	negentien	half	un demi	een half
20	vingt	twintig	a third	un tiers	een derde
21	vingt et un	een en twintig	a quarter	un quart	een kwart

Time

What is the time?	Quelle heure est-il?	Hoe laat is het?
today	aujourd'hui	vandaag
yesterday	hier	gisteren
tomorrow	demain	morgen
morning	matin	morgen/ochtend
afternoon	après-midi	namiddag
evening	soir	avond
night	nuit	nacht
day	jour	dag
week	semaine	week
month	mois	maand
year	an/année	jaar
century	siècle	eeuw
early	tôt	vroeg
late	tard	laat
Monday	lundi	maandag
Tuesday	mardi	dinsdag
Wednesday	mercredi	woensdag
Thursday	jeudi	donderdag
Friday	vendredi	vrijdag
Saturday	samedi	zaterdag
Sunday	dimanche	zondag
public holiday	jour ferié	feestdag
New Year	Nouvel An	Nieuwjaar
Easter	Pâques	Pasen
Christmas	Noël	Kerstmis

Countries, Nationalities and Languages

I am ...	Je suis ...	Ik ben ...
Britain/British	Grande-Bretagne/britannique	Groot Brittannië/Brits
England/English	Angleterre/anglais(e)	Engeland/Engels
Scotland	Ecosse/écossais(e)	Schotland/Schots
Wales/Welsh	Pays de Galles/gallois(e)	Wales/Welsh
Ireland/Irish	Irelande/irlandais(e)	Ierland/Iers
America/American	Amérique/américain(e)	Amerika/Amerikaan
USA	Les Etats-Unis	Verenigde Staten
Canada/Canadian	Canada/canadien(ne)	Canada/Canadees
Australia/Australian	Australie/australien(ne)	Australië/Australisch
New Zealand	Nouvelle-Zélande	Nieuw-Zeeland
South Africa	L'Afrique du Sud	Zuid Afrika
Belgium	Belgique	België/Belgisch
France/French	France/français(e)	Frankrijk/Frans
Flanders/Flemish	Flandre/flamand(e)	Vlaanderen/Vlaams
The Netherlands/Dutch	Les Pays-Bas/néerlandais(e)	Nederland/Nederlands

Miscellaneous Small Words

very	très	erg/zeer
much	beaucoup	veel
too much	trop	te veel
little/few	peu	weinig
enough	assez	genoeg
expensive	cher/chère	duur
cheap	pas cher/chère	goedkoop
old	vieux/vieille	oud
new	nouveau/nouvelle	nieuw
little	petit	klein
big	grand	groot
quickly	vite	snel
slowly	lentement	langzaam

Directions and Transport

I want to go to ...	Je voudrais aller à ...	Ik wil naar ...
Where is ... ?	Où est ... ?	Waar is ... ?
left	gauche	links
right	droite	rechts
straight on	tout droit	vooruit
near	près	dichtbij
far	loin	ver
airport	aéroport	luchthaven/vliegveld
railway station	gare	station
platform (five)	quai (cinq)	spoor (vijf)
ticket	billet	kaartje
single/one way	aller simple	enkel
return/round trip	aller et retour	heen en terug
car	voiture	auto
car hire	location des voitures	auto verhuur
driving licence	permis de conduire	rijbewijs
petrol	essence	benzine
petrol station	station d'essence	benzinestation
unleaded	sans plomb	loodvrij
car park	parking	parkeerplaats
diversion	déviation	wegomlegging
bicycle	bicyclette/vélo	fiets

Emergencies

police	police	politie
doctor	médecin	dokter
dentist	dentiste	tandarts
ill	malade	ziek
I'm not feeling well.	Je ne me sens pas bien.	Ik voel niet lekker.

ambulance	ambulance	ambulance
hospital	hôpital	ziekenhuis
medicine	médicament	geneesmiddel

Shopping and Services

shop	magasin	winkel
bakery	boulangerie	bakkerij
cake shop	pâtisserie	banketbakkerij
grocer	épicerie	kruidenierswinkel
bookshop	librairie	boekhandel
I'm looking for ...	Je cherche ...	Ik zoek ...
pharmacy	pharmacie	apotheek
clothes	vêtements	kleding
shoes	chaussures	schoenen
It's too big/small.	Il est trop grand/petit.	Het is te groot/klein.
lace	dentelle	kant
bank	banque	bank
post office	bureau de poste	postkantoor
postage stamp	timbre	postzegel
letter	lettre	brief
postcard	carte postale	ansichtkaart
air mail	par avion	luchtpost

Notices and Labels

closed	fermé	gesloten
open	ouvert	open
entrance	entrée	toegang/ingang
exit	sortie	uitgang/uitrit
No smoking	Défense de fumer	Niet roken
street	rue	straat

Food and Drink

The language of cuisine in Belgium is predominantly French. In restaurants in Flanders and Flemish-speaking Brussels, French terms tend to be used for the dishes, but the Flemish terms are used in shops.

General

English	French	Flemish
restaurant	restaurant	restaurant
to eat	manger	eten
to drink	boire	drinken
I would like ...	Je voudrais ...	Ik wil graag ...
to pay	payer	betalen
Could I have the bill, please?	L'addition, s'il vous plaît.	De rekening, alstublieft.
vegetarian	végétarien	vegetariër

breakfast	petit déjeuner	ontbijt
lunch	déjeuner	middagmaal/noenmaal
dinner	souper	avondeten
beer	bière	bier
wine	vin	wijn
a bottle of wine	une bouteille de vin	een fles wijn
red wine	vin rouge	rode wijn
white wine	vin blanc	witte wijn
glass	verre	glas
coffee	café	koffie
tea	thé	thee
milk	lait	melk
soft drinks	limonades	limonaden
orange juice	jus d'orange	sinaasappelsap
mineral water	eau minérale	mineraalwater
It is/tastes good!	C'est trés bon!	Het smaakt lekker!
soup	soupe/potage	soep
starter	hors d'oeuvre/entrée	voorgerecht
main course	plat principal	hoofdgerecht
dessert	dessert	nagerecht
dish of the day	plat du jour	dagschotel
bread	pain	brood
butter	beurre	boter
cheese	fromage	kaas
egg	oeuf	ei
jam	confiture	jam
salt	sel	zout
pepper	poivre	peper
sugar	sucre	suiker

Fish

fish	poisson	vis
bass	bar/loup de mer	zeebaars
cod	cabillaud	kabeljauw
eel	anguille	paling
haddock	aiglefin/églefin	schelvis
herring	hareng	haring
lobster	homard	kreeft
mackerel	maquereau	makreel
monkfish	lotte	lotte/zeeduivel
mullet (red)	rouget	roodbaars
mussel	moule	mossel
oyster	huître	oester
pike	brochet	snoek
plaice	plie	pladijs/schol
salmon	saumon	zalm

scallop	coquille Saint-Jacques	Sint-Jacobsoester/Jacobsschelp
sea bream	dorade/daurade	dorade/zeebrasem
shrimp/prawn	crevette	garnaal
skate	raie	rog
sole	sole	zeetong
squid	calamar	calamar/inktvis
trout	truite	forel
tuna	thon	tonijn
winkles	bigorneaux	kreukels/alikruiken

Meat

meat	viande	vlees
game	gibier	wild
beef	boeuf	rundvlees
chicken	poulet	kip
duck	canard	eend
goose	oie	gans
guinea fowl	pintade	parelhoen
hare	lièvre	haas
ham	jambon	ham
lamb	agneau	lamsvlee
partridge	perdrix	patrijs
pheasant	faisant	fazant
pork	porc	varkensvlees
quail	caille	caille/kwartel
rabbit	lapin	konijn
snails	escargots	escargots/slakken
veal	veau	kalfsvlees
venison	cerf/chevreuil	ree(bok)
wild boar (young boar)	sanglier (marcassin)	wildzwijn/werzwijn
brains	cervelle	hersenen
leg	gigot	bout
liver	foie	lever
kidneys	rognons	nieren
sausage	saucisse/saucisson	worst

Vegetables

vegetables	légumes	groenten
aubergine/eggplant	aubergine	aubergine
asparagus	asperges	asperges
Belgian endive/chicory	chicon	witloof
broad beans	fèves	tuinbonen
Brussels sprouts	choux de Bruxelles	spruitjes
carrots	carottes	worteltjes
cauliflower	choufleur	bloemkohl
chard	bette/blette	snijbiet

chervil	cerfeuil	kervel
chives	ciboulette	bieslook
courgette/zucchini	courgette	courgette
fennel	fenouil	venkel
garlic	ail	knoflook
green beans	haricots princesse	princesbonen
haricot beans	haricots	snijbonen
leek	poireau	prei
mushroom	champignon	champignon
onion	oignon	ui
peas	petits pois	erwten
potatoes	pommes de terre	aardappelen
potato chips/french fries	frites	frieten
rice	riz	rijst
sorrel	oseille	zuring
spinach	épinard	spinazie
tomato	tomate	tomaat
truffle	truffe	truffel

Fruit

fruit	fruits	fruit/vruchten
apple	pomme	appel
banana	banane	banaan
cherry	cerise	kers
chestnut	marron	kastanje
orange	orange	sinaasappel
peach	pêche	perzik
pear	poire	peer
pineapple	ananas	ananas
plum	prune	pruim
raspberry	framboise	framboos
strawberry	fraise	aardbei

Dessert

cake	gâteau	koek
cheesecake	tarte au fromage	kaastaart
tart	tarte	taart
whipped cream	crème Chantilly	slagroom
ice cream	glace	ijs
pancake	crêpe	pannekoek
waffle	gaufre	wafel

Preparation

rare	saignant	rood
medium	à point	half doorbakken
well-done	bien cuit	gaar

plain (without sauces)	nature	natuur
minced	haché	gehakt
stuffed	farci	gevuld
grilled	grillé	geroosterd
steamed	à la vapeur	gestoomd
smoked	fumé	gerookt

French/Walloon Dishes and Specialities

à l'ardennaise	cooked with Ardennes ham (and sometimes cheese)
à la liégeoise	cooked or prepared with strips of bacon
à la nage	(fish) served in a delicately flavoured stock
américain préparé	raw minced steak mashed up with egg yolk, onions, capers, etc.
andouillettes	rich sausages made of offal
anguilles au vert	eels in green herb sauce
assiette anglaise	a selection of cold meats
bisque de homard	thick, creamy lobster soup
blanquette de veau	a casserole of veal in a white sauce
boudin/boudin noir	sausage/black pudding
boulettes	meatballs
brochette	shish kebab
caille aux raisins	quail cooked with grapes
carbonnades flamandes	beef stew cooked with beer
civet (de lapin etc.)	game stew enriched with blood and red wine
cochon de lait	suckling pig
cramique	raisin bread
croque monsieur	grilled cheese (and sometimes ham) on toast
cuisses de grenouille	frogs' legs
entrecôte à l'os	a huge rib steak
(poissons) en escavèche	(cold fish) cooked in a jellied stock flavoured with herbs
faisan à la brabançonne	pheasant cooked with braised Belgian endives
flamiche aux poireaux	a kind of quiche made with leeks and cream
gratin de/au gratin	browned in the oven, usually dotted with butter or cheese
jambon d'Ardennes	cured ham (like Parma ham)
jets de houblon	hop shoots
magret de canard	sliced duck breast
moules marinière	steamed mussels, cooked with celery, onions and parsley
moules parquées	mussels grilled with garlic butter
navarin d'agneau	lamb stew
oiseaux sans tête	slices of beef rolled around a meat stuffing
pâté de foie gras	rich pâté made from the livers of force-fed geese or ducks
plateau de fruits de mer	platter of mixed cold shellfish and other seafood
printanier	cooked with spring vegetables
quenelles (de brochet)	rolls of poached paste flavoured with pounded fish (pike)
salade liégeoise	green salad made with green beans and bacon pieces
salmis (de bécasse)	roast meat (woodcock) recooked in a rich wine sauce

sauce béarnaise	egg and butter sauce with vinegar, shallots and tarragon
béchamel	creamy sauce made with butter, flour and milk
bordelaise	rich sauce made with bone marrow and red wine
chasseur	'hunter's' sauce made with wine, mushrooms and onions
hollandaise	sauce made with butter, egg yolk and lemon juice
madère	sauce made with butter, flour, stock and madiera wine
Mornay	béchamel sauce with cheese
mousseline	a light, whipped sauce of egg yolk, lemon and butter
Nantua	sauce made with crayfish and cream
Soubise	béchamel sauce with onion purée
tartare	mayonnaise with mustard, gherkins, capers and green herbs
sole meunière	sole fried in butter
steak à l'américaine	raw minced steak
steak tartare	raw minced steak (steak à la américaine is the usual term)
tartare (de thon)	raw and minced (tuna)
tarte tatin	baked apple tart turned upside-down on a pastry base
(cuisine du) terroir	local/regional (cooking)
tartine	slice of bread and butter (for open sandwich)
toast cannibal	raw minced steak on toast
tourte	savoury pie made with meat and vegetables

Flemish Dishes

bloedpens	blood pudding
boterham	a slice of bread and butter (for open sandwich)
fricandel	meatballs
Gentse stoverij	rich beef stew from Ghent cooked with beer and mustard
hutsepot	hearty stew (perhaps oxtail or pig's trotters) with root vegetables
paling in 't groen	eels in green herb sauce
speculoos	hard biscuits made with butter, brown sugar and spices
karbonaden	braised beef with onions, usually cooked in beer
rijstpap	rice pudding flavoured with cinnamon
stoemp	mashed potato mixed with vegetable and/or meat purée
waterzooi	chicken (now also fish) cooked in a soup-like cream sauce

Bruxellois Dishes and Specialities

boddink	a sort of bread-and-butter pudding
caricolles	whelks, cockles (any snail-like seafood)
choesels	casserole of mixed offal
faro	*Lambic* beer flavoured with sugar and caramel
gueuze	beer made from matured and blended *lambic*
kipkap	jellied meat made of unpopular cuts (ears, tail, cheeks etc)
kriek	*lambic* beer flavoured with cherries
lambic	beer brewed in the Senne Valley, fermented by natural yeasts
pistolet	bread roll
plattekeis	fromage blanc (a kind of cream cheese)
smoutebollen	deep-fried pastries dusted with icing sugar (fairground food)

amigo	police cell
braderie	sale of goods a knock-down prices
brol	something worthless, worn out; junk
brusseleir	a bruxellois (person)
carabistouilles	worthless remarks, rubbish
(faire sa petite) commission	'spend a penny'; urinate
dégobiller	vomit, throw up
dikenek	arrogant know-it-all
drache	a downpour
drève/dreef	an avenue lined with trees
estaminet	a cosy kind of pub
fritkot	chip shop or van
froucheleir	a man with wandering-hand trouble
impasse	alleyway
kaberdoech	cabaret, bistrot
ketje	young lad
kiekerfretters	archaic term, occasionally heard, for Bruxellois people
klachkop	bald
maboule	mad
manneken/menneke	little boy, rascal
pachacroute	idle worker, loafer, skiver
patapoef	fat
patraque	unwell, weak
pei	man/person
schieve lavabo	idiot (literally, 'twisted/bowed basin')
schieve architek	despicable person (*see* p.136)
snottebelle	snot running from a (child's) nose
strondzat	very drunk (literally, 'shit drunk')
tof	very pretty, good
volle gaz	at full speed
zieverier	a jerk/flake
zwanze	a joke

Place Names

Many places in Belgium have two versions of their name, Flemish and French. Signposts tend to be based on the assumption that you know that Mons is the same as Bergen, or that Mechelen is Malines—which can cause instant panic to the navigator. In Brussels all names—districts, streets, institutions—have two versions. Many of these pairs are clearly recognizable as one and the same—others are totally different from each other. Below is a list of the principal cities and towns in Belgium, and some of the place names in Brussels, where the two versions are noticeably different and might cause confusion.

Cities and Towns

French	Flemish/English	French	Flemish/English
Alost	Aalst	Lierre	Lier
Anvers	Antwerpen/Antwerp	Malines	Mechelen
Bruges	Brugge	Mons	Bergen
Bruxelles	Brussel/Brussels	Namur	Namen
Gand	Gent/Ghent	Ostende	Oostende/Ostend
Ypres	Ieper	Tongres	Tongeren
Courtrai	Kortrijk	Tournai	Doornik
Louvain	Leuven	Veurne	Furnes
Liège	Luik	Zeebruges	Zeebrugge

Brussels Place and Street Names

French	Flemish
Berchem-Sainte-Agathe	Sint-Agatha-Berchem
Botanique	Kruidtuin
Bourse	Beurs
Forêt	Vorst
Gare du Midi	Zuidstation
Grand' Place	Grote Markt
Ilot Sacré	Vrije Gemeente
Ixelles	Elsene
La Hulpe	Ter Hulpen
Molenbeek-Saint-Jean	Sint-Jan-Molenbeek
Notre-Dame-au-Bois	Jezus-Eik
Parc du Cinquantenaire	Jubelpark
Place de la Monnaie	Muntplein
Place Royale	Koningsplein
Quai au Bois à Brûler	Branthoutkaai
Quai aux Briques	Baksteenkaai
Rhode-Saint-Genèse	Sint-Genesius-Rode
Rue au Beurre	Boterstraat
Rue de Flandre	Vlaamsesteenweg
Rue de la Montagne	Bergstraat
Rue de l'Etuve	Stoofstraat
Rue des Eperonniers	Spoormakersstraat
Rue du Fossé aux Loups	Wolvengrachtstraat
Rue du Marché aux Fromages	Kaasmarkt
Rue du Marché aux Herbes	Grasmarkt
Rue du Marché aux Poulets	Kiekenmarkt
Rue Montagne aux Herbes Potagères	Warmoesberg
Rue Neuve	Nieuwstraat
Sablon	Zavel
Saint-Josse-ten-Noode	Sint-Joost-ten-Node
Watermael-Boitsfort	Watermaal-Bosvoorde
Woluwé-Saint-Lambert	Sint-Lambrechts-Woluwe
Woluwé-Saint-Pierre	Sint-Pieters-Woluwe

59 BC	Julius Caesar begins his campaign against the Gauls (Celts).
57 BC	Caesar comes close to defeat by the Belgic tribe, the Nervii.
54 BC	Revolt against the Romans by the Eburones under Ambiorix. After its suppression by Caesar, the Belgae are subdued.
AD 15	Creation of Roman province of Gallia Belgica.
Late C5th	Collapse of the Roman Empire.
c. 500–751	Merovingian dynasty of the Franks, ruling from Tournai.
Late C6th	According to legend, St Géry builds a chapel on an island in the River Senne-- the origin of the settlement that is to become Brussels.
c. 751–987	Carolingian dynasty of the Franks.
768–814	Reign of Charlemagne, centring upon Aachen.
843	Treaty of Verdun splits Frankish Empire along the line of the River Scheldt: first division of Belgian lands into what will become Flanders and Wallonia.
979	The date of the official foundation of Brussels.
Late C11th	Count Lambert of Leuven builds first fortress on the Coudenberg, Brussels.
1100	First ring of defensive walls raised around Brussels.
1302	Tension in French-dominated Flanders develops into a revolt in Bruges led by Pieter de Coninck and Jan Breydel, culminating in victory at the Battle of the Golden Spurs.
1337	Start of the Hundred Years' War (to 1453)
1338	Revolt in Flanders against French, led by Jacob van Artevelde.
1356	The Flemish under Count Louis de Male seize Brabant but are removed from Brussels after two months by rebels led by Everard 't Serclaes.
1379	Completion of the massive new set of city walls around Brussels.
1384	Philip the Bold, Duke of Burgundy inherits Flanders through his marriage to Louis de Male's daughter.
1406	The Dukes of Burgundy inherit Brabant through marriage, and go on to take over most of the Low Countries.
1419–67	Reign of Philip the Good, high point of the Burgundian period. (First) construction of Grand' Place and Hôtel de Ville, Brussels. Era of Jan van Eyck.
1477	Mary of Burgundy marries Maximilian I of the German-Austrian Habsburg family; beginning of Habsburg rule of the Low Countries (until 1794).
1506–55	Reign of Charles V: Brussels is at the hub of his mighty empire.
1556–98	Philip II rules from Spain.
1568	Execution of Counts Egmont and Hornes in Brussels.
1579	United Provinces (modern Netherlands) declare independence.
1585	Capitulation of Antwerp and Brussels to the Spanish under the Duke of Parma leads to the creation of the Spanish Netherlands (approximately equivalent to modern Belgium; lasts until 1713), with Brussels as the capital.

Chronology

1598–1633	Beginning of rule of the Infanta Isabella and Archduke Albert. Period of prosperity; age of Rubens.
1648	Spain formally recognizes United Provinces through the Peace of Münster. Closing of the River Scheldt by the Dutch (until 1794) cripples Antwerp.
1695	During the War of the Grand Alliance, French troops under Marshal de Villeroy bombard Brussels, destroying the Grand' Place and city centre.
1713	At the end of the War of the Spanish Succession, the Treaty of Utrecht assigns the Spanish Netherlands to Austria. Belgium is known as the Austrian Netherlands until 1794.
1719	Execution of François Anneessens puts an end to resistance to Austrian rule.
1741–80	Rule by Charles of Lorraine: a period of prosperity and stability.
1780–90	Unpopular rule from Vienna by reformist Emperor Joseph II.
1790	French Revolution of 1789 triggers the Brabançon Revolt; the United States of Belgium declared independent; the revolt is crushed by the Austrian army.
1794	The French Revolutionary Army defeats the Austrians at Fleurus.
1795	Belgium is incorporated into France.
1815	Final defeat of Napoleon at Waterloo. The Congress of Vienna makes Belgium a part of the United Kingdom of the Netherlands (until 1831).
1830	On 25 August a performance of the opera *La Muette de Portici* in Brussels incites the audience to revolt. Dutch troops finally forced out of Brussels on 27 Sept. Provisional Government declares Belgium independent on 4 Oct.
1831	At the London Conference the international community accepts Belgium's independence. Leopold of Saxe-Coburg becomes King Leopold I (r.1831–65).
1865–1909	Reign of King Leopold II, marked by rapid economic and industrial development, grand building projects and the modernization of Brussels, and the acquisition of the Congo (in the 1880s).
1909	Accession of King Albert I (r.1909–34).
1914–18	First World War: Germany ignores Belgian neutrality to overrun much of the country. King Albert I leads spirited resistance in northwest Belgium.
1934	Death of Albert I in a climbing accident; accession of Leopold III (r.1934–51).
1940–45	Second World War: Germany again ignores Belgian neutrality.
1951	Violent controversy leads to the abdication of Leopold III in favour of his 21-year-old son, Baudouin I (r.1951–93).
1958	The European Economic Community (EEC) is created; Belgium is a founder member, and Brussels is established as the EEC headquarters.
1962	The Belgian Congo (now Zaire) wins its independence.
1993	The 'Saint-Michel Accords' formalize the on-going devolution of government to the three regional governments: Flanders, Wallonia and Brussels. The death of Baudouin I and accession of Albert II reveal the breadth of popular support for the preservation of Belgian unity against increasing federalization.

History, Art and Architecture

Aron, Jacques, with Patrick Burniat and Pierre Puttemans, *Bruxelles et Environs: guide d'architecture moderne*, Didier Hatier, Brussels,1990. Excellent pocket guide with map and itineraries, describing buildings of interest from Art Nouveau to the present day.

Dictionnaire de la Peinture Flamande et Hollandaise, Larousse, Paris, 1989. Well-illustrated paperback, which includes brief accounts of all Belgian painters of any significance.

Le Nouveau Dictionnaire des Belges, Le Cri/RTBF, Brussels, 1992. Win that parlour game! Over 800 pages of compact biographies of hundreds of Belgians who have been famous for something since the birth of the nation in 1830.

Martiny, Victor-Gaston, *Bruxelles: architecture civile et militaire avant 1900*, J. M. Collet, Braine l'Alleud, n.d. Well-illustrated account of historic architecture in Brussels, especially of those buildings no longer with us. (Shame there's no index.)

Souillard, Colette, *Kunst in België*, Lannoo/Tielt, 1986. A good introduction to Belgian art and architecture, with plenty of large colour illustrations. There is an English translation of the Flemish text at the end of the book.

Quievreux, Louis, *Dictionnaire du Dialecte Bruxellois*, Editions Libro-Sciences, Brussels, n.d. Both erudite and amusing explanations of this earthy dialect.

Van Nieuwenborgh, Marcel, *A Bruxelles: guide pratique et littéraire des itinéraires poétiques*, Didier Hatier, Brussels, 1990. A short, readable and entertaining volume which recounts the various exploits and misdemeanours of selected writers in Brussels, including Victor Hugo, Alexandre Dumas, Baudelaire, Rimbaud and Verlaine, Charlotte Brontë and Karl Marx.

Literature

Baudelaire, Charles, *Les Fleurs du Mal et autres poèmes*, Garnier Flammarion, Paris 1964. This paperback collection includes the group of poems entitled *Amoenitates Belgicae*, in which the wretched poet vents his spleen famously over the nation to which he had exiled himself.

Further Reading

Brontë, Charlotte, *The Professor*, Oxford Paperbacks, Oxford University Press, 1987. The prototype for *Villette*, also set in a school based on the Pensionnat Héger, in Brussels where Charlotte taught. Not published until 1857, after her death.

Brontë, Charlotte, *Villette*, Oxford Paperbacks, Oxford University Press,1984. First published in 1853, this intense internal drama follows the life and emotions of the heroine as teacher in a *pensionnat* for girls in Villette, capital of Labassecour. The novel relates closely to Charlotte's own experiences in Brussels.

Thackeray, William Makepeace, *Vanity Fair*, Penguin Classics, London, 1968. The delightful and witty account of the fortunes of Becky Sharp and Amelia Sedley. The central chapters take place in the social whirl of Brussels on the eve of the Battle of Waterloo.

Food and Restaurants

Gordon, Enid, and Midge Shirley, *The Belgian Cookbook*, Macdonald, London, 1982 (O/P). With James Ensor's *Woman Eating Oysters* on the cover, and illustrated by old photographs of markets and *potagers*, this is a guide to how it is really done. Plenty of classic recipes.

Guide Delta: Bruxelles, hôtels et restaurants, Editions Delta, Brussels, published annually. A reliable guide to most of Brussels' 3000 restaurants.

Main references are shown in **bold**; numbers in *italic* indicate maps. Churches in Brussels are indexed under their names.

Index